Search Out the Land
The Jews and the Growth of Equality
in British Colonial America, 1740–1867

Until now, Jews and Jewish contributions to the early development
of Canada and the British colonies have been marginalized in Canadian history. In *Search Out the Land* Sheldon Godfrey and Judith
Godfrey begin to redress this situation by illustrating and analysing
the struggle by minorities for equal civil and political rights as seen
through the eyes of Canada's Jewish founders in pre-Confederation
British North America.

Mapping the history of Canadian Jews from the arrival of the
first settlers before 1750 through to the 1860s, *Search Out the Land*
introduces a new set of colourful players on Canada's stage. Ezekiel
Solomons, John Franks, Jacob Franks, Chapman Abraham, Rachel
Myers, Moses David, Samuel Hart, Elizabeth Lyons, and a host of
others now take their appropriate place in Canadian history. Focusing on the significant role played by Jews in British North America
in the fight for civil and political rights, the authors compare the
development of Canadian rights with those in other British jurisdictions of the time and set the contribution of Jews within the
context of other minority groups, including Presbyterians, Methodists, French-Canadian Catholics, and Quakers.

Using extensive archival, genealogical, and legal research, the
authors prove that settlers of other than British or French origin
were building, exploring, and developing Canada from its inception.

SHELDON J. GODFREY, chair of the Heritage Canada Foundation, is
a Toronto lawyer with a postgraduate degree in Canadian history.
JUDITH C. GODFREY is a heritage conservationist living in Toronto.

And Joshua the son of Nun sent out from among the acacia trees two scouts, secretly, saying: "Go view the land and Jericho ..."
And it was told the King of Jericho, saying: "Behold there come in hither to-night men of the children of Israel to search out the land."

Joshua 2: 1–2

Search Out the Land

The Jews and
the Growth of Equality
in British Colonial America
1740–1867

SHELDON J. GODFREY
& JUDITH C. GODFREY

McGill-Queen's University Press
Montreal & Kingston • London • Buffalo

ISBN 0-7735-1201-1

Legal deposit fourth quarter 1995
Bibliothèque nationale du Québec

Printed in Canada on acid-free paper

This book has been published with the help of a grant
from the Social Science Federation of Canada, using
funds provided by the Social Sciences and Humanities
Research Council of Canada.

Funding has also been received from the Department of
Canadian Heritage, Multiculturalism Programs, and the
William G. Cole Foundation.

McGill-Queen's University Press is grateful to the Canada
Council for support of its publishing program.

Canadian Cataloguing in Publication Data

Godfrey, Sheldon, 1938–
  Search out the land : the Jews and the growth of equality
  in British colonial America, 1740–1867
  (McGill-Queen's studies in ethnic history,
  ISSN 0846-8869 ; 23)
  Includes bibliographical references and index.
  ISBN 0-7735-1201-2
  1. Jews – Civil rights – Canada – History – 18th century.
  2. Jews – Civil rights – Canada – History – 19th century.
  3. Jews – Canada – History – 18th century. 4. Jews –
  Canada – History – 19th century. I. Godfrey, Judith C.,
  1940–   . II. Title. III. Series.
  FC106.J5G64 1995 323.1′1924071′09033 C95-900729-6
  F1035.J5G64 1995

Typeset in New Baskerville 10/12
by Caractéra inc., Quebec City

To the memory of
Ruth Godfrey
who in her own way searched out the land
for the rest of us

Contents

Tables and Illustrations

Acknowledgments

The writing of this book has involved an exhaustive and exhausting ten-year-long pursuit of an enormous number of faint – even far-fetched – leads amongst official documents and private papers. We are also indebted to an extensive network of individuals who were drawn into our quest in various ways and for many different reasons. Those who participated in the network helped spontaneously by sharing their research or by going out of their way to give us direction. Others, working at institutions, did much more than duty required to assist us. Still others read portions of the manuscript and offered constructive comments or helped in other ways. Finally, we acknowledge the help of some of the descendants of Canada's early Jewish settlers. We offer them all our thanks in print even though, because of the number of individuals and length of time involved, some may be inadvertently omitted.

HONORARY MEMBERS OF THE NETWORK

Henry Strauss Quixano Henriques (1866–1925), Samuel Oppenheim (1859–1928), Cecil Roth (1899–1970), Benjamin Gutl Sack (1889–1969), and Malcolm Henry Stern (1915–1994).

THE NETWORK

Anthony Adamson, Toronto; Mary Allodi, Canadiana Gallery, Royal Ontario Museum, Toronto; P.R. Aloof, Plymouth Hebrew Congregation, United Kingdom; Ken H. Annet, Quebec City; David A. Armour, Mackinac Island, Michigan; Warren Baker, Montreal; Arthur Barat, Windsor, Ontario; Professor David Bell, Faculty of Law, University of New Brunswick, Fredericton; Gerald E. Boyce, Belleville, Ontario; Dennis Carter-Edwards, Cornwall, Ontario; Edward Challenger, Basseterre, St Kitts; Seymour Craimer, Montreal and Albany, NY; Jerry L. Cross, North Carolina Cultural Resources, Raleigh, NC; Robert Dallison,

Fredericton; Ken Donovan, Fortress Louisbourg, Sydney, NS; Bill Draiman, Toronto; Fernand Drouin, Montreal; Harry W. Duckworth, Winnipeg; Patricia L. Fleming, Toronto; the late Phil Franklin, Toronto; J. Brian Gilchrist, Ontario Genealogical Society, Toronto; Bill Gladstone, Jewish Genealogical Society of Canada, Toronto; Gary Griesdorf, Toronto; Ron Greene, Victoria; Dr Donald Heldman, Fort Michilimackinac, Michigan; Estherelke and Bob Kaplan, Toronto; Abraham and Sera Kellermann, Windsor, Ontario; Patricia Kennedy, National Archives, Ottawa; Turner Kirkland, Union City, Tennessee; Marcia Koven, Saint John Jewish Historical Museum; Bernard Kusnitz, Newport, RI; Donald and Elaine Lake, Toronto; Malcolm Lester, Toronto; Peter Linegar, St John's, Newfoundland; Jane MacNamara, Ontario Genealogical Society, Toronto; Marion Macrae, Toronto; Dr Allan E. Marble, Halifax; Jacob R. Marcus, American Jewish Archives, Cincinnati, Ohio; Rosemary Malaher, Winnipeg; Mary Martin, Green Bay, Wisconsin; David Mattison, Public Archives of British Columbia, Victoria; Dr Richard Menkes, Vancouver; the Rev. C.J. Mersereau, Newcastle, NB; Evelyn Miller, Montreal; Dr John S. Moir, St Catharines, Ontario; Julie Morris, Public Archives of Nova Scotia, Halifax; William J. Olmstead, Riverview, NB; Chris Raible, Toronto; David Rome, Montreal; M. Jackson Samuels, Toronto; Ruth Saturley, St John's, Newfoundland; Miriam Schmidt, Elliot Lopes, and Bernard Roosevelt, St Eustatius Historical Foundation; John Sewell and Charlotte Sykes, Toronto; David Spector, Hove, United Kingdom; Allan Steinhart, Toronto; Bernard Susser, Devon, United Kingdom and Jerusalem; Lawrence Tapper, National Archives, Ottawa; Daniel T. Tweel, Charlottetown; John Ulock, Newcastle, NB; Kathryn Wilson, Toronto; William P. Wolfe, Montreal; Joyce and Fred Zemans, Toronto.

STAFF OF INSTITUTIONS

Twila Buttimer, Public Archives of New Brunswick, Fredericton; Anne Crocker, Law Librarian, University of New Brunswick, Fredericton; John Crosthwait, Baldwin Room, Metropolitan Toronto Reference Library; the staff of the Dictionary of Canadian Biography, Toronto; Diane Eacret, National Museum of American Jewish History, Philadelphia; Tim Dubé and Tom Hillman, National Archives, Ottawa; the late Nathan Kaganoff and Gina Hsin, American Jewish Historical Society, Waltham, MA; Julie Kowrak, Wills and Records, Philadelphia City Hall; Christian Lalancette, Archives du Séminaire de Trois-Rivières; Eugene Martel, Cathy Shepherd, and Leon Warmsky, Public Archives of Ontario, Toronto; Judith Nefsky and Janice Rosen, Canadian Jewish Archives, Montreal; Margaret Murphy, Legislative Library, Halifax, NS; Catherine Reid, Old Manse Library, Newcastle, NB; Jeanne Roberts and Daniel N. Rolph, Historical Society of Pennsylvania Archives; Miriam Rodrigues-Perreira, Honorary Archivist, Spanish and Portuguese Jews' Congregation, London, United Kingdom; Steven Speisman, Ontario Jewish Archives, Toronto; the staff of the Legislative Library of New Brunswick, Fredericton; Susan Tobin, Archivist, Shearith Israel Congregation, New York; Sylvie Tremblay, Archives nationales du Québec, Quebec City; Lucille Vachon and Luc Lepine, Archives nationales du Québec, Montreal; Louis M. Waddell, Pennsylvania Historical and Museum Commission, Harrisburg; Fanny Zelcer and Kevin Profit, American Jewish Archives, Cincinnati, Ohio.

DESCENDANTS

Nancy Erdrich, Ethel Olive Elwell, Henry Joseph, and Sarah McColl, descendants of Levy Solomons and Rebecca Franks and Rachel Solomons and Henry Joseph; Georgia Fralick, Nancy Cooper, and Dorothy Orr, descendants of George Benjamin and Isabella Jacobs; Herbert H. Franks, descendant of John Franks and David Salusbury Franks; Joan E. Gilday and Howard Chapman, descendants of Jacob Hirschfelder; Jo Hebert, descendant of Ezekiel Solomons; Lady Jessica Mellor, descendant of Abraham da Sola, Levy Solomons and Rebecca Franks, and Rachel Solomons and Henry Joseph; Barton Myers, descendant of Hyam Myers, Moses Myers, and Elizabeth Judah; Betti Paull and William Marsh, descendants of Benjamin and Rachel Myers and Judith Montgomery; David Ritchie and Basil B. Stead, descendants of Michael Samuel.

READERS

Phyllis Bruce, Paul and Sandra Druckman, Rabbi Baruch Frydman-Kohl, Bert Godfrey, Jonathan Godfrey and Melanie Karp, Michael Godfrey, William and Beth Godfrey, Jane Griesdorf, Morton and Bonnie Gross, Christine Hebscher, Ronald Hume and Penny Shore, Martin and Estelle Kosoy, Lynda Kovacevic, Malcolm Lester, Pearl Lester, Jim Lyons, Phyllis Mankoff, Phyllis Meiklejohn, Ruth and Eric Miller, Paula Pike, JoAnn Posen, David Roberts, Helaine Robbins, Noa Schwartz, Margaret Talley, and Elaine Waisglass.

THE PUBLISHER

Finally, we offer our thanks to Donald Akenson, Philip Cercone, and Joan McGilvray of McGill-Queen's University Press for making a complicated process appear simple and above all to Marion Magee whose editing skills turned an uneven manuscript into a story.

Preface: The Search Begins

It is not my purpose to branch off here into an extended review
of the legal status of Jews in England during the colonial period
... It may be observed, however, that thus far no earnest treatment
of the subject has appeared although without it it is impossible to
understand the development of religious liberty in America as far
as it is applicable to the Jews ... It may be doubted whether anyone
except a trained lawyer will be able ... to pick out the isolated
cases ... involving the rights of Jews.

Max J. Kohler, 27 January 1897[1]

In the summer of 1986, we stood at the edge of a partly excavated
area in the midst of a number of restored buildings surrounded by a
stockade, the remains of Fort Michilimackinac, an eighteenth-century
British fort. Not far away water lapped against rocks at the edge of an
ancient thoroughfare, the Straits of Michilimackinac, which joins
Lakes Huron, Michigan, and Superior. Over the ages the straits had
formed a strategic narrows on the water route from the Atlantic Ocean
to both the interior of North America and the headwaters of the
Mississippi River that led to the south. The Indians, the French, the
British, and the Americans, having recognized the geographic, military, and economic importance of the area, had all built their camps
and their forts along these shores.

Within the excavation in front of us, a number of archaeologists
and their helpers poked through the soil with small trowels, cleared
dirt with brushes and water, and made notes on clipboards. A small
sign announced that the Mackinac Island State Park Commission of
the Department of Natural Resources of the state of Michigan was
undertaking an excavation of the foundations of the Solomons-Levy
house prior to its reconstruction as a historic site. Behind us, just
outside the stockade, a larger sign, erected some years previously,
commemorated Ezekiel Solomons as "Michigan's First Jewish Settler."[2]

Solomons may have been the first Jewish settler in the area that *later* became Michigan, but the region was considered British by its occupants until it was reorganized as the Michigan Territory in 1805. He had spent almost all his working life in what he knew as British North America.[3] We were very interested in Ezekiel Solomons because the story of Solomons and his fur trade consortium is *Canadian* history.

Solomons had been born in Germany and by 1761 was based in Montreal. There, he and four other Jewish merchants had established Gershon Levy & Company. This consortium was one of the first organized fur trade companies on the Great Lakes after the British conquest of New France, its members setting themselves up with outposts at Niagara, Detroit, and Michilimackinac. These Jewish men were responsible for almost one-half of the British fur trade on the Great Lakes from 1761 until Pontiac's uprising two years later brought ruin to the consortium.

Fifteen years later, Solomons and three of his former partners were recorded as active members of Montreal's Shearith Israel Congregation. By that time he had become the most important individual in the fur trade of what is now northwestern Ontario. In fact he was so successful that he threatened the dominance of the Hudson's Bay Company in that area. He had supported Britain throughout the American Revolution. In later life he moved to Mackinac Island and died during the winter of 1804–5. His son William, an Indian interpreter, joined the British forces that recaptured Mackinac Island in 1812 and moved with his family to the new British post on Drummond Island after the British returned Mackinac Island to the Americans in 1815.

Ezekiel Solomons and his family gave their loyalty to British North America. He and his consortium played an important role at the very beginning of the development of the new "British" Quebec after 1760. Yet Solomons has received so little attention from scholars that he did not warrant a biography in the *Dictionary of Canadian Biography*.[4] Canada had forgotten Solomons along with the rest of his consortium and his community.

CANADA'S FORGOTTEN HISTORY

Why was Solomons forgotten by his country of choice? Most of those writing on the early history of Canada have assumed that there were very few Jews in Canada in the first years of British control and settlement and that consequently Jews had virtually no impact on the country's early development. As a result, interpretations of this period – if they pay any attention to Jewish history – have tended to be tied to general themes such as the absence of early Jewish roots in Canada or the issue of anti-semitism, themes whose existence or degree are not justified by further examination of the facts. The few previous studies of Jews in this period of Canadian history have left most of us with the belief that the larger Jewish community which arrived in Canada after 1880 was somehow grafted onto a country founded by non-Jews, a country in which the Jewish presence had hitherto made no impact.5 Yet this is not the case, and the integration of the history of these early Jews into the broader Canadian story is still to be done.

Until the 1970s, in the words of Michael Bliss, Canadian history concentrated on "the great men and events that had created our country and our identity." It documented the part played by statesmen and politicians in the development of the country, leaving the impression that Canada's history was largely that of white men who were either anglophone and Protestant or francophone and Roman Catholic. Bliss went on to observe that this point of departure "seemed to neglect the historian's higher obligation to search for documentable truth about the past." He concluded by suggesting that "we should renew our appreciation of the history of Canada ... but we must not do it at the cost of leaving out those Canadians who were excluded from the old history and whose integration into our historical and national consciousness is the finest achievement of our history-writing since the 1960s ... We cannot envisage a Canada of the future whose constitution and history books do not embrace the multiple identities of our people and the bonds they share."6

Canada was described as "a mixed race" almost two centuries ago when William Lyon Mackenzie wrote that "the town and country consists of persons of many sects and denominations in respect to religious belief – and who are either natives of Canada, or emigrants from other parts of North America, or from Europe Asia and Africa, – a mixed race, neither amalgamated in manners customs nor habits – doubtless containing many enlightened and well informed men, as well as others of very different character."7 But official British and colonial records and the correspondence of the public figures of British North America prior to Confederation do not adequately reflect the role played by racial and religious minorities, women, blacks, aboriginal peoples, and immigrants from the Far East and other lands. All were here in numbers, many from the earliest period of Canada's development. This fact alone should cast doubt on the more recent idea of "two founding peoples."

To look at our early history only through official records is to have a warped view, as only a few at the beginning of the colony were allowed to hold the offices on which that history has been based. The history of the others is to be found in other sources. As the histories of these other groups become better known, the forgotten story of the development of the country's tradition of freedom and equality will be revealed. Further research into the country's roots will give Jews and others their place among those who began the building of the Canadian nation.

It was apparent to us, as we watched the excavation at the Solomons-Levy house, that the unknown story of the importance of the settlement of the Jews to British America in its early years had yet to be told.

UNCOVERING THE STORY

In *Search Out the Land* we study the growth of freedom and legal equality in British America and examine how, in its infancy during the eighteenth and early nineteenth centuries, Canada developed into a nation where the civil rights of its religious minorities were an integral part of its nationhood, a central part of its self-image. This book combines history and law to elucidate this progression of rights so as to understand the legal framework as the underpinning of the Canadian experience.[8] At the same time, it provides a look at the early history of Canada through Jewish eyes and Jewish documents, as the role of Jews in the development of Canadian society parallels the development of legal equality of persons of the different religious groups in British North America. Jews of the eighteenth century, in their search for a place to call home, were at the leading edge of the movement for equality of citizenship.

From the little we already knew, we believed that the main motivation of Jewish settlers who came to North America in the eighteenth century was to escape the civil and political restrictions, injustices, and inequalities of the Old World and to find equal opportunity as Jews in the New. We supposed that before the first Jews arrived, they had made it their business to know the laws, to learn whether they could buy land and settle without restriction, to find places where they could carry on trades, professions, or enterprises that would permit them to earn a livelihood.

We supposed that there were pressures on all minorities to assimilate before the middle of the nineteenth century. Thus, communities of Jews with whom new arrivals could affiliate were the exception rather than the rule. A profile of the Jewish pioneer of the period would likely reveal a European man, perhaps even a refugee, whose priority lay in exploring the economic and political benefits for Jews in the American colonies, rather than in participating fully in Jewish communal life. The acquisition of the full rights held only by the members of the established Church of England developed too slowly for both Jew and non-Jew, and the lack of access proved a potent force for assimilation for all groups as some of these individuals, growing impatient at the delay, became Anglicans so as to increase their personal opportunities and to share rights otherwise denied.[9]

We surmised that the pioneers among all the peoples who were the first to test the land and its freedoms reported back to others through the usual informal networks such as letters home to family and friends or chance conversations with a stranger of the same culture who had been in some other place and had searched out the land. Such conversations would inevitably have centred on the topic of where it would be good to live and set down roots. Then some of these came as well, settled, and in turn reported on the conditions by letters home – and so we are all here today.

Our first step in testing our hypotheses was to determine where Jews did in fact settle in Canada. Over time, we were able to document the families of more than 100 Canadian Jewish pioneers between 1750 and 1840 – representing only a portion of those Jews who had come to Canada.[10] We discovered the places they chose to settle, the rights that were and were not allowed them throughout the period, and the reasons some areas were preferred for settlement.

Our second task was suggested by the fact that Jews tended to settle in some of the British American colonies and not in others. We were therefore obliged to review the laws relating to each colony to determine the restrictions for Jews and others or the inducements to settle. Why, to name a few examples, did Jews of the early period settle in Jamaica, Nevis, New York, Rhode Island, South Carolina, Quebec, Nova Scotia, and Pennsylvania? Why did they avoid Massachusetts, Maine, Maryland, North Carolina, Bermuda, and St Kitts?

Our third area of investigation was much more complex and was the more difficult because the "powers" of the day had seen to it that many of the "rules" governing political and civil rights were obscure. Prior to the introduction of responsible government in the British North American colonies by about 1850, the laws of a colony could not be determined simply by reference to colonial and imperial statutes and court cases as they are today. Many rules and practices did not arise from legislation but were founded in the authority of colonial governors who exercised arbitrary power in accordance with secret royal instructions drawn up by the Colonial Office in Great Britain.[11]

From the beginning, equality was the stated goal of the New World societies – allowed in theory to aliens who became naturalized as well as to religious nonconformists. It was this vision which prompted emigrants fleeing the inequalities of the Old World to come to the

New. In practice, however, from the time of the inception of the new colonies, the Colonial Office denied full equality to those who did not adhere to the established church while in theory maintaining the ideal. The device used by the Colonial Office to assert its control was an intricate system of oaths and declarations whose effect was to prohibit others from securing these higher rights unless they became members of the Church of England.[12]

We therefore discovered a complex and at times almost unintelligible patchwork of rights that shifted as the colonies developed. From the outset, the followers of the Church of England were officially promoted because of the establishment of their church. At the same time, the rights of those of other religions shifted according to the exigencies of British policy. In 1774, for example, the Quebec Act recognized the equal civil and political rights of French-Canadian Catholics, but not of other Catholics. During the same period Protestant Dissenters and Jews in Quebec were recognized as equal by government policy as well as by the governor's instructions. In 1791, again by virtue of the governor's instructions, all Catholics in Upper and Lower Canada were given legal equality to Anglicans, but equality was taken from Protestant Dissenters and Jews, not to be returned for almost forty years.

DISCOVERING THE SOURCES

Some of the material on which this book is based, including the governor's instructions, was originally not in the public domain and was thus not available to people of the time, or for that matter to scholars of past generations. Many of these documents as well as the private papers of pioneers of the early period have since been transferred to public archives and so were available to us, their accessibility enhanced through data banks, photocopies, and facsimiles. Until recently, scholars would have had only a limited glimpse of this patchwork of devices to deprive the "non-established" of equal access to the offices and rights allowed to the "established." Up to the middle of the nineteenth century, anti-disestablishmentarianism was still a factor in British policy. As time progressed, the system changed to eliminate such inequities. This book is a record of that development.

To provide an overview of where Canada fit into the colonial picture, some research into comparative rights in England and its colonies was required. Our conclusions are based on extensive research across Canada, the United States, the Caribbean, and England using materials uncovered in previously unexplored primary sources. We started with an exhaustive genealogical effort to identify and document the Jews in Canada during the period, using conventional as well as legal sources. We reviewed court records, land records, and probate records; we proceeded to archival research to establish the context; we concluded with a comparative examination of common law, statutes, and regulatory authorities to find the countries that were more advanced in granting equal rights to Jews and to see whether settlement patterns were affected as a result.

A STORY ON MANY LEVELS

This book has been written on several levels and may be read in many ways. The underlying argument determining the legal basis on which equality developed is largely unknown and necessarily complex, but it had to be thoroughly and unequivocally detailed as the framework upon which the country evolved. Thus, several of the chapters, particularly near the beginning of the book, offer an intensive exposition of the background of that aspect of our story. The remaining chapters are narratives which show how these legal developments affected the lives of individuals. While the expositive chapters are different in style, they explain this previously unknown framework. We believed it necessary to put the narrative in this context. Tables 1 (p. 19), 2 (p. 42), 3 (p. 55), and 4 (p. 132) offer a ready reference for following the development of rights described in chapters 1, 2, 3, and 10. Table 5 (pp. 216–17) provides a summary of the removal of disabilities in the colonies of British North America by 1867, and table 6 (pp. 238–40) is a summary of the Jewish role in the progression of the granting of specific rights in Britain and the various colonies of British America.

For those readers who do not choose to follow all the threads of the legal argument, the narrative chapters portray Jewish participation in the development of the nation and can be followed without digesting the background detail or thoroughly understanding the framework.

As our main story is the development of a just society based on equal rights, we were obliged to place some of the previously unknown details of the histories of individual Jews in the footnotes. In many cases, these can be read separately to add another dimension to the text. Many of these stories personify and humanize this very successful struggle for equal rights by giving additional glimpses of the society in which the earliest Jewish settlers lived and worked. These stories predate the organization of Jewish communities but are not isolated vignettes. They document a clear and consistent pattern that is part of the very foundation of Canadian history. They portray the depth and value of Jewish participation in Canada's early life and the significance of the Jewish contribution in building the kind of Canadian nation we know today.

REMEMBERING OUR HERITAGE

Canada has no plaques or public guideposts to commemorate the role that Ezekiel Solomons and many others played in the development of our exemplary tradition of equality. Like the story of Ezekiel Solomons, the history of the development of Canada's freedoms is found in the lives of countless individuals and groups who left other countries and came and worked together in a new land where discrimination as a political idea was intolerable – a country whose form of nationalism was merely political, not cultural or religious. Although many rules had yet to be established to "fine tune" the system, the land became free of many of the established religious and cultural biases and restrictions still existing in its mother country and its neighbours.

It is a story that begins with an invitation by Britain to Jews to settle its colonies in America, to bring their expertise in trade to provide a missing element in the development of colonial society. Jews were needed and actively sought after as colonists at the beginning of British settlement in the Americas, whether in the Caribbean, the Thirteen Colonies, or the area to the north, now Canada. Jews were seen as indispensable to a prosperous and vibrant colonial trade because of their experience, their international contacts, their access to capital, their willingness to take risks, and their loyalty to whichever imperial power would offer them a measure of equality.

Jews formed a significantly larger percentage of the English-speaking population of many of the earliest colonial settlements than has been previously known. They became, and were encouraged to become, an integral part of life in British North America from its very first moments. Consequently they played an important role in the development of equal rights. At a time when the right of a Jew to own land in Great Britain was in question, the first building lot granted in the very first English settlement in Canada was alloted to a Jew. We established that there was a community of religious Jews in Canada's first British settlement at Halifax from its inception in 1749 and that there may have been Jewish settlers in Nova Scotia even before the founding of Halifax.[13] In the 1760s Jews were integrally involved with the beginnings of the English fur trade on the Great Lakes, and they hurried home by canoe from the Upper Country a thousand miles away to be in Montreal for their High Holidays.

The story continues with colonial officials who bent the rules sent from Britain by the Colonial Office so they could be fair to the Jews in their midst. In 1768 the governor of Quebec appointed a Jew to public office while all the other British colonies of the time followed a restrictive policy. We learned that the province of Upper Canada was the first jurisdiction in the British empire to appoint a Jewish officer to the militia and to develop an unorthodox method of granting equality to Jews in order to avoid the imperial restrictions. From the formative years of the country, French-Canadian majorities in elected assemblies, using their numerical power to champion rights of other minorities, were among the first to work for the equality of others, successfully passing statutes granting equality to Protestant Dissenters and Jews over the objections of the British governors.

The many cultures and faiths of the peoples who settled in British North America led them to reject the policy of the Colonial Office, to seek full equality in practice as well as in theory, and to bring to an end the discrimination which was based on the rights of the Church of England as the established church. By 1867, when Canada was officially formed, British North America was already advanced and enlightened in its attempts to ensure that all minorities were legally equal.

The equal integration of people of all cultures and creeds into our country is our heritage as a nation. With a greater awareness of our roots, this heritage will take its proper place at the forefront of our national consciousness.

The book is written from the perspective of those of the Jewish religion in Canada, who through the millennia had wandered from one place to another, searching for a land where they could be granted equal status and put down roots. All of those who came and tested the country's freedoms spread the word to others still in the "old country" that they had searched out the land and that it was good. Let their story become a monument to our freedom, a guidepost to our Canadian identity, a beacon for our future.

In our minds this work is a legacy to the future from those whose stories we tell in *Search Out the Land*. We hope that your search will follow theirs, ultimately providing us with a nation where the opportunities can be limitless for all people.

SG/JG

Definitions

The same words can mean different things in different contexts and at different moments in time. The word "Jew" is defined differently in an observant Jewish community in Toronto or Montreal in the 1990s than it was on the Canadian frontier in the 1790s. The phrase "British North America" meant different things both politically and geographically at different times. Even the phrase "civil and political rights" requires further clarification to define which rights are concerned in the context of this inquiry. Before pursuing the presence and the role of Jews in the development of civil and political rights in British North America, it would be prudent to define the ways in which these terms are used in our analysis.

BRITISH AMERICA
This term refers to all the British colonies in the Americas at the time under discussion. It might therefore refer to some or all of the colonies in the Caribbean and South America and the Thirteen Colonies prior to 1775, as well as the colonies of British North America.

BRITISH NORTH AMERICA
This term refers to those parts of North America roughly equivalent to present-day Canada. While it is common among American writers to refer to British North America as "the fourteenth colony," at the time of the Treaty of Paris in 1763 British North America consisted of three colonies. The first was Nova Scotia, an area that included present-day New Brunswick as well as present-day Prince Edward Island and Cape Breton Island, which had both been captured from the French in 1758. The second was Quebec or Canada, captured from France in 1760, covering the area of present-day Quebec as well as most of present-day Ontario and the American states of Michigan and Wisconsin. The third colony was Newfoundland, captured from France in 1762.

By 1791, British North America consisted of six colonies, although its total area was no greater than it had been in 1763. Newfoundland was unchanged. Nova Scotia had been split into three, with the Island of St John (now Prince Edward Island) becoming a separate colony in 1769 and New Brunswick in 1784. Quebec was split into two colonies, with Upper Canada occupying most of the area of present-day Ontario and Lower Canada corresponding roughly to present-day Quebec. These colonies continued to exist in similar from until 1867, except that Upper and Lower Canada were united into a single Province of Canada in 1841.

British North America also included the territories of the Hudson's Bay Company, which while not technically colonies, covered the northern part of the continent from Hudson Bay to the Pacific Ocean. The replacement of the French empire in North America by British rule was won over a period of about fifty years, ending in 1760. British North America, therefore, existed as a place where Jews would come as early as 1710, when the British captured Nova Scotia from France during Queen Anne's War.

CANADA

This term was first used to describe the territory held by the French in North America which lay to the west of the French territory of Acadia in New Brunswick and Nova Scotia. The area corresponded roughly to the southerly parts of the present-day provinces of Quebec, Ontario, and Manitoba as well as parts of northern Michigan, Illinois, and Wisconsin in the United States. From 1791 to 1867 the term was used to describe the southerly portions of present-day Ontario and Quebec under the names of Upper and Lower Canada from 1791 to 1841, or Canada West and Canada East from 1841 to 1867.

NEW FRANCE

This term was usually used to describe Canada by contemporaries in France.

QUEBEC OR THE OLD PROVINCE OF QUEBEC

These terms, as used in this book, refer to the French colony of Canada or New France after it came under British rule in 1760 and had its boundaries expanded by the Quebec Act in 1774 to include large areas of what is now the American midwest. Under the Constitutional Act of 1791, the portion of this territory that had remained in British North America following the American Revolution was divided into Upper and Lower Canada (subsequently Canada West and Canada East).

EQUALITY; EQUAL CIVIL AND POLITICAL RIGHTS

In the context of the period before 1867, the notion of equality in the civil and political rights of citizens was limited to the removal of legal or official disabilities. Disabilities had the effect of preventing individuals, because of their religion or origin, from exercising rights made available by government. In this sense individuals were assumed to be equal before the law as long as no disabilities stood in their way, even though discrimination may have continued to exist in the private sector. Equality so defined was therefore more restrictive than the "equality rights" defined in the Canadian Charter of Rights and Freedoms of 1981. A contemporary usage is offered by a letter from Rabbi Isaac Lesser in the *Philadelphia Gazette* of 12 December 1839: "Where equality is the law of the land, there is no privileged class. Liberty precludes the idea of *toleration*, and the majority, no matter how large, have no right to claim any merit for leaving the minority undisturbed in the enjoyment of equal rights." See below, TOLERATION

CIVIL RIGHTS

At this period, these rights included the right to become a citizen by naturalization or other means, the right to reside freely in any area, the right to own land, the right to accept a grant of land from the crown, and the right to sue and be sued in the courts; the free exercise of religion and the freedom to worship publicly for religious minorities in a state with an established religion; the right of appointment to an office or place of trust, civil or military – the phrase used in English law to refer to appointments to high, non-elected positions. Examples of the latter include jurymen, lawyers, notaries, judicial officers, and government officers as well as commissioned officers in the military. With respect to Jews, these rights include the right to be sworn on the Pentateuch or the Old Testament as a witness in court, and the right to leave property by will for non-Christian religious purposes.

POLITICAL RIGHTS

These rights include the right to vote in elections as well as the right of election to office or of appointment to political office, whether municipal, or provincial, or federal.

TOLERATION

The definition of toleration arises historically from the toleration acts in force in Britain from 1689 to the middle of the nineteenth century. The definition implies the existence of an official "established" religion and other "non-established" religions. The latter, while not entitled to the official advantages of the established religion, are "tolerated" or allowed to engage in public worship without threat of prosecution. Toleration is not equivalent to equality of rights because it suggests a state where the rights of one group are officially promoted and the others are merely tolerated or preserved. In the twentieth century, tolerance is commonly used to describe the acknowledgment by one individual of the differing views or status of another, without accepting the other's position or view as equal or acknowledging the equal validity of the other's own self-definition. A contemporary usage is found in *Bell's Weekly Messenger* (London) for 29 June 1834: "The principles of toleration require us to abstain from all penal laws and active persecution, but in no degree require the abandonment of our national religion, nor the sacrifice of its pre-eminence by a concession of equality to all adverse sects and still less so when the concession of such equality must necessarily lead to the ruin of our own church." See above, EQUALITY.

JEW

As a rule, Jewish immigrants in the eighteenth and early nineteenth centuries lived apart from an organized Jewish community. For practical purposes, "Jew" was defined in the eighteenth century in British North America in four ways.

Jew by religion or profession. Such individuals were a rarity in eighteenth-century British America. Most Jews of the time observed only a few of the traditions of their faith. Of the twenty or so individuals listed as members of Montreal's Shearith Israel Congregation between 1778 and 1782, for example, less than half were married to Jews and at least six were married to Christians. Marriage to Christians apparently occurred because of the lack of Jewish women in the colony. An example of the mixed attitude to religious observance is the decision of the congregation to allow the burial in its cemetery of a baptized child of Ezekiel Solomons and his Christian wife but with the accompanying resolution that it was not to be considered a precedent for future burials. See below, 115.

Jew by birth. This phrase refers to an individual who, though born of Jewish parents, did not practise his religion. It is often difficult for a researcher to verify the religious origin of such persons. For example, Moses Jacobs lived near Kingston, Upper Canada, from about 1793 until his death in 1823. There is no evidence about his religion, but his signature identifies him as Jewish by birth because he wrote his name "Moshe" in Hebrew characters, although from left to right. See below, 164.

Jew by perception. This definition depends not on a person's conduct or birth but on the perception of others. It could apply to a professing Christian with Jewish ancestors – as long as that person was considered a Jew by others. John Lawe was baptized in 1779 at Trois-Rivières. His father, Captain George Lawe, was a Protestant, but his mother, Rachel, the daughter of John Franks and Appolonia Seymore of Quebec, was half-Jewish. John Lawe worked in the fur trade of the Upper Great Lakes with his uncle, Jacob Franks. Thomas Anderson, an associate who knew them both, recalled that "an English gentleman, Jacob Frank [*sic*], and his nephew John Lawe, Jews, were extensively embarked in the fur trade here." ("Personal Narrative of Captain Thomas G. Anderson," 145–6). The definition of Franks and Lawe as Jews was not derogatory but merely descriptive. They were perceived as Jews but were nevertheless members of the community. See below, 162, 315–16.

Jew by descent. There are many individuals of Jewish ancestry who were important participants in the development of the British colonies but who do not play a role in this book because they were not Jews, nor were they perceived as such by others. For example, Moses Mendes, the paternal grandfather of Sir Francis Bond Head, the lieutenant governor of Upper Canada in the 1830s, was of Jewish birth. In our research we found references to a large number of Jews by descent who were pioneers in the British as well as French, Spanish, and Portuguese colonies. In other cases we suspected Jewish ancestry but were unable to find documentation.

MARRANO

According to the *Jewish Encyclopedia,* "Marano (plural Maranos, generally written Marranos) were Crypto-Jews of the Iberian Peninsula ... The name was applied to the Spanish Jews who, through compulsion or for form's sake, became converted to Christianity in consequence of the cruel persecutions of 1391 ... who yielded through stress of circumstances, but in their home life remained Jews ..." Morris Gutstein states (*Jews of Newport,* 60) that "some of the Marranos intermarried with families of the higher and lower nobility to such an extent that after a few generations very few families in Spain were without Jewish blood. They took part in all forms of political and social life. Economically they acquired wealth and at times were entrusted with the financial policies of the country. In the royal Court and Chancery, the Marranos occupied exalted positions in many capacities. They became high dignitaries in the Catholic Church, to the extent that at one time the rumor arose that a Marrano had reached the position of Pope."

PLANTATION

In Britain during the eighteenth century, this term was used inter-changeably with the term colony or original settlement in a new country. A contemporary definition is to be found in Joshua Monte-fiore's *Commercial Dictionary*: a "plantation may be defined as a district, settlement or colony, frequently an entire island in some foreign part, dependant upon some mother country from whose inhabitants it was originally peopled, or by whom it was originally acquired or con-quered. Plantations or colonies are now used as synonymous terms." The Plantation Act, for example, is the short title of the British statute of 1740 known as "An Act for Naturalizing such foreign Protestants and others therein mentioned, as are settled or shall settle in any of His Majesty's Colonies in *America*."

Prologue

In the infancy of the trade of any country, it is right to encourage the Jews to come and settle ... But in a country where trade and commerce have been fully and long established ... it is madness, if not worse, to put Jews or any other foreigners upon an equal footing with natives.

Sir John Barnard, House of Commons, 7 May 1753[1]

"If the Jews were possessed of the best estates and finest houses in every county," Edward Vernon, MP for Ipswich, long-time admiral of the Royal Navy, told the British House of Commons in 1753, "there is some reason to doubt that the people of this nation would long continue Christian."[2]

On 27 November 1753, the date of Vernon's speech, there were no Jews among those of the 572 members of parliament who were present. The house was, as Sir Edmund Isham remarked, "a Christian Assembly,"[3] and indeed, to a man, the members of the House of Commons at Westminster were white, male, and overwhelmingly Anglican. There were no Mohammedans or pagans among their number; they included no "Papists" as Roman Catholics were often called; they included a group of Presbyterians from Scotland and a few scattered adherents of other Protestant dissenting sects who could count on representation in the house as a privilege, though not as a right.[4] There may have been one or two Jews watching the proceedings from the public gallery upstairs,[5] and there were likely some Catholics and Dissenters as well, for this was a debate which might have important consequences for all those whose religious beliefs in some way curtailed their opportunities.

Vernon was speaking on the question of the repeal of the Jews Naturalization Act, passed some six months earlier, which had allowed Jews to be naturalized as citizens for the first time in the history of the United Kingdom.[6] "It would be of the most dangerous consequence to the liberties and privileges of the Christian people of this nation, to have the Jews possessed of a great part of the landed property of this kingdom," he said. "But really, in that case, I do not know how long the people of this nation might continue Christian; for in all countries, the religion of the common people depends very much upon the religion of the people who feed and employ them."[7] Other members participating in this debate agreed "that this was a most unchristian, dishonourable and dangerous law,"[8] although some gave different reasons for supporting repeal. Many opposed the purpose of the act: "putting Jews upon an equal footing with the best Christians, and for giving them a preference to those of every other religion."[9] Thomas Prowse argued that "Christian charity and benevolence obliges us to wish that all Jews, Turks, and Pagans may become Christian and even to take proper methods for converting them, yet by the precepts of Christianity we are expressly commanded not to associate with such people." He reminded members of the prophecy in the New Testament that "the Jews shall be scattered among all nations without finding any ease or rest for the sole of the foot" and argued that "the Jews will never obtain a fixed settlement in any country whilst they continue in their present perverse obstinacy." The passing of the Jews Naturalization Act had therefore been "as great an affront as we could well put upon our established Church, or indeed upon any Christian establishment."[10]

For a listener in the gallery, these comments must have seemed academic, even irrelevant. As many of the speakers noted during the debate, a person born in England or within the realm of British sovereignty had the status of an Englishman, even if his parents were aliens. This custom or doctrine had been applied to the Jews as well in the century since their return to England. Thus the children of aliens, born in England or its colonies, were citizens by birth even though their parents would need to be naturalized to acquire the same status.[11] Under this custom, the community of Jewish Englishmen would grow as more and more Jewish children were born in England. In fact, however, the Jewish community in England had grown slowly during the first half of the eighteenth century, whether by immigration or natural birth.

In contrast to developments in Britain, many European countries had adopted a contrary principle, founded on the Roman law, whereby children, wherever born, were always deemed to possess the nationality of their parents. Under this principle a Jew could never become a citizen in these countries, and this was in fact the legal position of many nations. English authorities were naturally aware of the many Jews who could not become citizens in their nations of residence and might potentially migrate to Britain if a general law of naturalization were enacted. As a result, in the years between 1656 (when the Jews, banished in 1290, returned to England) and the debate on the Jews Naturalization Bill, citizenship had been granted to individual Jews by letters of denization from the sovereign rather than by naturalization under an act of parliament. In this manner, citizenship had been granted to individual Jews almost as a royal favour.

One concern at the root of the debate about the Jews Naturalization Act, therefore, was the fear that England might be flooded by alarming numbers of stateless foreign Jews. Another was that Jews, once they were citizens, might acquire too large a role in government for, as one member pointed out, "in this country every freeholder, and indeed every freeman of any city or borough, has a share in our legislature."[12] "But if those of true English blood have not now the power to prevent opening this sluice for letting the torrent in upon us," as Sir Edmund Isham had said in the original debate on the bill's passage, "can we hope that they will have power enough to shut it up, after the torrent is broke in, and the Jews are become possessed not only of all the wealth, but of many, perhaps most of the land-estates in the kingdom?"[13] Building on this theme, Sir John Barnard had asked the house: "if Jews should come to be possessed of a great share of the land estates of this kingdom, how are we sure that Christianity will continue to be the fashionable religion, or that the profession of it will continue necessary for qualifying a man for any honour or preferment; for fashion, we know, depends upon nothing but whim: and if the Jews should become our chief landholders, they will, probably, become the leaders of our whim. As landholders they will have the chusing of most of the members of this House, and may themselves be chosen; and then to intitle themselves to posts and preferments, they have nothing to do but to join with the other dissenters in getting the test act, and all the other laws for securing our established church, repealed."[14] Thomas Potter, son of the archbishop of Canterbury, was one of the few who spoke against repeal of the act, saying that the clamour against Jews, which had arisen since the passage of the act in May, would have the effect of causing many Jews already established in England to "retire with all their effects from this state of persecution, into some more reasonable, more civilized country, where they would only have the inquisition to fear."[15]

Beyond the rhetoric, the debates on the passage and the repeal of this act were of exceptional significance for both Jews and the common man in England. There had been no similar, open public discussion regarding the rights of Jews since they had returned to England almost a century before. And there was to be no similar discussion for the next hundred years. More than that, this was the first debate on the status of Jews to take place since the process of political reform in England had made the laws of Parliament superior to the edicts of the sovereign. With that change in Britain's system of government had come the fear, "no chimerical apprehension" as Barnard had put it in May, "that Jews would have a view to get possession of the whole strength and power of this nation."[16] The outcome of the debate ultimately would have a bearing on the future status of immigrant Jews in Britain's American colonies.

As a matter of historical record, from the time of William the Conqueror in the eleventh century, Jews had been invited into Catholic England to act as financiers to the monarch. They were banished from the country in 1290, during the reign of Edward III, a period that was known for its religious fervour, its crusading zeal, its wars, and its socio-economic upheaval. From that time until 1656 – over 350 years – Jews were not legally allowed to live in England, although there may well have been Jews living there secretly.[17]

When the Commonwealth government allowed Jews to return to England, they came back with same status they had had when they lived in England before. They were still considered aliens and thus had no more civil or political rights than when they had left in 1290.[18] Their occupations were limited. They were allowed to live only in specified areas in the city of London. They were not allowed to own real estate except for a dwelling house. They were not allowed to sue for debts in the courts or to be sworn as witnesses. They could not vote, serve on juries, or become citizens. They were prohibited from holding any office or place of trust, whether civil or military. Election to any form of public office was out of the question. Each of these rights would have to be won.

Even a century after the Jews had returned to England, they were merely tolerated in the country. They participated in trade, owned real estate, and were allowed to worship openly in synagogues only because of a tacit suspension of the laws that could be applied to prohibit these activities at any time. There were, however, some methods of giving relief. In addition to the right of persons born in England or its colonies to be considered natural-born Englishmen, a small number of aliens including a few Jews and foreign-born Protestants had been made "free denizens" and received special royal permission to obtain some or all of the rights of citizens under letters patent of denization. These rights included the right to sue and be sued, the right to own land, and the right to carry on business, sometimes in a particular area. However, denizens are "in a middle state between an alien and a natural born subject." Unlike the status given by naturalization, the rights of persons "endenized" were personal and did not include family members unless specifically named in the letters patent. Denizens continued to be liable to pay the alien duties on goods exported or imported.[19]

None of these methods of granting citizenship was designed to make Jews or Dissenters equal to Englishmen who were members of the established church. Britain in fact had two classes of citizenship. Those in the first class, the members of the established churches in England and Scotland, were entitled to be appointed to high office upon taking their oath in the authorized form. Those in the second class, made up of Protestant Dissenters, naturalized or natural-born Jews, and Roman Catholics, were theoretically equal to the first class of citizens, except they were unable to assume high office or exercise many other privileges because the tenets of their own creeds prevented them from swearing the oath of office whose form was designed to be acceptable only to adherents of the established churches. In fact, during the original debate on the Jews Naturalization Bill, one of the bill's supporters, Horace Walpole, reminded the house that there was nothing to fear from the Jews even if they should become naturalized. Naturalization would merely "allow them to live amongst us, and to enjoy the protection of our laws as to their persons and properties." Beyond that, he continued, they could "never have any share in the government of this country" because they are "by the laws now in being sufficiently excluded from ever having any share in it; for unless they become Christian, they cannot be so much as excisemen or customhouse officers."[20]

The Jews Naturalization Act (popularly known as the Jew Bill) had been passed by the House of Commons on 22 May 1753. It applied only to Jewish aliens living in England, Scotland, and Ireland, and it was intended to allow Jewish aliens who had established residence for more than three years to obtain the civil rights of citizenship without receiving the sacrament of the Lord's Supper which was a usual requirement of naturalization. It was not intended to allow Jews the right to have "any share in the government" by appointment or election to public office.[21]

Three years earlier, legislation for the naturalization of Jews in Britain had been introduced and defeated on the same day. The background of that attempt was recollected by Robert Nugent[22] during the debate on the repeal of the Jews Naturalization Act:

I remember when [in 1747] I had the honour to receive the commands of this House to prepare and bring in a Bill for a general naturalization of foreign Protestants (and I shall always look upon it as an honour) the Jews applied to me for a clause in their favour, and I was inclined to have added some clause for that purpose; but I was afraid lest it might obstruct the Bill, and therefore I refused to comply with their request. Yet I afterwards found that the *want* of such a clause was made one of the chief arguments against my Bill; for the Jews were then represented as a most innocent, harmless and useful people, and many advantages were talked of, which might accrue to this nation from their naturalization.[23]

In February 1750 Nugent revived the bill for the naturalization of foreign Protestants in Britain, which he had presented in December 1747. Although the bill was not originally designed to naturalize Jews, an amendment to that effect was introduced on 15 March 1750 after second reading of the bill but rejected after division on the same day.[24]

The naturalization bill of 1753 aroused little opposition when introduced in the House of Commons, with the recorded vote on second reading on 7 May indicating 95 in favour and only 16 opposed. It was passed quickly on 22 May, by a vote of 96 to 55, and received royal assent on 7 June. However, over the summer recess a storm of popular disapproval swept the country. As Walpole recalled: "The whole Nation found itself inflamed with a Christian zeal, which was thought happily extinguished with the ashes of Queen Anne and Sacheverell. Indeed this holy spirit seized none but the populace, and the very lowest of the clergy. Yet all these grew suddenly so zealous for the honour of the prophecies that foretell calamity and eternal dispersion to the Jews, that they seemed to fear lest the completion of them should be defeated by Act of Parliament and there wanted nothing to their ardor but to petition both Houses to enact the accomplishment. The little Curates preached against the Bishops for deserting the interests of the Gospel: and Aldermen grew drunk at county clubs in the cause of Jesus Christ, as they had used to do for the sake of King James."[25]

For almost the first time, the common people of England had a chance to speak and to see the results of political action in Parliament. The countryside told its leaders through pamphlets and debates that enough was enough. "No Jews! No Jews! No Wooden Shoes!" was the cry throughout the land.[26] "I believe there never was a law made in any country that produced so general a murmur among the people," one member of parliament felt moved to say.[27] Britain's leaders in 1753 – the aristocracy, the gentry, the members of parliament, the hierarchy of the established churches – had seen no danger to the established order in allowing Jews to settle freely in England and its colonies. They had actually encouraged them to settle in the plantations of North America in 1740; they had stood by while Jews were allowed almost complete equality in the settlement of Halifax only four years before; they had now passed the Jews Naturalization Act. But it had come to the test of the common people themselves. Six years of Parliament's term had elapsed and a new general election was imminent. England's leaders were about to be rebuffed by those members of the populace with new political power who were eager to test it on this issue on which there was a time-honoured, religiously based, historical consensus. Walpole, somewhat embarrassed at the degree of popular opposition to an act which he had supported, put the issue on the basis of party politics, telling the House of Commons that "it was not many years since, rightly observed by a very consummate politician, who said to his friends, we shall never get the better of the present government unless we can raise a dispute about religion."[28]

By the time the house reconvened in November, both the governing Whig party and the opposition Tories had agreed to repeal the unpopular measure. As a face-saving step, Henry Pelham, the prime minister, as well as the other Whig leaders who had supported the act, inserted a preamble in the repealing bill acknowledging that the effect of the act had been "to raise discontents and to disquiet the minds of many of His Majesty's subjects" – that the government had been forced by "popular clamour" to reverse itself.[29]

A bill repealing the Jews Naturalization Act was passed on 28 November 1753 by 113 votes to 47.[30] In the future, as in the past, citizenship was to continue to be granted by denization to individual Jewish immigrants to Britain only as a royal favour.

In a sense, this debate represented the beginnings of democracy at a time when Britain had recently emerged from the feudal age and had not yet entered the period of political and social reform which followed the Industrial Revolution. Sir George Lyttelton set out the maxim of the new age: "A wise government will know where to yield as well as where to resist." And he continued: "Public wisdom, on some occasions, must condescend to give way to popular folly, especially in a free country, where the humour of the people must be considered as attentively, as the humour of a king in an absolute monarchy."[31] The popular will had forced the government to change its course, but the new direction was not yet towards increasing rights for all. Rather the aim was to preserve the status quo for those experiencing their own new status for the first time. The public had exercised its new power against a traditional scapegoat because it was not politically mature enough to favour an enlightened new concept of citizenship. Bitter memories of the debate would remain for another century. It would not be until 1826 that Jews in England could be naturalized without having to take a Christian oath. It would not be until 1858 that an English Jew would be allowed to swear a non-Christian form of oath of office in order to take his seat in the House of Commons – that crowded chamber where a hundred men had voted for the Jews Naturalization Act, as well as its repeal, 105 years earlier.

On 4 December, the enemies of the "Jew Bill" sought to press their opposition to rights for Jews even farther. Lord Harley and Sir James Dashwood moved for the repeal of the Plantation Act of 1740,[32] which had allowed Jews in the British colonies of North America to become naturalized and thereby gain the rights of citizenship in those colonies, although not in England itself. This statute, by far the most important law of the eighteenth century relating to the rights of Jews in British America permitted foreign-born Jews and foreign Protestants to become naturalized as citizens after seven years' residence in those colonies.

However, the members of the House of Commons in 1753 were vocal in their support of the Plantation Act and the dangers of its repeal.[33] In the words of Henry Pelham, "a repeal will revive the intolerant principles of the High Church, which have produced such pernicious effects." "My maxim," stated William Pitt, "is not to grant more consideration to the church than it actually enjoys: for if a High Church spirit should revive, the fate which threatens the Jews today will menace the Presbyterian tomorrow, and the country will be agitated by a septennial church clamour."[34] Perhaps the real reason why a repeal of the Plantation Act could not be considered had best been expressed by the lord chancellor on 15 November 1753 during the debate in the House of Lords on the repeal of the Jews Naturalization Act:

The Plantation Act is of a nature very different from the act now proposed to be repealed. It has been in force for many years, and many Christians as well as Jews are concerned in its preservation. Many of both religions have in consequence thereof transported themselves, and embarked their whole fortunes in our plantations. With regard to them, therefore, the public faith is engaged, that the act shall never be repealed. A repeal of it even with regard to the Jews would be breach of public faith, and would prevent any Protestant Christian from trusting to it for the future.[35]

When the vote was taken, the attempt to repeal the Plantation Act was soundly defeated, 208 to 88.

Although a week earlier Parliament had been willing to repeal the act that had allowed naturalization of Jews in England, the members saw a distinction between that and allowing Jews to be naturalized in the colonies. Naturalization of Jews in England would open the floodgates for countless wanderers who could not obtain the rights of citizenship in other lands. Naturalization of Jews in North America, however, was a means of advancing the wealth and strength of the British empire. The preamble to the Plantation Act had stated the aim in plain words: "many Foreigners and Strangers ... might be induced to come and settle in some of His Majesty's Colonies in America, if they were made Partakers of the Advantages and Privileges which the natural born Subjects of this Realm do enjoy."

The message of the repeal of the Jews Naturalization Act and the defeat of the attempt to repeal of the Plantation Act within a single week was clear: naturalization of Jews in North America was to be encouraged; naturalization of Jews in Britain was to be left to another time.

England had nevertheless come much farther than most of the countries of Europe in its treatment of its Jewish and other religious minorities, even though it was by no means ready to grant civil equality at home to those of differing faiths. In most European countries, Roman Catholic hierarchies paralleled the civil establishment and in many respects rivalled the power of the state. In most of those countries, citizenship was defined to include adherence to only the Roman Catholic faith; "inquisitions" run by the church using the apparatus of the state had at one time or another rooted out those who secretly professed other religions – and Jews had no right to exist. But in the England of 1753, some Nonconformists were accepted as having rights, close in some respects though not equal to rights enjoyed by adherents of the Church of England; the Jewish religion was tolerated, Roman Catholicism somewhat less so. Christianity as defined by the Church of England was still the law of the land. The sovereign was still head of the Church of England, the established church, and full civil and political rights were available only to the adherents of that church.[36]

The message was plain. If there was to be an experiment in allowing equality to people of other faiths, England itself was not yet ready to be the proving ground. If there was to be a new order in democratic countries, that order was to be in the New World, not the Old.

SETTING THE STAGE

1 Obstacles to Equality for Religious Minorities in Britain in 1750

The word toleration, which, after so many centuries and so many acts of intolerance, appeared to be a word full of humanity and reason, is no longer suitable to a nation that wishes to firmly place its rights upon the eternal foundations of justice. America, to which politics will owe so many useful lessons, has rejected the word from its code, as a term tending to compromise individual liberty and to sacrifice certain classes of men to other classes. To tolerate is, in fact, to suffer that which you could, if you wished, prevent and prohibit.

Petition of French Jews to
National Assembly of France, January 1790[1]

Jews in Britain would not have been treated equally with other Englishmen even if the Jews Naturalization Act had remained the law of the land. When Horace Walpole told the House of Commons that English Jews, whether natural-born or naturalized, "could never have any share in the government of this country" and "cannot be so much as exercisemen or custom-house officers" unless they became Christians,[2] he was referring to the legal and administrative system of "disabilities" which had the effect of placing obstacles in the way of the exercise of the rights of citizenship by non-Anglicans, including of course Jewish people, in England. These obstacles were not designed to undermine Jewish equality in particular, and were in no way specifically "anti-semitic," but were aimed at dealing with the real problem of determining the status of religious dissenters in a state where the Anglican form of Protestantism was established by law.

EXPRESS PROHIBITIONS

The system of disabilities practised in Britain in the eighteenth century was quite different from the outright prohibitions that had kept Jews

---

For a schematic representation of this chapter, see p. 19.

out of England from 1290 until 1656 and were still common on the continent. Jews had been expelled from France in 1306 and repeatedly banished or severely restricted over the years until they found toleration in France at the beginning of the eighteenth century; their expulsion from Spain in 1492 and from Portugal in 1497 remained in effect well into the nineteenth century. Throughout the period, other European states adopted laws whose intent varied from outright banishment or expulsion to the imposition of direct restrictions and taxes upon Jews and other minorities.

After the Jews returned in 1656, England, unlike the Catholic countries of Europe, passed no laws directly affecting Jews either by tax or by prohibition. Only on one occasion, in November 1689, did the House of Commons consider imposing a special tax of £100,000 on the Jews of England in order to raise money for the war against France. A petition on behalf of the sixty to eighty Jewish families then in England, stating that if the tax were proceeded with they would be utterly ruined, was presented to the Commons by Paul Foley, the member for Hereford, on 19 November. The projected tax was withdrawn a month later, as the dangerous precedent of a special tax on a small unrepresented class was acknowledged.[3]

There was, however, one express prohibition against Jews in the laws of England which may have survived from the thirteenth century. It affected the *holding of land.*

In the early days after their return, the question of owning land had not been of practical importance to the Jews because the newcomers were all foreigners and, as aliens, could not own land in England.[4] But once the British-born children of the newcomers grew up, the question arose whether they were legally capable of holding land under English law as natural-born Englishmen.

The feudal system of landholding, which had been the rule in England during the Middle Ages, had been replaced by the mid-seventeenth century with a system of freehold tenure. The feudal system had been closely tied to parallel social and religious systems in which higher authorities commanded an elaborate range of duties from individuals who had few rights. Under this system the serfs at the bottom of the economic or social pyramid were allowed to work their land only because someone higher on the scale permitted it. The more flexible system of freehold tenure, in contrast, allowed persons to hold land granted directly from the monarch without owing any personal duties to others in the hierarchy.

By about 1725, the English courts had determined that Jews could also hold land, whether granted by the monarch or acquired by direct purchase from another landholder. In 1718 the attorney general had given his opinion that a person born in England, though a Jew, could own real estate in England and that on his death it would descend to his issue in the same manner as the lands of other English people, and not be forfeited to the crown as it would if there were no such right to hold land.

However, in 1738, two mediaeval statutes or ordinances were unearthed in manuscript form; these dated from 1271 and 1275, before the Jews' expulsion from England.[5] These statutes, which had never before been published, provided that Jews could own "Houses and Curtilages in the Cities and Boroughs where they abide" but no other freehold lands. From 1738 until 1846, when these two statutes were repealed, legal opinions in England were inconclusive as to whether they should apply to prevent Jews born in England from owning land. As a practical matter, Jews did openly and with impunity hold and enjoy landed estates other than houses in the cities and towns in which they resided. As a legal question, the opinion of most English lawyers of that time was that the status of villeinage, upon which the two statutes were based, no longer existed in England.[6] During the debate on the Jews Naturalization Act in 1753, Nicholas Hardinge, a member of parliament, had reviewed ancient English records and found that Jews had owned land in England since the twelfth and thirteenth centuries and perhaps even earlier. "We must conclude," he told the Commons, "that Jews who are not aliens, that is to say, such as are born within the British dominions, or naturalized, may still purchase and hold land estates, as well as any other of his majesty's natural born subjects."[7] But the question was not raised directly in any court of law and, until 1846, a segment of the legal profession considered that there was some doubt as to the right of Jews to hold land in England.[8]

DISABILITIES

The system that had evolved by the second half of the eighteenth century prevented non-Anglicans from participating equally in English society in a way that was much more subtle than the methods used by other countries which expressly prohibited or banned religious non-conformists from their territories or at the very least denied them legal equality by statute or by the assessment of special taxes. In practice, non-Anglicans were denied equal treatment only by specific obstacles to the exercise of various rights, sometimes by inadvertence, sometimes by design. In either case the effect of these disabilities was to prevent the full exercise of civil and political rights by Jews, Roman Catholics, and Nonconformists.

The distinction between substantive rights and procedural rights was at the root of the problem. In substance, religious minorities other than Catholics were allowed the rights of natural-born Englishmen. A number of statutes and court cases over a period of time had confirmed these rights. However, religious minorities frequently found that they were nevertheless unable in practice to fulfil the requirements necessary to the exercise of those rights; thus the rights allowed them in substance were denied them by the procedures that were in place. There were five types of such procedural impediments.

1 The first of these obstacles or disabilities was based on ancient custom and operated to keep strangers such as Jews from opening shops in the cities or *municipal* corporations of England.

2 The second disability arose from the concept of *toleration* itself – that is, the concept of whether legally to tolerate a particular religious belief by providing an exemption from the punishments that the law required for non-Anglicans.

3 The third disability hindered minorities from exercising the rights of citizens because of their *alien status* or because of the laws relating to denization, naturalization, and birth in England.

4 The law created a fourth layer of disabilities for those otherwise entitled to share in the exercise of authority by holding office but disabled by their refusal to take the *sacrament of the Lord's Supper according to the rites of the Church of England.*

5 Finally, the *state oaths*, a condition of holding any office or place of trust, were cast in terms which effectively barred those not of the ruling class or religion.

1   Municipal and Guild Restrictions

Some restrictions faced by Jews and other dissenting religious sects were particular to the nature of English cities and were tied to the control of trade. These restrictions arose from the ancient prerogatives of municipal governments. In one sense, they derived from the *privilegia*[9] that had, since the time of the Persian empire, allowed limited rights to individuals or groups to trade in cities and towns at different times or places. In another sense, these restrictions originated in the growth of self-governing cities or city-states in Europe during the Middle Ages, in that merchant and craft guilds in many cities had led citizens to achieve a degree of independence from the restraints of the feudal system. By the eighteenth century, even though cities or city-states had been absorbed into countries, they still retained the power to control trade within their municipal boundaries. Trading cities could decide who was to be allowed the freedom of the city and who could keep a shop and sell at retail.

Table 1
Obstacles to Equality for Religious Minorities in Britain in 1750

EXPRESS RESTRICTIONS – substantive laws
1. Prohibition on residence in certain areas (rare)
2. Special taxes (rare)
3. Prohibitions on land holding remaining from feudal times

DISABILITIES – procedural difficulties to the exercise of rights
1. *Municipal and guild restrictions* on the practice of trade, crafts, or retail sale of goods.
2. *Establishment of the Church of England* and the penal laws supporting that establishment. There was "toleration" (or *limited* rights to freedom of worship without punishment) for some dissenters. The Toleration Act of 1689 allowed legal toleration for Protestant Dissenters. There was no toleration for Roman Catholics (encoded in statutes). Toleration for Jews existed in practice but not by statute and was subject to the discretion of authorities.
3. *Alien status* – aliens had no political rights and severely limited civil rights. A Jew was an alien (1656–1740) unless
   (*a*) born in England or its colonies
   (*b*) able to obtain a letter of denization which allowed the individual some privileges of citizenship by royal prerogative
   (*c*) naturalized under an act of parliament and so obtaining citizenship as a right. This process allowed *only* in British colonies. Those naturalized in the colonies who returned to Britain were no longer aliens but still could not hold offices or places of trust.
4. *Prescription of the Anglican sacrament and a declaration against transubstantiation* as a condition of holding civil or military office and places of trust as required by the Test Act of 1673 (An act for preventing Dangers which may happen from Popish Recusants).
   (*a*) unacceptable to Roman Catholics because it denied a central tenet of their faith
   (*b*) unacceptable to Roman Catholics, Jews, and Protestant Dissenters because taking the sacrament of the Lord's Supper ("according to the Usage of the Church of England – in some publick Church, upon some Lord's Day, commonly called *Sunday*, immediately after Divine Service") was precondition of making the declaration.
5. *State Oaths* as a condition of holding civil and military office or a place of trust
   (*a*) Before 1701 the state oaths (oath of allegiance and oath of supremacy) were sworn under the Test Act and required the taking of the Anglican sacrament as a precondition, thus disabling Protestant Dissenters, Jews, and Roman Catholics.
   (*b*) After 1701 the state oaths were no longer sworn under the Test Act but a new oath, the oath of abjuration included the phrase "upon the true Faith of a Christian," thus disabling Jews.

Throughout history, whether the reason given was that Jews were aliens or that they refused to take the customary oath(s), the power of municipal governments to control trade had had the effect of excluding Jews from retail trade. In England, in the eighteenth century, the by-laws of the city of London excluded all from the retail trade but those who had been granted the freedom of the city and been made its citizens or freemen. The local usage of that city required that the oath tendered to all those entitled to its freedom be administered on the New Testament, rendering it impossible for a professing Jew, who would only swear upon the Pentateuch or the Old Testament, to pursue any retail trade within its boundaries. In practice this meant that Jews were forced to become wholesale merchants instead of retail shopkeepers.

In 1739 an attempt was made to have a duly qualified Jew named Abraham Rathom admitted to the freedom of the city of London by being sworn on the Old Testament, but the city administration refused to accept the oath. In the ensuing court case, it was decided that Jews did not have the right to swear the oath required for the freedom of the city on the Old Testament, even though they did have that right when giving evidence as a witness in court. The chief justice, in giving the judgment of the court, explained that the reason Jews were allowed to swear on the Old Testament when giving evidence was "because all courts desire to have the best security they can for the truth of the evidence; and therefore, as it is known they [Jews] have a more solemn obligation to speak the truth when sworn on the Old Testament, it is for that reason allowed." However, this case, as the chief justice noted, related to being sworn as a condition of obtaining the freedom of the city – a case of the ancient custom of taking an oath in the usual manner by swearing on the New Testament. It was not a case where the truth of the evidence was at issue. The custom of taking the oath in the usual manner was thus not "unreasonable upon the face of it" and therefore the court "ought not to interfere to allow the oath to be sworn on the Old Testament."[10] As a result, Jews were totally excluded from the retail trade in the city of London until 10 December 1830 when the city's council passed an act allowing them to swear the oath required for the taking up of the freedom of the city "according to the forms of their own religion."[11]

The involvement of Jewish artisans in skilled crafts was also usually limited by restrictions imposed by craft guilds, even when the craftsman did not keep a retail shop in the cities.[12] These guilds were self-regulating organizations which had been given exclusive rights to control the trade in a particular craft usually in a designated area. Before the expulsion of the Jews, the guilds had prevented Jews from following any trade or handicraft in towns. And some guilds maintained mediaeval restrictions on membership based on Christian oaths well into the eighteenth century.

For example, the Worshipful Company of Goldsmiths in London had the authority to regulate workers in gold, silver, and copper and to require the registration of marks by plate workers, spoon workers, watchcase makers, buckle makers, hilt makers, and sword cutlers. The regulations of the company had the effect of restricting Jews from entering these occupations in London. In consequence, only two Jews had their marks registered at Goldsmiths' Hall during the eighteenth century. One, Abraham de Oliveyra, had been a noted goldsmith and maker of Jewish ritual objects in silver for many years before his mark was entered in 1724 or 1725, and it is likely that he took a Christian oath in order to be qualified as a gold worker by the company.[13] The second, Naphtali Hart, had his mark recorded in 1791, and that may have occurred after a change in the company's regulations.[14] Restrictions were apparently less severe for "provincial" makers, notice of whose marks appeared in the registers of the London company. The mark of Merducea (Mordecai) Samuel of Portsmouth, for example, was entered in April 1759.[15]

The London Gunmakers Company maintained similar restrictions. One of the great eighteenth-century London gunmakers was Israel Segalas, who had come from France with the Huguenots after the revocation of the Edict of Nantes. According to some he was a Jew – as his name, a variation of "Segal" or "Levy," suggests – but on 14 June 1702, Segalas, described as an "arquebusier" or maker of muskets, took the oath of abjuration attesting to his true faith as a Christian in the Church of the Tabernacle, Leicester Fields, apparently so that he could carry on his trade in the city of London in accordance with the rules of the company.[16]

2   Establishment of the Church of England and the Practice of Toleration

In the twentieth century, "toleration" or "tolerance" has acquired the meaning of one equal accepting the differing practices of another equal with an open mind. In the eighteenth century, however, it meant the opposite of the word "establishment." Toleration of the religious beliefs of others amounted to a denial, rather than an advancement, of religious equality. To paraphrase the petition of the French Jews in 1790, toleration was a privilege not a right; the grant of toleration by authorities to persons or groups may appear superficially to be an act of humanity and reason, but it is no substitute for equality entrenched in law.

By the beginning of the eighteenth century, Anglicanism had long been established as the official religion of England. The first statutes passed during the reign of Elizabeth I in the sixteenth century, the Act of Supremacy and the Act of Uniformity, had provided that the monarch of England was the head of the Church of England and that the Book of Common Prayer was the only prayer book authorized for public worship.[17] The established character of the Church of England was reinforced by later statutes which provided for its support from public money and set out criminal sanctions against anyone in England who deviated from the norms of the Anglican faith.

After the restoration of Charles II to the monarchy in 1660, attitudes towards religion began to change. Dissenters who had supported the revolution deserved some reward and were in any event seen as allies in the continuing controversies with the Roman Catholics. While maintaining the establishment of the Church of England was seen as essential, ordinary Englishmen were concerned about "friendly" Nonconformists and softer attitudes towards Dissenters were prevalent – exemplified at the extreme by the English philosopher, John Locke. A *Letter on Toleration*, first published in 1689, was Locke's plea for individual religious liberty. Toleration, Locke believed, was "the chief distinguishing mark of a true church." In Locke's ideal commonwealth there would be no connection between church and state, and no religion would be favoured above any other. The state would tolerate all religions equally. "The toleration of those who hold different opinions on matters of religion is so agreeable to the Gospel and to reason," he wrote, "that it seems monstrous for men to be blind in so clear a light." Even non-Christians should be tolerated: "Indeed, to speak the truth, and as becomes one man to another, neither pagan nor Mohometan nor Jew should be excluded from the commonwealth because of his religion. The Gospel commands no such thing."[18]

While Locke's views represented the opinions of only a small minority of Englishmen, it was generally acknowledged by that time that the laws establishing the Church of England would make criminals of friendly Nonconformists unless they were legally tolerated. So, in 1689, toleration in England was defined by a statute which stated simply that people of a particular religious persuasion that was outside the established church could exercise their religion freely without running afoul of the English penal laws that applied to all Nonconformists. Toleration gave no higher rights than the right of these others to hold a public religious service. The Toleration Act of 1689 – An Act for exempting their Majesties' *protestant* subjects dissenting from the Church of England from the penalties of certain laws[19] – allowed freedom of worship to Protestant Dissenters by granting them an exemption from the penal laws that compelled attendance at Anglican church services and that outlawed the holding of church services not in accordance with the Book of Common Prayer. Protestant dissent was "tolerated" without repealing the penal laws; the laws were retained but Protestant Dissenters were exempted from them.

Toleration did not mean that Dissenters would be allowed to share political power with the Anglicans by sitting in Parliament, by holding any political or municipal office, or by accepting any place of profit under the crown. Nonconformity was still to be regarded as a crime, but exceptions were now put in place that allowed Protestants the right to practise without punishment forms of that religion that were not in conformity with the Anglican rite.

The Toleration Act specifically denied any exemption to Roman Catholics. "Nothing in this act," it read, "shall extend or be construed to extend to give any ease, benefit or advantage to any papist or popish recusant whatsoever." Similarly, the act did not grant any exemption to Unitarians "or any person that shall deny in his preaching or writing the doctrine of the Blessed Trinity." Jews were not mentioned at all in the act, either as persons fit to be exempted from the penal laws or as persons to be expressly denied relief; but there can be no doubt that Jews were deliberately excluded from the act and, according to the letter of the law, were not entitled to tolerance.[20] It was many years before the benefits of the act were finally extended to Catholics (1791), to Quakers (1812), to Unitarians (1813), and, finally, in 1846 to Jews.[21]

Although the Toleration Act did not extend to Jews, Jews in England had been allowed to worship in a synagogue, open to the public, since 1673, although this practice was permitted only at the discretion of the king-in-council. This permission was therefore a privilege rather than a right. At the beginning of 1673 the leaders of the London Jewish community had been "indited of a riot for meeting together for the exercise of their religion in Duke's Place, and a true bill was found against them by the grand jury." The Jews petitioned Charles II, and the king-in-council ordered the attorney general to "stay all proceedings at law against the Petitioners who have been indicted as aforesaid and to provide they may receive no further trouble in this behalf."[22] Still, because the Jewish religion was not officially tolerated, the right of Jews to worship in synagogues had not been granted expressly. The penalty had been waived, but the crime remained on the books. "The Jews are permitted to have dwellings and private houses; why are they denied synagogues?" Locke would ask sixteen years later. "Is their doctrine more false, their worship more abominable, or their combination more dangerous if they meet in public rather than in their private houses?"[23]

As Judaism was not officially tolerated in England until 1846, it followed that prior to that date the law could not be relied upon to allow gifts or bequests that advanced the Jewish religion, and during the eighteenth century there were a number of judicial decisions that bequests advancing the Jewish religion were void. Perhaps the most bizarre case was that of Da Costa v. De Paz in 1744.[24] Elias De Paz left a sum of money in his will to be used "in the maintenance of a Yesiba or assembly for daily reading the Jewish law, and for advancing and propagating their holy religion." In his judgment, the lord chancellor came to the conclusion that "the intent of this bequest must be taken to be in contradiction of the Christian religion, which is a part of the law of the land." As he determined that the legacy was not good in law, he decided that it should be applied to some other charitable uses rather than allowing it to become part of the residue of the estate and go to De Paz's heirs. The crown gave most of the legacy to the Foundling Hospital to support a preacher and instruct the children in his care in the Christian religion, thereby doing the opposite of what the testator intended. This was not an isolated case. In Isaac v. Gompertz in 1753, it was decided that legacies for the support and maintenance of a synagogue were similarly invalid because they advanced the Jewish religion.[25]

3   Alien Status

The Jews who returned to England in 1656 were aliens because they had been born outside the monarch's dominions or allegiance. Under English law at the time, and British law thereafter, aliens possessed no political rights and their civil rights were severely limited.[26]

Aliens had no right to enter or remain in England save as merchants who were international traders and who were allowed to enter and depart from the realm freely in times of peace. The right of the state to expel a foreigner from its territory was recognized by international law as the *droit de renvoi*. A foreigner could hold no real property although an alien merchant was entitled to lease a house for himself and his family or for carrying on his trade. An alien who was not a merchant could occupy a house for no more than a year, by agreement rather than by lease. Aliens could not sue to enforce real property claims. They could, however, hold or acquire personal property other than a British ship and could use the courts to protect personal property, although those rights were frequently curtailed by statute. Finally, aliens, particularly alien merchants, were liable to pay an additional tax on imported goods as an "alien duty" until it was abolished by statute in 1784.[27]

Since the return of the Jews to England, there had been two competing legal theories as to their status as citizens. One, a simple theory, was that Jews were not citizens unless they were naturalized by statute or were born in England or its colonies. Under this theory, Jews born in England held the rights of natural-born Englishmen. Though it was true that the exercise of some of these rights may have been impossible for Jews because they entailed the swearing of a Christian oath, this incapacity, the argument ran, was based solely on the form of the oath. The second theory was based on the decisions of Sir Edward Coke, the eminent English jurist of the first half of the seventeenth century. Writing in 1647, before the Jews returned to England, Coke argued that Jews, as "infidels," "are in law *perpetui inimici*, perpetual enemies" of the monarch and that because Christianity was the law of the land, those who did not profess it could never have the rights of Englishmen.[28]

Jews who had acquired the status of citizens of England, whether by birth in England, by naturalization in the colonies and return to England, or by denization in England, were entitled to more rights than those allowed to aliens. As Henry Pelham put it during the debate on the passage of the Jews Naturalization Act, Englishmen were "indulging them so far as to allow them to live amongst us, and to enjoy the protection of our laws as to their persons and properties."[29] The extent of these rights was not the same for all but depended on the facts of each case. By 1700 the courts had decided to overrule Coke's doctrine that Jews were perpetual enemies of the sovereign, thus allowing them to be sworn as witnesses, sue for debts, and participate as litigants. The right of Jews to swear an oath on either the Pentateuch or the Old Testament in order to give evidence in these instances had been finally agreed to in a case in 1680.[30]

But most Jews remained aliens in Britain and were far from equal to Englishmen. William Pitt summed up the situation at the middle of the eighteenth century: "By our laws, as they stand at present, were they to be strictly put in execution, no alien Jew could easily follow any employment in this country: he cannot export or import any goods without paying the aliens duty, except only those goods that are exempted by particular acts of parliament: he cannot so much as take a lease of a house or shop, nor can anyone let him such a lease: and indeed, as Jews are not included in the Toleration act, no Jew could so much as live in this kingdom, if our laws relating to religion were to be strictly carried into execution."[31]

The repeal of the Jews Naturalization Act in 1753 only a few months after its introduction meant that Jews could acquire the status of other Englishmen only by birth in Britain or its colonies, or by letters of denization given by royal authority as a privilege rather than as a right, or by naturalization in the colonies under the Plantation Act. It would not be until 1825 that Parliament would pass a statute making it unnecessary to receive the sacrament of the Lord's Supper according to the Anglican rite as a condition of naturalization,[32] with the result that Jews who had immigrated to Great Britain would be able to end their alien status by becoming naturalized.

4   The Prescription of the Anglican Sacrament and a Declaration against Transubstantiation

If anything was clear about the extent of minority rights in the England of the eighteenth century, it was that Jews, like Roman Catholics and many of the Protestant Dissenters, had no political rights. Jews were excluded from holding any office or place of trust, not through any express prohibition, but because of the operation of two statutes passed shortly after they were readmitted to England. The Corporation Act of 1661 and the Test Act of 1673 created a number of legal requirements for persons assuming office. None of these requirements was expressly intended to apply to Jews, but they had the effect of disabling Jews, as well as the Catholics and members of some dissenting Protestant sects at whom they were directed, from exercising many of the civil and political rights that would otherwise have been attached to citizenship.

The Corporation Act,[33] the first of these two statutes, was passed in 1661 to deal with the extreme Dissenters, such as Puritans and Republicans, who had remained in control of England's cities and municipal corporations after the Anglicans had regained control of the country with the restoration of Charles II in 1660. Section 2 of the act provided that "no person shall be elected or chosen in or to any office or place in any corporation unless he has within one year next before his election taken the Sacrament of the Lord's Supper according to the rites of the Church of England." Any election to any corporation, municipal or otherwise, was declared void if the individual was not so qualified. Because the more moderate of the Dissenters were willing to take the sacrament according to the Anglican rite, the statute posed no difficulty for them. But its provisions did act as a bar to extreme Dissenters as it would to Jews born in England after their community was re-established in 1656.

The Test Act[34] also required that the taking of the Anglican sacrament of the Lord's Supper as a condition of accepting certain offices, but, in contrast to the Corporation Act, it was aimed specifically at Roman Catholics: indeed, it was officially entitled An Act for preventing Dangers which may happen from Popish Recusants. It was passed in 1673, shortly after James, Duke of York, and heir presumptive to the throne, had publicly declared his adherence to the Catholic faith. In the wake of the public excitement aroused by the prospect of a Catholic becoming king and thereby supreme head of the Church of England, Parliament passed the Test Act. Section 2 provided that to be admitted to any office, employment, or place of trust under the crown, whether civil or military, a person had to take the oaths of allegiance and supremacy in open court. Before such a person was able to take these oaths, he was required to file a certificate that he had received "the Sacrament of the Lord's Supper, according to the Usage of the Church of *England*, within Three Months after his or their Admittance in or receiving their said Authority and Employment, in some publick Church, upon some Lord's Day, commonly called *Sunday*, immediately after Divine Service and Sermon." Further, section 9 of the act provided that at the same time as the oaths of allegiance and supremacy were taken, a declaration against transubstantiation was to be made and subscribed, thus denying the belief that the bread and wine used in the sacrament of the Lord's Supper were actually changed into the body and blood of Christ. Noncompliance with these requirements of the Test Act brought a penalty of £500 as well as forfeiture of the office and a number of civil disabilities, including a prohibition on prosecuting legal proceedings or receiving any legacy under a will. The declaration that there "is not any transubstantiation in the elements of Bread and Wine" could not be made by Roman Catholics. And, as the sacrament of the Lord's Supper according to the rites of the Church of England had still to be taken, the act also effectively stood as a procedural "disability" barring Jews and some Protestant Dissenters from those offices for which this observance was a requirement.

England's fear of Catholicism, even when practised by native-born Englishmen, rested on the view that Roman Catholics were in some sense citizens of a foreign power – the Church of Rome – and thus a threat to the security of the state. It drove Parliament to protect access to positions of influence from adherents of that church. The combined effect of the Corporation and Test Acts was to ensure that all Catholics were excluded from office in any corporation as well as from any office or place of trust under the crown. As a consequence of the insistence on the taking of the sacrament, the acts also subjected some Nonconformists and the Jews to the same penalties. The results were often ironic. For example, after the union of England and Scotland in 1707, adherents of the Presbyterian Church (the established church in Scotland) continued throughout the eighteenth century to be barred from holding any office in England because of the requirements of the Test and Corporation Acts. At the same time, however, Englishmen were able to hold office in Scotland because it had no similar legislation.

Although subsequent statutes in 1701 and 1714 meant that the oaths of allegiance and supremacy were no longer taken under the Test Act, the law in Britain continued to require the taking of the Anglican sacrament as a precondition to making and subscribing the declaration against transubstantiation. It was not until 1828 that the political disabilities of Protestant Nonconformists were swept away by the repeal of the Test and Corporation Acts as they affected this group. The Sacramental Tests Repeal Act removed the requirement that office holders take the sacrament according to the rite of the Church of England. It was replaced by a declaration, to be made "upon the true faith of a Christian," not to use any power or influence possessed by virtue of the office held to "injure or weaken" the established church.[35] The following year Parliament passed the Roman Catholic Relief Act, freeing the Catholics from the disabilities they had suffered under the Test and Corporation Acts,[36] including the declaration against transubstantiation. Though restrictions against the civil and political rights of Protestant Dissenters and Catholics were now relieved, Jews and other non-Christians were still not able to hold civil or military offices or places of trust because the new declaration included the phrase "upon the true faith of a Christian." The repeal of the Test and Corporation Acts did, however, allow Jews to obtain naval and military commissions below the ranks of rear admiral and major-general, as these did not require any declaration.[37]

Because of the phrasing of this declaration, Jews in England continued to be effectively barred for another seventeen years from holding political office in England until the Jewish Disabilities Removal Act of 1845 amended this requirement with respect to Jews elected to municipal office.[38] David Salomons had been elected an alderman for the city of London in 1835 and again in 1844, but both times he was unable to subscribe to the declaration required and was not admitted to office. Elected again in 1847, he was finally able to take office.[39] In one sense, Salomons's election as mayor of the city of London in 1855 marked the end of an era.

5   The State Oaths

The last act passed during the reign of King William III bore the lengthy title, An Act for the further Security of his Majesty's Person, and the Succession of the Crown in the Protestant Line, and for extinguishing the Hopes of the pretended Prince of Wales, and all other Pretenders, and their open and secret Abettors.[40] This act required three state oaths to be sworn as a condition of appointment or acceptance of any office or place of trust with the government in England: the oath of allegiance, the oath of supremacy, and the oath of abjuration.[41]

Oaths of office had originally been instituted to ensure that office holders were loyal to the sovereign, a tradition that remains today in

Canada although in a different form. By the act of 1701 the state oaths were required to be sworn by persons appointed to any civil or military office, or to receive remuneration by reason of any royal grant or patent, or to have any command or place of trust under the authority of the crown, and by all ecclesiastical persons, all preachers, all members of colleges and halls at a university that were of at least eighteen years of age, all teachers, schoolmasters, and ushers, and all court officers such as barristers, solicitors, proctors, clerks, advocates, and counsellors-at-law.

The oaths of allegiance and supremacy had been in use long before 1701. After 1688, the oath of allegiance amounted to a simple declaration of allegiance to the sovereign: "I, *A.B.*, do sincerely promise and swear, That I will be faithful and bear true allegiance, to [the sovereign of the day]. So help me God." The oath of supremacy constituted an acknowledgment that no English monarch, though excommunicated by the pope, could be murdered or deposed by his subjects and that no "foreign prince" had any ecclesiastical or spiritual jurisdiction, power, or superiority within the realm. The purpose of this oath, which had its roots in the Act of Supremacy of 1558, was to deny that the pope had any higher authority than the Protestant sovereign of England. By 1672 the oath had already taken the form to be adopted in the act of 1701, namely: "I, *A.B.*, do swear That I do from my heart abhor, detest and abjure as impious and heretical that damnable doctrine and position, That princes excommunicated or deprived by the Pope, or any authority of the see of Rome may be deposed or murdered by their subjects or any other whatsoever. And I do declare That no foreign prince person prelate state or potentate hath or ought to have any jurisdiction power superiority preeminence or authority ecclesiastical or spiritual within this realm. So help me God."

The oath of abjuration was introduced for the first time in the act of 1701, largely to prevent Roman Catholics from assuming office.[42] After the death of James II, who had been deposed in the revolution of 1688, the claim of his son James, the Old Pretender, to be king was supported not only by the Jacobite party in Britain but by the French monarch. To undermine the Pretender's claim, a new oath was drafted "abjuring" or denying that claim. This oath was designed to reinforce the oath of supremacy. To prevent a suspected practice of the Jesuits to encourage Catholics to take the oath with a secret inner mental reservation or by crossing their fingers, the oath of abjuration concluded with these words: "And all these things I do plainly and sincerely acknowledge and swear, according to these express words by me spoken, and according to the plain and common sense and understanding of the same words, without any equivocation, mental evasion, or secret reservation whatsoever. And I do make this recognition, acknowledgment, abjuration, renunciation and promise heartily, willingly and truly *upon the true Faith of a Christian*. So help me God."[43]

There was nothing in the wording of either the oath of allegiance or the oath of supremacy that would have been objectionable to the most devout Jew or to any non-Christian. However, observant or professing Jews were naturally unwilling to swear the oath of abjuration because of that penultimate phrase and were thus caught in the net designed for the Catholics. Consequently, they would remain barred from the exercise of rights otherwise allowed them.

In 1715, the Catholic supporters of the Old Pretender failed in their attempt to win the throne for him. The following year, the Parliament at Westminster passed the first of a series of acts to assure the crown of the loyalty of all its subjects. These acts required "Papists, and other persons who had been Notoriously concerned in Continuing, Stirring up, and Supporting the late Rebellions, Insurrections, and Conspiracies" and those who had refused to swear the state oaths "to Register their Names and Real Estates" in default of which they should "forfeit the Fee Simple of Inheritance of, or such estate and interest in, all such Lands Tenements or Hereditaments, not registered."[44] Loyal Catholics, Jews, Quakers, and Protestant Dissenters who for reasons of conscience could not swear the oaths were caught by these statutes along with those Catholics who had supported the rebellion.

By 1723 the need for an exemption from the inflexible wording of the oath of abjuration had been recognized. The act of 1723 was intended to give relief to those who had not supported the rebellion in 1715 but who could not take the state oaths.[45] The act in fact did more than that as far as Jews were concerned. For the first time Jews were exempted by statute from the state oaths, although the exemption was allowed only for a particular purpose and for a limited time. After dealing with Quakers and other Protestant Dissenters, the act of 1723 specifically referred to "his Majesty's Subjects professing the Jewish Religion" – the first time any British statute had acknowledged Jews to be British subjects.[46] Jews were now allowed to take an oath of abjuration from which the words "upon the true Faith of a Christian" were omitted.[47] The exemption allowing Jews to amend the oath did not apply in other situations, however, and after 28 November 1724, when the deadline for taking the oaths had passed, the act no longer had any force.

In 1728 the British Parliament gave some relief to Protestant Dissenters and Jews with the passage of the first of the indemnity acts. The act allowed all persons who had neglected to qualify themselves for an office or an employment in the previous year by failing to take the oaths and perform the necessary obligations under the Test and Corporation Acts to be indemnified and recapacitated provided that they qualified themselves on or before 28 November 1728.[48] Indemnity acts with similar wording were passed by Parliament in every subsequent year until the repeal of the Test and Corporation Acts in 1828.[49] These statutes had the effect of ratifying appointment to *some* offices or employment in *some* professions during the previous year even though the required oaths and other obligations had not been discharged. Despite the long duration of this ad hoc arrangement, it was nonetheless true that Protestant Dissenters and Jews who held such office or employment lived under continual threat that an indemnity act might not be passed.

Some of the Protestant sects were given relief from the disabilities imposed by the requirements for swearing the state oaths as long as they were not perceived as a threat to the security of the state or to the ascendancy of the established church. Quakers, for example, believed that a society of friends, not a hierarchy of bishops, had authority in religious matters. Because they thereby rejected the ecclesiastical structure of the Church of England, they were seen as a threat to the established religion. The Quakers' beliefs also kept them from accepting offices or places of trust because they interpreted the words "swear not at all" in the New Testament to mean a prohibition on swearing any oaths. Their preference, in cases where it was allowed, was to "affirm" the contents of an oath. Parliament allowed Quakers in England some relief from these disabilities in 1748, but it was not until 1833 that they were given equal civil and political rights by a statute that enabled them to substitute an affirmation in all cases where an oath was required.

Even as late as 1855, however, the year that David Salomons was elected mayor of London, Jews continued to be excluded from the House of Commons because the parliamentary oath of office required that members acknowledge adherence to the Christian religion. In 1847 Baron Lionel de Rothschild had been elected to the Commons and he was re-elected in subsequent elections. However, he had not been able to take his seat because of the oath required. Finally, in 1858, the form of oath was amended in a manner acceptable to Jews and Rothschild was able to take his seat.[50]

CONCLUSION

Such was the system of obstacles in the middle of the eighteenth century for members of religious minorities seeking to participate fully in English society. It was the result of ancient restrictions, a lack of official toleration, alien status, and disabilities created by the state oaths and other statutory requirements. Disabilities were the mechanism whereby rights were seemingly allowed but were actually denied. This system amounted to a denial of equality to some British subjects in England. It put members of these minorities at a great disadvantage and increased the pressure for their assimilation.

Alexander Schomberg was a case in point. One of the five sons of Meyer Low Schomberg, a physician who had immigrated to London from Germany, he was raised in the Jewish tradition. He entered the navy in 1743, was promoted to captain in 1757, took part in the siege of Louisbourg and was knighted for his role as commander of the frigate *Diana* which covered the landing of the British forces under James Wolfe at Quebec in September 1760. However, in order to pursue a naval career and obtain his commission, Schomberg had been obliged to abandon his Judaism and be baptized as an Anglican.[51] Ralph Schomberg, a brother of Alexander, was more fortunate. On 24 June 1737 he had been appointed a notary public after having been allowed to strike the words "in Christ" from his appointment.[52]

As a result of the system of disabilities, there are no recorded examples in Britain of Jews elected or appointed to civil or military office, until the announcement in the London *Gazette* of August 1807 that Joshua Montefiore, Esq., had been commissioned in the York Light Infantry Volunteers as paymaster.[53] There were apparently other Jews who obtained commissions before the repeal of the Test and Corporation Acts in 1828, either because they concealed their religion and fulfilled the requirements despite their Christian content, or because the rigours of these legal requirements were somehow overlooked. When Jewish emancipation was being discussed in Parliament in 1833, for example, the Duke of Wellington surprised the House of Lords by admitting that fifteen Jewish officers had fought under him at Waterloo.[54]

Despite these possible exceptions, the requirements laid down by statute and other means to ensure that those in authority in eighteenth-century England were adherents of the established church meant that members of religious minorities were denied many rights. Most of these restrictions were directed, in the first instance, towards the exclusion of Protestant Dissenters or Roman Catholics. But the barriers they set up excluded Jews and other non-Christians as well. Moreover, as the debates over the Jews Naturalization Act in 1753 made clear, most of the people in England would have supported this exclusion if the question had been put directly. It was in the New World that those who sought to escape these restrictions would seek relief. For as one historian put it, the "American Colonies had not really been founded as extensions of England and of the English way of life in North America. Rather, they existed as rejections of that particular way of life. Those men who had established the original settlements along the Atlantic seaboard had done so with the deliberate object of escaping from the restrictions which England had imposed upon them; restrictions, religious, political and social which had become intolerable."[55]

2 The New World before 1740

[In order that] Jews, heathens and other dissenters from the purity of Christian religion may not be feared and kept at a distance from it – therefore any seven or more persons agreeing in any religion shall constitute a Church or profession to which they shall give some name to distinguish it from others.

John Locke, *Fundamental Constitutions*, Carolina, 1669[1]

The British colonies of North America, in which Jews might find a more welcoming environment than existed in the Old World, consisted of the West Indian islands of Jamaica, Barbados, and the Leeward Islands and the Thirteen Colonies on the eastern seaboard of North America, south of New France and northeast of the Spanish territories. As far as the treatment of the Jews was concerned, the British colonies also offered an entirely different environment from the colonies of Spain, Portugal, and France.

Catholic Spain and Portugal did not allow Jews at home or in their colonies. State policies ensured that even those who had been forcibly converted to Catholicism were found and expelled or killed.[2] Nevertheless, both countries relied on the skills and involvement of Jews for voyages of exploration as well as for international trade. Cecil Roth records how "voyages of exploration at the close of the Middle Ages were dependent in large measure on Jewish maps, Jewish nautical instruments, and Jewish astronomical tables; how hardy Jewish travellers paved the way for, and skilled Jewish interpreters accompanied Albuquerque and Vasco da Gama; how Columbus's expedition was patronised by Jews, financed by Jews, and in large measure manned by Jews; how it was a crypto-Jewish sailor who first sighted the New World, and the ex-Jewish interpreter who first set foot on it." Roth notes that "Jews were among those who were consulted by Amerigo Vespucci and among the *Conquistadores* who followed Cortez."[3] Spain

For a schematic representation of this chapter, see p. 42.

had its share of citizens of Jewish descent; the most celebrated was Christopher Columbus who made his first discoveries in the new world in the very year of the expulsion of the Jews from Spain. According to one source, a high proportion of the first settlers in the Spanish colonies of the Caribbean were Spanish New Christians. Jews as well as Phoenicians and Egyptians had been to the Cape of Good Hope long before Bartholemew Dias of Portugal sailed around it in 1488; Gamar da Gama, a Grenadine Jewish pilot who was forcibly baptized, accompanied Vasco da Gama of Portugal on his second voyage around the Cape of Good Hope to India in 1502.[4] Portuguese merchants of Jewish background had become so common in the international markets of the seventeenth century that "Portuguese" became a common name in France for Iberian Jews and "New Christians."[5]

While Catholic France seems to have accepted merchants of Jewish descent on its own territory, it officially allowed no Jews at all in its colonies in the Americas. The Jewish Gradis family of Bordeaux, to take one example, was relied upon by France to finance and supply the defence of its empire in North America throughout the Seven Years' War from 1754 to 1760. There is no evidence, however, that any Gradis ever set foot upon the soil of New France.[6] Nevertheless, there were undoubtedly persons of Jewish descent, or even secret Jews, in New France, as is attested by the "street of Jews" at the French fortress of Louisbourg on Cape Breton Island, identified in a court case of 1719.[7] In the French colonies, the few recorded instances of Jews arriving in North American outposts invariably resulted in attempts to convert the outsider to Roman Catholicism. However, when the occasional Jew was found in French colonies, the remedy was less severe than that employed by Spain or Portugal.

Esther Brandau was one Jew in New France who refused to convert. Her record showed that she had "shipped as a boy" for about five years before she landed in Quebec in 1738. At age 15 she had been sent to visit relatives in Amsterdam. Her ship had been lost on a sand-bar, and after her rescue she had worked on ships – some French, some Spanish – dressed as a man as well as spending time as a tailor's apprentice in Nantes. According to a declaration dated 15 September 1738, given before the marine commissioner of Quebec, a person had arrived in Quebec, "aged about twenty years, who embarked at La Rochelle as a passenger, dressed in boy's clothes, under the name of Jacques La Fargue, on the vessel Saint-Michel, Sieur de Salaberry commander, and declared her name to be Esther Brandau daughter of David Brandau, a Jew, trader of St Esprit, diocese of Daxe, near Bayonne, and that she is of the Jewish religion." After her discovery in Quebec, Brandau stayed for about six months, but as she refused to convert to Catholicism, her case became a cause célèbre and she was deported by order of the king of France.[8] Esther Brandau's statement to posterity was that she preferred deportation to the renunciation of her religion. The message of the French government was that Jews could live in its colonies only if they accepted Catholicism.

Marianne Periou, a Jewess and native of the Xaintes region north of Bordeaux, was found in Louisbourg in July 1749 by the French forces when Île Royale (as Cape Breton Island was known) was returned to French control by the English as a result of the Treaty of Aix-la-Chapelle. Two weeks later, on 14 August, Marianne Periou, now renamed "Marie," was baptized "after being instructed in the Roman Catholic faith." She signed her name with a crossed mark ("X") on her baptismal certificate, either because she was illiterate or as a gesture of defiance as in "crossing one's fingers."[9]

Joseph Jean Antoine Moise, a soldier at Louisbourg who had been born Jewish in Maastricht, was baptized in the presence of French authorities at least three times. He was first baptized at sea on board *La Fripponne* by the new governor, the comte de Raymond, after "he had been enlightened with the truth of the Roman Catholic and Apostolic faith, and had recognized the falsehood and horror of the Judaic religion in which he had hitherto professed faith." Immediately upon his arrival in Louisbourg he was again baptized, with the governor standing as godfather. Raymond then learned that Moise had already been baptized and named at Louisbourg at about the same time as Marianne Periou. Moise's story evoked the comment from Louisbourg's troop major, Colonel Michel Le Courtois de Surlaville, that "from a bad Jew, you get a worse Christian."[10]

The Netherlands and Britain, unlike France, Spain, and Portugal, recognized that Jewish merchants could be advantageous to imperial trade and selectively provided incentives for Jews to settle in their colonies. England, like other European countries, had relied on Jews in voyages of discovery even before Jews were allowed to return in 1656. A Moroccan Jew, who had been brought to England as a prisoner, had served as interpreter for the expedition of the English to the East Indies led by Captain James Lancaster of the East India Company in 1601 and was responsible for the negotiation of a treaty with the sultan of Achin which was a landmark of British expansion in the East. Israel Lyons, another Jew, accompanied Constantine John Phipps as principal astronomer or navigator in his explorations towards Spitsbergen in 1773.[11] Jews were recognized as skilled international traders who had networks of contacts in other trading countries and were thus often organized to withstand the risks to ships and cargoes in dangerous voyages across oceans. As they were rarely encouraged to settle in most of the world's countries at this time, it is not surprising that Jews chose to come – in numbers out of all proportion to their world population – to those British and Dutch colonies whose laws were more welcoming.

Where the Dutch encouraged Jews to settle in their American possessions, they flocked in large numbers and general prosperity resulted. For some two decades after the Dutch conquest of Brazil in 1603, Jews experienced the beginnings of a "golden age" in America. Jews, particularly traders, were encouraged to settle in this colony by the unprecedented toleration and equality of civil rights offered by the Dutch. The largest immigration of Jews came from Amsterdam in 1642. The Brazil trade supported the Netherlands' access to the British West Indies and reinforced Amsterdam's position as the counting-house of Europe. However, the Portuguese reconquest of the colony in 1654 ruined the flourishing Jewish communities of Recife and Bahia; all the colony's Jews were expelled – five thousand from Recife alone.[12]

Later, in 1730, Jewish settlement on the tiny island colony of St Eustatius was given unprecedented encouragement when the Netherlands proclaimed that Jews on the island were to be allowed complete civil and political equality. St Eustatius thus became the first territory in the Americas to give Jews equality with other citizens. Similar rights were not offered to Jews on the larger Dutch island colony of Curaçao until 1825, almost a century later.[13] By the time of the outbreak of the American Revolution in 1775, the Dutch colonies in America, by then restricted to half-a-dozen small West Indies islands and Surinam which offered little opportunity for growth, had the largest Jewish population in the New World.[14]

THE BRITISH COLONIES IN AMERICA

From the point of view of any specific group of non-Anglicans, it might be tempting to view the British colonial system of disabilities and restrictions for religious Nonconformists as arising from prejudice: as anti-semitic, anti-Papist, anti-Quaker, anti-Puritan. The reality was that Britain felt it needed these devices to control an enormous and growing empire composed, unlike England itself, almost entirely of non-Anglicans. England, in its evolution from its Catholic past, had made the unity of church and state a high government priority, and the powers of the monarch, no longer absolute, were being increasingly shared by a Parliament elected by landholders. The system of disabilities that allowed a paternalistic society in England to suppress potential Roman Catholic insurgents and to keep Protestant Dissenters from government office could easily and logically be extended to distant parts of the empire to give loyal Anglicans in the colonies the reins of government, while allowing the appearance of equality to subjects of different religions and cultures.

Nevertheless in the early years of settlement, British authorities permitted the colonies considerable latitude in determining the extent of the civil rights of their settlers. Non-Anglicans were thus able to receive more liberal treatment in certain British American colonies than in England itself: in some cases groups of Dissenters had been granted specific colonies where they could settle and where they were not subject to the restrictive laws that applied in England. This policy allowed people of differing faiths to choose different colonial jurisdictions. Inevitably, however, it led to a patchwork of laws that was by no means uniform and that could place religious dissenters in a *worse* position than they had in England if they were unfortunate enough to choose the wrong colony.

Jews were known to have been in Barbados around the time it was settled by the English in 1627.[15] In 1650, six years before Jews were allowed to return to England, the assembly of Barbados, dominated by Cromwell's Puritan supporters, passed an act that permitted the immigration of Dutch, Quakers, Huguenots, Catholics, and Jews "providing they do not commit public scandal on our days of worship."[16] As a result, Jews formed about 10 per cent of the European population of Bridgetown, the island's main town, by the late seventeenth century. According to the census of 1679–80, 54 of the 404 householders in Bridgetown were Jews, clearly forming a vital force in the colony's development.[17]

After Cromwell's forces captured Jamaica from Spain in 1655, Jewish settlers went there as well. In 1623 St Christopher's, or St Kitts, was the first of the West Indian islands settled by England. Although Jews were still not legally allowed in England itself, a number of Jewish families settled on St Kitts by 1628, at which time they were removed to the adjoining island of Nevis by the governor where they formed the nucleus of a new English settlement.[18] By 1688, three of the four Jewish communities in the English-speaking world known to be large enough to support synagogues were in the West Indies, with two in Barbados, one in Jamaica, and one in Nevis.[19] Jews settled in areas where they were welcome and which allowed them the greatest measure of equality.

While some of the Jews expelled from Brazil by the Portuguese after 1654 returned to Amsterdam or moved to Dutch territories such as Curaçao or New Amsterdam (now New York), most sought refuge in British territories, spurred by unprecedented attempts on the part of British colonial officials to encourage Jews to settle in Surinam.[20] This territory, a part of Guiana known to English navigators of the day as "the Wild Coast," was settled by the English after its conquest from the Dutch in 1650. From that time, until the territory was returned to the Dutch in exchange for New Amsterdam in 1667, Surinam was the first British colony after Barbados that openly encouraged Jewish settlement. In 1654, the English government's Committee of Trade and Plantations issued a charter of "Privileges Granted to the People of the Hebrew Nation that are to goe to the Wilde Cust."[21] This charter offered Jews willing to be transported to the new English colony of Surinam liberty of conscience and the right of public worship, the right to govern themselves according to the law of their own religion, the legal right to observe their sabbath as the Lord's day, the same civil liberties as enjoyed by citizens of the Netherlands, and the same privileges as those granted to settlers in the colony from "anny Nation." In addition, the Jews were granted free passage, free building materials for as much land as they wished to purchase, and freedom for a period of time from all taxes, customs, and duties if they should establish sugar plantations or mines. Eleven years later, in August 1665, the governor and assembly of the colony gave another charter to the Jews of Surinam which included the grant of "every privilege and liberty which we ourselves enjoy."[22]

Under the Treaty of Breda (1667) Surinam was returned to the Netherlands. After some delay those who were English subjects were allowed to leave in 1674. At first, the Dutch governor indicated that the 270 or so Jews in the colony could also leave, but perhaps realizing that the colony would be left with only a similar number of Dutch settlers, he soon changed his position. He refused to allow all the Jews to leave, saying that the treaty had given the right to leave only to "English subjects"; those Jews who had not actually been made denizens of England must stay. The English and the Dutch both believed that they needed the Jews. The English emissaries concluded that the governor found "more of the Jews would depart than he expected [and] did feare it might much weaken the Colony." However, the English finally succeeded in being able to take all the "Hebrew Nation" from Surinam to the English colony of Jamaica.[23]

From the seventeenth century, English colonies were granted to proprietors by royal charter, sometimes to establish a settled area that could support the trade of England and sometimes to establish a trade monopoly like the charter given in 1670 to the Company of Adventurers of England trading into Hudson's Bay. This charter gave its proprietors the right to establish an English fur trade monopoly in the territory to the north and west of New France. There may have been Jews at some Hudson's Bay posts.[24] Charters which established settlement usually encouraged religious dissenters to set up their own English colonies in North America in order to encourage an adequate population. Maryland was granted by royal charter to Cecil Calvert, second Lord Baltimore, in 1632 as a Roman Catholic colony. Rhode Island was established in 1636 by Roger Williams, a dissenting Protestant minister. The practice of granting proprietary colonies by royal charter continued even after the passage of the restrictive Corporation and Test Acts. Pennsylvania was chartered to William Penn, an English Quaker, in 1682, and Labrador was chartered to Joseph de la Penha, an Iberian Jew who lived in Rotterdam, in 1697.

The charter given to de la Penha was perhaps the most unusual of the English colonial charters. According to the Dutch text of the document, on 1 November 1697 William III of England granted all of Labrador from the 54th to the 60th degree of latitutde to de la Penha in perpetuity.[25] The grant was likely a reward for de la Penha after the captain of one of his ships had defended the English coast by fighting a victorious battle with two French ships off Dunkirk in February 1696. De la Pehna was known to have sent large numbers of Sephardic "poor Jews" from Holland to London. A letter from the wardens of the London Sephardic Congregation to de la Penha in 1692 warned him to discontinue forwarding poor people to London as "His Majesty's Council have just passed a new Order forbidding entry at the ports without a passport which costs £3 10s. od., a sum which the congregation cannot possibly afford for all the would be immigrants who are detained thereby on entry."[26] It was likely anticipated that de la Penha would settle Labrador with Sephardic "poor Jews." Notwithstanding this extraordinary gesture by the English crown, it is not known whether de la Penha took any action to attempt to establish Labrador as a Jewish colony.

EXPRESS RESTRICTIONS ON RELIGIOUS MINORITIES

Although most of the laws of England applied automatically to the colonies during the seventeenth and eighteenth centuries, those respecting religion did not, thereby encouraging settlement of religious dissenters in the colonies. The established rule was that statutes of the British Parliament with respect to religion applied only to the Mother Country unless specifically stated to apply to the colonies as well. In consequence, the English laws respecting the establishment of the Church of England did not apply in the British American colonies; nor did the Corporation and Test Acts or the laws respecting the state oaths. Thus, while Dissenters in the British American colonies could not claim the benefit of the Toleration Act of 1689 as that law was similarly applied only in England, the restrictive laws of England did not apply in the colonies, which were thus free to pass their own laws, subject of course to the assent of the governor, acting in accordance with his instructions from the Colonial Office in the case of colonies under direct royal control. In many cases the colonial laws continued to encourage the immigration and settlement of religious dissenters, although Roman Catholics continued to be severely restricted from the exercise of political and even civil rights. Indeed, by 1750 Catholics were excluded by express restriction even in Maryland. Quakers, Baptists, and Jews were occasionally denied rights but were often allowed toleration in varying degrees.

Jews were explicitly restricted to a degree by colonial legislatures in the British West Indies. Jewish settlers in Barbados, for example, were not allowed to give evidence or to sue in cases other than those involving the businesses of merchants. In 1674 the governor, council, and assembly of that colony passed a law providing that "all persons of the Hebrew Nation resident in this Island that are made her Denizens may be admitted to give testimonies on their oaths, in all courts and causes, in such manner and form as the religion of the Hebrews will admit" as long as the courts and causes were limited to those "relating to Trade and Dealing, and not otherwise." Jews were not able to use the courts for personal causes, except in the case of personal injury.[27] Jews had been encouraged to settle in Barbados in order to assist the expansion of British trade, but the trading rights they received were construed so literally that they were not treated equally to non-Jewish traders. Notwithstanding strenuous objections by the community of Jews on the island, this law was not repealed until 1786.

In Jamaica, inequality took other forms. From 1688 onwards, the assembly adopted the practice of levying a special annual tax on "the Jewish nation" over and above that levied upon the other inhabitants of the island. Other acts of the assembly provided for the encouragement of immigration of all white men "except Jews, non-jurors, Papists and convicts." In 1711 Jamaica enacted an express provision excluding Jews from political rights.[28] The assembly persisted, levying an additional "Jews Tax" in 1739 and 1740. The Jewish inhabitants of the island complained bitterly and finally obtained the support of the lords of the Board of Trade in England which ordered the assembly to end the practice in 1739.[29] A special tax was also authorized by Bermuda in 1695 for "Jews and reported Jews." No Jews were known to object to being affected by the act, but it had still not received royal assent by 1707.[30]

Table 2
The New World before 1740

INTRODUCTION
• Notable role of Jews in age of exploration and discovery
• Jews not accepted as settlers in the colonies of Spain, Portugal, or France
• Jews encouraged as settlers in colonies of the Netherlands
• Britain encouraged religious dissenters to settle in its American colonies: Jews in Barbados (1627), Jamaica (1656), Nevis (1630s), Surinam (1654–69); charter for Labrador to Joseph de la Penha (1697)

OBSTACLES TO EQUALITY
Express restrictions on Jews and Protestant Dissenters rare in British colonies despite partial examples in Jamaica, Barbados, and Bermuda
Disabilities
1. Municipal restrictions
   • aliens not allowed to operate retail shops in some towns
2. Established churches/Toleration
   • established churches in the colonies created limits on various rights; most allowed liberty of conscience and freedom of worship to all. In the Thirteen Colonies, for example, the Church of England was established in six colonies and the Congregational Church in five; two colonies had no established church.
   • by 1740 Jews and Protestant Dissenters were "tolerated" in the British colonies but Roman Catholics were increasingly not "tolerated."
3. Prescription of the Anglican sacrament/Making the declaration against transubstantiation as a condition of holding office
   • rarely used because most colonies proprietary
   • lack of direct royal control over colonies and lack of government control over colonial affairs
4. State oaths as a condition of holding office
   • individual colonies established their own requirements
   • British acts of 1701 and 1714 specifying the wording and use of state oaths did not apply to colonies
   • most colonies required a Christian form of oath, thus disabling Jews. *Exceptions:* Carolinas, New York, Rhode Island, Georgia
5. Alien status
   • Navigation Acts shut out aliens from British colonial trade, so from 1660 Britain provided letters of denization for colonial aliens
   • those born in Britain or its colonies were automatically British, that is, non-alien
   • each colony made its own laws on naturalization, but naturalization was not frequent
   • naturalization often required a Christian form of oath

Despite the absence of express prohibitions against Jews in the colonies on the American mainland, several laws indirectly had the same effect. Voters had to be Christians in Pennsylvania after 1682, in South Carolina from 1716 to 1759, and in Rhode Island after 1719. A resolution of the New York assembly in 1737 actually disenfranchised Jews, but the resolution did not amount to a law passed by the colonial legislature and signed by the governor.[31]

DISABILITIES

Instead of express restrictions, legislatures in British colonies in America increasingly denied civil and political rights to religious minorities in the years after 1700 by imposing indirect restrictions on the exercise of those rights. Just as in Britain, these limitations were imposed by devices such as municipal restrictions, toleration laws, and the state oaths. Collectively, the different colonies employed a hodgepodge of restrictions that must have required careful study by prospective immigrants but that did allow a greater degree of equality than in England to those prepared to search for it. While the restrictions may have initially been applied haphazardly in the different colonies, by the time of the American Revolution they were applied almost uniformly and amounted to an important element of colonial policy that would continue to be systematically applied to the remaining colonies in British North America.

Municipal Restrictions

At least two municipal jurisdictions in New York maintained restrictions similar to those of the English trading cities. New York City and Albany limited retail trade within their boundaries to those who had been granted "freedom of the city," a restriction based upon alien status rather than upon a requirement for swearing a Christian oath. The New York City restrictions, which lasted until the outbreak of the Revolution in 1775, were based on two ordinances. The first prohibited the sale of "any Goods wares and Merchandizes by Retaile" unless by citizens who were "Freemen or made Free or Burghers of this Citty." The second provided that "none were to be made freemen, but his Majesty's natural born subjects, or such as shall be first naturalized by Act of the General Assembly or shall have first obtained Letters of Denization from the Lieutenant Governor."[32]

An example of the enforcement of these retail trade restrictions in Albany is to be found in the testimony of Solomon Hays, a Jewish merchant, given in a New York court in 1756. Hays referred to "two strange Jews one Ephraim Champman the other named Levi who offered to set up Shops at Albany as natural born Subjects of the King, but the Corporation of Albany mistrusting that they were Aliens and not born at Plymouth as they pretended, they sent for Mr Hayes [*sic*] and examined him and he declaring that he always understood that they were born in Holland they were obliged afterwards to apply for an Act of the Assembly to naturalize them."[33] Immigrant foreign Protestants and Jews who had come from places other than England or other English colonies were unable to engage in retail trade, even in some of the cities of North America, unless they became naturalized British subjects. That process required a period of residence in the colony. This may explain the preponderance of Jews in the fur trade outside the organized towns and settlements.

Newport, like New York and Albany, imposed retail trade restrictions against aliens. And by the middle of the eighteenth century, the colony of Rhode Island would refuse to allow aliens in the colony to become naturalized. The combined effect of these policies kept Newport Jews from owning retail shops.

Establishment of Churches

Because the laws of England respecting religion did not apply to the colonies unless specifically stated to do so, each colony had its own laws and traditions respecting religion. The only restriction was that colonial legislatures were generally required not to pass laws repugnant to the laws of England.

The power of the established church in England was not duplicated in the colonies, even though each of the Thirteen Colonies eventually acknowledged in one way or another that a Protestant form of Christianity was the law of the land and should be supported by the colonial government. The Church of England was established in New York (1686), Maryland (1691), New Jersey (1702), Virginia (1702), South Carolina (1720), North Carolina (1730), Georgia (1754), and New Hampshire (1761), although only in Virginia was a majority of the population actually Anglican. The Congregational Church was established in the New England colonies of Maine, Massachusetts, New Hampshire until 1761, and Connecticut. Pennsylvania and Rhode Island had no formally established church.

Colonies in which the Congregational Church was the established church were governed by church members on the theory that the Bible was the supreme law, from which the right to govern was derived. Only church members were eligible to vote, to hold public office, and to sit on juries. The government, like the church, was composed of local self-governing congregations (hence the name "Congregational"). Church attendance was compulsory, although non-attendance was rarely prosecuted. Church membership was zealously limited: only the most devout, the Elect, having first established their orthodoxy through interrogation by other members on the floor of the meeting-house, were received into membership. Thus, only a small percentage of the total population of each colony actually became church members, and they governed that colony. In these circumstances, it is not surprising that there were few Jews known to have lived in the four New England colonies in which the Congregational Church was the established church during the eighteenth century.[34]

The Practice of Toleration

In the early years of settlement, most of the laws for the protection of Protestantism in the Thirteen Colonies were not so severe as to require toleration laws for dissenters. In the colonies where dissent had not been expressly prohibited, toleration developed through practice rather than law. The distinction between the English and colonial law on this point was dramatically illustrated in New York in 1737 when a Jewish woman named Rachel Luis died. Her will, probated in a New York court on 13 April, ordered her furniture to be sold by her executors "and the money arising therefrom to be applyed to buy a Shefer Tora for the use of the Kall Kados of Sherith Ysraell in New York."[35] This legacy, which advanced the Jewish religion, would undoubtedly have been contrary to law in England as the decision in Da Costa v. De Paz would confirm seven years later.[36] The court, however, saw no problem with Rachel Luis's bequest. In New York the right of Jews to leave religious bequests by will was thus confirmed over 100 years earlier than in England.

In England, where the Jewish religion was not officially tolerated until 1846, synagogues for public worship existed only because the attorney general had been ordered by the king not to prosecute Jews for meeting together for the exercise of their religion. In the Thirteen Colonies, in contrast, the first Jewish congregation started to function in New York in 1692, after various issues as to its legality were resolved. The Jews of New York had been recorded holding services as early as 1682, although in 1685 the mayor and common council of the city had ruled "the Jews worship not to be allowed."[37] Seven years later any doubt as to the right of Jews to worship publicly had been removed.

Several of the charters or constitutions of the American colonies had expressly or implicitly given Jews, along with Protestant Dissenters, the rights of liberty of conscience and free expression of religion. In other colonies the instructions to the governor sent from England specified that he was to ensure that colonial legislatures tolerated the religions of minorities as long as it was not Roman Catholicism. Statutes enjoining toleration were less necessary in the colonies than in England in any event because the power of an established church to enforce conformity in England was not duplicated in the colonies – at least in the early years.

In New York, although the Church of England was established in 1686, there were no special statutes allowing religious equality and toleration had been allowed in practice from the beginning. In 1663 Charles II gave the charter of the colony to his brother James, Duke of York, who ten years later instructed New York's governor, Edmund Andros, to "permit all persons of what Religion so ever, quietly to inhabit within ye precincts of yor jurisdiccion wthout giving ym any disturbance or disquiet whatsoever, for or by reason of their differing opinion in matter of religion: Provided they give noe disturbance to ye public peace nor doe molest or disquiet others in ye free exercise of their religion."[38]

Carolina's Fundamental Constitutions, drawn up in 1669 by John Locke, recognized the Church of England as the established church but allowed unprecedented free expression of religion to Jews as well as others. Article 97 read: "But since the natives of that place who will be concerned in our plantation are utterly strangers to Christianity, whose idolatry, ignorance and mistake gives us no right to expel or use them ill and those who remove there from other parts to plant will unavoidably be of different opinion concerning matters of religion, the liberty of which they will expect to have allowed them – and also that Jews, heathens and other dissenters from the purity of Christian religion may not be feared and kept at a distance from it – therefore any seven or more persons agreeing in any religion shall constitute a Church or profession to which they shall give some name to distinguish it from others."[39] This document was never adopted by the assembly of the colony, but it nonetheless had some legal standing and reflected the need to offer religious liberty to prospective colonists.[40] In 1697 the Carolina assembly passed "an Act for the making aliens free of this part of the Province [South Carolina] and for granting liberty of conscience to all Protestants."[41]

Maryland's Toleration Act of 1649, which prohibited non-Christians from exercising their religions, provided that any person blaspheming or denying Jesus Christ to be "the Son of God" should be punished with death and forfeiture of land and goods. But toleration was allowed in practice. By 1747 there were a few Jews in Baltimore, one or two of whom had been naturalized under the Plantation Act.[42]

At the time of the charter to Roger Williams in 1636, the colony of Rhode Island was based on religious liberty. It had no established religion. "We agree," ran one of its laws adopted in 1641, "as formerly hath been the liberties of the town, so still to hold for the liberty of conscience." Between 1655 and 1657, when Williams served as president of the colony, the first Jews to emigrate to a British colony in

North America arrived in Newport. One historian has suggested that during this period, Jews enjoyed absolute freedom of religious expression, their civil and political rights being equal to those of their Christian fellow citizens.[43] However, no evidence has yet appeared to demonstrate such equality of civil and political rights during the colony's early years, and attitudes certainly changed quickly after Williams's administration. The Rhode Island charter of 1663, granted by Charles II, made the colony undeniably Christian. That charter guaranteed to the inhabitants of the colony that, while it secured them "in the free exercise and enjoyment of all theire civill and religious rights," it would "preserve unto them that liberty in the true Christian faith and worship of God which they have sought with so much travail."[44] Later that year the legislature decided to restrict admission to the colony to those professing the Christian religion.[45] Yet, on 24 June 1684, the general assembly of Rhode Island resolved that Jews in the colony "may expect as good protection here as any strangers being not of our nation residing amongst us, in his Majesty's colony ought to have, being obedient to his Majesty's laws."[46] Then, in 1719, the colony passed a law to deny political rights to Catholics, although the wording also excluded Jews. The law provided that "all men professing Christianity (Roman Catholics only excepted)" were entitled to be admitted as freemen "and shall have liberty to choose and be chosen Officers in the Colony both civil and military."[47]

In Pennsylvania, toleration of religious dissent, including dissent by Jews, was written into the law as a result of the Quaker influence. In 1696 the governor and assembly of the colony enacted a Constitutional Frame of Government paying deference to those who, like the Quakers, would not take an oath, and allowing those like the Jews who would not take a Christian form of oath to exercise greater rights than usual.[48] It allowed any person who "cannot, for conscience sake, take an oath, upon any account whatsoever" to make a solemn affirmation instead of swearing. Penn's Charter of Privileges of 1701, which was approved by the assembly and remained in force until the American Revolution, allowed "Freedom of their Consciences, as to their Religious Profession and Worship" to all those who "acknowledge One Almighty God, the Creator, Upholder, and Ruler of the World."[49]

In Georgia, the charter granted by George II in 1732 to the trustees for establishing the colony had allowed "liberty of conscience" in the worship of God to all settlers and had provided that "all such persons, except papists shall have a free exercise of their religion." At the time time, however, the charter specified the swearing of the state oaths, including the oath of abjuration, when oaths were required.[50]

The State Oaths

Although Parliament had adopted a statute in 1701 setting out the three state oaths for use in England, each colony had been left to determine its own requirements on this matter. It will be recalled that the English form of the oath of abjuration, to be sworn as a condition of the exercise of most privileges of citizenship, ended with the words "upon the true Faith of a Christian," words that a professing Jew could not swear in good conscience.

Within five years of the passage of the act of 1701 in Britain, most of the Thirteen Colonies had followed suit and adopted some form of the state oaths. As a result, Jews in these colonies were unable to be elected or even appointed to high office. In none of the colonies, to paraphrase Horace Walpole, could Jews ever have any share in the government. A Protestant form of Christianity thereby became the official religion of all the Thirteen Colonies.

Although most of the American colonies adopted a Christian form for their oaths of office, there were exceptions. Carolina's act of 4 November 1704 allowed foreign-born Jews to become citizens on the sole condition that they swear oaths acceptable to them according to their own religion. This act gave aliens "all the rights privileges powers and immunities as if they had been and were born of English parents within this Province." Section 4 specified that no person should have the benefit of the act "until he or they shall on the Holy Evangelists, or otherwise according to his form of profession," take the oaths of allegiance and supremacy.[51] However, in the same year, the assembly of Carolina passed an act preventing Jews and Protestant Dissenters from serving as members of the assembly. The act for the "more effectual preservation of the government" required members to take the oaths conforming to the Church of England and to take the sacrament according to the rite of that church.[52] After 1712, when the colony was split into North and South Carolina, both parts continued to require the state oaths as a condition to the exercise of political, as opposed to civil, rights. Between 1716 and 1759 South Carolina required voters to be "Christians" and after that to be non-Catholic "Protestants."[53] In view of this history, Elzas's conclusion that "in South Carolina from the day of its settlement, the Jew has never labored under the slightest civil or religious disability whatsoever" does not appear to be borne out by the facts.[54]

New York adopted the Christian form of the state oaths, but in 1727 it specified an exception for Jews. There is considerable evidence that New York was willing to relax the rigorous requirements of alien status and the restrictions of the state oaths usually employed by British authorities to exclude Jews and other Nonconformists. In fact, New York was willing to naturalize Jews by special statute even before the Plantation Act was passed in 1740 and was willing, at the same time, to grant a form of exemption from the state oaths. On 15 November 1727 the legislative council was considering a bill passed by the assembly to authorize the naturalization of eight individuals born outside the British empire by allowing them the rights of natural-born British subjects. During the debate, it appeared to the council that Daniel Nunez da Costa, one of the individuals, was of the Jewish faith and would be unable to benefit from the statute because he could not in conscience swear the oath of abjuration. Without hesitation, the council amended the bill by adding a clause, whose words were similar to those used by the British Parliament in the act of 1723 and would again be used by Parliament thirteen years later in the Plantation Act:

AND WHEREAS the following words are contained in the latter part of the Oath of Abjuration vizt [upon the true Faith of a Christian] be it further enacted by the authority aforesaid that whenever any of his Majesty's Subjects professing the Jewish Religion Shall present himself to take the said Oath of Abjuration in pursuance of this present Act the said words [upon the true Faith of a Christian] shall be Omitted out of the said Oath in administring [sic] the Same to such person and the taking of the said Oath by such person professing the Jewish Religion without the words aforesaid in the like manner as Jews are to be admitted to be Sworn to give evidence in Courts of Justice Shall be deemed to be a Sufficient taking of the Abjuration Oath within the meaning of this Act.[55]

The New York assembly passed the act as amended by the legislative council on 25 November.[56] The act answered some questions but raised others. Did the right of Jews to amend the oath of abjuration apply only "in pursuance of this present Act," that is to the one Jew who had actually been naturalized thereunder? Or had the act given all naturalized and natural-born Jews in the colony the right to alter the oath for all purposes flowing from the status of citizen?

Rhode Island and Georgia did not adopt the oath of abjuration as a requirement for holding land or offices. Thus, when Daniel Nunes was made "waiter of the Port of Savannah" by a vote of the assembly of Georgia in 1765 he was not required to swear the state oaths and was able to take the post.[57]

Pennsylvania's Frame of Government allowed exemption from the oath requirements as a political right, in the case of election or appointment to "offices of State and trust," only to persons who were prepared to "make and subscribe the declaration and profession of their Christian belief" in the form required by the Toleration Act of 1689. Similarly, the Charter of Privileges stopped short of allowing those who were granted liberty of conscience, such as the Jews, the political right to participate in government. That right was reserved to "Persons who also profess to believe in Jesus Christ the Saviour of the World."[58]

Alien Status

The Navigation Acts, passed from 1651 onwards, were stated to apply and therefore did apply to the British colonies in the Americas. The first of these acts, passed during the Commonwealth, shut out from the London market all merchandise and produce which was not shipped to England directly, thus barring goods which passed through the great distributing centres on the continent. This act was aimed chiefly at Amsterdam, forcing a great many Dutch merchants, largely Jews who dissembled about their religion, to attempt to settle in London. Subsequent Navigation Acts in 1660 and 1661 denied aliens (which included those Jews who had recently come to England) the right to trade with English colonies, with the object of preventing merchants of competing trading nations such as the Netherlands from profiting from trade with English colonies.[59] The loss of Brazil by the Dutch in 1654 and the subsequent expulsion of the Jews combined with the English Navigation Acts were a terrible blow to the trade of Amsterdam and a corresponding gain for England. In the English colonies to which Jewish refugees now flocked, trade took a great bound forward, all to the profit of the London market.

As England wished to continue to encourage merchants, whether foreign Protestants or Jews, to trade with the American colonies in spite of the restrictions of the Navigation Acts, the government made a practice of liberal grants of letters of denization to Jewish merchants trading in the American colonies in order to end their alien status. Denization, unlike naturalization, left the recipient subject to alien duties. By 1740, almost 300 Jews had been granted letters of denization, although almost all of these appear to have gone to substantial merchants who sought the right to trade in the West Indies rather than to residents of the Thirteen Colonies.[60]

Alien status was not used in the colonies to exclude foreign Protestants and Jews to the same extent that it was in England. At first, the imperial government attempted to encourage the American colonies to pass their own laws dealing with naturalization. And several of the American colonies did so.

Carolina's Naturalization Act of 1697 allowed aliens, including Jews, the right to become citizens in the southern part of the colony without special royal permission. At least four of the sixty-four men made citizens under this act were Jews.[61] Some have concluded that Jews were even allowed limited political rights based on the evidence of Simon Valentine, a Jewish citizen, being appointed one of the commissioners in charge of the Charleston guard and patrol.[62]

As we have seen with the case of Daniel Nunez da Costa, New York's legislature proved willing to relax the rigorous requirements of alien status on a selective basis rather than by general statute. Pennsylvania passed a law in 1696 giving relief to aliens so that their status improved somewhat even though they were unable to become citizens. New Jersey also granted rights of naturalization to individuals in specific cases.[63]

Nevertheless it was becoming less likely as settlement progressed that the individual American colonial legislatures could be relied upon to naturalize aliens, thereby exempting them from the restrictions of Britain's Navigation Acts and allowing them to assist in the expansion of British trade. By 1737 New York was becoming much more restrictive, and on 23 September of that year, the assembly resolved that "Persons of the Jewish Religion ... ought not to be admitted to vote for Representatives in this Colony."[64] The resolution had been provoked by a contested election in New York City as well as by the observation that the "Jewish vote" may have been decisive in giving an apparent victory to a candidate not favoured by the assembly. The resolution was passed unanimously after an impassioned speech by William Smith, acting as counsel on behalf of Cornelius Van Horne, one of the candidates. Smith held the legislators spellbound with a description of the death of Christ at the hands of the Jews. He then argued that since the curse still clung to the race, Jews were not fit for political duties.[65] The resolution, having achieved its purpose of reversing a particular election result, was never embodied in a statute. It remained unrepealed, however, and thus left the matter in a state of uncertainty.[66]

Britain's desire for world trade ascendancy required a concerted policy of encouraging experienced traders to settle in its American colonies. But by 1740, South Carolina was still the only one of the Thirteen Colonies with a general naturalization law. Apart from specific laws passed to deal with individual cases by New York, Pennsylvania, and New Jersey, Britain's other North American colonies had not given status to aliens in the period. There was even some likelihood that the New York legislature was entering a restrictive mode and could not be counted on to increase the incentives for Jewish traders who Britain hoped would immigrate to the colony.

England decided that more drastic action was required.

3 The Plantation Act, 1740: An Invitation to the Thirteen Colonies and the West Indies

> And as the Jews by their great command of money, and by their extensive correspondence in all parts of the known world, do increase the commerce of every country they repair to, it is certainly the interest of every trading or manufacturing people to invite, or at least to render it possible for the rich Jews to come and live amongst them.
>
> Lord Dupplin, House of Commons, 7 May 1753[1]

In 1740 the British Parliament announced its assumption of complete authority over alien status in the American colonies when it passed An Act for Naturalizing such foreign Protestants and others therein mentioned, as are settled or shall settle in any of His Majesty's Colonies in *America*, commonly known as the Plantation Act.[2] Hereafter, the American colonies could no longer pass their own laws concerning alien status, as the British had removed that disability for Jews in the colonies. The Plantation Act was Britain's invitation to the Jews to come and live in its American colonies even though they faced many disabilities in Britain itself. While the act occasioned no debate at the time of its passage through Parliament, the evidence which emerged in the debate over naturalization in 1753 indicates it was passed solely to encourage Jews to emigrate to the British colonies in America.[3]

Britain, observing the success of trade in the Dutch colonies, perceived that it needed the Jews to enhance its trading position which was at once a source of its wealth and of its power in the world. During the debate on the Jews Naturalization Act, the prime minister would acknowledge that "it would be of great service to us, to have the Jew brokers in all countries engaged both in interest and in inclination to recommend our manufactures." And in that same debate, Nicholas Hardinge was to give Jewish traders glowing, though mixed, praise: "no people can be supposed more capable, or more ready than the

---

For a schematic representation of this chapter, see p. 55.

Jews, to make new experiments [in commerce], because of their great propensity to trade, and because of the curse that attends them. By being dispersed through all nations, and by being the chief traders in every nation where they sojourn, they know what sort of fabric in every kind of manufacture is best suited to the taste of the people in every country." Jews, he would conclude pithily, "are more likely to improve and extend our foreign trade than any other set of people whatever."[4]

Moreover, the Jewish traders were perceived to have an incomparable international network. "As they are dispersed over the whole world, and keep up a correspondence with one another," noted Sir John Barnard in this same debate, "they know where all sorts of manufactures may be sold to the best advantage; therefore by lending their money to the native manufacturers, they may enable them to extend their manufacture, and by their foreign correspondence they may increase the exportation."[5] "The Jews may be of advantage to our commerce," echoed Lord Temple in the House of Lords, "for there are some of them settled as brokers or traders in almost every country, and as they keep a general correspondence with one another, they have a better opportunity than any set of people whatever, for learning where any of our manufactures may be disposed of to advantage, and where all sorts of foreign commodities may be purchased at the cheapest price." Or, as Nicholas Fazakerley put it in the Commons: "Their brethren are almost the sole brokers between merchant and merchant in all countries."[6]

Finally, Jews would be loyal to any country that would provide them with a permanent home. "As they have no country they can call their own," said Hardinge, "we are in no danger that after they have gained an opulent fortune by trade they will retire to spend the income of it in any other [country]."[7]

So even though the members of parliament saw a danger in 1753 that Jews would take over too much of the trade in Great Britain itself if they were allowed to be naturalized, it was recognized that "in the infancy of the trade of any country, it is right to encourage the Jews to come and settle amongst them."[8]

Robert Nugent also told the Commons of his perspective of the importance of the Jews to Britain's trade: "The Jews, Sir, by their knowledge, in trade, and their correspondence over the whole known world, have been of great service in all countries where they have been encouraged to settle. They contributed greatly towards the establishment of the Dutch trade and commerce in the infancy of that wise republic; and it was they chiefly that raised the city of Amsterdam to that height of splendor and riches, at which it has now arrived. On the other hand, we know that Spain and Portugal have been in some measure ruined by banishing them their country; for neither of these kingdoms have now any trade but to their own colonies, and even a great part of that is carried on by foreigners under the borrowed names of Spaniards or Portuguese."9

In 1753, when it was proposed to repeal the naturalization rights for Jews in British America contained in the Plantation Act, the lord chancellor was quick to tell the House of Lords that a repeal "even as to the Jews, from the very beginning of its commencement, would be of such fatal consequence to our plantations, and such a breach of public faith, that I am sure no man who has any regard to the happiness, the credit, or the character of his country would desire it." "Even with respect to the Jews," he added, "the discouraging of them to go and settle in our American colonies, would be a great loss, if not the ruin of, the trade of every one of them."10

The decision to act in 1740 appears to have arisen from two causes. One was the evidence that the individual colonies could not be relied on to naturalize aliens and exempt them from the restrictions of the Navigation Acts so as to encourage them to assist in expanding Britain's trade. The other was the success of Dutch policy in the West Indian island of St Eustatius. The Netherlands, Britain's main trading rival, had experimented with a liberal policy on St Eustatius. As a first step in establishing that island as a free port, Jews had been granted equality in 1730. Within eight years the Jewish community was large enough to build a synagogue.11 By 1750 the island was on the way to becoming one of the busiest ports in the Americas with resident merchants in addition to Jews from the Netherlands, France, Spain, England, Turkey, Greece, and the Levant. With an area of only nine square miles, the island was known as "The Golden Rock." The town of Oranjestad formed a great market with diverse wares exposed for sale in its shops and warehouses. According to one account, a traveller could buy rich draperies, silverware, French gloves, English yarn, French wines, iron pots and shovels, sailor pants and shoes.12 There seems little doubt that the policy of encouraging alien traders to become citizens of St Eustatius was the reason for its success.

Nor is there much doubt that Britain was aware of the significance of this successful experiment on St Eustatius as the island provided critical assistance to the Thirteen Colonies during the American Revolution by breaking the British embargo.13 For Admiral Sir George Rodney, commander of the British fleet sent to capture the island in 1781, St Eustatius was no Golden Rock but a "Nest of Vipers, which had preyed on the Vitals of Great Britain."14 On taking over the island, the British singled out the Jewish merchants, showing Britain's estimation of their importance to the success of St Eustatius. They deported

Table 3
Obstacles to Equality in British America after the Plantation Act, 1740

THE PLANTATION ACT 1740

- enactment signified assumption of imperial control over naturalization in colonies as a means of encouraging Jews and foreign Protestants to settle and assist Britain in its trade competition with the Netherlands
- allowed naturalization after seven years' residence in a colony, thus overriding the reluctance of some colonial legislatures to naturalize Jews and Protestant Dissenters
- encouragement of Jewish traders to come to British America was its primary purpose
- allowed Jews to amend the oath of abjuration, at least for the immediate purpose of naturalization and perhaps for all purposes, although the ambiguous wording made such interpretation debatable, opening the way for colonial authorities to use their own discretion for good or ill

ROYAL INSTRUCTIONS AND IMPERIAL CONTROL

- transformation of proprietary colonies into royal colonies brought them and their governments under the control of the Colonial Office
- restrictions against Roman Catholics increased
- imposition of state oaths and Test Act requirements for office holders by means of instructions, leading to:
  (*a*) exclusion of non-Anglicans from colonial positions of influence
  (*b*) policy of conversion of religious dissenters to Church of England in order to hold office

---

thirty Jewish men to the British garrison at St Kitts, forcing them to leave their families and possessions behind, and after holding the remaining seventy-one heads of Jewish families under arrest for a few days, they confiscated their possessions as well.[15]

The preamble to the Plantation Act left no doubt as to its purposes. It gave two logical reasons for a drastic change in Britain's policy regarding aliens in general and Jews in particular. The first premise was that "the Increase of People is a Means of advancing the Wealth and Strength of any Nation or Country." The second premise was that "many Foreigners and Strangers from the Lenity of our Government, the Purity of our Religion, the Benefit of our Laws, the Advantages of our Trade, and the Security of our Property, might be induced to come and settle in some of His Majesty's Colonies in America, if they were made Partakers of the Advantages and Privileges which the natural born Subjects of this Realm do enjoy." The conclusion that followed justified relaxing the restrictions against foreign Protestant and Jewish traders in the American colonies. It is interesting to note, however, that the sections which included Jews in the Plantation Bill in 1740 were added without debate. The earl of Egmont, a member of parliament at the time, felt that the administration of the day had not wanted the public to know of its overture to the Jews. "That part of the [Plantation] act which relates to Jews," he told the House of

Commons at the time of the debate over repeal of the Jews Naturalization Act, "was passed as it were by stealth, without ever making its appearance either in the votes of this House, or in the title of the act, so that very few of the people know that there is such an act."[16]

Despite this lack of frankness, the Plantation Act was to be the most important statute of the eighteenth century relating to the rights of Jews in the British colonies in North America. The act allowed Jews to become naturalized and assume the rights of natural-born Englishmen after seven years' residence in the colonies, although by all accounts only a small number of individuals actually took advantage of the naturalization rights in the act. The records sent to the Board of Trade each year by the secretaries of the different colonies show that 185 Jews were naturalized under the act between 1740 and 1753. Of these, 150 resided in Jamaica; of the balance, 24 lived in New York, 8 or 9 in Pennsylvania, 1 or 2 in Maryland, and 1 in South Carolina. There are records of another 22, from New York and Pennsylvania, who were naturalized under the act by 1770. Jews were naturalized in other colonies as well, although the records have not been discovered.[17]

Despite the passage of the Plantation Act, there was clearly a reluctance in some of the Thirteen Colonies to naturalize Jews. There is no record of any Jew being naturalized under the Plantation Act in Rhode Island. Indeed, Aaron Lopez and Isaac Elizer (or Elizar), both Jewish merchants from Newport, were refused naturalization by the colony's Superior Court in March 1762. In dismissing their petitions, the court stated that it was "unanimously of the opinion that the said Act of Parliament was wisely designed for increasing the number of inhabitants in the plantations but this colony being already so full of people that many of his Majesty's good subjects born within the same have removed and settled in Nova Scotia, and other places, cannot come within the intention of said act." The court also noted that the colony's charter had referred to "the free and quiet enjoyment of the Christian religion" and that this "first principle" was amplified by a colonial law in 1663 providing that "no person who does not profess the Christian religion can be admitted free of this colony."[18] Lopez secured naturalization in Massachusetts a few months later, and the following year Elizer was naturalized in New York. Both men had evidently studied the patchwork of rights in the Thirteen Colonies and learned through their network where freedom was to be found.[19]

Two other sections of the Plantation Act had even greater long-term significance than that allowing Jews to be naturalized, for they allowed Jews in the American colonies greater rights than those available to them in Britain at this time. Section 6, for example, was open to a liberal interpretation. It provided that "no Person who shall become a natural born Subject of this Kingdom by virtue of this Act, shall be of the Privy Council or a Member of either House of Parliament, or capable of taking, having or enjoying any Office or Place of Trust within the Kingdoms of Great Britain or Ireland."[20] By stipulating that naturalized "foreign Protestants and others" could not be given these rights within Great Britain or Ireland, did not this section acknowledge that these people were entitled to those rights in the British colonies?[21] The implication was there, even if not expressed. This question was finally decided by the British House of Commons in 1773 when an act was passed specifically to remove doubts that every person naturalized under the act of 1740, including Jews, "shall be deemed to be capable of taking and holding any Office or Place of Trust, either Civil or Military, and of taking and holding any Grant of Lands, Tenements, and Hereditaments, from the Crown to himself or themselves, ... any Law or Act of Parliament to the Contrary notwithstanding."[22]

Section 3 of the Plantation Act was also of long-term significance in that it allowed "any Person professing the Jewish Religion" to amend the oath of abjuration required as a condition of accepting British citizenship to omit the words "upon the true Faith of a Christian." Unfortunately, this section was ambiguous, for it allowed Jews to amend the oath of abjuration "in pursuance of this Act."[23] There were two opposing interpretations of that phrase. A strict interpretation would restrict the rights of Jews to amend the oath of abjuration solely in situations where they applied for naturalization ("in pursuance of" the act) and in no others. If this was what the statute meant, then Jews would still be excluded from office, not because of any lack of right but because they would still be required to swear a Christian oath as a condition of accepting office. A more liberal interpretation would allow that amendment to be made whenever a Jew was appointed or elected to any office and required to take the state oaths. If the liberal interpretation were to prevail, then the Plantation Act had given full equality to the Jews in the British colonies of North America in 1740, and no further law was necessary.

British statutes normally did not over-rule the religious rights of people in the British American colonies, but the Plantation Act was expressly designed for that object. There is little doubt that, at the time of its passage, the act was understood to allow Jews in the colonies the right to amend the state oaths to conform to the requirements of the Jewish religion and that, as a result, Jews were entitled to assume full political rights in colonies where the restrictions were based on oaths worded in the same form as the English state oaths.

ROYAL INSTRUCTIONS AND
IMPERIAL CONTROL

Ironically, at almost the same time as Jews were being given an incentive to come to the British colonies in North America, a new disability for non-Anglicans in these settlements was being established through the direct intervention of the Colonial Office.

All thirteen of Britain's colonies on the eastern seaboard had originally been chartered by the crown either to an individual or to a corporate proprietor. Throughout the eighteenth century some were converted to royal colonies under the direct control of the monarch, so that by the time of the American Revolution only five of the original thirteen were still proprietary colonies. Georgia, settled in 1733, was the last of the corporate proprietary colonies. All Britain's subsequent colonies in America were to be royal colonies. Georgia itself became a royal colony in 1752.[24]

The advantage of a royal colony for the imperial authorities was that it had a governor appointed by and responsible to the sovereign and his ministers in Britain. Even though the governor did not control colonial legislation, he could be instructed to require oaths and declarations of all serving under him in the colony. Moreover, legislation which had been passed only to apply in Britain could be given extraterritorial effect by being applied to the colonies through the office of the governor.[25]

The Church of England was established in only eight of the thirteen colonies.[26] In consequence, the requirement that officials provide a certificate that they had taken the sacrament of the Lord's Supper according to the rite of the Church of England could only be required by the British government in these colonies. The Test and Corporation Acts applied only in Great Britain, and no imperial statute was ever passed to apply those laws in any of the colonies. Nevertheless, the trend to changing the American colonies from proprietary to royal control gave imperial authorities the opportunity to use the governor's instructions to require – as a condition of holding office in the colonies – the state oaths and the declaration against transubstantiation as prescribed by the Test Act. The phrasing of the governor's instructions usually did not specifically mention the manner of making and subscribing the declaration. It appears nevertheless that in practice the making of the declaration remained linked to the taking of the sacrament of the Lord's Supper according to the Anglican rite. However this ambiguity – which may well have been deliberate – allowed the governor and other colonial officials some latitude in practice with respect to the imposition of this requirement.

The experience of Simon Valentine (Vallentine) illustrates the point. A resident of Albany, then of New York, in the 1680s, there is no doubt as to his religion. He was the son of Rabbi Jerachmel Falk, a relative of Asser Levy of New York, and was described as "Valentijn Vander Wilde, Joode" or "Jew" in official documents. He was apparently a skilled tradesman because he was able to purchase burgher rights in the city of New York in 1682 as a "handy craftsman." He subsequently moved to Charleston in Carolina, where he was naturalized in 1697 as "an alien of the Jewish Nation borne out of the Crown of England." Notwithstanding his religion, in 1703 he was appointed one of the commissioners in charge of Charleston's guard and patrol, an unprecedented appointment for a Jew.[27] Valentine's appointment was made during Queen Anne's War (1702–13), at a time when the settlers in Charleston were required to turn back attacks from French and Spanish forces without the assistance of the colony's proprietors. Valentine appears to have had little difficulty being appointed to the position, which may not actually have been created by commission from the sovereign. In any event, no religious test seems to have been required. In 1704 the colonial assembly would adopt the English form of oath of abjuration and the declaration against transubstantiation as requirements for subsequent appointments.[28]

After a rebellion by the colonists against the proprietors in 1719 the colony was purchased by George I and became a royal colony. When the new governor, Francis Nicholson, arrived in Charleston in May 1721, his instructions required him to ensure that colonial officials swore the state oaths and subscribed to the declaration against transubstantiation as required by the Test Act. Nicholson's instructions on this point were quite specific: "without the doing of all which you are not to admit any persons whatsoever to any public office nor suffer those that have been formerly admitted to continue therein."[29] Simon Valentine had died by 1715. If he had survived till South Carolina had become a Royal colony, he could no longer have held public office.

British policy, like the policy of the Church of England, encouraged colonists to convert to the established church. The church, manifesting Christian charity and benevolence, obliged its members simply, "to wish that all Jews, Turks, and Pagans may become Christian."[30] The state, reflecting the legal connection with its established church, had reasons of its own for encouraging converts to the Anglican religion. Britain administered territories throughout the world that were many times the size of the British Isles. Their populations were composed of overwhelming numbers of non-Anglicans; their languages and customs were frequently incompatible with those of Britain.

The small number of British officials in the colonies and their circle of Anglican supporters were not enough to ensure loyalty of the general populace, even if appointments to positions of authority were restricted to Anglicans and the cultures and creeds of the general populace were tolerated by the colonial government. The long-term interests of the British rulers of the colonies lay in the maintenance of order and stability, not enforced by arms but encouraged through adherence to a common Anglican faith and a common acceptance of the English system of values.

Britain's target group for obtaining converts to the Church of England in the colonies was not, therefore, limited to Jews, Turks, and pagans, but included the much larger group of non-Anglicans. British policy would welcome converts to the Church of England from among the best of the Roman Catholics and Protestant Dissenters as well as non-Christians. In this way, order would be preserved in the colonies without force of arms, and the commercial advantages of empire would continue to flow to the Mother Country.

Britain's policy of conversion diverged sharply from the objectives of the colonists. Many had come to the colonies for the very reason that they wanted to be free from the religious restrictions of Britain. Britain needed a steady stream of colonists, even though few Anglicans could be encouraged to emigrate. Prudence on the part of the authorities therefore dictated that secrecy was to be an important element of British policy in order not to publicize the limits of the diversity that was allowed. The policy of conversion was contained in the secret instructions to the governors of the colonies and in rules that resembled a code more than an intelligible law. The instructions were used to mandate oaths and declarations as a condition of holding office that could only be taken by Anglicans. The true meaning of the code would be revealed only to non-Anglican colonists whose abilities brought them to the point where equality with the ruling group was a requirement for the continuation of the upward ascent of their careers.

British policy in this sense had the same objectives as the policies of the Catholic colonial powers of Europe, Spain, Portugal, and France, although the latter had used force to obtain converts while Britain used a subtle policy of disabling competent candidates for office unless they would conform to the tenets of the Church of England.

THE INVITATION

The Plantation Act of 1740 was an invitation to the Jews to come to the British colonies in North America. Britain needed Jewish entrepreneurs to enhance its international trade. Britain therefore encouraged

Jews to come to the Americas. On the one hand, the Plantation Act could be treated as the Magna Carta of the Jewish people in the British colonies of North America. On the other hand, it could be treated simply as a statute providing for the naturalization of "Foreign Protestants and others" including Jews. How Britain would handle Jews after they settled there was another matter. The wording of the act itself was ambiguous. The draftsman had kept Britain's options open. If the former was intended, Jews would be welcomed as equals. If the latter, the numbers and rights of Jews, and of others for that matter, would be subject to control. Perhaps it had been left open so that decisions could be made depending on individual cases.

While there was no doubt that the Plantation Act constituted an invitation to the Jews, the significance of that invitation had not been publicly debated and remained for most of the public a well-kept secret. Nor was the long-term significance of the act for the development of civil and political rights evident at the time. Over the next century, governments would be forced many times to choose between the two possible interpretations of the act. But in the middle of the eighteenth century, the British colonies in North America seemed the most likely place for those searching out a new land which would offer equality.

4 The Characters Take Their Places, 1747

> Toleration is not the opposite of intolerance, but is the counterfeit of it. Both are despotisms: the one assumes to itself the right of withholding liberty of conscience, the other of granting it.
>
> Thomas Paine[1]

On Sunday, 11 December 1748, eight years after the passage of the Plantation Act, three men sat in a room at 8 Devonshire Square in the city of London.[2] Solomon da Costa Athias finished reading the letter, written to them the previous Thursday on behalf of the commissioners of the Board of Trade, a committee of the Privy Council responsible for developing the North American colonies,[3] and looked up at his associates, Joseph Salvador and Benjamin Mendes da Costa. The letter, addressed to da Costa, said that before the commissioners would consider an application for land to be used for Jewish settlers in South Carolina, they wanted to know positively whether he and his associates would advance the sum of £6,000 to defray the costs.

A standing committee to further emigration and colonization had been struck in 1732 by the Spanish and Portuguese Jews' Congregation in Bevis Marks in London. Part of the mandate of the committee was to search out the possibilities of using the British colonies in America as a refuge for the Jewish poor.[4] The congregation's action had been prompted by the growing number of "sick poor" Jews who did not have the resources to lift themselves out of the cycle of poverty that seemed to accompany life in London and was reinforced by the lack of opportunity resulting from the alien status and disabilities that confronted many Jews. In 1732 these sick poor had numbered over 250, their dependants over a thousand.[5]

Then, in 1744, Maria Theresa, empress of Austria and hereditary ruler of Bohemia, issued a decree expelling all Jews from Prague. That decree was followed in 1745 by an order for the expulsion of the remaining Jews from Bohemia. These decrees, which affected over 40,000 Jews, were partly carried out despite the intercession of the British and Dutch governments. London's Sephardic community was not idle during the time of distress of the Bohemian Jews and raised nearly £900 for the relief effort.[6] But it was Moses Hart and Aaron Franks, the leaders of the Ashkenazi Jews of the Great Synagogue in London, who had championed the cause of the Bohemian Jews with the English authorities and who could claim some of the credit for the successful intervention by the king of England with the empress.[7]

By 1748 many thousands of Bohemian Jewish expatriates were seeking a new land, with England and Holland their most likely places of refuge.[8] It was actually this potential immigration that had prompted the governments of both Britain and Holland to instruct their ambassadors to urge the empress to revoke her decree. And it was the prospect of an influx of Bohemian Jews that would cause some members of the House of Commons to see the Jews Naturalization Bill of 1753 as "opening this sluice for letting the torrent in upon us."[9] As the refugees began to arrive in England, there was an increase in the activity of the congregation's committee to further emigration and colonization. Hence the meeting of 11 December 1748.

None of the three men who constituted the emigration committee is known to have visited the Americas. Just over 50 years of age, Solomon da Costa was the acknowledged leader of the committee. By the age of 50, he had completed an extremely successful business career and also become England's third Jewish notary. He was held in great respect by his contemporaries. During his lifetime he was described in *Gentleman's Magazine* as "a man of knowledge and virtue; and of such rare ability that he has acquired by it, during the course of his life, one hundred thousand pounds; and this without public scandal or private fraud or meanness." Moreover, da Costa was a person of considerable influence: "To this same gentleman, several of our leaders in the House of Commons have been in no small degree indebted for their fame there, in funds and money matters and by his credit with them he has been able to effect at times even national good offices." As an active member of London's Sephardic Jewish community, he was well known as a Hebrew scholar, scribe, Talmudist, and communal magnate.[10]

Joseph Salvador was twenty years da Costa's junior. Although he had inherited a considerable estate from an uncle and worked for his father as a merchant trader, by the age of 30 he had established himself in his own right. He had served as parnas or president of the Bevis Marks Congregation in 1746 and about the same time he had replaced his father, Francis, as a member of the emigration committee.

He played the leading role in the establishment of Beth Holim, the Jewish hospital in 1747 and served on its committee. A few years later he was to play a leading role in lobbying for the passage of the Jews Naturalization Bill.[11]

The third member of the committee, Benjamin Mendes da Costa, had come to London at the age of 20 and was endenized in 1725. He was an exceptionally prosperous merchant, noted for his philanthropy.[12]

With the resources available to the committee, Solomon da Costa was in a position to obtain information from Jews already settled in British America and to undertake a thorough review of the colonial jurisdictions of America in order to select the areas that would allow the greatest freedom to potential Jewish emigrants.

In 1747 Jewish communities existed in only four of the Thirteen Colonies: New York, Rhode Island, Pennsylvania, and South Carolina. There were also small numbers of individual Jews in Georgia and Maryland.[13] In none of these colonies were Jews granted full equality with other settlers. In some ways New York, with the largest Jewish population of any of the colonies and the only permanent synagogue building in North America, was the logical place for the committee to consider first. Jews had come to New York in 1654 when it was still the Dutch colony of New Amsterdam.[14] Under Dutch jurisdiction both New Amsterdam and the neighbouring area (later to be Pennsylvania) had allowed substantial advances in rights for minority religions. In Pennsylvania, as we have seen, toleration of religious dissent, including that of Jews, had been written into the constitution in 1696. Asser Levy had established the precedent for Jews holding land in the area by taking up a grant in Albany in 1661, two years before the English captured New Amsterdam and renamed it New York.[15] A century later, New York City unquestionably had the largest Jewish population in America: at least 300 souls representing some 60 families, just over 2 per cent of the city's population of 13,000.[16] In practice, the political and civil status of the Jews in New York was perhaps the most advanced of the Thirteen Colonies.

There were Jews in Rhode Island by 1657. By 1747, when Newport challenged New York as the second most important seaport in the northern colonies, its Jewish population numbered about two dozen families of almost 100 souls.[17] It thus had the second largest Jewish population of the American colonial settlements. In Pennsylvania at least a dozen Jewish families, representing about 50 persons, lived in Philadelphia by 1747, and they had begun to hold regular religious services in a house on Sterling Alley.[18] About ten more families had settled in Lancaster, a frontier post for the western fur trade.[19] Although Jews had been recorded in the area of South Carolina in the 1670s and a small group had settled in Charleston before 1700, there were probably still not more than ten Jewish families in South Carolina by 1747.[20]

Georgia, the last of the colonies to be established on the eastern seaboard, had been founded in 1732. Its colonial charter had allowed full liberty of conscience but it still required the swearing of the state oaths as a condition of holding office. What actually happened when the first settlers arrived in the colony the following year was probably not anticipated. The Bevis Marks Congregation's standing committee to further emigration and colonization was composed of three of the congregation's wealthiest officers: Francis Salvador (the father of Joseph), Alvaro Lopez Suasso, and Anthony da Costa. The committee had sought and obtained a commission to raise money for the sending of the poor – presumed to be the Christian poor – to the new colony. There is some evidence that the committee members actually broached the subject of sending Jews to Georgia, but before a decision could be made by the government, the committee had already sent two boatloads of Jews to Savannah.[21]

William Oglethorpe, the governor of the colony, had not been advised of the coming of Jewish colonists. Because of the liberal charter of the colony, he allowed them equality with the other colonists, contrary to the practices of the day and against the wishes of the trustees who held the charter of the colony for the proprietors. As a result, Jews had rights in Georgia at the very beginning of its settlement, including rights in the land allotment of Savannah. Ten Jewish families actually received land from the government of Georgia in 1733, at a time when the ownership of land by Jews in England was being questioned.[22] Notwithstanding the liberal attitude of Oglethorpe and most of the settlers, legal toleration of the Jewish religion could not be taken for granted during the twenty years Georgia remained a proprietary colony. There is some doubt, for example, whether the Jews were given the right to build a synagogue.[23] By about 1740 many of Georgia's original Jewish settlers had left the colony, some to resettle in Charlestown, South Carolina. At most four families remained. The reasons for their departure were the economic difficulties that almost caused the failure of the colony itself rather than any illiberal treatment.

An examination of the treatment of Jews in the Thirteen Colonies by Solomon da Costa and his committee would have shown that all but two allowed toleration of Jews. Pennsylvania, Delaware, and Rhode Island allowed toleration by charter. The instructions from the Colonial Office mandated the governors "to permit liberty of conscience to all persons except Papists" in another eight of the colonies. And there was no reference to toleration in the instructions to governors of Connecticut or Maryland.[24]

Among the six colonies with numbers of Jewish settlers in 1747, New York, Pennsylvania, and South Carolina had affirmative policies on two of the three issues that concerned Jews in Britain – toleration and alien status – but had negative policies with regard to the other disabilities. Georgia had an affirmative policy on toleration, but there is no evidence about its policy on alien status as most of its Jewish settlers had left the colony by 1740 when the Plantation Act came into force. The remaining two colonies, Maryland and Rhode Island, had affirmative policies on only one issue each – alien status in Maryland and toleration in Rhode Island – but were negative on two of the issues. All the Thirteen Colonies had negative policies on disabilities. The attitude in these colonies was reported by an observer in Marblehead, Massachusetts, who referred to a young man who was "shamefully abused, by being Stoned through the Street, because he is a Jew. I have Advised him to go to Newport, where I hope he will meet with better Treatment."[25]

While New York and Pennsylvania might seem to lead the list of likely places for Jewish settlement, they had drawbacks as well. A resolution of the New York Assembly in 1737 had attempted to prohibit Jews from voting, even though the resolution had not become a statute. The Pennsylvania Charter of Privileges limited participation in government to those who "profess to believe in Jesus Christ the Saviour of the World."

In South Carolina, however, restrictions on voting and holding political office were based solely on oaths of the same form as the state oaths which could be amended, if the liberal interpretation of the Plantation Act was accepted, to allow Jews to use an alternative form.[26] From the point of view of legal equality for Jews, South Carolina must have appeared to Solomon da Costa and his associates in 1747 as the clear winner among the Thirteen Colonies. Its charter, drawn up by John Locke, even though not clearly adopted by the assembly was the only one that allowed equality rather than mere toleration for minority religions. It was the only colony to have encouraged naturalization as a right for members of religious minorities. Now, admittedly not by its own act but through the Plantation Act, the state oaths might no longer be considered a disability to other free and equal civil and political rights. By this reasoning, South Carolina was the only one of the colonies that had the potential to allow equality to Jews.

It was against this background that in the autumn of 1747 a London merchant named James Peyn petitioned the British government on behalf of himself and unnamed associates for a grant of 500,000 acres of land in South Carolina. The petition suggested that "amongst other Benefits which will accrue to the Crown, they will be enabled to settle thereon such Foreign Protestants and others as will shew themselves attached to His Majesty's Person and Government."[27] The choice of words – identical to the description of persons who had the right to be naturalized in North America under the Plantation Act – was unmistakably deliberate. Though Peyn himself was apparently not Jewish, if the Board of Trade were to approve this petition, Jews could not be denied the right to qualify as settlers on the 500,000-acre tract in South Carolina.

In December, when its commissioners considered the petition, Peyn did not appear before the Board of Trade but was represented by John Hamilton, one of his associates, as well as by Joshua Sharpe, barrister, of Lincoln's Inn. According to the board's journal, "Mr Hamilton being called in, informed the Board that he was the principal person concerned and had agreed with several Jews and others in this under-taking, and that Mr Solomon da Costa was Trustee for them." In response to the board's summons, Hamilton returned the following Tuesday, 22 December, accompanied by Solomon da Costa as well as Sharpe. Da Costa told the board that he, together with Joseph Salvador and Benjamin Mendes da Costa, "had agreed with Mr Hamilton for the settlement of several of their poor in South Carolina and sub-scribed a sum of money for that purpose." Instead of responding, the board suggested that Hamilton should submit new proposals in writing "with respect to the terms whereon he desired a grant might be made to his associate Mr Peyn."[28] At this point, the affair seemed to lose momentum. Hamilton did not submit his proposals to the board until the following March, when he wrote that he "has engaged with some Merchants of Fortune and Integrity who have agreed to Advance a large Sum of Money to make an extensive Settlement and to Advance necessary Sums from time to time for transporting Inhabitants." He asked for 200,000 acres, rather than the 500,000 acres in Peyn's original petition, and he requested that the land be made available in tracts of no less than 12,000 acres each.[29]

In the face of repeated questioning over the summer by the com-missioners, the delegation gradually shifted their requirement from an area that would be set aside exclusively for Jewish settlers to an area for "Jews as well as Christians." Hamilton suggested that a Dr Hempe represented the Protestant families involved in the coloni-zation scheme, but when Hempe finally came to address the board he confirmed only that "he had not entered into any agreement with Mr Hamilton, but if he obtained a grant, would furnish him with five or six Protestant families, provided their passage was paid and their property secured when they arrived there." Hamilton's agreement was clearly not with "several Jews and others" as he had told the Board of Trade; his real clients were unmasked as exclusively Jewish. Hamilton was pressed to make further reductions in his proposal from 200,000 acres available in parcels of at least 12,000 acres to 30,000 acres available in tracts of 200 acres. A day later, this was reduced to 100 acres.[30]

On 8 December 1748 the Board of Trade decided to write Solomon da Costa and advise him of their requirement that the "eminent Jews" start by making an unprecedented advance of £6,000 to support the Jewish settlers "in case the Board shall think proper to recommend the making of a grant to Mr Hamilton, according to his said proposal."[31] Although notes of da Costa's meeting with his associates the following Monday have not been discovered, the emigration committee was apparently struck by the lack of trust in the negotiations with the Board of Trade. It was clear that the board was reluctant to recommend that Hamilton be given a large tract in South Carolina to which Jews were to be allowed free access unless there were tight restrictions over those who would settle each 100-acre lot. Moreover, the board might never recommend that Hamilton get any land on which Jews could settle once the committee had paid out its entire fund in advance. With the notable exception of Jewish immigrants to Jamaica, the British government had usually paid many of the costs for the settlement of colonists, even Jewish ones. Could the government not share in the cost of establishing the colony? Was a new rule now to prevail – that Jewish settlers, unlike others, were to be responsible for all their own costs of settlement?

Da Costa's reply, dated 12 December, was considered by the Board of Trade the next day. His letter advised the board "that the intention of himself and his associates was to make the first Outsett for Two Thousand Pounds, laid out in things necessary for the establishment of our undertaking, in such manner as Mr Hamilton should have advised, and should not have scrupled to encrease it to three times that sum or ever more, if we found it answered our expectations, as well with regard to the Publick good, as to our Advantage." The commissioners were unwilling to proceed and they immediately decided that the petition "will not be for his Majesty's service to comply with, Mr Hamilton not having laid anything before the Board, that can induce them to think that he can carry his proposals into effect."[32]

If there was to be a migration of Jews to the English colonies in North America, it would not be with the encouragement of the British government. Solomon da Costa's committee now turned its attention to Nova Scotia, the next British colony to be settled in North America.[33] The granting of civil and political rights to Jews in the land later known as Canada came much earlier than in England and, contrary to popular belief, often earlier than in the future United States of America.

Georgii II. Regis.

An Act for naturalizing such foreign Proteſtants, and others therein mentioned, as are ſettled, or ſhall ſettle in any of His Majeſty's Colonies in *America.*

Hereas the Increaſe of People **Preamble.** is a Means of advancing the Wealth and Strength of any Nation or Country : And whereas many Foreigners and Strangers from the Lenity of our Government, the Purity of our Religion, the Benefit of our Laws, the Advantages of our Trade, and the Secu- rity of our Property, might be induced to come and ſettle in ſome of His Majeſty's Colonies in America, if they were made Partakers of the Advantages and Privileges which the natural born Subjects of this Realm do enjoy ; be it therefore enacted by the King's moſt Excellent Ma-

C t 2 jeſty,

The Plantation Act 1740: "It was either an act for naturalizing Jews, or a charter of rights for Jews in British North America." (American Jewish Historical Society Archives, Waltham, MA, by permission)

Joseph Salvador, the prime Jewish promoter of the Jews Naturalization Act of 1753. (*Jewish Historical Society of England: Transactions* vol. 21, 1968)

William Hogarth, "An Election Entertainment," 24 February 1755. A section of this etching showing a Tory election mob carrying an effigy of a Jew on whose breast is written "No Jews" – a reference to the repeal of the Jews Naturalization Act. (Fisher Rare Book Library, University of Toronto)

E187-L

N Ew-England Rum	Mould Candles	
Leeward Island Do.	Philadelphia hard Soap	
Jamaica Ditto	New-England Ditto	
Moloffes	Cafteil Ditto	} per Pound.
Linfeed Oyl	Indico	
Sweet Oyl	Allfpice	
Clove-Water	Ginger	
Mint-Water	} per Gallon.	
Oringe Ditto	Water-Bread	} per Quar-
Cinnamon Ditto	Milk Ditto	ter Cafk.
Annifeed Ditto	Butter Ditto	
Brandy		
Ginn	Indian Corn	
Limejuice	Barley	
	Oats	
Madiera Wine	Rye Meal	
Lifbon Ditto	Indian Ditto	} per Bufhel.
Port Ditto	} per Pipe	Salt
Claret	Peas	
Vidonia Ditto	White Beans	
	Onions	
Common Brown Sugar		
Midling Ditto	Bricks	
Mufcovado Ditto	18 Inch Shingles	
Rice	3 Foot Ditto	
Ship Bread	} per Hun-	Clapboards
Hay	dred.	Pine Boards
Fine Flower	Oak Ditto	
Common Ditto	Pine Joice	} per Thou-
Rye Ditto	Oak Plank	fand.
Cornell	Hoops	
	White Oak Staves	
Pitch	Red Ditto	
Tar	White Oak Heading	
Turpintine		
Beef	Sweeds Iron	} per Tun.
Pork	} per Barrel	Whippeny Ditto
Beer		
Porter	Stone-Lime	per Hogfh.
Cyder		
Indian Meal	Lemmons	per Box.
Butter	Onions	per Roap.
Chefhire Cheefe		
Gloucefter Ditto	**Produce of** *Halifax*.	
Rhode-Ifland Ditto		
Gammons	Pickle Cod	
Smoak'd Beef	Mackrel	
Smoak'd Mutton	Fifh Oyl	} per Barrel.
Single refin'd Loaf Sugar		
Double refin'd Ditto	} per Pound.	Jamaica Fifh
Chocolate	Merchantable Ditto	} per Quintal
Bohea Tea	Refuge Ditto	
Green Ditto	Toliqual Ditto	
Cut Tobacco		
Virginia Leaf Ditto		
New-England Ditto	*Your Humble Servants,*	
Roll Ditto		
Pigtail Ditto	**Nathans and Hart.**	
Dipp'd Candles		

Nathans and Hart, "Price Current," Halifax, 1752. The oldest known artifact relating to Jews in Canada. (Massachusetts Historical Society, Boston, by permission)

THE
FORM
OF
PRAYER,

Which was performed at the

JEWS Synagogue,

IN THE

City of *NEW-YORK*,

On Thurſday *October* 23, 1760;

Being the Day appointed by Proclamation for a General Thankſgiving to Almighty GOD, for the Reducing of *Canada* to His Majeſty's Dominions.

Compoſed by D. R. **JOSEPH YESURUN PINTO;**
In the Hebrew Language :

And-tranſlated into Engliſh, by a Friend to Truth.

NEW-YORK:

Printed and Sold by W. WEYMAN, at his New Printing-Office, in Broad-Street, not far from the Exchange, 1760. (Price 4d.)

No. 39.

The Form of Prayer in the Shearith Israel Congregation, New York, 23 October 1760 – Upon the Capture of New France. (American Jewish Historical Society, Waltham, MA, by permission)

Chapman Abraham narrowly escapes being burnt at the stake. (Drawing by Harvey Dunn for Stephen Vincent Benet's "Jacob and the Indians," *Saturday Evening Post*, 14 May 1938)

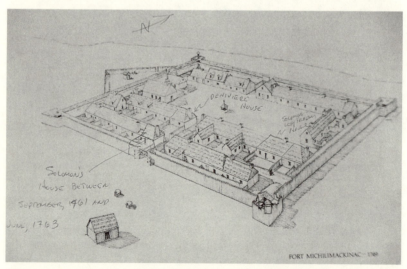

The Scene of Ezekiel Solomons's Capture, Fort Michilimackinac, June 1763. (Sketch by Donald Heldman; Colonial Michilimackinac, courtesy of Mackinac State Historic Parks)

Plaque, entrance to Fort Michilimackinac. (Photograph by author)

The Trade House purchased by Ezekiel Solomons and Gershon Levy, Fort Michilimackinac, 1765. (Colonial Michilimackinac, courtesy of Mackinac State Historic Parks)

Levy Solomons, c. 1780. (Private Collection, by permission)

Probably Rebecca Franks, who married Levy Solomons in Montreal, 31 May 1775. (Private Collection, by permission)

Dorothea Judah Hart, aged 60 years, 1 March 1809. (Metropolitan Museum of Art, New York, Fletcher Fund, 1935, by permission)

Aaron Hart of Trois-Rivières, c. 1770. (A.D. Hart, *The Jew in Canada*, 1926)

"State Oaths for Persons of the Jewish Persuasion," signed by John Franks, Quebec, 1768. (National Archives of Canada, RG 1, E 11, vol. 1, by permission)

"Torah" or Pentateuch belonging to the Shearith Israel Congregation, Montreal. Hand lettered in Hebrew on leather with wooden rollers, c. 1700. (National Library of Canada, Lowy Collection, by permission)

A page from the Minute Book of the Shearith Israel Congregation, Montreal, 1778. (Corporation of Spanish and Portuguese Jews, Montreal, by permission)

Seal of Samuel Jacobs from a document in November 1783. The seal was apparently made in 1761: in a letter dated 18 September 1761, Hyam Myers writes to Jacobs that "Mr Finlay's sudden departure makes me write in haste to aquaint [*sic*] you that with him I send your seal which costs four dollars." (National Archives of Canada, MG 19A, series 3, vol. 22, by permission)

David Salusbury Franks, c. 1778. (Private Collection, by permission)

Moses Myers of Montreal, 1785. (The Chrysler Museum of Art, Moses Myers House, Norfolk, VA, by permission)

Elizabeth Judah Myers of Norfolk, VA, 1803–4, by Gilbert Stuart. (Chrysler Museum of Art, Norfolk, VA, by permission)

"Elizabeth Judah Finished This Work March 6 1771 In Montreal": the oldest known Canadian sampler. (From the Collection of The Gershon and Rebecca Fenster Museum of Jewish Art, Tulsa, OK, by permission)

Certificate of Marriage of Henry Joseph and Rachel Solomons, Berthier, Lower Canada, 28 September 1803: "According to the Laws of Moses and Israel, being agreeable to the laws of England." (Private Collection, by permission)

Henry Joseph, c. 1810. (A.D. Hart, *The Jew in Canada*, 1926)

Rachel Solomons Joseph, c. 1815. (Private Collection, by permission)

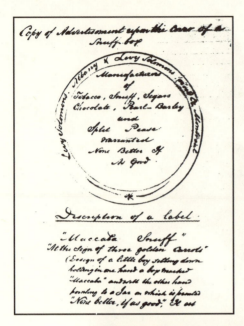

"Copy of Advertisement upon the cover of a Snuff box," for Snuff Manufactured by Levy Solomons and Co., Montreal, c. 1815. (Lyons Collection, American Jewish Historical Society Archives, Waltham, MA, by permission)

Sarah Solomons McCord, c. 1800, oil by Louis Dulongpré. (Collection: McCord Museum of Canadian History, Montreal, by permission)

British North America
1749–1790

5 Remember Halifax

British plans for colonizing Nova Scotia in 1749 struck a respon-
sive chord in Jewish circles in England, although not a single Jew
was among the founders of Halifax in that year.
C. Bruce Fergusson, Provincial Archivist of Nova Scotia, 1961[1]

It was August 1749. The representative of the emigration and colonization committee of the Spanish and Portuguese Jews' Congregation
of London, England, stood on the shore of Chebucto Bay in Nova
Scotia and contemplated the new settlement being carved out on the
south shore.

With the loss of Louisbourg to the French in 1748 under the Treaty
of Aix-la-Chapelle, the British government had seen the necessity of a
permanent British settlement and military station on the Atlantic coast
of Nova Scotia. A scheme for the settlement of Halifax at Chebucto
Bay was organized by the government and £40,000 was allocated by
Parliament. The structure of the venture was similar to Britain's most
recent colonization scheme in North America – the settlement of
Georgia under Oglethorpe in 1733.

The *Sphinx*, carrying Colonel Edward Cornwallis, MP, recently
appointed captain general and governor-in-chief of the province of
Nova Scotia, had dropped anchor in Chebucto Bay on 21 June 1749.
A fleet of 31 transport ships carrying more than 2,500 passengers,
which had shipped out from England in mid-May at the same time as
the *Sphinx*, had arrived at the new town site before the first of July.
There were no Jews among the passengers.[2]

However, Isaac Solomon, John Franks, and Samuel Jacobs were
already in the new settlement of Halifax by the end of July 1749,
having arrived even before Cornwallis's transports. All three were Jews.
Solomon had lived in Boston and New York.[3] Franks, a son of the New
York merchant, Jacob Franks, had probably come from Philadelphia.[4]
The name of Samuel Jacobs, Canada's first permanent Jewish settler,

runs through a half-century of Canadian history as if he himself were a theme. His origins are shrouded in mystery, but he had already been in Britain's North American colonies for some years before Cornwallis's ships arrived. He was born about 1710, apparently in Alsace. He was probably involved in shipping to Newfoundland in the 1730s, for, according to the "Slade Journal," a Samuel Jacobs, owner of the 80-ton schooner *Minorca Snow* of Bristol, England, made several voyages between Bristol, Barbados, New York, and Newfoundland between 1733 and 1738.[5] Jacobs was likely established as a trader at Annapolis before 1745 and at Louisbourg during its occupation by the British which began in 1745 and ended in 1749 with the evacuation of the garrison to Halifax.[6] As a resident of Halifax, he was an example of a committed Jew on the frontier: he boarded with other Jews on Sabbaths and holy days; and his signature invariably included the Hebrew "Shmuel" for Samuel.

Cornwallis was clearly disappointed with the settlers he had brought. Within a month of arrival the number of colonists had shrunk to 1,400. "Amongst these," Cornwallis reported to his superiors in London, "the number of industrious active men proper to undertake and carry on a new settlement is very small. Of soldiers there is only 100. Of tradesmen, sailors and others able and willing to work, not above 200 more, the rest are poor worthless vagabonds that embraced the opportunity to get provisions for one year without labour, or sailors that only wanted a passage to New England. Many have come into a hospital to be cured, some of Venereal Disorders, some even incurables." To stop desertions, Cornwallis was obliged to issue a proclamation advising that anyone who was absent from the settlement for two consecutive days without permission would forfeit all his rights and privileges as a settler.[7]

The situation was critical. Halifax had to be carved out of the forest on the shore of Chebucto Bay. When Cornwallis landed he found the country to be "one continued wood, no clear spot to be seen or heard of." Even though the French fleet had stopped there previously, they had "cleared no ground," but "encamped their men upon the beach." No one had lived on the bay. A few French families had lived "on each side about three leagues off."[8] By the end of July the situation was starting to improve. After the transport ships had unloaded their passengers at Halifax, they had gone north to evacuate Louisbourg. Many of the mustered-out soliders, as well as the few settlers at the fortress, decided to stay in Halifax, adding to the ranks of those committed to making the new colony work. "A good many people from Louisbourg have settled here, and several from New England," Cornwallis reported in August.[9]

The representative of the Spanish and Portuguese Jews' Congregation, whose identity remains unknown, had come to search out the land. He arranged a meeting with Cornwallis so that he could make proposals for the settlement of a number of Jewish families. Back in England his congregation had been advertising for poor families which would be willing to emigrate to Halifax with a promise of three years' support from the synagogue.[10] It was not the only set of proposals Cornwallis was to hear during the summer. When a French merchant had come at about the same time and proposed that a group of French Protestants from Martinique settle in Halifax, Cornwallis had "promised them all encouragement and protection." When word reached him that a thousand New Englanders desired to come before winter, he "ordered all vessels in the Government's Service to give them their passage." Again, when a proposal was made for the immigration of Germans to Halifax, Cornwallis recommended to his superiors in London that it might answer the purpose "to make it Known through Germany that all husbandmen, tradesmen, or soldiers, being Protestants, should have the same rights and privileges in this Province as were promised on His Majesty's Proclamation to His natural born subjects, besides which, at their embarkation at Rotterdam or Plymouth or at their arrival here (as Your Lordships shall think proper), each man should receive 40 sh or 50 sh, and 10 sh for every person in his family, they to be at the charge of their own passage."[11]

Undoubtedly knowing that Jews did not have full rights in England, Cornwallis chose his words carefully in reporting to his superiors on the proposals of the one who had come to search out the land. "A Jew has likewise been with me with proposals," he wrote. "He goes to London and I have referred him to Your Lordships."[12] However, there was no prospect of the representatives of the Spanish and Portuguese Jews' Congregation returning to the Board of Trade for another rebuff, for the experience with the South Carolina colonization scheme was still fresh.[13] Indeed, the minutes of the Board of Trade indicate no further application by them. But Cornwallis seemed ready to wink at the rules because of the urgent need for committed settlers. However cautious he may have been in his official response to Jewish settlement, in practice he welcomed Jewish immigrants to his new settlement without restriction.

Thus, when the official allotment of land in the new settlement of Halifax was made on 8 August 1749, John Franks, Samuel Jacobs, and Isaac Solomon were among those receiving grants. Franks, named on page 1 of the allotment book, obtained the first land granted to a settler in what is now Canada.[14] Samuel Jacobs is listed on page 2 and Isaac Solomon on page 31.[15] This right of Jews to obtain land from the government as equals was unprecedented after a history of Jewish diaspora in countries where church and state shared jurisdiction and where landholding was restricted to those whose beliefs were acceptable to these official bodies.

Although the Board of Trade might well have not have responded favourably to an approach from the Jewish community in London, the evidence seems to establish that the British officials in Halifax undertook a unique experiment on their own. For the first time, Jews were encouraged to settle in a British colony, not merely as individuals, but as a community. This may explain that arrival of a number of additional Jews shortly after the founding of Halifax. Those from Newport, Rhode Island, included Israel Abrahams and his brother Emanuel,[16] Nathan Nathans,[17] Isaac Levy,[18] Nathan Levy,[19] Abraham Andrews, and Naphtali Hart Jr. Joseph Jones and his sons, Mordecai and David, were probably from New York.[20] Isaac Judah had lived in Boston, Newport, and New York.[21]

In Halifax, Jews were allowed to become shopkeepers engaged without restriction in retail trade, at a time when "two strange Jews" were not allowed to set up shops in Albany without being naturalized.[22] Thus, in these early years of the colony, we find Isaac Levy and Nathan Nathans "Joyntly concern'd in the Trade of the Shop" as Nathans & Levy until Levy's death in 1751.[23] Abraham Andrews, an alien and a Jew, was maintaining a shop that sold to the public in 1752,[24] and Mordecai Jones and John Franks were described, respectively, as a "shopkeeper" and "retailer."[25] Indeed, if one takes account of the very high percentage of court cases in which Jews were involved – some 20 per cent of the total in peak years during the 1750s – it seems clear that the Jews formed a significant portion of the settlement's merchant community, even though they constituted no more than one per cent of the population.[26]

Although there is little evidence of them being granted this privilege in other British colonies, Jews in Halifax were frequently called upon as jurors. Jewish jurors in court cases between 1755 and 1763 included Nathan Nathans, Naphtali Hart Jr, Nathan Levy, Joseph Jones, and Mordecai Jones.[27]

Perhaps the most striking feature of early Jewish settlement in Halifax was that the members of the community were to a considerable degree observant Jews. Though it is not possible to draw out an accurage count from the 1752 census, there were evidently at least twenty Jews in the settlement by then.[28] Certainly, there is little doubt that there was a minyan of more than ten men willing to gather for prayer in a religious congregation – the basis of any Jewish community. No record of a Jewish synagogue in Halifax has been found, and the evidence indicates that the Jews of Halifax continued to look to the synagogues in Newport and New York as their actual congregations. However, in another example of the freedom allowed by the government, it seems likely that an official Jewish burying ground had been set aside in the 1749 Halifax allotment of lands.[29]

Israel and Emanuel Abrahams appear to have been the leaders of the minyan in the colony. Their father was Rabbi "Isaac Brisker" Abrahams of Brest-Litovsk and a brother, Abraham Isaac Abrahams of New York, who was a tobacconist and distiller like Israel and Emanuel, acted as the mohel, performing ritual circumcisions for the New York and Newport Jewish communities and for some of the sons of the Halifax community.[30] An unexpected glimpse into the community's existence is to be found in documents relating to Samuel Jacobs. Apparently he did not live with his family in the colony and for a time boarded with Israel and Nelly Abrahams, both observant Jews. In 1752 he was sued by Israel Abrahams for payment for "6 months board, Sabbaths & holy days."[31]

In contrast to other similar early communities, Halifax was also exceptional in that many of the Jewish traders brought wives with them and, further, that most of these women were also Jewish. Israel Abrahams was married to Nelly, the daughter of Ephraim Solomons.[32] His partner, Joseph Jones, was married to Judith, who was Jewish and was likely a sister of the Abrahams.[33] Emanuel Abrahams was married to Bilah, who was Jewish, although it is not known whether they were married while he was in Halifax.[34] Abraham Andrews, who signed his name in Hebrew as "Avraham Bar Asher," was married to a Jewish woman who was probably another sister of the Abrahams and who died before mid-1761.[35] Isaac Levy, Nathan Nathans, and Naphtali Hart Jr[36] were all bachelors. However, the 1752 census indicates that Nathan Nathans, who had no family, had five males over sixteen years of age, possibly Jewish, living with him.[37]

Even some of those with Christian wives remained observant Jews. Isaac Solomon, who had brought his Christian wife with him when he came to Halifax from New England in the summer of 1749, was undoubtedly the "Solomons from Halifax" noted in the records of the Shearith Israel Congregation of New York during the High Holidays in October 1755.[38] John Franks, who married a Christian shortly after he arrived in Halifax, also remained a professing Jew.[39] In later years, he was an active member of Montreal's Shearith Israel Congregation which drew participants for the High Holidays from as far west as Michilimackinac deep in the fur trade hinterland. Franks himself is known to have travelled back to Montreal by canoe for these celebrations.[40]

How does one account for the acceptance of a religiously observant Jewish community in Halifax at a time when Jews were little more than tolerated in England? Three possible explanations come to mind. One is the passage of the Plantation Act nine years earlier which indicated a more accepting attitude in the British government by actively encouraging the settlement of foreign Protestants and Jews in the colonies. A related explanation might be found in the extension of policies established during the settlement of the proprietary colony of Georgia in 1733. There the precedent of allowing a number of Jewish settlers to share in the allotment of lands had been reluctantly established. It may be that officials in Halifax were aware of the practice and chose to continue it in Nova Scotia.[41] Finally, Cornwallis needed willing and hardworking settlers if his new colony was to survive. The Jews who came to Halifax in these early years had much to contribute to a frontier economy and were therefore welcome. The civil rights which they were allowed no doubt encouraged them to come and to remain.

Despite the vigour of the early Jewish settlement in Halifax, it flourished for only a few years. By the mid-1750s there was no longer a minyan in Halifax and the Jewish community as such thus came to an end. Isaac Levy had died in 1751. There is no trace of Isaac Judah after 1752.[42] By 1756 Isaac Solomon was in New York. When the flourishing Nathans and Hart partnership ended in debt in May 1754, Naphtali Hart Jr returned to Newport.[43] Abraham Andrews stayed in the colony at least until 1756, but he left shortly thereafter.[44] The partnership between Israel Abrahams, Emanuel Abrahams, and Joseph Jones ended in debt in 1755.[45] The Abrahams stayed in the colony a while longer then left as well.[46]

During the first years of its existence, when the Seven Years' War between England and France raged about the colony, the economic health of the settlement ebbed and flowed with the arrival or departure of the British fleets supplied by local merchants. The population of the colony shrank despite the best efforts of the British government to bring in new settlers. According to one account, by December 1755 "the inhabitants did not then exceed 1300, many having gone to the other settlements."[47] Samuel Jacobs had left by 1758 to pursue his career as a supplier to the British army, first in New Brunswick and later in Quebec.[48] John Franks had "suffered great losses in trade" as a tobacconist and merchant by February 1751; in 1752 and again in 1754 he advertised his intention "to leave this Colony very soon." His business improved somewhat and he delayed his departure until 1758, a year after the stagnation in commerce caused when the British fleet left Halifax to occupy Louisbourg. He sent his wife to Philadelphia and followed later when he had cleared up his business affairs.[49]

On 2 November 1758 a committee of Nova Scotia's Assembly and Council recommended that the land set aside as the "Jews' burying ground" be used "as a site for a Workhouse."[50] There was no longer a communal need for a Jewish burying ground. And when, on 20 May 1758 and 22 August 1759, Nova Scotia's Executive Council required all voters to take the state oaths, at the option of any candidate, there was no longer any Jewish community to complain that the state oaths, which still included the oath of abjuration to be sworn "upon the true Faith of a Christian," were prejudicial to non-Christians.[51]

A few of the Jewish settlers stayed, but not as part of a Jewish community. On 27 June 1759 Nathan Levy married Sarah Dunn, a Christian, at St Paul's Anglican Church in Halifax, and they moved a few miles south, to Chester, where he died in 1787.[52] Nathan Nathans remained in Halifax as a merchant until 1768, when his former partner, Naphtali Hart Jr, recovered an enormous judgment against him for not rendering proper partnership accounts.[53] Nathans then moved to Russell's Island (now Horseshoe Island) in the bay across from Halifax and became a fisherman. He died in Halifax in 1778, never having married.[54]

Joseph Jones stayed in Halifax longer than the other members of the community. In partnership first with his elder son, Mordecai, and then with his youngest son, David, Jones prospered as the owner of Jones Wharf in Halifax harbour. On 23 October 1758 Joseph Jones and Robert Campbell were given a government grant of a waterfront lot on the harbour to build "a Brest Work on the Beach from the Fish Market in Length 125 feet and 40 feet in Width, as also to Build from the Centre of said Brest work a Wharf for the Accomodation [sic] of Shipping." The grant came with the proviso that the two men "shall on that part of it next to the Fish Market lay down a slip of Ten foot wide for accomodation [sic] of Boats and landing which is to be for public & common use."[55]

Jones was a colourful character, as well known for his temper as for his success in business. In May 1760 his attorney, Daniel Wood, sued him for slander as a result of a dispute about the lawyer's fee. An extract from Wood's claim described the tone of their altercation, alleging that Jones had said:

He the said Daniel was a Cheat and had received his Money, meaning the money of the said Joseph, and kept it and would not repay it him and that he the said Daniel had Robbed and Cheated him the said Joseph of his Money – and that he the said Daniel was a Damn'd Scoundrel and an Insignificant

Puppy or fellow not fit for an Attorney. and that he the said Joseph would put the said Daniel behind the fire meaning the fire then Burning in the Chimney of the Court House at Halifax aforesaid and kick the said Daniel's Arse or such other Words to the same and like Effect.[56]

In 1761 Jones and his wife, Judith, moved to New York, where his attendance was recorded at Shearith Israel Synagogue.[57] After his wife's death in 1767, however, Joseph returned to Halifax, married a Christian, had two more children, and died in 1771. His four children by his marriage to Judith all married Christians. Mordecai Jones died in 1770.[58] Joseph's younger son, David, is recorded as attending Shearith Israel in New York in 1764,[59] but he continued to live in Halifax until his death. His primary occupation was tavern keeper or "publican" – owner of the "Halfway House to Horton." When his parents had returned to New York, his father sold half of his property on the beach near Jones Wharf to David "in consideration of natural love and affection" and five shillings. David Jones then rented the property to his parents but lost his interest in it to a creditor. However, after his father's death in 1771, he sued the estate from which he had been excluded in favour of his father's second wife and their two children. He obtained a judgment for the rent for the five years and eight months that his parents had rented the house on the beach.[60] David Jones died in Halifax in August 1782.[61]

Despite the exodus of many of the early Jewish settlers in the mid-1750s, the records show that Jews continued to come to Nova Scotia although most did not stay for long. For example, in May 1760, one Nahum Israel joined Mordecai Jones as surety for Joseph Jones in support of his appeal against a judgment of the Nova Scotia Inferior Court.[62] And by his own account a builder and master mason named Isaac da Costa, or Decosta, lived in Nova Scotia in 1765–6, employed in construction of the fortress at Annapolis Royal. He possessed vast tracts of land, one of 20,000 acres by the side of a smaller domain of 2,000 acres, but he left the colony by 1771.[63] Even later, we find some descendants of the earlier Abrahams carrying on business in Halifax.[64] Samuel Hart, who will play a prominent role in our story at a later date, arrived in November 1783.[65] And there were others – such as Jacob Calnek[66] and Solomon Jacobs,[67] Isaac and Alexander Levi, and Aaron Moses.[68]

Some of these people considered themselves Jewish; some were merely considered Jewish by others. Nevertheless, using this broader definition, it is fair to say that there has been virtually continuous Jewish settlement in Nova Scotia since 1749. Although the minyan or religious community had lasted only a few short years, it had provided an exceptional and successful precedent in allowing Jews to settle as equals on a new frontier. The reasons for the community's failure appear to have been economic and military rather than lack of support on the part of the British government. The minyan had lasted for only five or six years, but in the history of the Jews it had been a shining moment. Even though a century would pass before there would be another minyan in Nova Scotia, for those who had come to search out the land looking for freedom, a start had been made.

6 Founding People, 1760–1763

Mr: Levi Solomons, a Jew of very good character, who in partnership with three other Jews had carried on a large trade in North America, and had been much concerned in furnishing provisions to the army, had been ruined by unavoidable accidents that befell him in the Indian war in 1762 and 1763.

Francis Maseres, attorney general of Quebec, 30 March 1768[1]

The first light of dawn could barely be seen through the crack in the wall, but it felt damp and cold. The room, prison-like, had no windows, no furniture, the layer of single boards beneath being at once the flooring of the garret and the ceiling of the room below. Sleep had been all but impossible for Ezekiel Solomons. It was Friday morning, 3 June 1763, the day after the massacre of the British garrison at Fort Michilimackinac,[2] one of the incidents in the uprising by Indians who had remained loyal to the French.

As the morning broke, Solomons began to distinguish shapes and forms outside from his vantage point in the garret. It was quiet now, but dead and mangled bodies seemed to lie everywhere, some scalped, some ripped open. Through the crack, Solomons could clearly see the front of his own house immediately to the south, beside the south gate of the fort.[3] There was no doubt that the front door was ajar. As Solomons strained against the crack he recognized "Cote the Frenchman,"[4] as Solomons called him, coming out the door, his arms laden with Solomons's trade goods. Cote returned again and again, each time taking more. Then Solomons recognized "Sanpear" or St Pierre, one of the Indians. He also entered Solomons's house and came out with furs. As Solomons later recalled, he watched as Sanpear "carried the Peltry from my House to the House of Aimable Denivierre in whose garret I was then concealed."[5]

Not long after Solomons heard a stirring below. Then his door opened. Ariek, one of the French Canadians, stood before him.

Solomons had a debt that was accruing to Ariek but was not yet due. Now Ariek, seizing the moment, demanded payment. Solomons, saying the debt was not yet due, refused until the time contracted for. Ariek, aware of his advantage, replied that if Solomons would not pay now, he would exact payment by force. The fort's commanding officer, said Solomons, somewhat hopefully, would prevent that. Ariek rose to his full height. The commanding officer is nothing, he said: "Moi, je suis le Commandant."[6] It was nonsense of course. Ariek was not in control of the fort. But nor, of course, was Solomons. That may have been Ariek's point.

Ezekiel Solomons was arguably the first English-speaking person who reached the Upper Great Lakes after the British conquest of New France. He had moved his base from Albany to Quebec in August 1760 shortly after the British captured Montreal and was among the first four traders to obtain a "passport" to trade in furs in the Upper Country from General Thomas Gage in the spring of 1761.[7] Gage, as military governor of Montreal, had responsibility for the former French territory on the Great Lakes, and he had opened the trade on 1 April 1761 by an ordinance which declared that "all merchants, inhabitants or others, who purpose continuing their residence in this country, who wish to go to trade in the Posts of the Upper Country, that they may go there, the trade is free for everybody."[8] Solomons and his partners had borrowed heavily from Samuel Jacobs and his company, and he had hastened to Michilimackinac with his canoes. Based on the account of Alexander Henry, one of the other traders, Solomons may have arrived first at Fort Michilimackinac.[9] Solomons, a professing Jew born in Germany,[10] was a very unlikely representative of the British at the post, but his presence symbolized the French traders' loss of status arising from the British conquest.

Two years earlier, at the end of the summer of 1761, just before the British had established a garrison at the post, Solomons had been involved in an incident that could also have developed into a massacre. Solomons, Henry, and James Stanley Goddard,[11] together with about thirty of their voyageurs, had stood off two hundred furious warriors of the Ottawa nation for two days and nights until 28 September 1761, when a larger force of British troops arrived to take control of the fort for the first time.[12]

On the day of the 1763 massacre, Thursday, 2 June, the fort had been held by a small garrison of thirty-five soliders under the command of Major George Etherington, supporting a group of not half a dozen British traders among a large number of French-Canadian residents. Now the garrison was decimated, its commander was in hiding, the fort was ignored by several hundred Indians who joined in celebration outside the stockade, exhausted by their efforts, leaving three hundred or so French Canadians, who had traditionally been their allies, inside the fort.

Solomons should have seen it coming. The day before the massacre, unusual numbers of Chippewa had appeared at the fort. They had come to his trading house, as they had to the houses of Alexander Henry, Henry Bostwick, and one Tracy, the other English merchants.[13] They had examined his trade goods, particularly the silver arm bands and more valuable ornaments, noting with interest where they were kept, but they had bought only trade axes or tomahawks. Then, on Thursday there was a game of *baggatiway*, called *le jeu de la crosse* by the French Canadians, played outside the stockade between the Chippewa and the Sauk nation. Some of the French Canadians and almost all the English garrison had gone outside to watch, leaving their weapons inside. At a prearranged signal – Chief Madjeckewiss threw the ball over the pickets into the fort – a chilling war cry was heard and the Indians rushed after the ball, tomahawks and knives appearing in their hands amid screams and general confusion.[14] In the ensuing mêlée more than half the garrison of thirty-five was slaughtered, amid shouts of rage and victory and shrieks of fear from the dying.[15] Solomons, Henry, Bostwick, and an Englishman from Detroit who had just arrived at the fort had not gone to the game and were in hiding. Tracy, who was outside, was killed. None of the three hundred French Canadians was attacked. "The Fury of the Savages fell only on the British soliders & Traders," noted the governor of Montreal a few weeks later: "They neither hurt the Canadians nor plundered their Goods."[16]

His hiding place discovered, Solomons needed all his courage just to stay alive over the next few days. The following day, 4 June, Solomons, Henry, the Englishman from Detroit, and a soldier were all taken west towards the "Isles du Castor" by canoe, accompanied by seven Chippewa warriors. The soldier was bound to a thwart of the canoe by a rope around his neck. The other three prisoners, most of their clothes having been taken from them, were required to paddle. It was very cold; a thick fog required the canoe to keep close to the shore. While they had not been told the purpose of the trip, the Chippewa were taking them, according to Henry, "only to kill and devour us." Part way through the trip, the Chippewa offered bread to the prisoners who had eaten nothing for two days. Henry recorded the offer: "They had a loaf which they cut with the same knives that they had employed in the massacre – knives still covered with blood. The blood they moistened with spittle, and rubbing it on the bread offered this for food to their prisoners, telling them to eat the blood of their countrymen." At Fox Point, about eighteen miles west of the fort, the fortunes of the prisoners changed. The Chippewa canoe was overwhelmed by warriors of the Ottawa nation, who were insulted at not having been consulted about the attack on the English.[17]

The prisoners were returned to the fort but obliged to remain in the hands of the Chippewa, their lives at risk until a guard of friendly Menominee, Sauk, Foxe, and Winnebago from Baie des Puants (Green Bay) arrived on the evening of 30 June 1763 to protect the surviving English. On 18 July Etherington and the remaining British soldiers departed for Montreal under a guard of sixty Ottawa warriors.[18] According to Henry, Solomons was also taken to Montreal by the Ottawa and there ransomed.[19] He had escaped with his life, but his goods were lost and he would soon face a large number of claims from creditors.

While Solomons was held prisoner at the fort, his partner Gershon Levy,[20] unaware of the Indian uprising, had arrived from the east, his canoes laden with trade goods. Levy was taken prisoner, and his goods were confiscated. While the date of his capture has not been confirmed, there is every reason to believe that he was treated like the English traders who had arrived at the fort on 4 June, suspecting nothing, and "were seized, dragged through the water, beat, reviled, marched to the prison Lodge, and there stripped of their clothes, and confined."[21] Levy found that payment of debts not yet due was demanded by one of the French Canadian traders, and on 12 July he was obliged, under duress, to sign a promissory note for £1,200. He remained at the fort, virtually alone among the French Canadians, after the British troops left on 18 July.[22]

About a month before the massacre at Michilimackinac, another of the traders allied with Solomons, Chapman Abraham, was coming up the Detroit River from Lake Erie when he, too, was captured by Indians. The diary of John Porteous, one of the Detroit merchants, noted tersely: "Friday 13th May. Had account this morning that Chapman Abrams and a Dutch trader named Barkman, with five Batteaux and horses were taken at the lower settlement by the Hurons there, the enemy got seventeen Barrels of Powder besides all the other merchandise." The "Diary of the Siege of Detroit," written by Major Robert Rogers three months later, offers scarcely more detail, saying only that on 13 May 1763, "Mr Chapman a trader from Niagara was taken Prisoner by the Waindotes, with five Battoes loaded with goods."[23]

From 9 May, Fort Detroit, the fur trading post between Lake Erie and the Upper Great Lakes, had been under seige by hundreds of Indian warriors led by Pontiac, who was still loyal to the French. Earlier, the 120 British soldiers and English traders inside the fort had

watched helplessly as the "English" unlucky enough to be found outside the fort, including Sir Robert Davers,[24] Captain Robertson, and
at least a dozen more, were killed and scalped. Then, on Wednesday,
11 May, five or six hundred Indians attacked the fort but withdrew
with three men killed and more than a dozen wounded. From then
on, Pontiac's men waited, hoping to starve out the defenders of the
fort.[25]

Chapman Abraham, a forty-year-old trader, had been in the Detroit
area for at least a year, having come from Holland to New York by
1756 after a stay in Plymouth, England, where his brothers settled.[26]
He was proudly Jewish and was so known on the frontier.[27] His own
account of the incident was set out in his affidavit of 9 August 1763,
which was presented to the military court at Detroit under Major
Henry Gladwin:

Mr. Chapman Abraham being sworn informs the Court, that in coming up
Detroit River, having put on shore at the place of Monsieur St. Lewis, he [St
Lewis] acquainted this Deponant [Abraham] that the Fort was besieged by
the Indians & Capt. Robertson, Sir Robert Daviss [Davers] and a great many
more English were killed, & that they intended to kill all the English that
would come up Detroit River. This Deponant immediately told his men to go
back with him; but the before mentioned soldiers told his men if they returned
that all would be killed, as the Indians were round the whole Lake and at
Niagara, upon which they absolutely refused to return with him. In consequence of which this Deponant put all his goods in said St. Lewis's house,
who told him he could do his best to save them from the Indians; Then this
Deponant asked him where he should go to hide himself to save his life. He
and Madam Esperame (who was present) answered him he should go to her
home and hide himself in her cellar; where he continued about ten minutes
and then was told by said Madam Esperame to go out of the house; which he
obeyed and in going out she perceived his watch chain & told him to give it
to her that she was certain the Indians would kill him; upon which this
Deponant told her he would make her a present of it, if she would let him
stay in the cellar to save him from the Indians. She answered he should stay
no longer in the House; upon which he endeavored to gain the woods; she
followed him, demanding the watch a second time, which I again refused. By
this time the Indians discovered him, took him prisoner and carried him to
St. Lewis's house, where he found some of his goods were put in his canoe.[28]

The story is then picked up by the missionary, the Reverend John
Heckewelder, who wrote that he had first heard it from the inhabitants
of Detroit, the facts being "afterwards confirmed to me by Mr Chapman himself":

About the commencement of the Indian War in 1763, a trading Jew, named Chapman who was going up the Detroit River with a batteau-load of goods he had brought from Albany, was taken by some of the Indians of the Chippeway nation and destined to be put to death. A Frenchman impelled by motives of friendship and humanity, found means to steal the prisoner, and kept him so concealed for some time, that although the most dilligent [sic] search was made, the place of his confinement could not be discovered. At last, however, the unfortunate man was betrayed by some false friend, and again fell into the power of the Indians who took him across the river to be burned and tortured. Tied to the stake and the fire burning by his side, his thirst from the great heat became intolerable and he begged that some drink might be given to him. It is a custom of the Indians, previous to a prisoner being put to death, to give him what they call his last meal; a bowl of pottage or broth was therefore brought to him for that purpose. Eager to quench his thirst, he put the bowl immediately to his lips, and the liquor being very hot, he was dreadfully scalded. Being a man of very quick temper, the moment he felt his mouth burned, he threw the bowl and its contents full in the face of the man who handed it to him. "He is mad! He is mad!" resounded from all quarters. The bystanders considered his conduct as an act of insanity, and immediately untied the cords with which he was bound, and let him go where he pleased.[29]

Abraham may have been free, but like Ezekiel Solomons he had lost all his trade goods and furs. His affidavit before Gladwin named a number of French-Canadian residents of the fort whom he had seen wearing or trading goods he recognized as his. But he was not able to recover anything.

Just a week after Abraham was taken prisoner, another associate of Ezekiel Solomons, Levy Solomons, was captured by the Indians at almost the very same spot. Lieutenant James McDonald of the 60th Royal American Regiment noted that on 20 May, "Messrs Leveys, with two Servants were taken prisoners by the *Wandots*, within a League of the Fort."[30] These "Leveys" were Levy Andrew Levy, a Pennsylvania trader from Fort Pitt,[31] and Levy Solomons, a New York trader based at Niagara who was commonly known simply as "Mr Levy." Like Abraham, he was a Dutch Jew, and though about ten years younger than Abraham, he was similarly firm in his religious beliefs despite his distance from an organized Jewish community.[32] Like Abraham, he had risked his life. A report received at Fort Pitt several months later advised that "we hear from D'Troit that Levy Solomon and H. Crawford with three of his Men made their escape and got into D'Troit after remaining with the Indians some time."[33] Levy Solomons had escaped with his life but he, too, had lost everything.

Ezekiel Solomons, Gershon Levy, Chapman Abraham, Levy Solomons. Four stories, but really one story. Together with Benjamin Lyon[34] they had been associated in a partnership known as Gershon Levy & Company and had been by far the most influential of the Jews who came to Quebec during the years immediately after the conquest of New France. These men had dominated the New York Indian trade before 1760 and as sutlers or provisioners of the army had provided crucial support to the British in the war with France. In the three years following 1760, the consortium moved its trade into the former French territories surrounding the Great Lakes, filling the void left by the French. They reoriented the Indian trade in furs towards Montreal, thereby assisting the new British government which had not yet had an opportunity to establish its jurisdiction.[35]

The consortium's use of Albany as a base by 1756 had met with considerable resistance in the colony of New York, as at least two of its members were prevented from opening shops by reason of the municipal trade restrictions against foreigners who had not been naturalized. Solomon Hays, a New York Jewish merchant, had been brought to testify at court in Albany in 1756 regarding "two strange Jews ... one Ephraim Champman the other named Levi," because the corporation of Albany did not believe they were natural-born subjects of the king; Hay was not helpful for he declared that he always understood that they were born in Holland. "Ephraim Champman" and "Levi" seem from the evidence to have been Chapman Abraham and Levy Solomons.[36]

Within the next two years, however, the consortium had been more formally organized and had opened two shops in Albany. A notice found in a New York journal, dated in the spring of 1758, advised the public of "Fine hard soap, dip't and Mould tallow, spermecetae Candles, sold by LEVY, SOLOMONS and COMPANY; by LYON, LEVY and COMPANY at their stores in Albany as cheap as at New York."[37] While both Abraham and Levy Solomons may have commenced their qualifying period for the seven-year residence requirement and applied for naturalization under the Plantation Act, the unusual juxtaposition of the names of the two firms in the advertisment suggests the possibility that they had gone directly to opening stores in Albany by splitting into two firms each "fronted" by a natural-born British subject. In this way, Levy, Solomons was composed of Gershon Levy who was native born and Ezekiel Solomons who was born in Europe. Lyon, Levy, later also known as "Lyons, Levy & Chapman,"[38] was led by Lyon who was born in either Britain or one of the colonies.

By 1760 the consortium, though still based in Albany, was sending out representatives who summered at Oswego[39] and Fort Niagara[40] on the south side of Lake Ontario and probably traded even farther west. Their trade goods included molasses and rum as well as a range of products such as iron "peace pipe" tomahawks not locally available.[41] There is evidence that they maintained a close connection with traders in England, the Thirteen Colonies, and the Caribbean – a trading triangle with merchants overseas. Albany had served as trading centre for the British fur trade to the north and west. The consortium had led the British effort which had broken the French monopoly of the Great Lakes fur trade with the Indians. Moreover, because of their trade contacts among the Indians on the north side of the lake, the consortium had been well positioned to supply the British and colonial forces prior to the conclusion of the war in 1760. The consortium, according to one account, "during the late war with France ... were employed to furnish divers necessaries to His Majesty's Armies in North America."[42]

Upon the capture of Montreal by the British in April 1760, France lost its great commercial empire on the Great Lakes. The Jewish consortium was free to move north and use Montreal as their base – Levy Solomons and Chapman Abraham establishing themselves at Forts Niagara and Detroit, respectively, Ezekiel Solomons and Gershon Levy setting up at Michilimackinac, and Benjamin Lyon working from Montreal and Albany. Their departure from Albany in the summer of 1760 to move north to Quebec was a great loss to the New York merchants, causing considerable consternation and evoking some sharp complaints. One account written from New York noted that as a result of their departure "it is computed our merchants in New York lose between £18 and £20,000, a great loss ... suffered." It was, the letter continued bitterly, "about three weeks since the Jew traders at Albany shut up shop and made them selves scarce."[43] Yet only four years earlier the town of Albany had complained that they had been allowed to open up shops at all. The new territory of Quebec to the north was to have no such restrictions and was ripe with opportunities.

In the spring of 1761, the partnership of Samuel Jacobs and Alexander Mackenzie[44] staked a large advance to the consortium of Gershon Levy & Company, relying on a promissory note due on 9 July 1761 as well as the guarantee of Hyam Myers,[45] but anticipating that Jacobs would become the major Canadian purchaser for the consortium's furs. When Jacobs found the following year that the consortium had in fact "consignd their Beavor & other furrs to Isaac Levy," Gershon Levy's brother, in anger he petitioned the governor, asking that the company's goods be secured for the payment to him of the balance of the debt.[46] The debt to Jacobs was still outstanding at the time of the Indian uprising in 1763.

Although statistics on the fur trade were not systematically kept by the British until after 1766, there is nevertheless some indication of this consortium's relative importance in early British fur trading ventures in what is now Canada. In 1768, the members of the group testified that because of the Indian attacks in June 1763 they had lost "a great quantity of goods which they were carrying to the said forts [Detroit and Michilimackinac] to the value of £18,000 of lawful money of this province." A report in 1766 by a British official regarding the value of the total British trade at the western posts indicated that for more than two seasons, between the start of the fur trade in the spring of 1761 and June 1763, "the Aggregate fur trade did not exceed £100,000."[47] Based on that report, the consortium's annual sales amounted to almost 40 per cent of the entire trade on the Lakes. It was later officially acknowledged that during this period it "carried on a large trade in North America."[48]

There is also evidence that the consortium's intended line of supply reached across the continent to the Pacific Ocean – from sea to sea – several years before others attempted to do this. On 10 July 1762, Ezekiel Solomons, acting for himself as well as Gershon Levy, signed an *engagement* or fur trade contract with Jean-Baptiste Proulx to travel to "la mer du Ouest," intending that he should reach at least as far as Fort Dauphin, the former French post on the northwest shore of Lake Manitoba at the portage to Lake Winnipegosis or the North Saskatchewan River. The trip was unsuccessful as Proulx had stayed at Rainy Lake, as Lake of the Woods was then known, because of perceived dangers to the west.[49]

In June 1763 the success of the consortium of Jewish fur traders came to an abrupt end. Four of its members were taken prisoner by the Indians, and although all miraculously escaped, the consortium had, according to their own account, lost goods to the value of £18,000 in the Indian uprising "through unavoidable losses and misfortunes." They had "preserved another considerable part of their effects," but they faced demands for payment from their voyageurs in the field[50] and from their suppliers in Montreal and New York.

Other traders had losses that were similarly devastating. Although there were many individuals involved, repayment by the government was out of the question: compensation for war losses did not become government policy until after the American Revolution. Nor was there any insurance. As they were unable to obtain payment from the Indians to whom they had given credit, four English trading firms at Michilimackinac, including Gershon Levy, petitioned General Gage at the end of 1763 "to hint to you what we think may be to our private Advantage without any Detriment to the Nation and wherein our

Losses may be in some Measure repaid without any Retardment to the publick Peace." The traders suggested: "If your Excellency thinks proper, when they [the Indian nations] propose Terms of Peace, to mention to them to pay their Debts."[51] Six months later, however, we find sales of the goods of "Levy & Solomon" for the benefit of their creditors being announced in the *Quebec Gazette* on 10, 19, and 26 July, to take place on 10 August 1764.

By 1767 Gershon Levy & Company had clearly recovered some of their trade in that they had the second largest volume of beaver skins sent from Michilimackinac to Montreal.[52] However they remained deeply in debt, and in 1768, five years after the consortium had suffered its losses, the owners petitioned the governor and council, asking to be declared bankrupt so that they could be relieved of their debts.[53] A question had arisen whether an ordinance of 1764 that introduced the laws of England into the colony meant that English bankruptcy laws applied in Quebec. The members of the consortium, among many others, asked for the English law to apply to them.[54] Samuel Jacobs, however, had been a major creditor of the consortium at least two years prior to their default, and he was unwilling to take the loss.[55] In November 1767 he and 20 other merchants had therefore petitioned the governor and council, expressing their alarm at the prospect of English bankruptcy laws being applied in the province. They suggested "that such a step would be extremely detrimental to the General trade of this Province" and set out "some of the many reasons why these Acts should not be introduced into this Province."[56] Lieutenant Governor Carleton jumped to the defence of the merchants and decided to hold the operation of the bankruptcy laws in suspense while he wrote to the government in England recommending that the laws should not be brought into operation.[57]

The five merchants of the consortium, having no alternative, decided to withdraw their petition and remain responsible for the entire burden of their debt.[58] They were never permitted to declare bankruptcy. Gershon Levy was not heard from again.[59] The others spent years trying to repay their debts.[60] Chapman Abraham[61] and Benjamin Lyon[62] both remained fur traders and died in Montreal. Levy Solomons retired to Montreal as a merchant, where he died in 1792.[63] Ezekiel Solomons moved to the new British fort on Mackinac Island, although it appears he returned to New York just before his death to end his days among his people.[64] All four were members of Montreal's Shearith Israel Congregation.

None of these five men became rich, but their legacy was enormous. The consortium was the first large-scale organized fur trade enterprise after the British gained sovereignty over the western posts. Almost forgotten today as Canadian patriots, the five members of the consortium risked their lives in an attempt to found a British North American fur trade that could give Canada an economic justification as a country. The nation's existence from sea to sea is based not on manifest destiny, or on the spread of empire, or on the spread of the gospel, but rather on the economic fact that exploration and the fur trade in Canada were historically one and the same thing. Exploration in British North America was not the search for the western sea or the Northwest Passage. Exploration was dictated by the fur trade which itself determined boundaries, established east-west thinking, and was the precursor of the bands of steel that would later bind a country from end to end. In this sense, the members of the consortium were among Canada's "founding people."

In the grand works attempted by this small band of brave souls, they found that they were accepted as equals, not merely tolerated. They were welcomed by their fellow "English traders" and earned the respect of the French residents of the western posts as well as of the Indians. They had been encouraged to enter the trade in the Upper Country by the new government of the province of Quebec. They had been treated equally in obtaining fur trade licences, in being given the protection of British troops – as well as in the lack of compensation for their losses! When they needed help, their champion was none other than Francis Maseres, the attorney general of the province.

"Damned Jew," a close, non-Jewish, friend had joked to Chapman Abraham, months before the Indian uprising at Detroit: "I thought you should act like a Christian." The Jewish members of the consortium that entered the fur trade of the Upper Country in 1761 had come to pursue their trade freely on the frontier. They found no obstacles. They acted with full rights, not as Christians, but in the same manner as Protestants. In short, they were among the "Protestant" Jews of Quebec.

7 The "Protestant" Jews of Quebec, 1763–1774

> A Jew is a Protestant. Therefore is Entitled to Enjoy all offices.
> Gershom Mendes Seixas, 13 January 1783[1]

A small group of men stood in a room in the Castle of St Louis, the residence of the governor of the province of Quebec. It was 18 November 1768. John Franks bowed his head, placed one hand on the book containing the five Books of Moses, and took the oath of office: "I, John Franks, do swear that I will faithfully and truly execute the office of Overseer of the Chimnies for the Town of Quebec, according to the best of my abilities. So help me God." Then Franks read the three state oaths from a large sheet of parchment. The first was the oath of allegiance to the sovereign, the second the oath of supremacy, the third the oath of abjuration. When Franks came near the end of that oath, he read "and promise heartily, willingly, and truly upon the true faith of a Jew." Then he signed his name at the bottom.

On the back of this parchment was a title, "State Oaths for Persons of the Jewish Persuasion." George Allsopp, deputy provincial secretary and assistant clerk, then signed a document certifying that Franks had personally appeared before him and "being of the Jewish Religion, and Sworn on the Pentateuch or five Books of Moses, took and subscribed the Oaths of Office, Allegiance, Supremacy & Abjuration According to Act of Parliament." The governor, Guy Carleton, signed a commission acknowledging that he was "well assured of the Integrity, Diligence and Ability of John Franks" and appointing him overseer of chimneys for the town of Quebec and suburbs pursuant to an ordinance passed earlier in the year. Then the governor handed the commission to Frank.[2]

What had just happened was absolutely unprecedented in Great Britain or in any of its colonies. Franks had been appointed to high office by commission, had sworn upon his faith as a Jew, and had been granted his office by the king's representative. This was the first such appointment to a Jew in the British empire.[3] More than that, the governor of the province had officially amended the state oaths used for appointments to all offices so that they would not be offensive to Jews and so that they could be used by other Jews in the future.

In 1766 an act of the British parliament altering the oath of abjuration had been passed. Among its provisions was a requirement that the colonies follow the British practice with regard to the state oaths and "no other." Thus, for the first time the colonies would have to use the oath of abjuration which included the phrase "upon the true Faith of a Christian." The new state oaths were adopted without qualification in almost all of the American colonies, even in those where the oath of abjuration had not previously been a requirement. Even though Allsopp certified that Franks had taken the oath of abjuration "According to Act of Parliament," the act that dealt with that oath had not specifically provided for its alteration for Jews in these circumstances.[4] In Quebec, the lone exception to this new rule, the government, disregarding the prescription that the Christian form of oath "and no other" should be used, had adopted a different form of the oath of abjuration that would be acceptable to persons of the Jewish persuasion.[5] In 1768 the last step had been completed in ensuring that Jews had rights equal to those enjoyed by other British subjects in Quebec.

Of course Quebec was different from the other British colonies in North America. British administration of the colony had started immediately after the capture of Quebec in September 1759. Before that Quebec had been controlled by France and had allowed only French Catholic settlers. Even though the French still controlled the area around Montreal, about a hundred British civilians, including a substantial number of Jews, had arrived in the town of Quebec to supply the British army. Over the winter of 1759–60, it appeared that France might retake the town of Quebec, and the British were required to protect, as well as to provide support for, these merchants or sutlers who had come to supply them. After the capture of Montreal in the spring of 1760 the war was over and a military administration was instituted for the whole colony of Quebec. More Jewish merchants had come in 1760, and more again in 1761, this time to Montreal.[6]

By 1762, however, the immigration of English-speaking civilians had stopped. A census two years later showed that while there were slightly more than 60,000 French-speaking Catholics in Quebec, there were only 133 male Protestant "house keepers" in all the colony. Of these, 99 were in Montreal; the other 34 were in the town of Quebec and spread throughout the upper half of the province. One-half were merchants; three-quarters were civilians. As well, there were some 18 or more Jewish adult males.[7]

Clearly, Britain had a problem. Quebec was populated by French-speaking Catholics. In the short term there was no hope of encouraging enough English-speaking Protestants as settlers to create a stable new colony. The French had been the enemy of Britain in the Seven Years' War just concluded, and Catholics were treated with great caution in England itself. As we have seen, the Roman Catholic religion was not tolerated in Protestant Britain. Catholics were excluded from all offices and places of trust, whether civil or military; they were excluded from sitting in Parliament and voting at elections; and they were excluded from purchasing or inheriting estates. The preamble to the 1766 act for altering the oath of abjuration began with the statement that new legislation was required because the Catholic James Stuart, the Old Pretender, had died in 1766. The continuing objective of the oath of abjuration was to exclude Catholics from authority. In dealing with the French Catholic Acadians in Nova Scotia just a few years earlier, Britain had used the traditional European method of expelling those who did not conform to the state religion. The status of the Acadians, who found themselves in a British colony in North America after the founding of Halifax in 1749, had been doubtful because of their religion. Moreover, they had been reluctant to swear allegiance to the British king. In 1755 Britain therefore decided to deport or expel all the Acadians to ensure that Nova Scotia would be a Protestant colony. At this time all of the Thirteen Colonies also excluded Catholics from civil rights.

When the treaty concluding the Seven Years' War was under negotiation, however, it was clear that the French-speaking Catholics of Quebec would not renounce their religion. Section 4 of the treaty of 1763 thus provided that "His Britannick Majesty, on his side, agrees to grant the liberty of the Catholick religion to the inhabitants of Canada; he will in consequence give the most precise and most effectual orders, that his new Roman Catholick subjects may profess the worship of their religion, according to the rites of the Romish Church, as far as the laws of Great Britain permit."[8] The Roman Catholic religion was to be tolerated, although the hierarchy of the church was not recognized and the church was not legally established or entitled to collect tithes. It was a unique situation: the acceptance of the Roman Catholic religion to a degree that would not have been contemplated in England.

By the end of the year the British government had made an administrative decision. There was to be no elected assembly: the new province was to be ruled by a civil governor and a council composed of the chief justice and surveyor general of the province together with eight other appointed councillors.[9] It would not be necessary to

decide whether His Majesty's "new Roman Catholick subjects" were to
have the right to be elected to office or to vote because there were to
be no elective offices and no one was to have the franchise. There was
to be no question whether membership in any assembly would be
limited to Protestants because there would be no assembly. The council that the new governor, James Murray, appointed on 10 August
1764, when the military regime ended and civil government began,
was composed entirely of Protestants, although some of those
appointed were of Huguenot ancestry and one of them spoke
French.[10] To a remarkable degree for the time, the laws, institutions,
and customs of the French Canadians were retained by the new
government. French Canadians were entitled to retain their language,
their system of landholding, and their organization into rural parishes.
Although English criminal law was introduced, French laws and customs were still to be the rule in many civil cases, and French-Canadian
advocates, proctors, and attorneys were to be entitled to practise in
the courts of the province.[11] The Catholics in Quebec, although they
were not yet to be appointed to high office or given complete equality,
had been treated with a degree of latitude in an attempt to win their
support for the British administration. For the time, it was a generous
gesture from the winners to the people who had lost a war.

The Jews of Quebec were also important to the British administra-
tion because Jews had been Britain's supporters throughout the Seven
Years' War.[12] The small community in Halifax had supplied the navy
until the capture of the fortress of Louisbourg. Merchants in the
Thirteen Colonies such as Moses and David Franks of New York and
Philadelphia and a group of Jewish fur traders based in Albany in New
York had all played an important role as sutlers in provisioning the
British armies in the field.

Samuel Jacobs, as we have seen, had established himself as a prosperous merchant by provisioning the British forces at Halifax from
1749, and after the navy left Halifax for Louisbourg in 1757, by
provisioning the army at Fort Cumberland on the Bay of Chignecto.
His later movements confirm his pattern of moving to a new area as
soon as it was opened for trade or settlement by the British. From
December of 1758 he followed the 43rd Regiment into Quebec,
supplying it with provisions through arrangements with Major Skey
and Captain Dunbar.[13] He arrived in the town of Quebec very soon
after the battle of the Plains of Abraham in September 1759. By 11
October he was running a schooner from Quebec to Oporto, Portugal,
sending fish and bringing back supplies. We know this because his
schooner, *Betsey*, was diverted by the orders of the British adjutant of
the town of Quebec and sent to the Island of Orleans to bring cattle

and stores for the army in November. On 7 June 1762, Governor Murray endorsed Jacobs's petition certifying that his schooner "was pressed into the Government's service some time in November, 1759 to bring Cattle and Stores to Quebec from the Island of Orleans and that she was also detained and Loaded with Provisions after the Action of the 28th of April, 1760 [when the British captured Montreal], to attend the Retreat of the Troops in case the enemy had obliged us to abandon the Town."[14] In 1760 Jacobs received one of the first land patents in Quebec and in 1765, in partnership with two Christians, a licence for a distillery. When the Jewish community moved from Quebec to Montreal by about 1765, Jacobs moved on to St Denis. He bought a store on the Richelieu from Charles Curtis and operated it until his death in 1786.[15]

Other Jews who supplied the army, such as Aaron Hart[16] and his partner, Isaac Levy,[17] are also known to have arrived in the province before 1760 and helped to create the fledgling British colony. The consortium of Gershon Levy, Ezekiel Solomons, Levy Solomons, Chapman Abraham, and Benjamin Lyon was similarly engaged. According to their petition of 1768 they were employed "during the Time of the late War with France and the subsequent Indian War in the Year 1763 ... to furnish divers Necessaries to His Majesty's Armies in North America."[18] The British troops at Fort Niagara knew Levy Solomons as a sutler.[19]

Whether sutlers or settlers, Jews had quickly become indispensable. There were so few English and non-Catholic residents that the Jews made up a significant and "loyal" population. All Protestant adult males in the districts of Quebec and Montreal numbered only 133 in 1764, and as adult male Jews numbered at least 18, they comprised about 12 per cent of the non-Catholic adult male population.[20] And many of them were men of substance, welcome in any colony.[21] By 1764 the Jewish population at the town of Quebec included John Franks,[22] Elias Solomon,[23] Lazarus David,[24] Eleazar Levy,[25] Hyam Myers,[26] and a man with the surname Aaron who worked for Samuel Jacobs.[27] As well as the partners of Gershon Levy & Co., the community at Montreal included Levy Simons,[28] Elias Henry,[29] Levy Michaels,[30] and Andrew Hays.[31] The need of the administration for loyal supporters meant that Jews in Quebec were allowed considerable economic and civil equality with the other English settlers and were central to the British efforts to administer their new colony. Quebec appears to have called Jews as jurors,[32] and that they possessed a position of unusual equality at the time may be presumed from the somewhat resentful comment of a later French-Canadian nationalist: "Entreprenants et audacieux, et sans doute favorisés par cette politique de protection anglaise qui accordeait aux conquérants et à leur amis des avantages qui étaient persistamment refusés aux anciens colons français, les Juifs surent obtenir quelques fonctions officiels ou lucratives."[33]

Samuel Jacobs certainly found virtually no restrictions placed on his economic ascent. In 1765 he joined a distillery venture with John Hay, a Quebec merchant, and Benjamin Price, one of the governor's councillors. Jacobs and his influential partners had "improved certain Ruinous buildings and erected certain Houses for making Malt and Distilling Spirits from corn upon a Lott or Piece of Ground in the Province of Quebec Situated near the Intendant's Palace within the Garden wall of the same." The three merchants had spent over £1,500 on the enterprise in the town of Quebec without owning the land. When they petitioned for rights to use the land as a distillery, Governor Murray recommended that the king grant them a 99-year lease at a rent of £5 a year. They received the patent to the land and buildings as a "lot under tenure" on 23 November 1765.[34]

In August 1763 Aaron Hart became probably the first Jewish office holder in the new British colony of Quebec when he received an appointment as postmaster of Trois-Rivières.[35] There were only four post offices in Quebec until the 1780s; the appointment was therefore of some importance. Hart had been appointed by Hugh Finlay, the postmaster at Quebec who was himself appointed by the postmaster general in England.[36] The appointment is significant for our story because it was the most senior given to any Jew in England or any of its colonies to that date. His appointment seems to have originated in the need of the government to find a qualified individual who would be loyal to the administration in Trois-Rivières, a town with few English inhabitants. According to Frederick Haldimand, the military governor at Trois-Rivières, Hart was at the head of "the group of British merchants in Three Rivers ... composed of a Jew and of a Sarjeant and of an Irish Soldier on half pay."[37] The governor felt he had few to choose from and Hart seemed the only one available with the necessary qualifications: he was not a French Canadian, he was able, and he was loyal. There is a possibility that Hart had held a position with the British army that invaded Montreal in 1760 under General Amherst.[38] If that were true, it would have provided an additional reason for the choice of Hart. Hart held the position of postmaster until 1780.[39]

Three years after Hart's appointment, on 24 December 1766, Eleazar Levy, who lived in the town of Montreal, received an imperial commission as a notary. The authorities in England had erased the words "in Christ" from his appointment.[40] He thus became the first

Jewish notary in North America, as none had been appointed in the Thirteen Colonies. Although the position of notary was not a high government office, notaries performed an important function among the merchants by officially recording contracts, wills, and land records.[41]

This appointment may be even more significant than it at first appears. A few Jews had been appointed as notaries in England in the previous twenty-five years, notwithstanding the wording of the act of 1701 which named notaries as among those required to take the state oaths, a requirement that was reaffirmed in the act of 1766. Even though the Jewish notaries had not taken the requisite Christian oath of office, the indemnity acts, passed annually in England after 1727, allowed these irregular appointments of some officials to be confirmed retroactively for the following year. In this way Jewish notaries were able to continue practising in England from year to year, although they did not know at any given time whether the indemnity act would be passed the following year to allow them to continue in office.[42] Levy's status as a notary was even more anomalous. Although appointed in England, he resided in Quebec. He was subject to the state oaths by virtue of the act of 1766, but could not obtain the benefit of the indemnity acts because they applied only in Britain.[43]

Levy's appointment may have had something to do with a bizarre act of official insensitivity almost three years earlier. Though the facts of the case seem to have little to do with Levy's religion, he achieved considerable public notice as the hapless victim in a textbook case of the abuse of power by colonial officials. In January 1764, General Ralph Burton, then lieutenant governor of Montreal, wrongly seized goods from Levy's store to a value in excess of £700. There was no question but that Levy was an innocent party and that the governor had made an error. On 24 August 1765, after a trial in the Supreme Court before Chief Justice William Gregory and a jury in Levy's joint action against Burton and the officers who had seized the goods under his authority, Levy was given judgment for £500 sterling and costs. Burton and his co-defendants then appealed to the lieutenant governor of Quebec and his council on 5 December 1766, the very month that Levy obtained his commission as a notary.

Altogether Levy spent eleven years in litigation. The defendants won on appeal to the governor and council in May 1767, whereupon Levy appealed to the Privy Council in London. Ultimately, after two trips to London and much additional expense, Levy's judgment for damages was confirmed by the Privy Council in 1771, but he was unable to collect. Burton and the other officers had left Canada in the interval, depositing a bond to cover the possibility that the case might go against them, but the bond had been lost. The chief justice had inexplicably returned it to the officers and they had destroyed it. Levy's expenses amounted to more than £2,500, none of which was recovered. To add bitterness to gall, he discovered that the officers had been reimbursed for their legal expenses because the case had arisen out of their actions in an official capacity.[44] Levy left Quebec for New York in 1772 and started over again. In that year he loaned £1,000 to the owner of 1,080 acres of land at West Point on the Hudson River. When that land was expropriated by the American army during the Revolution, Levy lost his security.[45]

There may have been other important appointments of Jews to public office in this period,[46] but none surpassed that given to John Franks in November 1768. His appointment had been preceded by a particularly disastrous fire that swept through Montreal on 13 May 1765, destroying 121 houses and causing damage estimated at £87,580 Sterling. Burning with "unrelenting fury" for two hours, the fire left many of the inhabitants in "the most deplorable State of Want & Misery" and left the merchants' warehouses open to looting.[47] Other smaller fires had occurred in Quebec and Trois-Rivières. As a result, in February 1768, the council at Quebec passed an "Ordinance for preventing Accidents by Fire," which required each resident to be provided with a five-gallon skin-covered bucket, a hatchet, fire poles, and ladders. It was the duty of the overseer or inspector of chimneys to visit each house, to ensure the presence of the necessary equipment, and to "observe whether or no any Hay or Straw is kept in the Garrets or Cellars or in any other part of any Dwelling House."[48]

On 18 April 1768 two merchants applied to be surveyor of chimneys for the town of Quebec: Franks and J. LaBat.[49] The council chose Franks, and he was granted his commission on 18 November. A week later Franks was back at the governor's residence. Additional appointments as overseer of chimneys for the towns of Montreal and Trois-Rivières made him the chief fire prevention official in the province. As he was being granted two additional commissions, he swore two additional oaths of office – one for Montreal and one for Trois-Rivières. Again he signed his name to the "State Oaths for Persons of the Jewish Persuasion." Again he read aloud that he was entitled to swear "upon the true faith of a Jew." Again George Allsopp certified that Franks had personally appeared before him and "being of the Jewish Religion, and Sworn on the Pentateuch or five Books of Moses, took and subscribed the Oaths of Office, Allegiance, Supremacy & Abjuration According to Act of Parliament."[50] It would be at least ten years before a commission would be granted to a Jew in what soon became the United States.[51] It would be forty years more before another Jew would be granted an office by commission in an English colony.[52] It would not be until 1828 that the laws of England would be amended to allow lower level government offices to be granted by commission to Jews in England itself.

During this period government officials included Jews whenever they considered the Protestant population of Quebec. In December 1773, Hector T. Cramahé, lieutenant governor of the province, wrote to the earl of Dartmouth in London and enclosed copies of petitions by Protestant inhabitants for an elected assembly. According to Cramahé, the petitions had originated in the town of Quebec out of a series of meetings of "the Principal Inhabitants of this Town, that are Protestants"; these were seconded by another petition signed "by some of their Fellow Subjects at Montreal."[53] The petitioners included three Jews. Samuel Jacobs signed the Quebec petition of 29 November 1773; Levy Solomons and Ezekiel Solomons signed the Montreal petition of the same date.[54] Though the lieutenant governor had not said that Jews would be treated as Protestants, he was comfortable including Jewish signers among the "Principal Inhabitants of this Town, that are Protestants." It seemed only logical to expect that Jews could participate in government, just like any other Protestant.

The Reverend Gershom Mendes Seixas, the renowned Jewish spiritual leader, was even more explicit in explaining a contemporary definition. "A Jew is a Protestant," he would write in 1783, and "Therefore is Entitled to Enjoy all offices."[55] Seixas believed that when a law referred simply to Protestants, it meant non-Catholics, including established Christian denominations, Dissenters, and Jews. However, when legislation referred to Christian Protestants it meant only Christians and not Jews. Seixas, who had been schooled in the English colonial system, was in a position to know. Born in the province of New York in 1745, he had become cantor and spiritual leader of the Shearith Israel Congregation in 1766 at the age of twenty-one.[56] By 1774, only two of the Thirteen Colonies allowed Jews broad civil rights, and even these colonies maintained restrictions. None allowed Catholics anything approaching equality. Quebec, however, seemed like the place to go for those searching for a new land where they could live in freedom.[57]

The passage of the Quebec Act in 1774 confirmed many of the decisions made in the aftermath of the Proclamation of 1763, such as religious freedom for Roman Catholics and maintenance of the seigneurial system of land tenure and French civil law. As well, the state oaths were amended such that Roman Catholics could hold office which made them eligible for appointment to the Legislative Council. Somehow in the dynamics of the relationships between the English-

and French-speaking, between Protestant and Catholic, between Anglicans and Dissenters, an acceptance of minorities, inconceivable in the Old World, had made its appearance. The need to disregard differences had become an imperative if the British colonization of Canada was to succeed. It mattered little that Jews had no written declaration of their rights; their rights were being established by precedent. The basis of their liberty in Quebec was subtle, perhaps, but its existence was real.

8 The Liberty Boys

> I have to acquaint you that the yankees have been drove out of this place. tho Stated themselves Liberty Boys: but their liberty turned to robbery.
>
> Chapman Abraham, 30 June 1776[1]

On 1 May 1775, as dawn broke over the Place d'Armes in Montreal, those first reaching the square noticed a shocking transformation. In the centre of the square stood a wooden kiosk sheltering a marvellous marble bust of the monarch, George III. In the dark of the night of 30 April, some person or persons had blackened the white marble face with paint and placed a bishop's mitre upon its head and a wooden cross and rosary of potatoes around its neck. At the base of the statue these words appeared: "Voici le Pape de Canada, ou le Sot Anglois" – "Behold the pope of Canada, or the English fool."[2]

There could be no doubt that the desecration of the statue was in some way linked to the fact that the Quebec Act, passed by the imperial parliament to set up a new constitution for the province, had come into force that very day.[3] It had been passed at the insistence of Guy Carleton, governor of the province, and had been signed by King George on 22 June 1774. The act was not only a bid for the support of French-speaking Canadians and their leaders, it was also an unprecedented act of political and economic justice. It granted civil and political rights to the Catholics of Quebec fifty-five years before the same rights were granted to Catholics in England. A provision in the act gave the Roman Catholic Church full rights of public worship – to carry out its traditional services and rituals – as well as the right to collect tithes from the faithful. Though the act established English criminal law, the use of French civil law and the prevailing seigneurial system of land tenure were affirmed. Section 12 of the act set up a "Council of Affairs for the Province of Quebec," with the power to "make Ordinances for the Peace, Welfare, and Good Government" of the province. The council was to have a minimum membership of seventeen and a maximum of twenty-three. French-Canadian Roman Catholics were eligible for appointment to this body, and under Carleton's instructions of 3 January 1775 it was provided that "every member of Our said Council, being a Canadian, and professing the Religion of the Church of Rome," could take the oath specified in section 7 of the act instead of the state oaths and the declaration under the Test Act. Finally, and not the least important, for persons "professing the Religion of the Church of Rome," section 7 of the act replaced the state oaths, which had made it impossible for a Catholic to accept governmental office, with a new oath from which all objectionable features had been removed.

The Quebec Act gave the French Canadians almost everything they wanted. They could still not be elected to a Quebec assembly but only because there was no such assembly. If the act had provided for an elected assembly, there was nothing in the law of the colony, the oath qualification having been amended, to prevent French-Canadian Catholics from sitting in it.

The Quebec Act did not deal with those professing the Jewish religion because it was understood that Jews were already entitled to full civil and political rights without the necessity of a special statute. The government of Quebec had already appointed Jews to high office and instituted the special form of oath for those professing the Jewish religion. Although no Jews were appointed to the new Legislative Council in 1775, their numbers scarcely warranted this, and there seemed no legal impediment in any event.

There was some grumbling amongst the Montreal and Quebec merchants who had been among those who petitioned for an assembly or representative form of government in 1773. This request had been bluntly denied by the provision of the Quebec Act that stated: "at present it is inexpedient to call an Assembly." In fact, however, the merchants made up such a small proportion of the population that they could not have held control of an elected assembly. The new, appointed, Legislative Council would serve their interests just as well without putting them in a minority position. Moreover, the Quebec Act offered an advantage for the merchants in that it extended the boundary of the province from the Ottawa as far west as the Mississippi, bringing the lucrative fur trade area known as the Indian lands under Quebec's jurisdiction.

The act provoked opposition in the Thirteen Colonies, however, for two reasons.[4] First of all, the extension of the western boundary to the Mississippi gave Quebec an area that had formerly belonged to New France, and the Americans thought they had some rights there because they had fought against France on the side of England during the Seven Years' War. American opposition was based on simple prejudice fostered by two centuries of mistrust: on a fear that the Catholic ideas of the unity of church and state made citizenship by those of other faiths virtually impossible in countries where Catholic populations were in the majority. In sum, the enemy of just fifteen years ago was being rewarded and the allies punished.

Over the summer of 1774 the American colonies agreed to coordinate their opposition to British policies, including the Quebec Act. On 5 September their representatives met in Philadelphia and founded the Continental Congress. On 26 October they decided to bid for the support of the colony of Quebec by drafting a letter to the people of Canada, which was subsequently distributed in both English and French. The letter urged them to seize the opportunity presented by Providence to win freedom and gain representative government by entering into a union with the thirteen other colonies. "Our confederation," it stated, "has no other object than the perfect security of the natural and civil rights of all the constituent members." But the American offer was coupled with a threat. "You are a small people compared to those who with open arms invite you into a fellowship," the letter continued. "A moment's reflection should convince you which should be most for your interest and happiness, to have all the rest of North America your unalterable friends, or your inveterate enemies."[5] The letter was widely circulated in printed form throughout the province, but it generated little support. Most inhabitants of Quebec already enjoyed "the natural and civil rights" promised – indeed, enjoyed rights not yet available in most of the colonies.

The interest of both English and French in Quebec in what was happening south of the border changed dramatically towards the end of April 1775 with the first reports of the skirmishes between British troops and colonials at Lexington and Concord. The declarations of the Continental Congress had turned to armed conflict. It was only a matter of time until the people of Quebec would be drawn in.

When the loyal citizens of Montreal gathered around the defaced statue of George III in the early morning of 1 May, all were furious; everyone suspected someone else of being the culprit. The military blamed the merchants. French-Canadian Catholics blamed the English Protestants for the insult to the pope. Others thought French Canadians were responsible for the insult to the king. Some were convinced it was the work of Yankee malcontents. One man, a certain Sieur Le Pailleur, said it must have been a Jewish scoundrel. Le Pailleur levelled his charge at Ezekiel Solomons, the Jewish fur trader. Blows resulted and Solomons knocked Le Pailleur to the ground. In

Governor Carleton's report of the incident, Solomons was "appre-
hended and obliged to give Bail."[6]

Prompt official action followed. Two sergeants were sent from the
garrison shortly after the damage was discovered. Long before noon
the statue had been cleaned, its trappings removed. By afternoon
Carleton had issued a proclamation stating that a number of wicked
and ill-intentioned persons had defaced the statue and had affixed a
defamatory and scandalous libel. As a result he was offering a reward
of $200 to anyone who would bring the culprits to justice. By the end
of the day, the merchants had raised a subscription and added 100
louis as a reward.

The next morning, 2 May, a crowd waited by the garden of the
Séminaire which faced onto the square.[7] Suddenly a drummer
appeared in the street, accompanied by a crier and number of officers
of the 26th Regiment. The officers, the crier announced when the
drum roll had achieved its desired effect, were adding 50 guineas to
the reward money. The crowd buzzed for a moment. A small group
of men in the midst of the crowd spoke quietly in French. One of
their number, a blond man of superior bearing and finely chiselled
features, apparently in his twenties, wondered aloud what could be
done to the perpetrator of the deed if he was discovered. A man of
about sixty, standing nearby, overheard the remark. "Il serait pendu,"
he barked. He would be hanged. The young man, David Salusbury
Franks, John Franks's son replied sharply: "On ne pend pas pour si
peu de choses en Angleterre," that is, "In England, people are not
hanged for such small offences." (There is some dispute upon this
point. Franks's own recollection, written in English, is that he actually
said "that I thought by the law it was not death.") Franks repeated the
words, whatever they were.

The older man, François-Marie Picoté de Belestre,[8] had maintained
a prosperous fur-trading business and had had a distinguished career
in the military under the French régime, ending his role in the Seven
Years' War as commandant at Detroit in 1759. He had quietly resigned
himself to supporting the British conquerors during the 1760s and
had been rewarded for his loyalty by being appointed a legislative
councillor on 1 May. Picoté de Belestre rose to his full height in
defence of his government. You speak like a fool and a "babillard," or
idle prattler, he told Franks. Franks stepped backward, saying, again
in French, that he was not used to such language. Picoté de Belestre
pressed forward, pushing Franks's arm. And what, he growled, did
Franks know about the statue? Franks tried to retain his composure.
Picoté de Belestre and Franks exchanged increasingly inflammatory
remarks. The older man grabbed Franks's nose and twisted it. Franks

grabbed Picoté de Belestre's coat just as his own hair was being pulled. Each pummelled the other until, after Franks had gained the advantage, bystanders pulled the two men apart.

The next day, 3 May, Picoté de Belestre went before the conservators of the peace of Montreal and swore out a complaint, not because of the blow he had received, for he was conscious of the fact that he had given Franks cause by striking first. His complaint was based solely on the words Franks had used in saying that in England men are not hanged for such small offences. The conservators found themselves caught in the frenzy of loyalty that had gripped the town and issued a warrant for Franks's arrest. They decided "that every good subject ought to look upon the said insult to His Majesty's Bust as an act of the most atrocious nature, and as deserving of the utmost abhorrence; and that therefore all declarations made in conversation that tend to affirm it to be a small offence, ought to be esteemed criminal."

On the afternoon of 4 May Franks was arrested and taken at bayonet point by a file of soldiers to the public prison of Montreal. He protested "that my heart was truly loyal and upright; and I was so far from approving what was done on the 30th of April to the King's Bust, that I detested the action and would freely contribute my share of the reward offered by the merchants to find the authors of it." All to no avail. Franks's offer of bail was refused. He languished in jail but only for five days. On 9 May he was released by order of the governor. Defacing the statue was undoubtedly an act of sedition by some unknown culprit, but it was not a capital crime. Franks's words may have been ill chosen in the emotional climate of the day, but they constituted no crime at all.

Years later, however, Franks would recall the incident in a different light: "in the Spring of 1775 I suffered a short tho rigorous imprisonment on Account of my attachment to the Cause of America."[9] And when the Americans, led by General Richard Montgomery, captured Montreal the following November, Franks "did everything in my Power to promote their Success." The Americans remained in occupation for seven months. In January 1776 Franks accepted an appointment from the Americans as "Paymaster to the Artificers of the Garrison of Montreal." When Benedict Arnold's army left Montreal on 15 June 1776 and retreated from Canada, Franks, again according to his own account, "joined it as a Volunteer & continued attached to that army with some little intermission until the reduction of General Burgoyne" at Saratoga on 17 October 1777.[10] Franks reached Albany by 20 June 1776, travelling only with his manservant. He satisfied the Albany Committee that he was "a friend to the American cause" and was permitted to go to New York on private business. He reached New

York by 29 June and obtained a further pass to proceed to Philadelphia where he had relatives.[11] It appears from available evidence that Franks was the only person who might be considered Jewish who left Canada to support the American revolutionary cause.[12] The rest remained loyal to the British.

The army that captured Montreal appeared invincible during the closing days of 1775. The American invasion was seen to be a gathering of strength for an attack on Quebec; if it were successful, the whole province would fall into American hands. The people of Montreal were captives, their movements restricted, their freedoms dependent on the good will of the military government that had "liberated" them. In these circumstances the people were forced to deal with their captors as if they were the lawful authority. Paper money issued by the Continental Congress became legal tender and, in the absence of British specie, circulated widely, even though there was no person or government prepared to take responsibility for its redemption.[13] Some, thinking that their future security lay in assisting their new governors, lent their assistance to the new regime without reserve.

Levy Solomons was one of these. Despite the losses he suffered during Pontiac's uprising in 1763,[14] by the time the Americans captured Montreal, he had regained a measure of his former prosperity. His first wife, Lizette Loubière, a Catholic, had died at the end of 1772 after only five years of marriage, leaving him with two small children, and on 31 May 1775, he married Rebecca Franks, the daughter of Abraham Franks and the granddaughter of Jacob Franks, the wealthy New York merchant whose family were Loyalists opposed to the Revolution.[15]

One of General Montgomery's first acts after the capture of Montreal on 13 November was to send for Levy Solomons.[16] He asked Solomons to be "purveyor to the American Hospitals in Canada." He offered him two guineas per day as well as a salary for his clerk. In return Solomons would be responsible for, and would be reimbursed for providing, at least three completely furnished hospitals for the Americans as well as "everything necessary for the patients." Solomons had little choice. He and his fellow citizens were virtual prisoners of war. There appeared little doubt that their city was already American territory. If Solomons had been wondering what he would be doing after the Revolution, his doubts seemed to have been put to rest. He threw in his lot with the occupiers. By the end of December Solomons had established three hospitals and done everything asked of him. He had spent "all the hard money he could procure" and his own credit was, in his own words, ruined. It was at this point that the fortunes of the American army, having reached their peak, took a turn for the worse. The Americans attacked Quebec on New Year's Eve and were disastrously defeated. Montgomery was killed and Arnold wounded. The American army remained outside the walls of Quebec for several more months, but only because no British or Canadian army appeared to chase it away. It also remained in control of Montreal, but it no longer appeared invincible.

To help extricate Solomons from his financial morass and to help him obtain more hard currency for the "preservation of the sick," the American general, David Wooster, promised to indemnify Solomons if he would sell at below cost a large quantity of rum that he was holding on consignment for Quebec merchants. This little venture put Solomons 7,000 livres farther into debt, and no one made good on the indemnity. There were more losses for Solomons in the spring. Arnold's army, when it circled the area at Lachine, "found it necessary to appropriate sundry Goods and Arms & Ammunition" as well as other "Indians Goods" that Solomons had stored there, intended for the up-country trade.

Now hopelessly in debt, Solomons assisted the Americans in their evacuation from Montreal. He scoured the countryside for carriages and conveyances and thus enabled the American army to rescue its sick and salvage its hospital stores. He had been paid "upwards of fourteen Hundred Dollars in Continental Paper Money," all of it worthless. He was now exposed "to Insults and Injuries from people of every denomination in the Province." On the 1 July 1776, two weeks after the Americans had quit the city, Solomons received an order from General Burgoyne of the British army to leave his house in four days. He was then evicted with his family; their belongings were dumped unceremoniously in the street since he was, in his words, "under the Frowns of Government, deserted by everyone."

Solomons's case was not unique. Though many in Montreal and the surrounding area occupied by the American army kept to themselves, others were forced to deal with their occupiers and curry their favour. For example, Aaron Hart of Trois-Rivières, which was also occupied by the Americans, wrote to the American colonel, James Livingston, while the latter was engaged in the siege of Quebec: "I am glad to find you arrived in good health before Quebec and Hope ere this Comes to hand you are in Safe Quarters within Side the walls."[17]

Samuel Jacobs, at St Denis on the Richelieu River, found himself on the route that the Americans were using on their way north to Montreal. Towards the end of September, as the Americans laid siege to the fort at St Jean to the south, the parish of St Denis had sent a request to Carleton, the commander of the British forces, to pardon their lack of enthusiasm for the government. Then, by 20 October,

Fort Chambly, even closer than Fort St Jean, fell; the area in which Jacobs lived was occupied by the invaders. He furnished the Americans with supplies, apparently cheerfully, as his neighbours toasted "Congress and Liberty."[18] Despite outward signs of compliance with the new regime, Jacobs secretly kept a journal of the American occupation. Jacobs watched his neighbours and intended to report them to the British authorities. To avoid possible discovery, he used Hebrew characters in a code that not even American Jews have been able to unscramble.[19]

A few months later, when the Continental Army was marching through St Denis on the way to try to capture Quebec from the British, Colonel Moses Hazen, the American commanding officer of the district of Montreal, wrote to Jacobs requesting his support. "As many inconveniences now arise to the Continental Service for the want of Cash," he wrote, "and as you have it greatly in your power to support the Credit of the united Colonies in this part of the country, It is therefore my Desire and Request, (not Doubting your inclination) & I beg you will use your utmost endeavours to forward the Service in every Instance and in Particular, your Interest in forwarding the troops which are now on their march to Quebec, as they pass this place, That you will endeavour to support the Credit of the united Colonies by Taking up Such authentick Certificates as may appear to be sufficiently vouched for the afores'd Service, which I engage shall be paid to you with Thanks." It was an invitation Jacobs could scarcely refuse as the unruly Continental soldiers were literally at his door. Probably as a joke, but more likely as a reminder that Hazen could not be responsible for the consequences if Jacobs did not comply with his request, Hazen added the following postscript: "You will also please to stimulate the officers of militia to the implicit obedience of all such orders as they may receive from their General Commanders." His words were garbled, but the meaning was clear. Hazen would not be able to control the troops if Jacobs didn't give them what they wanted.[20]

Those who lived in Quebec, unlike their fellow citizens in and around Montreal, remained free of American domination throughout the invasion. With one exception, all the Jewish families known to be residing in Quebec threw themselves into the defence of the town when the Americans attacked at the end of December 1775. Isaac Judah, Elias Solomon, and John Franks were recorded among those who joined in the defence. Franks, almost fifty, was fighting for the side his son, David Salusbury, would soon oppose.[21] Solomon, in his seventies, undoubtedly did not play an active role in the defence.[22] Judah, however, served in the British militia and was part of the force led by Colonel Henry Caldwell.[23] The main American force of about

700 men under Benedict Arnold was defeated on the night of 31 December–1 January at the barricade at Sault au Matelot in the Lower Town. Caldwell's company, including Judah, played a critical role in the "compleat" victory over the Americans.[24]

Hyam Myers was also at Quebec after the Americans captured Montreal. He had come to New York from Holland and was naturalized on 17 January 1759. Originally a butcher and supplier of kosher meat to the Jewish congregation in New York, he had diverted his attention to Canada by the time of the British conquest of New France, and his position as the representative in New York of Quebec Jewish merchants justified his move to Quebec with his family by the spring of 1763. His ties to New York remained strong, however, for there is evidence of frequent trips back and forth between the two cities.[25] By 1775 his oldest son, Moses Myers, who had been born in New York in 1752, had returned to that city to seek his livelihood. On 23 April 1775, the same week as the skirmishes at Lexington and Concord, Moses enlisted in the New York militia. Though there is no evidence that he saw active duty, Moses Myers was committed as a soldier to fight on the side of the rebels.[26]

In December 1775 it was clear to everyone that the American army would soon be marching on Quebec to capture the seat of government and force the province to surrender. Hyam Myers was asked to join the British militia in defence of the city. He refused, undoubtedly not being willing to bear arms against an army that might have included his son. Colonel Allan MacLean, the commandant of the city, ordered Myers's arrest. Myers's loyalties, however, remained with the British. A year later he was in England, partly on business and partly to obtain a spiritual leader for the Shearith Israel Congregation in Montreal.[27] On his return, his ship was captured in the Gulf of St Lawrence by the *Harlequin*, an American privateer from Salem, Massachusetts, and Myers was brought to Boston as a prisoner of war. He petitioned the government of the new state for his release, stating that his son was "an officer in the American army, and he himself was imprisoned by Col. McLean [*sic*] at Quebec at the breaking out of these troubles, because he refused to bear arms against the Americans."[28] His petition was accepted. Myers was released from jail but required to remain "on parole" for another six weeks. At first he was required to remain in Salem, but then was allowed to travel to Boston. Unknown to his captors, Myers made detailed notes of the comings and goings of the American troops, the large contingent of French forces that had arrived to reinforce them, and the reports of American victories or defeats in other areas. When, in September, he was finally allowed to return to Quebec by land, he turned over all his information to British intelligence.[29]

The activities of Chapman Abraham during this period were in a class by themselves. After his adventures during Pontiac's uprising,[30] he had continued his activities as a fur trader, using Detroit as his base, for some years. However he had sold his house and moved to Montreal some time before the outbreak of the American Revolution.[31] By that time, even though he was already over fifty years old, he was physically fit from his years on the frontier where his experiences had trained him for work as a scout. Thus, from the time the Americans invaded Quebec at the beginning of September 1775 until they left in June of the following year, Chapman Abraham moved about the province joining with the Canadian militia to defeat the Americans wherever he felt his skills were needed. He was at Longue Pointe at the end of September 1775 when the Americans under Ethan Allen made an unsuccessful attempt to enter Montreal Island from the east.[32] When he got the news at Trois-Rivières in mid-November that the Americans were again at Montreal, he borrowed passage money from Aaron Hart and rushed to Montreal to join the defenders who had, in fact, surrendered four days earlier.[33] He was at Quebec as part of an advance party at the end of December when the American army suffered its disastrous defeat. He joined the battle at Trois-Rivières on 8 June 1776 when the Americans experienced their last major defeat on Canadian soil; they retreated from Montreal a week later and returned south.[34] At the end of June 1776, when it was all over, Abraham was exultant in a letter to a friend in Detroit: "I have to acquaint you that the yankees have been drove out of this place,"[35] he wrote from Montreal.

In the end, no one except David Salusbury Franks left to join the Americans, not even Levy Solomons. The Jewish community in Quebec had experienced an unparalleled development of its civil rights under British rule. If there had ever been a glimmer of hope that the Canadian Jews of the 1770s would see American liberty as superior to the rights they enjoyed in Quebec, the abrasiveness of the occupying army snuffed it out. Chapman Abraham, the frontiersman, said it most eloquently. The Americans "stated themselves Liberty Boys," he said, "but their liberty turned to robbery and a great many People has suffered by them as allso their own friends they plundered before they went off."[36]

9 Cries of War and Peace: The Establishment of a Permanent Jewish Community in Canada, 1775–1790

> Any Israelite that will not Sign these our Laws and Regulations that are Inhabitants of this Town within Twenty Days and those out of the Town within Six Months shall forever be Exempted from having any Privilege, Honour or Employment in this Congregation and be Looked on as No Member thereof. Except only Chapman Abraham and Benjamin Lyon who are at too great a Distance, – but allowing them Twenty Days – after their arrival in this Town.
>
> Regulation 13, Shearith Israel Congregation, Montreal, 22 December 1778[1]

If the Jewish community in Montreal learned anything from the American invasion of Canada, it was that they were on their own as far as the rest of the North American Jews were concerned. They were in some ways closer to England than to the states to the south, even though England was geographically much more remote. Living in Quebec was good for the Jews; they probably had greater freedom in the province than they could have experienced anywhere else. Most perceived no advantage in leaving Quebec or in joining the new United States.

There were, however, scarcely more than a dozen Jewish families actually living in Montreal. Since the beginnings of a Jewish congregation in Montreal 1768 their religious life had revolved around a minyan or group that became a holy congregation when at least ten men were present for prayer.[2] The arrangement had its advantages since the minyan would meet only when needed. There was no rabbi, no hazan or cantor; in fact, there were no employees and no synagogue building – but then a building was hardly necessary for such a small number of people.[3] There were one or two individuals among the group who were qualified to provide religious leadership on a voluntary basis. And, although he was based at Quebec, Hyam Myers appears on occasion to have acted as the lay religious leader of the Montreal minyan. As well as his experience as a shochet in New York, we know that he performed circumcisions for members of the Montreal community.[4] Nevertheless, until the American Revolution started, the links with New York's Shearith Israel Congregation were strong, and there is ample evidence of Jews from Quebec attending services in New York, where many of them had relatives and where the renowned cantor, Gershom Mendes Seixas, provided full-time religious leadership. After the invasion, however, the Jews of Quebec were isolated. They could hardly travel into enemy territory to attend services. Worse, the New York synagogue had voted to dissolve itself just before the British captured the city on 27 August 1776.[5] There was now no synagogue accessible to the Jews of Quebec.

Within months of the departure of the American army, the Jews of Montreal decided to become a formal community. They had searched out the land. Now it was time to put down Jewish roots in a secure society. They decided to build a synagogue.[6] Led by David Franks[7] and Ezekiel Solomons, they raised subscriptions among themselves, and by 1778 a low stone structure with a high red roof had been constructed on a plot of land on St James Street that belonged to the estate of Lazarus David.[8] At the same time they raised another subscription to purchase a safer torah, or scroll of the law, from the Spanish and Portuguese Jews' Congregation in London. They were surprised a year later when the London synagogue gave them three – the two additional ones being presents.[9] On 13 February 1778 Hyam Myers, "acting for and on behalf of the Jews in this Province," contracted in London with Jacob Raphael Cohen[10] to come to Montreal as the congregation's first "Shochet, Hazan, Teacher and Reader."[11]

By all accounts the Montreal congregation was an unusual one. Unlike the synagogue in Newport which had relied on New York's Shearith Israel Congregation in its early days, the Montreal Jewish community had to rely on London, rather than on the North American synagogues, for its spiritual and material support. In the first instance, this was undoubtedly because of the continuation of the Revolutionary War, but in another sense it reflected the emerging pattern of Canadian reliance on British as well as American resources. The Montreal congregation thereby retained links with, and independence from, both. The synagogue was unusual too because of its attempts to define its membership in a way that reflected the realities of Canadian geography. The Montreal Hebrew congregation was not just a synagogue in Montreal; it was the synagogue of the entire province that stretched from the town of Quebec to the Straits of Michilimackinac. Its members included not only those resident in

Montreal, but Heineman Pines[12] and Barnet Lyons,[13] who lived near Trois-Rivières, as well as John Franks and Hyam Myers in Quebec, Chapman Abraham at Detroit, and Benjamin Lyon at Michilimackinac.

The congregation's tolerance of Christians in its members' families was another indication of its adaptation to the realities of frontier settlement. Of the twenty or so individuals whose names appear in the records of the congregation as members at the time the synagogue was built, more than a quarter had wives who were not Jewish.[14] Moreover some of the children of these marriages were baptized Christians. Yet these men were active members of the congregation and accommodations were made as situations arose.

The case of Ezekiel Solomons illustrates the point. Solomons had married Louise Dubois at the Anglican church in Montreal in July 1769 and their children were baptized.[15] Having put the losses incurred with his fur trade consortium behind him, Solomons re-established his own formidable fur trading enterprise during the 1770s. With a summer base at Fort Michilimackinac, by 1771 he was sending canoes into the Nipigon country north of Lake Superior challenging the Hudson's Bay Company control of the area drained by the Albany River flowing into James Bay.[16] By the late 1770s, Hudson's Bay Company officials regarded Solomons as the dominant trading figure in the region which makes up most of present-day northwestern Ontario. In 1780, one official who was sent to explore the Nipigon country reported that "the trade here in the little north as they call it is Entirely carried on by an Illiterate Jew, one Ezekiel Solomon a kind of pedling merchant at mountreal ... he has got an old serjent in partnership with [him] on[e] Shaw, who winters this year at the Red or Oker Lake" Another company report a year later referred to Solomons as "master of all the Trading Houses in this part of the Country."[17]

Throughout this period Ezekiel Solomons continued to spend his winters in Montreal. Notwithstanding the baptisms of his children, he was elected as the gabay, or treasurer, of the Montreal congregation in 1777 during the construction of the synagogue. Then in 1778 Solomons, the "Illiterate Jew" of the Hudson's Bay Company records, was selected as hatan torah, to be honoured by reading the last portion of the Torah at the end of the High Holiday season in October.[18] When one of Solomons's sons died in 1778, the congregation was called to a special meeting to decide whether the child could be buried in the congregation's cemetery "according to the rules and customs of Jews, the said child not being circumcised." The congregation reluctantly agreed, at a meeting on 30 November, that Solomons's son could be buried in the cemetery, notwithstanding the circumstances, but also unanimously decided that the burial should not be a precedent.[19] A month later Solomons was elected as one of the three members of the congregation's junto or board.[20]

Another unusual aspect of Montreal's congregation was suggested by its name. The congregation was known as "Shearith Israel" although there is nothing in its surviving minute book of the period or in contemporary references to indicate that that name was ever formally adopted by the congregation.[21] As if to confuse the issue, the Montreal congregation was known by the same name as the nearest Jewish congregation – Shearith Israel of New York. "Shearith Israel" means literally "the remnant of Israel." To the congregants it was a term of optimism, "the remnant that is Israel," the people of Israel who are strong enough to preserve their faith in spite of the forces that cause their numbers to remain small over the years. Another interpretation of the name suggests an outpost of Judaism surviving in an unfamiliar environment.

The use of the name Shearith Israel by the congregation in Montreal would not, however, have confused contemporaries. The New York congregation had voted to disband itself in August 1776 and its "patriot" spiritual leader, Gershom Mendes Seixas, and many of his followers had left the city, most going to Philadelphia. According to a descendant of the family, "under the direction of Rev. Mr. Seixas the building had been stripped of everything that could be carried away. The essentials to constitute a synagogue were missing." New York remained in British hands, but had few Jews (mostly refugees from other centres controlled by the Continental forces), and its synagogue remained inactive until 1782 except for the occasional gathering of Loyalist Jewish refugees.[22]

In these circumstances, and according to available evidence, Montreal's congregation formed the only "loyal" Jewish congregation in British North America during the Revolutionary War, a fact which may explain why the war years were that congregation's halcyon period. It may also explain the level of support the Montreal congregation obtained from the Sephardic congregation in London and suggests the possibility that the Montreal congregation may have been known as Shearith Israel because it was commonly understood to be the New York congregation in exile. The evidence that the Loyalist David Franks, who had links with New York's Shearith Israel, may have been involved with the formation of Montreal's Shearith Israel, strengthens this possibility.

The Loyalist affiliations of many of the Montreal congregation may also explain the expulsion of Levy Solomons from the office of parnas or president in 1779. When the Americans occupied Montreal in

1775–6, Solomons had thrown in his lot with his captors to a degree not matched by others in the town and had been, in his words, "exposed to Insults and Injuries from people of every denomination in the Province ... under the Frowns of Government, deserted by everyone." Two years later, in September 1778, restored to the esteem of his peers and as the largest contributors in the purchase of a torah from England, Solomons was elected parnas. Yet, only a few months later, Solomons was once again rejected by his peers. In some way which has not been recorded, Solomons "made use of expressions to the manifest injury of this congregation." Led by John Franks and other members with known British sympathies, the congregation passed a resolution condemning Solomons and replacing him as parnas. Solomons later acknowledged that "notwithstanding the persecution [he] has suffered he always uniformly adhered to the American side."[23]

Shearith Israel functioned as a synagogue in Montreal only during the Revolutionary War. After the British surrendered in October 1781 and once a peace treaty was signed by Britain and the new United States of America in June 1783, relations were re-established with friends and families to the south. As a result, the members seem to have relaxed their enormous effort and to have reverted to a minyan.

The collapse of the Montreal congregation appears to have been accelerated by the changes occurring in the wider world. Levy Solomons, who was again elected parnas in the autumn of 1781, refused to pay Jacob Raphael Cohen his salary. Cohen sued Solomons and, with the support of Simon Levy and some of the members of the Judah family as witnesses, won his case in the Court of Common Pleas in September 1782.[24] Cohen and his wife, Rebecca Luria, left a badly divided community intending to return to England, but the British ship diverted to New York. Stranded in New York, Cohen gladly gave his services as hazan to the Loyalist remnant of the local congregation there.[25] After Cohen's departure, the Montreal congregation lost its sense of cohesiveness. The Jews of Montreal did not obtain the services of another paid employee until 1839 or 1840 when David Piza was brought from England. The minutes of the congregation, which had probably been recorded by Cohen, were no longer kept. Services became sporadic: between 1805 and 1825 there appear to have been few services at all. By 1825 the synagogue building no longer existed as such.[26]

With the victory of the new American republic and the return of peace it has been suggested that the Jews remaining in British North America after the Revolution "envied the new liberty of the Republic to the south."[27] Quite the contrary. It appears that the Jews who stayed in British North America as well as the Jewish Loyalists from the United States who joined them had chosen to remain under British rule. They believed they had a better opportunity for equal treatment as citizens in British North America than in the new republic, even though this equality was sometimes harder for a person to discern because it was to be found by examining British precedents and not simply from reading declarations. John Franks, who had led the Montreal Jewish congregation in impeaching Solomons in the interests of the "future welfare of our religion in this Province," was one who would have been able to make this distinction. He had been given conclusive evidence of the equal treatment offered to his people under British rule when the standard oath of office was formally amended by the governor to make it acceptable to Jews and thus allow him to accept an office.[28]

Jews to the south of the line, contrary to present-day perceptions, were not completely equal to other citizens in the newly independent United States. Whatever interpretation the Plantation Act may have been given relating to the rights of Jews, its protection was no longer available in the United States. The self-evident truth proclaimed by the Declaration of Independence that "all men are created equal" did not lead in practice to equality for all races and creeds in the new republic. Most of the new constitutions that the independent states had adopted by 1781, as well as the federal constitution adopted in 1787, left doubts as to the legal equality of Jews as well as others.

For Gershom Mendes Seixas, the acknowledged intellectual leader of the Jews in the new American republic, the moment of truth came in Philadelphia in January 1783. Seixas had left New York when the British took the city in August 1776. After four years in Stratford, Connecticut, he had moved to Philadelphia in 1780 to assume the position of religious leader of Congregation Mikveh Israel, which had been revitalized by the exodus of "patriots" from New York.[29]

On 13 January 1783, Seixas performed an exercise common to Jews throughout the world who sought the best places to go in search of equal rights. On that day he perused a book setting out the new constitutions of the several states and learned that the sum total of the new laws fell far short of the equality promised by the Declaration of Independence. Although he did not refer to the significance of the loss of the British Plantation Act, the new American state constitutions fell far short of its protections as well. Seixas's marginal notes on the pages of *The Constitutions of the Several Independent States of America* provide a revealing statement on the degree of rights afforded Jews in the new republic by a Jew who was a "patriot." He found that New Hampshire, Rhode Island, Connecticut, New York, and Virginia had ended all restrictions on Jews being elected to positions of "Honor, Trust or proffit [*sic*]."[30] Delaware, Maryland, Massachusetts, North Carolina, and Pennsylvania, however, effectively prohibited Jews from holding elected office because of the declaration required.[31] Perhaps to relieve his disappointment, Seixas decided that Georgia, New Jersey, and South Carolina, which restricted office to Protestants, did not intend that restriction to apply to Jews because article 38 of the South Carolina constitution referred specifically to "Christian Protestants" and the other restrictive articles referred only to "Protestant Inhabitants," presumably a general reference to non-Catholics.[32] On this line of reasoning, Seixas put forth a view that was apparently never tested in any court. "A Jew is a Protestant," he wrote, and "Therefore is Entitled to Enjoy all offices."[33] The constitution of New York (1777) was the only one to include a provision that granted Jews full equal rights: the first time in North America that rights of that nature were embodied in a statute.

The constitution of the United States, adopted in 1787, contained a declaration in article 6 that no religious test should ever be required as a qualification to any office or public trust in the United States. The first amendment to the constitution, adopted in 1789, provided that "Congress shall make no law respecting an establishment of religion, or prohibiting the free exercise thereof" – ensuring a separation of church and state in the federal government.

But these constitutional provisions applied only to the federal sphere. The federal government had no power to alter test oaths or to remove disabilities in the individual states, each of which had the power to make its own laws relating to civil and political rights. In the ten years following the end of the Revolution, some of the states did move dramatically to give equal treatment to Jews and other minorities. By 1785 Virginia had gone beyond the removal of restrictions and took the more positive step of enacting a declaratory act for religious liberty. Drafted by Thomas Jefferson and guided through the legislature by James Madison, the act established the principle of equality of all religions and the separation of church and state.[34] By 1790 Pennsylvania and South Carolina joined New York and Virginia in removing disabilities for Jews. But nine of the thirteen states still maintained restrictions. In 1792 Delaware passed an act declaring that those religious tests that affected Jews be removed, reducing that number to eight.

In the United States a citizen could obtain a reasonable idea of what his rights were through an examination of the constitution and other federal laws as well as the constitutions and statutes of the individual states. In Quebec, however, the laws relating to civil and political equality were much more subtle than in the United States. The law of contract was determined by the civil code, other matters were determined by ordinances passed by the governor and his council, and still others were determined by regulations proclaimed by the governor pursuant to his instructions. These last "laws" frequently had the effect of importing British law into the colony. The British "constitution" as it pertained to civil and political rights was not simply composed of statutes passed by Parliament, or of orders and regulations set down by the crown, but comprised as well the common law based on precedent established by court cases, published by reporters, and known by the legal network and by those motivated to know their rights. The provisions of the Plantation Act that could protect the rights of Jews were fully available in British North America.

In 1784, just after the war had ended, more than 500 of the English-speaking citizens of Quebec once more petitioned for "a Free, Elective House of Assembly." They asked as "affectionate Subjects of this Province, in the full enjoyment, of their rights as British Subjects." At least a dozen Jews signed the petition in the same character as their Christian neighbours.[35] They asked for no more than their non-Jewish neighbours because they already had equal rights.

In the United States, the Declaration of Independence had said that all men had the inalienable right to "life, liberty and the pursuit of happiness," but in the years immediately after the Revolution, there was no mass exodus of Jews heading south to the United States looking for freedom. Jews in British North America were optimistic about the continuing development of their equality at home. In fact, an examination of the only known cases of Canadian Jews moving to the United States after the war seems to suggest economic, religious, and family reasons as the motivating factor rather than the search for equal rights.

Abraham Judah offers a good example. He came to Montreal in 1780 after serving as liaison between the Montreal congregation and the London congregation.[36] He may have been in Quebec at an earlier time and returned to Britain during the war, but in any event, on his arrival in 1780 he joined his children, Uriah, Samuel, Dorothea, Isaac, Elizabeth, and Henry, who had all been in the colony for some time. Dorothea had married Aaron Hart of Trois-Rivières in London in 1768. Elizabeth was to marry Chapman Abraham in Montreal in 1781. Another daughter, Miriam, had married Emanuel Manuel, but had died at Quebec just before her father's arrival in Montreal.[37] In 1780 Judah was made a full member of the Hebrew congregation and was accorded the rights of a founding member.[38]

Abraham Judah moved to New York with is wife, Zelda, in the summer of 1784, but his departure was most likely connected with his desire to live near an active synagogue in his old age. Jacob Raphael Cohen had left the Montreal congregation two years previously and Gershom Mendes Seixas was once again to conduct High Holiday services at New York's Shearith Israel that September. The war being over, families could once again move across the border without restriction. In October 1784, Samuel Judah wrote to Aaron Hart: "You wrote me for a large candle – my father took them all with him – which was given to the shool [sic] at New York to burn Yom Kippur." Unfortunately, Abraham Judah had already died before the High Holidays.[39]

Samuel Judah, one of Abraham's sons, also moved to the United States, but his reasons for leaving related to his business. He had come to Montreal from England before the American Revolution; he probably came first to the colony to join his sister, Dorothea Hart. If we can believe the records, he was born in 1725 and arrived in Quebec at middle age although he had the vitality of a much younger man. He was regarded as "a very liberal man to almost every handsome woman."[40] When he was fifty years old, he went back to London to marry Elizabeth Ezekiel in March 1775. He returned to Montreal with his bride before its capture by the Americans the following October.[41]

Judah was undoubtedly a man of exceptional acumen.[42] During the American occupation he, along with many, probably most, of the merchants in Montreal, had business dealings with the occupiers, undoubtedly thinking Quebec might eventually become one with the Thirteen Colonies. As a result, the merchants were left at the end of the war holding worthless sums of Continental currency that could not be redeemed for specie. Others such as Aaron Hart[43] and Levy Solomons[44] would still be holding the worthless notes years later. Not Samuel Judah. On 9 June 1776, the day after the disastrous defeat of the Americans at Trois-Rivières and six days before the Americans evacuated Montreal, Judah wrote to David Franks, a trusted business acquaintance in Philadelphia. With the letter he enclosed $11,000 in Continental notes, amassed over the previous months. Rather than lose the entire sum, he sent the currency to Franks to discount before the British successes in the war made his Continental currency worthless: "I should be glad to have this paper money changed as soon as possible," he wrote.[45]

There was no doubt that the war disrupted his business: he suffered a number of losses, particularly near the end of the war when the Americans seized ships carrying his goods. Instead of consolidating his losses he began buying more and more on credit, taking the risk that if his goods avoided seizure, he would obtain large returns. By

June 1784 Judah had lost his gamble and was declared insolvent. He spent part of the next two years in the courts offering to repay his creditors a fraction of their loans. On 21 March 1786 he applied in New York for naturalization as a citizen of the United States of America which he received in April 1787.[46] He died in New York in 1789.[47]

Almost all of Abraham and Zelda Judah's other children chose Quebec as their home. Samuel's brothers, Isaac and Uriah, had arrived in Montreal shortly after he did and had joined him in business. They stayed when Samuel left. Uriah died in Montreal in 1824. Isaac moved to the United States after 1800 and died in New York about 1810. Henry, the youngest of the Judah brothers, died in Trois-Rivières about 1838. His son, Henry Hague Judah, would become a member of the legislature of the province of Canada in 1843. Dorothea Hart died in Montreal in 1827. Elizabeth Abraham was widowed in 1783; in 1787 she married Moses Myers, a son of Hyam Myers, and moved to Norfolk, Virginia. However she returned to die in Montreal at the home of Dorothea in 1823.[48]

Hyam Myers was another Jew who departed after the war, but his reasons also seem to have had little to do with a search for equality or liberty. Myers had supported the British during the war, but after the death of a child in 1786, the family went to join his eldest son, Moses, who had lived in New York since before the war and had supported the American cause.

When the peace treaty was signed in 1783, Hyam Myers was still in Quebec with his wife, Rachel, and two of their four children, Jacob and Bilah. He had an old debt for which Samuel Jacobs of St Denis, a merchant he had represented in the 1760s, had been dragging him through the courts for almost fifteen years. At the beginning of 1784, Jacobs finally obtained some settlement on account of the debt.[49] Then, during that summer the problems of the Myers were exacerbated by the death of Jacob, their youngest son.[50] Meanwhile, their eldest son, Moses, had had a devastating experience at the hands of the British just before the war ended. He and his partner, Samuel Myers of Amsterdam, had been among those Jews with a thriving branch of their mercantile business on the Dutch island of St Eustatius in the West Indies. During the war, it had built a reputation as a port where goods from Europe could be trans-shipped to the United States and avoid the British blockade. However, on 3 February 1781 when the British navy had occupied the island, Moses Myers was among the Jews singled out for harsh treatment – he was ordered to leave the island and his property was confiscated. By 1782 he was back in the United States and the firm of Samuel and Moses Myers was bankrupt.[51]

At the end of August 1784 Moses Myers journeyed to Quebec to try to persuade his parents to move to the United States. He found "times & people are very dull in this place. It does not look the same as it formerly did." He had not seen his parents for a long time: "Tho' am scarce able to undergo the afflicting pain of meeting my Dr. Parents my spirits are entirely Gone With all my fortitude & I almost determine not to see my Mother. I trust for support through a most afflicting scene. It will be impossible to remove My Mother by Land & the Greatest Sin to leave them in this country if to be avoided. Should I find It Practicable to Charter a Vessell I should manage by a clearance for Halifax to ship some furrs. In which case I can get money here. When below [the line] shall determine agreeable to circumstances & my Father's wish."[52] At first Hyam Myers decided to remain at Quebec, but by 1786 he and his wife had moved to New York.[53]

Abraham Hart left Montreal after the war and established himself in New York.[54] In 1784, he had joined other loyal citizens of the province of Quebec in petitioning for an assembly. His reasons for leaving are not known. The family of his brother, Aaron, remained to become prominent citizens of Trois-Rivières and Montreal.

Ezekiel Solomons also moved away. He left Montreal with his family in 1781 and moved west to Mackinac Island, an action that perhaps gave rise to the suggestion that he thus became Michigan's first Jewish settler. The records show, however, that Solomons was not motivated by a desire to move to the United States. Mackinac Island was then British territory, the site of the fort that had moved from Michilmackinac on the mainland the previous year. Solomons's move was prompted by his bankruptcy in 1781,[55] by the collapse of the Montreal Jewish congregation, and perhaps because the competition of the Montreal-based traders organized as the North West Company obliged him to move west to be closer to his source of furs.

While most Canadian Jews seemed satisfied with the development of their rights at home and did not move south, many Americans, known as Loyalists because of their continuing attachment to the British crown, left their homes in the United States looking for opportunities of a different sort. Some went to Britain, some to British colonies in the West Indies, and some moved northward to points all across British North America. Although many of the Jewish Loyalists who moved north came for social or economic reasons, others left states such as Massachusetts which had never granted them equality, and still others left states like Rhode Island that had withdrawn an earlier level of equal treatment. In this sense, the departure of these Jewish Loyalists followed the same pattern as the Jews who left South

Carolina after 1712 and Georgia after 1733. Some of these Jewish Loyalists stood out enough to be recorded.

Samuel Hart, a member of an illustrious Jewish family of Loyalists from Newport, Rhode Island, but not related to the Harts of Trois-Rivières, arrived in Halifax with his wife and infant daughter in November 1783. While he came without resources, he prospered in business, was elected to the Nova Scotia Assembly in 1793, and died in the colony in 1810.[56]

Isaac da Costa arrived in Boston from London in November 1777 but was imprisoned upon his refusal to take the oath of loyalty to the patriot government. He is remembered, however, more as an engaging ne'er-do-well than a prominent Loyalist.[57] Having originally settled in Boston by 1762, he had lived in Nova Scotia and worked as a master mason during the 1760s. He came to possess enormous tracts of land at Annapolis in Nova Scotia by 1765, but after work on the fortress at Annapolis Royal was suspended, he returned to Europe to press claims on family estates. When the American Revolution broke out his properties in Boston and Nova Scotia were producing no income, although apparently more from lack of management than as a result of the war. His petition for aid as a Loyalist indicated that he had a daughter in Nova Scotia.

Rachel Myers and her sons, Benjamin and Abraham, all obtained crown grants of land as Loyalists at Gagetown, Queen's County, New Brunswick, in the 1780s. She was the widow of Benjamin Myers, a Hungarian immigrant who had settled in Newport, Rhode Island, and was a professing Jew. She fled with her nine children along with the retreating British troops in 1779 and joined other Loyalist refugees in New York until its evacuation. She arrived at Gagetown, New Brunswick, with the first fleet in May 1783.[58] Her selection of New Brunswick may have been due in part to the fact that her daughter, Judith, had married Alexander Montgomery Jr, in New York and had gone to Gagetown with his family. As Benjamin Myers had served as a soldier in the 43rd Regiment, Rachel may have anticipated being eligible for grants of crown lands. Although the society of the day rarely considered women in questions of entitlement or in the exercise of civil or political rights, widows were entitled to exercise property rights.[59] The Myers, as professing Jews, undoubtedly found themselves isolated from their co-religionists. After a stay of four years, Rachel Myers and most of her family returned to the United States, leaving her daughter Judith, now with her own family, in New Brunswick.[60]

David Goebels, born in Holland in 1733, was "a German Hebrew" according to family tradition. In 1783, his name changed to Davy Gabel, he arrived in Saint John, New Brunswick, as a Loyalist from New York and obtained a crown patent to land in Saint John in 1783.[61]

He died in Saint John in 1816 and was buried in the Loyalist Burial Grounds.

Barrak Hays, a merchant and vendue master or auctioneer from New York, came to Montreal as a Loyalist in 1783, accompanied by two young children and a new wife.[62] He was the elder son of Solomon and Gitlah Hays and the brother of Andrew who had come to Montreal some ten years before. Like his father before him, Barrak Hays had sued the officials of New York's Shearith Israel Congregation for assault and battery in forcibly ejecting him from the synagogue in 1769.[63] He and his family remained in Montreal for about ten years after 1783.[64]

Lyon Jonas had come to New York from London by the summer of 1765 and had set up shop as a furrier in Broad Street by 1773.[65] He was joined by his wife, Sarah Jacobs, and his two sons.[66] Loyal to the British, he was recorded in June 1777 as a "supplier of necessaries and provisions to the British troops."[67] It was Jonas who became the unofficial parnas of the residual congregation and was responsible for opening the old synagogue building for Loyalist refugees on the few occasions when services were held between 1776 and 1782.[68] The Jonas family left with the other Loyalists when the British evacuated New York, and by the autumn of 1783 he had set up shop in St Paul's Street in Montreal.[69] Nonetheless he retained a connection with the New York congregation until August 1786 when he appears to have severed the relationship after he was disciplined and fined by the congregation for having "for a Considerable time past trespass'd on our holy Sabath."[70] Notwithstanding his naturalization in New York as an American citizen in March 1788,[71] he continued to live in Montreal and was active in the community. In 1794 he joined with other inhabitants of Montreal in signing a memorial for a land grant on which to build "a Court House Public offices and a Gaol," and in February 1798 he was among those subscribing for a new Hebrew burial ground.[72] However in the winter of 1799–1800 a serious fire in Montreal destroyed his shop. Though now aged seventy, he attempted to reestablish himself, and he applied for a land grant "as a suffering Loyalist" but his request was refused in 1802.[73] By 1809 he was back in New York and was relying on the charity of the Shearith Israel Congregation for support.[74]

Sergeant Samuel Moss of the King's Royal Rangers of New York obtained letters patent for the west half of lot 24, concession 2, Cornwall Township, in the province of Upper Canada on 22 May 1797.[75] Moss was apparently born to a Jewish family named Moses and came to the area around Cornwall as a Loyalist after the Revolution. Two hundred years later the Moss family, completely assimilated almost from the beginning, still lives in the area.[76]

Moses Jacobs, born in Falmouth, England, about 1746, emigrated to Massachusetts about 1773. When the Revolutionary War broke out, he was displaced[77] and finally arrived in Kingston, Upper Canada, in 1793. To support his wife and four children he obtained a job working for a distiller named Wickens. Beginning in 1797 he applied for land more than once but was unsuccessful until he obtained a lot in the township of Sophiasburgh in 1816. He died on 28 August 1823, felled by a tree he was chopping down in a field near Colborne.[78]

In summary, few Jews left Quebec to move to the new nation to the south. Many more came north from the Thirteen Colonies as Loyalists, viewing the provinces of British North America as their best chance for continued equality.

In 1791 the British government passed the Constitutional Act,[79] which divided the Old Province of Quebec into Upper and Lower Canada and changed the system of government by providing for elected assemblies in both provinces. There was no written restriction or disability for Jews set out in the act, as indeed there had been none by actual precedent. Section 24 provided that anyone could vote on the taking of a secular oath. Section 29 provided a secular form of oath for any member of the Legislative Council or the Assembly. Section 33 provided that the laws in force in the Old Province of Quebec were to remain in force. Presumably such laws included the decision of the governor in 1768 to establish state oaths for Jews. It remained to be seen whether practice would conform to appearances.

In a mood of hope, Gershom Mendes Seixas had noted in his search for equality in the constitutions of the new American states that "a Jew is a Protestant." In Quebec, precedents for equal treatment had been established in law. There was no need for a declaration of rights to include all religions as the Jews in Quebec appeared already to have the same rights as Protestants.

By 1790, although a lasting synagogue was yet to be established, a new generation of Jews born in the New World was reaching maturity in Quebec. They had not known the official discrimination that had afflicted their parents in the Old World before their naturalization under the Plantation Act. From 1760, through the time the state oaths for persons of the Jewish persuasion were officially introduced in 1768, and through the time of the American Revolution and its aftermath, they had been treated no differently from their fellow Canadians by the government of the time. Even if something were to stand in the way of their rights – civil or political – they had found a home in British North America. They were ready to test, and build on, their country's freedoms.

ENTR'ACTE

10 Exemptions from Oaths and Declarations: The Balancing Act for Colonial Equality 1750–1790

> The Test Act [is] the corner stone of the constitution which should have every preservation.
>
> Lord North, MP, 28 March 1787[1]

In many ways, Henry Beaufoy seemed the ideal champion of the rights of Dissenters in Britain. Born a Quaker, the son of a vinegar brewer, he had attended "nonconformist schools" in his youth. As an adult, he had joined the Church of England and become known as a great speech maker, a person with great potential for higher office. He had never lost touch with the Dissenters, however, and they were responsible for his election in 1784 as the representative of the voters of Yarmouth to the House of Commons at Westminster. At thirty-seven years of age, though still a backbencher, his abilities were manifest.[2] On 28 March 1787 he offered the Commons a chance to relax the restrictions that had prevented adherents of moderate religious minorities in Great Britain from assuming public office. His motion seemed innocuous enough. He moved that Parliament repeal the Corporation Act of 1661 and the Test Act of 1673 "so far as they concern Protestant Dissenters."[3] The motion was a response to a petition unanimously endorsed by the three main groups of Dissenters – the Presbyterians, the Independents, and the Baptists.[4]

Both the Corporation and the Test Acts required persons accepting an appointment or election to office to take the sacrament of the Lord's Supper according to the usage of the Church of England. This had effectively precluded Protestant Dissenters as well as Catholics and non-Christians from holding office, whether civil or military. Beaufoy made it very clear that his motion affected only Dissenters. "Catholics will continue as compleatly rejected as before" because other legislative provisions such as the oath of abjuration and the declaration on

For a schematic representation of this chapter, see p. 132.

transubstantiation would continue to provide the kingdom with security against "strange and preposterous appointments" to office. Nor would there be any opportunity for "persons who are not even Christians" to be admitted to situations of civil and military trust. The oath of abjuration, he reassured his audience, "operates as a bar to all but Christians," and there would thus be no possibility of the Jew, the "Mussulman," or "the worshipper of fire" being able to assume office. "I should not think," he said, "that the followers of Moses, of Mahomet, or of Zoroaster, would be the objects of the Sovereign's choice."[5]

Beaufoy's motion seemed to reflect the liberal trends developing in other parts of Europe. Prussia and Russia had recently renounced religious tests for office as had Ireland seven years earlier. France was considering following suit. Scotland and Holland had never had a religious qualification for civil office. Scotland's practice was actually a source of some embarrassment to the English because adherents of the Church of Scotland were excluded from office in England because of the Test and Corporation Acts notwithstanding the union of the two countries eighty years earlier, whereas adherents of the Church of England faced no such restrictions in Scotland. The limited repeal of the Test and Corporation Acts would give "complete toleration" – presumably something approaching equality – to Dissenters rather than just the toleration of liberty of conscience allowed under the Toleration Act.

Lord North, a former prime minister but rarely seen in Parliament for the past year because of poor health, appeared in his seat to lead the opposition to the repeal. At 55 years of age, North was by no means the oldest member of the Commons, but he had sat in the house since his election in 1754. North believed the suggested repeal was "dangerous in the extreme." His speech summarized a century of English policy: he started with the proposition that the "Test Act was the corner stone of the constitution which should have every preservation." His next premise was that the government has a right "to confirm the admission to public offices to men of particular principles." His conclusion was that if government offices were open to all, the English constitution would be at risk. "If Dissenters claim it as their undoubted, their natural right, to be rendered capable of enjoying offices, and that plea be admitted," he concluded, "the argument may run to all men."[6] In other words, admitting the right of Dissenters to appointment to office – and thus suggesting that the government had no right to impose restrictions – could mean that none could be excluded. Even Beaufoy's worshippers of fire might hold office.

At the end of the day, "the House growing extremely impatient for the question," Beaufoy's motion was put and defeated 178 to 100. The

Test and Corporation Acts, which denied non-Anglicans the right to hold office, would continue as "the corner stone of the constitution" in England for almost half a century more.

DISABILITIES IN BRITISH AMERICA

Beginning about 1750, just as Britain was starting to organize the settlement of its colonies in what would later be called Canada, a significant shift in its colonial policy began. Earlier the desire to stimulate the growth of colonies as a means of encouraging imperial trade had led to a policy of allowing the colonies to develop along their own lines. In 1740 the need for an imperial policy to stimulate immigration of skilled traders such as the Jews to the American colonies had led to the Plantation Act which superseded previous colonial laws with respect to aliens and allowed them to be naturalized. After 1750, however, Britain sought to exercise increasing control over the settlers of diverse cultures who were arriving in its American colonies. If the need for control was evident by 1750, when only one or two of the colonies had Anglican majorities, the need for a more defined policy became an urgent necessity once Britain's victory over New France was confirmed in 1763. By that time Britain held more than twenty colonies in the Americas,[7] including Quebec with its seventy thousand French Canadians whose Catholic religion was not tolerated in England.

As expected, Britain's policy for increasing control after 1750 relied on the very measures for controlling religious dissenters that had worked with such success in England: a set of rules affecting non-Anglicans, focussing on the "disabilities." The rules included the application of the Test Act to the colonies through instructions to the colonial governors, the application of the state oaths to the colonies by legislation, and the "establishment" of the Church of England in all new colonies, with toleration of religious dissent where it was deemed appropriate. What was not anticipated was that the variations in Britain's policy of disabilities required to meet the particular circumstances in Quebec left that colony in the unique position of being free of the Test Act. In Britain itself, as well as in almost all of its American colonies, Roman Catholics, Jews, and even Presbyterians and other Protestant Dissenters from the Church of England, could not hold office because the Test Act of 1673 remained "the corner stone of the constitution," as Lord North was to put it. Yet for almost thirty years, from 1763 to 1791, Catholics and Anglicans as well as members of other religious minorities in Quebec were legally equal, even though the Church of England was legally "established."

Table 4
Disabilities in Britain and British North America, 1750–90

DISABILITIES IN BRITAIN

1. Prescription of the sacrament and declaration against transubstantiation under the Test Act remain in force
   - keeps Protestant Dissenters from positions of authority and trust because of unwillingness to take the Anglican sacrament of the Lord's Supper
   - keeps Roman Catholics from exercising rights
   - keeps Jews from exercising rights
2. State oaths remain in force
   - keeps Jews from municipal and other offices
   - keeps Jews from being seated in the House of Commons

DISABILITIES IN BRITISH NORTH AMERICA

1. Prescription of the sacrament and declaration against transubstantiation under the Test Act applied through instructions to governors
   - keeps Roman Catholics, Jews, and Protestant Dissenters from offices or places of trust
   - *exception* Old Province of Quebec (1760ff) where such instructions were not issued and no one was thereby disabled from offices or places of trust except for appointments of non-Catholics to governor's council
2. State oaths applied as a condition of holding offices or places of trust throughout the empire by virtue of an imperial act of 1766
   - keeps Roman Catholics and some Protestant Dissenters from office or places of trust
   - keeps Jews from office or places of trust because the oath of abjuration includes the phrase "upon the true Faith of a Christian"
   - *exception* Old Province of Quebec: Roman Catholics not required to take state oaths and Jews (from 1768) allowed to amend oath of abjuration, allowing both to hold civil and military offices and places of trust
3. Establishment of Church of England/Toleration of dissent
   - Church of England established in all colonies of British North America
   - royal instructions to governors allowed toleration
     (*a*) to all in Nova Scotia and the Old Province of Quebec
     (*b*) to all but Papists in Newfoundland, New Brunswick, and Prince Edward Island

---

*Application of the Test Act
through Instructions to Colonial Governors*

By 1749 it had been determined that all new colonies established by Britain in the Americas were to be royal colonies. Even the first thirteen colonies, all of which had been founded on a proprietary basis, had been mostly converted to royal control. This enabled the Colonial Office in Britain to implement policy in the colonies through the commissions and instructions to the governors. The commissions appointing the governors were usually published in the colonies, but the instructions were given as secret orders to each governor and not made known, even to the governor's appointed council. As the governors exercised virtual arbitrary authority over their colonies and could ignore colonial legislatures, these commissions and instructions were in fact the basic constitutional documents in each colony. The instructions were not colonial statutes but had the same effect, either through orders or proclamations by the governor or by virtue of the governor's power to refuse assent to any law passed by the colonial legislature which was not in accordance with his instructions.

It was in a governor's instructions that the requirements were set out which would transfer the disabilities for non-Anglicans in Britain to its colonies. These requirements would likely have been unintelligible to any ordinary colonist who might have seen the instructions. References in a governor's instructions to "an Act for preventing Dangers which may happen from Popish Recusants" or to the statute of 25 Charles II, c. 2, or to the Test Act 1673, or to "subscribing the Test," or to "taking the Declaration" all meant the same thing – that "only Anglicans need apply" for offices. All this may have been complicated for those in the colonies who were made aware of the rules, and indeed the wording was not meant to be simple. British colonial officials had developed a code for excluding all but Anglicans from positions of influence in the colonies. This code would not be readily apparent to colonists seeking to know the true extent of their rights. Indeed, the nuances of this method of control through oaths and declarations have been largely ignored by historians although its impact on minority rights was significant.

The instructions dated 29 April 1749 which were given to Edward Cornwallis as governor of Nova Scotia made it clear that only those who were prepared to subscribe to the declaration against transubstantiation and to receive the sacrament of the Lord's Supper according to the rites of the Church of England would be eligible for any office in the province. His instructions required him on arrival in the colony to call his appointed council together and join them in taking the state oaths as well as making the declaration against transubstantiation specified in the Test Act of 1673. He was then to administer the state oaths and the declaration to all "persons that hold any office or place of trust or profit in our said province." "Without the doing of all of which," the instructions continued, "you are not to admit any persons whatsoever into any public office nor suffer those that have been formerly admitted to continue therein."[8] The other Maritime colonies also followed the British practice closely. Similar instructions to the governor of Newfoundland were issued in 1762, to the governor of

New Brunswick after its establishment as a province in 1786, and to the governor of St John's Island (Prince Edward Island) after its establishment as a separate colony in 1769.

However, the rules for the Old Province of Quebec were unique.[9] Faced with a British colony whose population was almost entirely Catholic, the Colonial Office made an exception and did not include the usual provision in the instructions to James Murray in 1763.[10] While Governor Murray was directed to call a council and administer the state oaths and declaration against transubstantiation to them, there was no requirement for subscribing the declaration or taking the state oaths as a condition of assuming other offices. Membership in the governor's council therefore was to be restricted to Anglicans, though not other offices. An amendment to the governors' instructions in 1775, after the Quebec Act had been passed, allowed them to appoint French-Canadian Roman Catholics to the council without requiring them to make the declaration against transubstantiation. But for all other offices, the Old Province of Quebec was unique in that it did not have the Test Act restrictions during the entire period from the conquest of Quebec in 1760 until the reconstitution of the colonial government by the Constitutional Act of 1791, thus allowing anyone to hold office.[11]

It was the lack of these restrictions that gave Dissenters in Quebec an equality they could not find in England. It was the lack of these restrictions that had enabled Aaron Hart to be appointed postmaster of Trois-Rivières in August 1763 and allowed Governor Burton to issue a proclamation confirming that a post office had been opened "in this town of Trois-Rivières in the house of Mr. Hart, merchant."[12] Although the postmaster was a senior position of trust in a British colony, Hart was not required to subscribe the declaration under the Test Act. Nor was there any requirement under the law of Quebec or in the governor's instructions that he swear the state oaths. No such appointment could have been made in England under the existing rules.

Application of the State Oaths by Legislation

In 1766, a new imperial act, the Act for Altering the Oath of Abjuration and the Assurance, required, for the first time, that the colonies follow the English practice with regard to oaths. The act, which came into force on 1 August of that year, stipulated that the form of oath ending with the words "upon the true Faith of a Christian" was to be the oath of abjuration "taken ... in his Majesty's Dominions, and no other."[13] The new oaths were soon adopted without qualification in most American colonies, even in those where the oath of abjuration had not previously been a requirement.[14] Thus it came to be that in the colonies, as well as in Great Britain, the oaths effectively barred Catholics, Jews, and Quakers from rights that they appeared to be entitled to exercise on the basis of substantive law alone.[15]

A strict application of this law meant Jews could no longer be appointed to any office or exercise any privilege of citizenship that required the swearing of the oath of abjuration. In Georgia, for example, which complied with the new act, the persons of Jewish origin who were appointed to high office between 1766 and 1773 all had to subscribe to the new Christian form of the oath of abjuration.[16] While the possibility exists that none of these individuals was a professing Jew, it is also possible that the individuals indicated were of the Jewish faith, but merely swore with a mental reservation – a figurative crossing of their fingers – in order to assume offices to which other citizens would have been entitled. This method had been employed by Jewish Marranos in Spain or Portugal in order to continue to avoid penalties by appearing to be Christian.

The state oaths were also used as a condition to restrict the franchise in Nova Scotia from 1757[17] and in Prince Edward Island from 1773.[18] In New Brunswick, Roman Catholics were allowed to vote at the first elections in 1785 but the election of an Acadian in Westmoreland by Roman Catholic voters led to his unseating by the English and Protestant Assembly and eventually to an act, assented to in 1795, that imposed the state oaths on all voters.[19] Although these restrictions were clearly directed at Roman Catholics, once again they had the effect of also excluding professing Jews from the exercise of these rights.

In the matter of the state oaths, Quebec once again provided the one exception to the imperial mandate for their use. At the time of the conquest the French Catholic inhabitants of Canada would undoubtedly have found the oaths offensive, not so much because the oath of allegiance was to the king of England but because the oath of supremacy was based on the idea that the king of England was superior the pope. Without any change in the statutes from 1763, and despite the act of 1766, the governor and council of Quebec simply adopted the custom of disregarding the state oaths for Catholics. "It may be stated to be a fact," reported a special committee of the Assembly of Lower Canada years later, "that from the time of the Cession of the country in 1763, down to this time, Justices of the Peace, being of the Roman Catholic Religion, have not been required to take this Oath [of abjuration]; and so far as the obligation of taking this oath is concerned, they stand upon the same footing as their Protestant brethren."[20]

Then, in 1774, the Quebec Act officially removed these disabilities by providing that "that no Person, professing the Religion of the Church of Rome, and residing in the said Province, shall be obliged to take the Oath required by the said Statute passed in the First Year of the Reign of Queen Elizabeth [oath of supremacy], or any other Oaths substituted by any other Act in the Place thereof" and by allowing Catholics to swear a short form of oath of allegiance in substitution for the state oaths and declaration against transubstantiation.[21] By this act, French-Canadian Roman Catholics were legally equal, subject to the fact that the Church of England was the official established church and that the act did not allow Roman Catholics to extend their hierarchical organization. Moreover, French-Canadian Catholics, unlike other Catholics, Protestant Dissenters, and Jews, could now be appointed to the new legislative council,[22] and if there had been an assembly in the Old Province of Quebec, nothing in the laws that applied to the province would have prevented Catholics from being elected as representatives. It was in fact the certainty that the French-Canadian Roman Catholics would have constituted a majority in any such assembly that caused petitions from the English in Quebec for an assembly to be rejected. French-Canadian Roman Catholics had virtual equality to do what was allowed in the colony, but not everything was allowed. That was the complexity of the British system of administration.

From the time of the Quebec Act, the position of Roman Catholics in Quebec was probably better than in any other English-speaking country. In 1776, the year of the Declaration of Independence, all of the Thirteen Colonies still maintained restrictions against Roman Catholics which excluded them from office. Even after the first amendment to the United States constitution guaranteeing religious equality came into effect in December 1791, some of the individual states maintained restrictions which prevented Catholics from holding office.

The act of 1766 amending the oath of abjuration had also posed an obstacle to the appointment of Jews in British America. However, in November 1768 the governor and council of the province of Quebec, flying in the face of the act of 1766, adopted an amended form of "State Oaths for Persons of the Jewish Persuasion" with a revised form of oath of abjuration which was acceptable to Jews in order to enable them to hold high office along with the Protestant establishment. This decision had been made possible, first of all, by the fact that Governor Carleton's instructions, unlike those given to all the other colonial governors, did not require him to apply the Test Act to appointments of officials in Quebec. His instructions, or rather a lack thereof, allowed him to overcome the second obstacle as well. Unlike the instructions to the governors of the other British colonies in America, Carleton's instructions were silent on the issue of whether he was to require provincial officials to swear the state oaths.[23] There was nothing in his instructions that prevented him from officially recognizing the equality of Jews as provincial officials, notwithstanding the 1766 act. Carleton may also have taken account of the fact that Roman Catholics had not been required to swear the oath of abjuration even in cases where the law required it. If Catholics were not required to swear the oath of abjuration, why should the Jews be? Finally, Carleton may have taken account of the importance of the Jews to the colony at this time when they formed 10 per cent of the "English" population. It was a time to encourage non-Catholic settlers, and Carleton was no doubt aware of the provision of the Plantation Act which allowed naturalized Jews to alter the oath of abjuration. Certainly Quebec's new oath for Jews took its wording from that act.

Nevertheless, the long-term effect of the act of 1766 was not entirely clear for Jews in Quebec, and this difficulty was not resolved by legislation as it was for Catholics in the Quebec Act. A liberal interpretation of the Plantation Act of 1740, specifically section 3, would give the right of Jews to alter the oath of abjuration not only to Jews who had actually been naturalized under the act but also to the children of naturalized Jews and to all natural-born Jews in the colonies. The question was whether persons naturalized by the act could have full rights in the colonies to a status not permitted to naturalized persons in England – namely, the right to "be of the Privy Council or a Member of either House of Parliament, or capable of taking, having or enjoying any Office or Place of Trust."[24] In the words of a committee of Lower Canada's Assembly that would adopt the liberal interpretation of the act in 1834: "It is not to be believed that the Parliament intended under any circumstances, to give to the naturalized foreigners, under this statute, rights which were denied to natural born subjects of the King."[25] If naturalized Jews had these rights, then Jews born in the colonies must surely have them as well.

The ambiguity surrounding this question was dealt with over a period of years but was not clearly resolved even in 1773 when the British Parliament passed a declaratory act to remove doubts as to the status of Jews in the colonies.[26] This act provided that persons naturalized in the British colonies in America under the Plantation Act of 1740, which phrase included Jews, "shall be deemed to be capable of taking and holding any Office or Place of Trust, either Civil or Military, and of taking and holding any Grant of Lands, Tenements, and Hereditaments, from the Crown to himself or themselves, or to any other or others in Trust to himself or themselves." The act made it clear that naturalized persons could hold high office, as described in the Plantation Act, as well as take grants of land from the crown, a right that was not so described in that act.

The Old Province of Quebec, unlike Britain's other colonies in America, did not apply the restrictions of the Test Act or the state oaths against the Roman Catholics, Jews, Presbyterians, and other religious dissenters within its boundaries save for appointment to the governor's council. In this sense, Quebec was unique. And, in consequence, it was ahead of its time in offering almost equal civil and political rights to subjects who were not members of the established church.

An Established Church and Toleration of Religious Dissent

Beginning with Nova Scotia in 1749, the Church of England was established in all the new colonies settled under British rule in North America. Cornwallis's instructions required him to ensure that the Church of England "be Established both in principles and practice" in Nova Scotia and to "take especial Care that God Almighty be devoutly and duly served throughout Your Government; the Book of Common Prayer as by Law Established be read each Sunday and Holiday; and the Blessed Sacrament administered according to the Rites of the Church of England."[27] Following the governor's instructions, the Church of England was established by law in Nova Scotia in 1758.[28] Identical instructions to establish the Church of England were given to the governors of Quebec, Newfoundland, Prince Edward Island, and New Brunswick, and in all these colonies the establishment of the church was supported by colonial legislation.[29]

At the same time as he was instructed to protect the Church of England as the established church, Cornwallis was directed "to permit liberty of conscience to all persons." This latter instruction was unique as contemporary instructions to governors in all the other colonies under royal control excluded "Papists" or Roman Catholics from that right.[30] Six years later, despite this leniency the government was unable to obtain the allegiance of the Acadian Catholics during the continuing war with France and the colonial administration eventually took the drastic step of expelling the Acadians from the colony.[31] Notwithstanding this use of the ultimate "disability" of banishment, the instructions of the governor of Nova Scotia continued to allow liberty of conscience to Roman Catholics in the colony.[32] Yet, at the same time, the instructions to the governor of Prince Edward Island when it was organized as a colony in 1769 allowed liberty of conscience "to all except Papists."[33] In Newfoundland, Roman Catholics were allowed public worship by 1784 when the first Catholic chapel was built in St John's.[34] Although Roman Catholics outnumbered Protestants in the District of St John's by more than two to one in the early years of the nineteenth century,[35] the removal of civil disabilities for Roman Catholics in that colony developed slowly.[36]

The law adopted subsequently for the treatment of religious minorities in the Old Province of Quebec was very different from that relating to the treatment of religious minorities in Nova Scotia, perhaps because of the lessons learned from the expulsion of the Acadians. In 1763 George III had agreed to "grant the liberty of the Catholick religion to the inhabitants of Canada." Section 4 of the Treaty of Paris had specified "that his new Roman Catholick subjects may profess the worship of their religion according to the rites of the Romish church, as far as the laws of Great Britain permit." Section 5 of the Quebec Act of 1774 carried forward the same liberty by providing that "for the more perfect Security and Ease of the Minds of the Inhabitants of the said Province, it is hereby declared, That His Majesty's Subjects professing the Religion of the Church of *Rome*, of and in the said Province of *Quebec*, may have, hold, and enjoy, the free Exercise of the Religion of the Church of *Rome*, subject to the King's Supremacy."[37]

Religious liberty for Protestant Dissenters and Jews in Quebec was not referred to in the Quebec Act or in the governor's instructions, but there is no doubt that in practice it was provided to an unparalleled degree. The Dissenters built churches. The Jews of Montreal founded a congregation in 1768 and had built a synagogue ten years later. Then, in 1787, religious liberty appeared in some additional instructions to the governor of Quebec in a manner that had no precedent in England. The instructions to Carleton (now Lord Dorchester) that year required him "to permit Liberty of Conscience and the free Exercise of All such modes of religious worship as are not prohibited by Law, to all Persons who inhabit and frequent the Province ... provided they be content with a quiet and peaceable Enjoyment of the same, without giving Offence or Scandal to Government." The wording was similar to a phrase in the first amendment to the American constitution, adopted two years later, providing that Congress shall make no law preventing the free exercise of religion.[38]

The unprecedented level of equality for Roman Catholics in the Old Province of Quebec had been clearly set out in the Quebec Act. The equality of Protestant Dissenters and Jews was not set out in any statute. In Britain, only Anglicans could hold office. In Quebec, alone among Britain's American colonies, offices could be held by Anglicans and

Roman Catholics. Presbyterians, Quakers, and other Dissenters and "the followers of Moses, of Mahomet, or of Zoroaster" could hold office as well, though not because of any statute or law. The plea had been admitted, to paraphrase Lord North, that Dissenters in Quebec were capable of enjoying offices, and the argument, it seems, had run to all men.

Capable of enjoying offices, but perhaps not *entitled* to enjoy offices? The problem was that almost none of the documentation on the rights of Dissenters in Quebec was published: not the governor's instructions from England, or the decisions of the governor and his appointed council. These decisions had stemmed from royal prerogative: they were documented, if at all, in manuscript form, and were kept secret, as if they were privileges, not rights, and could be removed at the royal whim. The decision to appoint Aaron Hart as postmaster of Trois-Rivières; the governor's decision to appoint John Franks to public office by commission; the governor's decision to establish "State Oaths for Persons of the Jewish Persuasion" as a substitute for the oaths prescribed by the act of 1766 which permitted no alternatives – none of these decisions was published. They were allowed in practice as long as no one objected. Few knew the rules and few understood the significance of the exceptions in the new colony.

But if there is to be equality under "a system of law based on the eternal foundations of justice," as the petition of the French Jews of 1790 stated, it must be known to all. For people of different cultures and creeds to be encouraged to make the commitment to share in the responsibility of building a new land, they have to know the rights that they and their children can expect. They have to know whether their hard-won achievements can be taken from them as easily as a privilege is withdrawn. The experience of other colonies in North America had shown that Jews did not remain after their privileges of equality were removed.

Before 1790, the body of court decisions that could have established legal precedents for equal rights binding on future administrations was similarly not published.[39] None of the judges was trained in the law. They were more noted as the political confidants and advisers of the governor, by whom they were appointed and supported, as well as for supporting the governor's interests in the council. A petition of Quebec residents, dated 30 September 1783 and presented to the authorities in Britain the following spring, was as much a symbol of a weakness in the system as a portent for future conflicts owing to the lack of documentation of the rules. "With the utmost fervency," the petition prayed, "Your Petitioners implore that Your Majesty will be Graciously pleased to appoint to the Court, and place on the Seats of Justice, Men of jurisprudent Learning."[40]

Without equality, without the knowledge of the laws giving rise to equality, a society based on the eternal foundations of justice could not develop. The issue was by no means restricted to Quebec. Jews in the colonies of British North America would continue to be confronted by events which caused difficulties because the rules were not known in advance. One by one, Jews in the colonies of Nova Scotia, Upper Canada, and Lower Canada would face situations of an epic nature that were as much a test of the legal system as of the motivation and good will of the people involved.

The stage had been set.

Grave of Moses David, Windsor, Ontario, 1814. (R.M. Fuller, *Windsor Heritage*, 1971, courtesy of The Herald Press and Dr Jack Fuller)

The removal of Moses David's remains to Shaar Hashomayim Cemetery, Windsor, 1978. (Photo by Cec Southward, *Windsor Star*, 6 October 1978, courtesy of the *Windsor Star*)

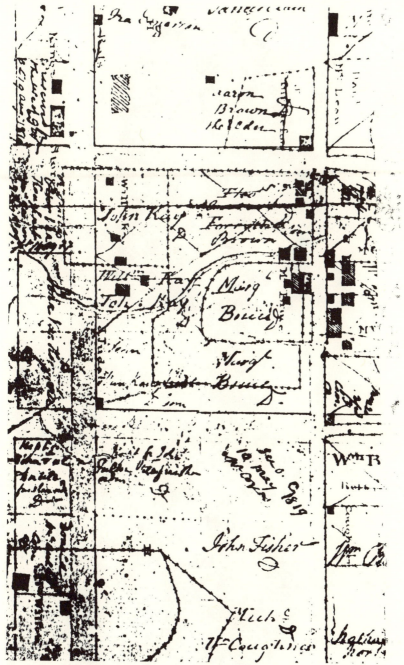

Plan of Town of Cornwall, by W. Chewett, showing Isaac Judah's cabin, 1790.
(Survey Records Office, Ministry of Natural Resources, Province of Ontario)

Jacob Franks. (A.D. Hart, *The Jew in Canada*, 1926)

John Lawe. (American Jewish Archives, Cincinnati, OH, by permission)

Ezekiel Hart, c. 1810. (A.D. Hart, *The Jew in Canada*, 1926)

Moses Hart, c. 1795. (Musée du Château de Ramezay, Montreal, by permission)

Benjamin Hart, c. 1820. (A.D. Hart, *The Jew in Canada*, 1926)

David David, c. 1810. (A.D. Hart, *The Jew in Canada*, 1926)

David David's Beaver Club Medal. (Private Collection, by permission)

Frances David Michaels, c. 1815. (*History of the Corporation of Spanish and Portuguese Jews, "Shearith Israel" of Montreal, Canada, Published on the Celebration of Its 150th Anniversary, 5679, 1918*)

Samuel David, c. 1815. (A.D. Hart, *The Jew in Canada*, 1926)

William Abrams (Abrahams) of Miramichi, New Brunswick, c. 1840. (Picture Collection, New Brunswick Museum, Saint John)

Michael Samuel of Chatham, New Brunswick, c. 1840. (Private Collection, by permission)

Joseph Samuel of Chatham, New Brunswick, c. 1855. (Picture Collection, New Brunswick Museum, Saint John)

Selim Franklin of Victoria, c. 1865. (Visual Records Unit, British Columbia Archives and Records Service, Victoria)

Lumley Franklin of Victoria, c. 1865. (Visual Records Unit, British Columbia Archives and Records Service, Victoria)

Selim Franklin's auction house at the foot of Yates Street, Victoria, c. 1861. (R.C. Mayne, *Four Years in British Columbia and Vancouver Island*, 1863)

George Benjamin of Belleville, Canada West, c. 1846. (Portrait by W. Sawyer; Private Collection, by permission)

William Hyman, c. 1870, Mayor, Township of Rosier, Gaspé, 1858–82 (A.D. Hart, *The Jew in Canada*, 1926)

Moses Judah Hayes, Chief Commissioner, Montreal police, 1845. (A.D. Hart, *The Jew in Canada*, 1926)

William Benjamin, Montreal alderman, c. 1848. (A.D. Hart, *The Jew in Canada*, 1926)

ACT TWO

British North America
1791–1860

11 The Retrenchment: Two Steps Forward, One Step Back

> You shall administer or cause to be administered the Oaths appointed by the aforesaid recited Acts to the Members and Officers of the Councils and Assemblies respectively of the Province of Nova Scotia ... and you shall also cause them to make and subscribe the aforesaid declaration mentioned in the aforesaid Act of the twenty fifth year of the Reign of King Charles the Second.
>
> Instructions to Lord Dorchester, 23 August 1786[1]

Sunday morning, 17 March 1793, immediately after the second lesson, St Paul's Anglican Church, Halifax.[2]

The rector, the Reverend Mr Robert Stanser, descends from the pulpit and waits in the chancel beside the gilded font. At the far end of the nave, a man in his early forties begins to walk down the centre aisle, his advance marked by the fine deep tones of a mahogany organ that appears at second glance to be a trifle too grand for its surroundings.[3] An expectant hush falls over the congregation. In both galleries running the length of the church, all eyes are upon him. He walks past pews occupied by well-dressed parishioners, heavily bundled against the cold because the church lacks a stove; he walks past the pews of the bishop of Nova Scotia, the Very Reverend Charles Inglis,[4] of members of the governor's council, of officials of the colony. He walks past the pew of the lieutenant governor, John Wentworth, ornamented with its canopy and the royal arms and furnished like "a miniature drawing room." To either side of the chancel where Mr Stanser waits, silhouetted by the great south window, are the square pews of the officers of the army and navy.[5] The man reaches the steps of the chancel and stands as the rector begins to speak.

St Paul's is indeed the church of the Nova Scotia establishment. Its designs have been copied from elegant churches in London, the plans conveniently provided to the governor by the Board of Trade and

Plantations. When the building was finished in 1755 its appearance was described as "very handsome." It is of brick foundation, the outside of wood, aisled and plastered within. Forty-eight mural tablets adorn its walls, eight hatchments are attached to its pilasters. In the twenty vaults beneath its aisles, several of the colony's notables (including its last governor, John Parr) have already been buried. St Paul's was built entirely at government expense, and over the years it has been repaired, enlarged, and refurbished by government funds, supplemented by a special annual levy on all inhabitants of the parish, even those who attend other churches.[6]

The priest asks: "Has the person here presented been baptized, or no?"

"I have not," says the man.

The priest pours fresh water into the font and speaks at some length, talking to the man in front of him as well as to the congregation. All remain standing.

The priest turns to the man and asks: "Dost thou renounce the devil and all his works, the vain pomp and glory of the world, with all covetous desires of the same, and the carnal desires of the flesh, so that thou will not follow nor be led by them?"

The man answers: "I renounce them all."

The priest asks: "Wilt thou be baptized in this faith?"

The man answers: "That is my desire."[7]

These answers are the responses required by a service known as "The Ministration of Baptism to Such as are of Riper Years, and Able to Answer for Themselves," set out in the Book of Common Prayer of the Church of England.[8] They had just been given by Samuel Hart, and the motivation for his decision was more complex than a simple change of faith. A Jew until that morning, Hart had been elected to the Nova Scotia Assembly just two weeks before, representing the town of Liverpool.[9] Immediately after his election, he had been surprised to learn that he could join the assembly and take his seat at the scheduled opening on 20 March only if he was a Christian.

Mr Stanser finishes the ceremony. Hart takes his seat with his family. A murmur, scarcely audible, runs through the crowd. There is general satisfaction at Hart's baptism: not only does it fulfil the mission of the church, but it gives visible support to government policy, manifesting the unity of those in authority in the colony through a common acceptance of English moral law and the Anglican faith.[10]

The priest again faces the congregation. The formal service ends. The priest calls by name on those present who have been elected to the assembly for the first time to join him in the chancel. Once again, Hart rises from his seat and walks to the front of the church, joining others. The priest turns to Hart and hands him a sheet of paper, signalling him to make his declaration. Hart intones: "I, Samuel Hart do declare, That I do believe that there is not any transubstantiation in the Sacrament of the Lord's Supper or in the elements of Bread and Wine at or after the consecration thereof by any person whatsoever."

Hart then proceeds to the desk near the pulpit and signs his name at the bottom of the sheet of paper, subscribing the declaration. Each new member of the assembly takes his turn making and subscribing the declaration. Each has thereby fulfilled the requirements of the Test Act "for preventing Dangers which may happen from Popish Recusants" passed in 1673. They had all made and subscribed the declaration against transubstantiation; they were soon to receive, in accordance with the regulations, "the Sacrament of the Lord's Supper according to the Usage of the Church of England ... in some publick Church, ... after Divine Service."

In a dramatic way, Hart's conversion was a demonstration of the rule that in the colony of Nova Scotia only Anglicans could serve as members of the assembly, or as appointed officials of any kind for that matter.

Samuel Hart, the youngest of three children, had been born in Newport, Rhode Island, in 1749, the year of the founding of Halifax. Prior to his birth, his father, Jacob Hart (the son of Moses Hart), and his mother, Esther (the daughter of Moses Raphael Levy), both professing Jews, had lived in Stamford, Connecticut, raising their children alone in a place far from any of their co-religionists. The move to Newport had brought the Hart family into a small but vibrant Jewish community that included Samuel's uncles, Naphtali, Samuel, Abraham, and Isaac, and their children.[11] Samuel's uncles were prominent members of this community. Naphtali was elected parnas or president of Newport's B'Nai Jeshrun Congregation in 1759; Isaac was one of the three trustees who acquired the land for the building of the synagogue in June 1759. Both were honoured, along with Jacob Rodrigues Rivera and Moses Levy, the other trustees, at the ceremony of the laying of the cornerstone of the synagogue in 1762.[12]

Samuel Hart remained closely linked with his extended family. He was trained as merchant by his Uncle Samuel[13] and was associated with his older brother, Moses, in a partnership when the American Revolution broke out in 1775. At this point, Samuel Hart's world fell apart. The whole Hart family, all loyal to the crown, fled Newport after its evacuation by the British army in 1777 and took refuge on Long Island. Meanwhile Hart had apparently brought himself to the attention of the revolutionary authorities to such a degree that in 1780 the newly organized legislature of Rhode Island noted, in one of its first acts, that he "had left this State and joined the enemies thereof" and banished him from the state along with seven others.[14]

Then tragedy struck his Uncle Isaac, with the rest of the family likely helpless witnesses. Just after dawn on 23 November 1780, a party of about fifty rebels, who had come across from Connecticut, arrived at Smith's Point at St George's Manor on Long Island and surprised a group of Rhode Island Loyalists in the process of "establishing a post, in order to get a present subsistence for themselves and their distressed families." By the time the rebels returned to Connecticut later that day with about forty prisoners, they had devastated the settlement, leaving five wounded and two dead. One of the dead was Isaac Hart. According to *Rivington's Gazette*, "Mr. Isaac Hart, of Newport in Rhode Island, formerly an eminent merchant, and ever a loyal subject, was inhumanly fired upon and bayoneted, wounded in fifteen different parts of his body, and beat with their muskets in the most shocking manner in the very act of imploring quarter, and died of his wounds a few hours after, universally regretted by every true lover of his King and country." Samuel Hart and the rest of the family were likely among the "body of respectable loyal Refugees belonging to Rhode Island" who were ambushed while building their settlement on Long Island. Later, Samuel's father was to talk of his brother who "was murdered at Long Island with great cruelty by the Rebels for his Attachment to Great Britain."[15]

The Hart family, once so closely knit, was now dispersed. Naphtali Hart Jr was already in St Eustatius. The family of Isaac Hart and his wife, Hannah (who had died in 1779), went to the British West Indies. Abraham Hart, who had earlier returned to England, was to die there. Naphtali Hart eventually returned to Newport.[16]

Samuel Hart and his immediate family first took refuge in New York. They were destitute and he and his father and brother were granted small subsistence allowances by Sir Guy Carleton, who was in New York as commander-in-chief in North America for some six months in 1782–3. It was here that Hart's sister Miriam met and married Lieutenant Montague Blackwell of London. It was here, amongst many other Loyalist refugees, that he himself met and married Rebecca Byrne, the daughter of William and Sara Byrne of Philadelphia.[17] According to the British officials in New York, his marriage disentitled him to his government allowance as "he had procured a livelihood by marriage, and was struck off."[18] When the British yielded New York to the victorious rebels in 1783, Samuel fled to England with his wife and infant daughter, Esther, in company with his parents and his brother Moses.[19] His parents – his father still a pensioner – were to die in London the following year.[20] However, Samuel and Rebecca

Hart had returned to North America with their child in November 1783 and were in Halifax by 1785.[21] In December 1786 Hart purchased a store at the corner of George and Hollis Streets.[22] But Hart's troubles were by no means over. Notwithstanding his marriage, he was still heavily in debt, and over the next five or six years he suffered significant business losses and was jailed for debt on more than one occasion.[23]

Halifax had changed significantly in the forty years since Samuel Hart's cousin, Naphtali Hart Jr, had settled in the town shortly after its founding. It was no longer needed as an English outpost among the French dominions in North America after France lost its empire there in 1763. Most of the original settlers had left, and the population had declined until 1783 when the town was flooded with Loyalists, bringing its population up to almost 8,000. Much of this influx soon dispersed, and by 1790 about 5,000 remained in the town.[24] After the loss of the Thirteen Colonies, Halifax again became a trading town, the major point in British North America on the triangle with the West Indies and the Mother Country.

Most of the Jewish settlers of the 1750s had gone many years before. Nathan Nathans had died in debt in Halifax in 1778. David Jones, the son of Joseph and Judith Jones, had died in the summer of 1782, just before Hart arrived. Both had lived among Christians for many years.[25] Jones's Wharf was just a name. Nor were there to be any additions to the Jewish population of Halifax during Hart's residence. Yet Samuel Hart survived, and by 1790 he had even begun to prosper. His skills as a trader became much in demand.

When the writ for a new election to the assembly was issued on 22 January 1793, Hart made known his aspiration to run in Halifax, where he lived, but in view of the strong claims of others, his friends urged him to run in the town of Liverpool, where he had solid business connections. According to an eyewitness, at the nomination meeting on 4 March, "Mr. Samuel Hart of Halifax, was Set up by Major Nathl. Freeman, as a Candidate for the Town, & no other Candidate Setting up, Mr. Hart then had all the Votes & was declared duly elected."[26]

When Hart was elected to the House of Assembly of Nova Scotia, he probably expected to be the first Jew to sit and vote in a British legislature. According to any law Hart could check, he was entitled to take his seat in the assembly as a Jew.

It was true that the commission given to Edward Cornwallis as governor of Nova Scotia over forty years earlier had provided that "no person shall be capable of sitting tho' elected" to the assembly until they had taken the state oaths and subscribed the declaration under the Test Act.[27] However, the commissions to subsequent governors, usually published in the *Journal* of the province's Legislative Council, had no similar restriction and were silent as to franchise and election requirements for the assembly. Moreover, the laws restricting voting had been recently liberalized. In 1758 Nova Scotia's Executive Council had passed an ordinance requiring voters to take the state oaths, but only at the request of any candidate in an election who challenged a voter's loyalty. Then, in 1775, a bill, which did not proceed to law, was introduced in the assembly that would have dispensed completely with the oath of abjuration as a prerequisite to the vote.[28] Finally, in 1789 the Nova Scotia Assembly had abolished the state oaths as a condition of the exercise of the franchise by enacting a secular voter's oath that could be taken by persons of any religion and by allowing Quakers to affirm, instead of swear, the contents.[29]

Hart, as a British subject born in His Majesty's dominions, was entitled to assume that the liberalization of the franchise adopted for voters only four years earlier would apply for the seating of members of the assembly as well, even though the legislature had been silent on the matter of the oath of office for members. The liberal British policy on the secular oath for members of the assemblies of Upper and Lower Canada set out in section 29 of the Constitutional Act of 1791 might well have been a precedent. Hart may even have been aware of an opinion by the law officers of the crown in the summer of 1792 to the effect that persons naturalized under the Plantation Act of 1740 could vote for and be elected to the assemblies in Upper and Lower Canada.[30] If foreign-born, naturalized Jews could be seated in the assemblies of the Canadas, surely Hart, a British-born Jew, could be seated in Nova Scotia.

Hart was likely aware of commission of the new lieutenant governor, John Wentworth, appointed 13 January 1792, as his commission had been published, as usual, in the *Journal* of the Legislative Council. That document made no comment on any conditions attached to taking a seat in the assembly, although it did say that in the event of the death of or during the absence of the governor-in-chief, Lord Dorchester, from Nova Scotia, Wentworth was to "exercise and perform all and singular the Powers and Directions contained in Our Commission to our said Captain General and Governor in Chief according to such Instructions as he hath already received from Us, and such further Orders and Instructions as he or you shall hereafter receive from Us." Dorchester's commission as governor-in-chief, dated 27 April 1786, had likewise been published, but it was no more explicit.[31]

Hart was of course unaware of any royal instructions to Wentworth who had arrived in the colony in May 1792, if indeed they existed.[32]

As we have seen, a governor's instructions remained secret, even though they were the fundamental constitutional document in a colony, particularly in the Maritimes where no British statutes similar to the Constitutional Act were in force. It was even more complicated. The instructions that did have the force of law in Nova Scotia were not, in fact, those of Wentworth, but those of the governor-in-chief, whose instructions were to be followed by the lieutenant governor when Dorchester was out of the province. Because Dorchester was governor-in-chief of the whole of British North America and resided in Quebec, not Halifax, he was rarely in Nova Scotia, leaving his duties to be performed by Wentworth. Article 3 of Dorchester's instructions of 23 August 1786, which were not of course published, read: "You shall administer or cause to be administered the [state] Oaths appointed by the aforesaid recited Acts to the Members and Officers of the Councils and Assemblies respectively of the Province of Nova Scotia ... and you shall also cause them to make and subscribe the aforesaid declaration mentioned in the aforesaid Act of the twenty fifth year of the Reign of King Charles the Second [Test Act]."[33]

There can be no doubt of Samuel Hart's surprise when, shortly after his election, he was informed that he was obliged to make and subscribe the declaration under the Test Act as well as to swear the state oaths as a condition of taking his seat in the assembly. While he may have sensed the existence of a code, as only Anglicans had been known to take office in the colony, Hart could not have determined the exact nature of the rules unless they had been explained to him by the governor. Once aware of the requirements, however, Hart was forced to choose. If he wished to take his seat, he would have to be baptized in order to make the declaration against transubstantiation and to receive the sacrament "according to the Usage of the Church of England ... in some publick Church, ... after Divine Service," as well as to take the oaths of office "as a Christian." He made his compromises and had no restrictions as a citizen. Hart held his seat until 1799 when he retired from public life.

There is little evidence that Samuel Hart had any connection with Judaism after his baptism in 1793, although one account suggests that Hart took his young son, Moses Montagu, to London in 1796 and left him with his brother Moses,[34] who remained an observant Jew until his death in 1825.[35] Hart would become a pathetic figure at the end of his days. He was unsuccessful in his attempts to be named a magistrate or to be elected to the executive of the Halifax Commercial Society. He failed commercially during the severe slump in the Halifax trade between 1805 and 1807. In 1809 he was declared a lunatic and spent the last days of his life chained to the floor of a room in his mansion in Preston, Nova Scotia. He died insolvent on 3 October 1810. According to his biographer, "Hart's tragic fate had underscored the difficulties facing Jews who aspired to social acceptance in early British North America."[36]

Samuel Hart's case was not unique. The rigorous enforcement of the oath qualifications for members of assemblies in British North America after 1791 found a parallel in the treatment of Lieutenant Philip Dorland of Adolphustown, Upper Canada, who was a Quaker.

The Constitutional Act, which had come into effect in 1791 with the express purpose of forming the new provinces of Upper and Lower Canada out of the Old Province of Quebec and of creating elected assemblies in both provinces, carried forward provisions for the protection of religious groups. Like the Quebec Act of 1774, this act ensured the establishment of the Church of England.[37] But it also carried forward section 7 of the Quebec Act which had allowed Roman Catholics to swear a simple oath of allegiance instead of the state oaths and section 5 which had allowed Roman Catholics to "enjoy the free Exercise of the Religion of the Church of *Rome*, subject to the King's Supremacy."[38]

The legal equality of French-Canadian Roman Catholics with Anglicans was continued in practice after the Constitutional Act; other Roman Catholics now joined them in possessing this special status not shared by Protestant Dissenters and Jews. From the time of the Quebec Act of 1774, a position on the governor's council was open only to a follower of the Church of England or to "a Canadian professing the religion of the Church of Rome." After the Constitutional Act, the governor's instructions for the Canadas required that members of the Executive Council swear the state oaths and make and subscribe the declaration against transubstantiation.[39] While there was no exemption from this requirement for Roman Catholics, the same instructions appointed a number of French Canadians to the first Executive Council in Lower Canada, apparently allowing them to swear the oath provided in the Quebec Act instead of the state oaths.[40] The instructions continued to allow "any of Our Subjects who may profess the Religion of the Church of Rome" access to all other offices or places of trust.[41] Protestant Dissenters and Jews fared considerably worse. With the exception of assemblies and legislative councils, they were now excluded in both new provinces from all offices or places of trust for which they had formerly been eligible in the Old Province of Quebec.

Section 29 of the Constitutional Act allowed one simple oath to be taken by all those wishing to be sworn as members of the legislative council or assembly in either Upper or Lower Canada. It was unique in form as a relaxation of the oath requirements that did not restrict any particular group by its words, except perhaps atheists. The introductory words of the section provided "that no member of either the Legislative Council or Assembly, in either of the said Provinces, shall be entitled to sit or vote therein until he shall have taken and subscribed the following oath." The oath read: "I, A.B., do sincerely promise and swear that I will be faithful and bear true allegiance to his Majesty, King George, as lawful sovereign of the Kingdom of Great Britain, and of these Provinces dependant on and belonging to the said Kingdom; and that I will defend him to the utmost of my power against all traitorous conspiracies and attempts whatever shall be made against his person, crown, and dignity; and that I will do my utmost endeavour to disclose and make known to his Majesty, his heirs or successors, all treasons and traitorous conspiracies and attempts which I shall know to be against him, or any of them; and all this I do swear without any equivocation, mental evasion, or secret reservation, and renouncing all pardons and dispensations from any person or power whatever to the contrary – So help me God." It was an oath that could be taken by Roman Catholics, Protestant Dissenters, and Jews.

In August 1792 Philip Dorland had been elected to represent Prince Edward County. Dorland, as a Quaker, had refused to swear the oath for members of the assembly set forth in the Constitutional Act, even though that oath presented fewer complications than the state oaths had done.[42] "From the religious principles I profess (being one of the persons commonly called Quakers)," Dorland stated in his petition of 19 September 1792 asking to take his seat as a member of Upper Canada's first House of Assembly. "I do not feel myself at liberty nor can I conscientiously take an oath in the form and manner usually prescribed although I would readily affirm and subscribe a declaration to the purpose and effect therein set forth."[43] Affirmation, Dorland's suggested alternative, had not yet been authorized as a substitute for swearing oaths in Upper Canada.

The debate on Dorland's petition occupied an entire day's business in the assembly. There were few precedents for denying a seat to an elected member in England, the most notable having occurred in 1688, over a century before, when Sir H. Monson and Lord Fanshaw, both Roman Catholics, refused to take their oaths of office to the House of Commons and were unable to take their seats. At the end of the day, the assembly resolved that Dorland was "declared incompetant [sic] to sit or vote in the House without having taken and subscribed the Oath set forth in the Act of Parliament aforesaid in the manner and form therein specified."[44] The house called for a new election, but Dorland did not run again. Upper Canada would not give formal relief to its Quakers until the Oaths Act of 1833 allowed them to affirm instead of swear whenever an oath was required by law.[45]

Some of the other colonies were more accommodating to Quakers. In 1786 New Brunswick had passed an act giving relief to Quakers by allowing them to affirm instead of taking an oath "in the usual form" if "required on any lawful occasion to take an oath."[46] At its very first session in 1793, the legislature of Lower Canada, with its Catholic majority in the assembly, gave equal rights to Quakers by allowing them to affirm, instead of swear, oaths.[47]

In one sense, British colonial policy following the implementation of the Constitutional Act was designed to ensure that the Test Act would continue to be, in Lord North's words, "the corner stone of the constitution." The Constitutional Act was silent as to the form of oaths to be taken by persons other than those of the Anglican or Roman Catholic faiths. The act was silent as to the form of declaration on transubstantiation to be taken by non-Anglicans or Roman Catholics. It was silent as to the toleration of those of other religions.

The respective instructions to Lord Dorchester as governor of each of the new provinces were ironic, however, perhaps reflecting in the sphere of civil rights one of those chronic cycles that affect economies. On the one hand, these instructions mandated religious liberty for Dissenters and Jews in the same words first introduced in the governor's instructions for the Old Province of Quebec in 1787.[48] On the other hand, the governor was also required to ensure not only that the state oaths for office holders were required in each province in accordance with the imperial statute of 1766, but that the Test Act for the suppression of dangers from "Popish Recusants" would be strictly enforced, except for "Subjects who may profess the Religion of the Church of Rome."[49] That act, which had been intended to apply only to Catholics when it was passed in 1673, was now to be applied not to Catholics but only to Protestant Dissenters and to Jews who had both been exempt from its provisions in the Old Province of Quebec. In almost all cases, Dissenters and Jews were now to be required to make the declaration against transubstantiation and take the sacrament according to the Church of England rite. Roman Catholics were required only to swear the simple oath of allegiance specified in section 7 of the Quebec Act.

As the eighteenth century drew to a close, the colonies of Upper and Lower Canada were turning back the clock on the Protestant Dissenters and Jews who had possessed virtually equal rights with Anglicans for thirty years in the Old Province of Quebec. The most recent instructions to the governor meant that Anglicans and Roman

Catholics would be able to assume appointed offices, but Jews and Dissenters such as Presbyterians were now to be excluded as they were in Britain. Roman Catholics had flourished under the British regime in Quebec and Roman Catholics were to flourish in the provinces of Upper and Lower Canada to a degree that had no precedent in any other English-speaking land. It is no coincidence, however, that the decline of the Jewish community in Lower Canada dates from the Constitutional Act.

The motives for Britain's abrupt change of policy towards minorities in British North America are easy to discern. Nova Scotia and Quebec had both been small beachheads of Protestant settlement in a sea of Catholics when they became active British colonies in the 1750s and 1760s. Britain had encouraged Jews and other Protestants to settle these colonies – waiving the usual rules designed to promote Anglicans – in order to counterbalance the numerical superiority of the French Catholic inhabitants. They had encouraged German-speaking Lutherans to settle in Halifax to counterbalance the Acadian French and, in 1752, even established a German Protestant colony at Lunenburg. These policies were intensified after 1763 when Britain became the ruler of the colony of Quebec peopled by 70,000 Roman Catholics loyal to France.

By 1790 Britain's colonial needs had changed substantially. It was no longer in such need of Protestant Dissenters and Jews in Quebec or its Maritime colonies. A wave of English-speaking Loyalists, many of them Anglican, had come to Britain's remaining "Mutilated Colony" as refugees from the lost British territory to the south.[50] By this time, the major threat to the British dominions in North America was no longer the French but the newly minted United States of America.[51] The English-speaking Protestant American infiltrators who came north after 1783 hoping to share in the benefits offered to Loyalists were indistinguishable from "loyal" British subjects and therefore presented a danger to the future control of the colonies by Britain.

There were two differences between "real" Loyalists and these Americans: the Americans would not take an oath of loyalty to the king of England and they would not accept the king of England as the head of their church. Because the oath of allegiance instituted for land applications by Loyalists in Quebec in 1783 was a secular one,[52] it had encouraged settlers of all religions to come north to take up land as long as they would accept British rule. But to allow such latitude among those holding office was another matter. The re-imposition of the state oaths and the provisions of the Test Act would prevent all but Anglicans and Roman Catholics from holding office and would thereby ensure that any American infiltrators did not gain government or military offices. The remaining colonies in British North America, by rigorously applying the Test Act "for preventing Dangers which may happen from Popish Recusants" as well as the state oaths, also excluded all but Anglicans from office. Thus, the laws relating to Roman Catholics in the colonies of British North America other than the Canadas remained as restrictive as they were in England.[53] That was the mood that had confronted Samuel Hart.

If the experiences of Samuel Hart and Philip Dorland had anything in common, they showed that colonial policy in British North America had retrenched from equality to toleration at the very time that toleration was rejected in favour of equality in the constitutions of the new republics of France and the United States of America.[54] A theme was beginning to emerge. By 1790, Britain no longer feared Roman Catholics; it feared the infiltration of the "rebels" of the former Thirteen Colonies. The rules that had worked so effectively in Great Britain to promote Anglicans to, and exclude Dissenters from, positions of influence were now to be strictly imposed on the remaining British colonies in America, although in a hybrid form that promoted Roman Catholics almost to the level of Anglicans in Upper and Lower Canada. The imposition of the English rules was an excess – a form of colonial dragfishing that caught in the same net not just the feared Americans but also the people Britain had earlier invited to establish and settle its colonies – the Jews, the Presbyterians, the Quakers, and the other Protestant Nonconformists. The net set for the "liberty boys" also caught those loyal subjects who had defended Quebec against them. Samuel Hart was not alone. It became common for Dissenters, even Presbyterians, to convert to the Anglican faith in order to be appointed to office in British North American colonies.[55]

The religious oaths and declarations that were in Lord North's words "the corner stone of the constitution" may have upheld the structure of social and political life in Britain. The use of that cornerstone as the basis of a transatlantic colonial policy showed that the structure had been built to its limits. Ideas of a more complete form of religious equality were still evolving, and the existing forms of administration would remain until several difficult years of transition had passed. Nevertheless, colonial officials increasingly gave their own interpretation to the British rules, winking at the letter of the law, based on a new understanding that equality of different cultures was the only policy that had currency in the colonies themselves and that would draw and retain a viable and productive population. The people of a large part of British North America had tasted equality and would accept nothing less.

As the world entered the nineteenth century, two events would bring matters to a head, at least for the Jews. The first arose from the use of the state oaths in connection with land grants in Upper Canada, the second from the use of these oaths in connection with political office in Lower Canada. In neither instance did the British and Canadian authorities appear to have anticipated the outcome of the challenges.

12 The Upper Canada
Proving Ground

When every remnant of Religious Intolerance is growing odious
in the eyes of every enlightened Government, when the sister
colony of Lower Canada has admitted all descriptions to a participation of the same rights, and the Government of Upper Canada
is knocking off with all their strength the Shackles from the
unhappy African, your Petitioners might reasonably hope to share
in this general philanthropy.

> Petition of the Baptists and Presbyterians
> to the Upper Canada Assembly to be included in
> the Marriage Act, 27 March 1796.[1]

"Jews cannot hold Land in this Province." These words came from the
pen of John Elmsley, chief justice of Upper Canada, on 5 January
1798. Elmsley was also chairman of the land board at York which
heard petitions for free grants of a portion of "the waste lands of the
Crown."[2] Of the 231 petitions reviewed that day, grants of as little as
100 acres and as much as 1,500 acres were recommended in 226 cases.
Two petitions were stayed pending a report on a boundary question,
and another petitioner was declared too young to apply.[3] The remaining two petitions came from Jews. Moses Hart's petition, based on
officers' rights to land that he had purchased, was simply "Not recommended."[4] It was the petition of Levy Solomons Jr, based on his own
merits as a resident of the settlement at Cornwall, that gave the chief
justice an opportunity to make this statement of policy on the right
of Jews to hold land.

Solomons was blasted by the words. This was the province of Upper
Canada, a new colony, sparsely settled. It was a proving ground[5] where
new ways were tested, sometimes with devastating results. Similar decisions were to follow. At a subsequent sitting of the land board, Elmsley
rejected the application of Moses David of Sandwich on the ground
that the "Pet[itione]r belongs to the Lower Province." The application

of Moses Jacobs of Kingston was simply deferred without reasons.[6] For Jews, Elmsley's decisions were potentially devastating. None of the four Jewish applicants was an alien. In fact, three had been born in Canada. They had been refused land because of their religion, and for no other reason.

For Jewish people, to search out the land meant to seek a place where citizenship was not defined in such a way as to exclude Jews, where land would be granted equally to Jews, and where there would be equality of opportunity. Those places where land would be granted freely to Jews were understood by them as places where nations more enlightened than those of the Old World were in the process of creation. For many years, natural-born colonial Jews had been obtaining patents to land. They had bought and sold land in all the British colonies, the earliest recorded transaction involving Asser Levy in Albany in 1661.[7] Land grants to Jews by the crown had been common in Nova Scotia from the time of the first English settlement. The same pattern had emerged in New Brunswick and in the Old Province of Quebec – even in the part that subsequently became the separate province of Upper Canada. However, it was to be expected that people schooled in the rules of the Old World, ignorant of the practices of the New, would come to the colonies in positions of authority.

John Elmsley was not a man of the frontier. Born in London, England, in 1762, he was called to the bar in 1790. In 1796 he secured the chief justiceship of Upper Canada through his connection with the home secretary, the duke of Portland. He arrived in Upper Canada on 20 November 1796 and took up his duties on 10 December. It was clear even to his contemporaries that he had brought his English notions with him.[8] "He was one of the few university graduates in the province," says a biographer, "and was much given to elegant phrases and Latin quotations, a habit that may not have endeared him to all his colleagues."[9]

It is not hard to determine what was in Elmsley's mind in his ruling on Jews and land. The decision reflected his views on a debate that had been going on in England for well over 100 years but had recently received additional attention. Two thirteenth-century statutes unearthed in manuscript form in England in 1738 suggested that Jews had possessed the status of villeinage in mediaeval times and therefore could not own freehold land. The issue had not been raised directly in any court and, indeed, many Jews in England held land at this time, but a segment of the legal profession considered the issue open to doubt.[10] Elmsley was apparently among them. He was seemingly unaware that section 43 of the Constitutional Act of 1791, under which Upper Canada was created, had made "free and common socage," rather than feudal forms of ownership such as villeinage, the only operative form of freehold tenure.

Nor does it appear that Elmsley was aware of the distinctions in the practice of landholding in England and in the colonies where the government was directly involved in granting land to Jews. The distinction was based partly on the fact that the grant of "any Lands, Tenements, or Hereditaments" by the crown to naturalized Jews was prohibited "within the Kingdom of Great Britain or Ireland" by section 6 of the Plantation Act of 1740 but was implicitly authorized for the colonies. Then, in 1773 Parliament had passed a declaratory act specifically to remove doubts as to the status of naturalized persons such as Jews with respect to grants of land from the crown in the colonies. That act provided that persons naturalized in the British colonies in America under the Plantation Act "shall be deemed to be capable of … taking and holding any Grant of Lands, Tenements, and Hereditaments, from the Crown to himself or themselves, or to any other or others in Trust for him or them." Naturalized persons could take grants of land, even though that right had not been expressly described in the Plantation Act and even though that right was denied to naturalized persons in England itself. The substantive law was clearly on the side of Jews being entitled to hold land in Upper Canada. Naturalized Jews certainly had taken advantage of that right. Their children, born in Britain or its colonies, could be entitled to no less in the colony.

Before Elmsley's decision on Solomons's petition, the British government's position had therefore been that crown grants to Jews were permitted by law. The only change had been the firm reactivation of the practice of requiring the state oaths as a condition of receiving such grants. From 1783, when the British turned to resettling the Loyalists, the instructions to governors had required that applicants for land take the oaths directed by law. Moreover, on 7 February 1792 a proclamation by the lieutenant governor of Upper Canada, John Graves Simcoe, had advised that persons "desirous to settle on the lands of the Crown in the Province of Upper Canada" were required to cultivate and improve the lands and to take "the usual Oaths."[11] If the applicant could not comply with procedure because of an unwillingness to take the state oaths, that was a matter for the applicant and his conscience. If anything prevented Jews from taking up grants of crown land, it was the procedural requirement for the state oaths as a condition of that grant. It was a subtle system. Perhaps because of his lack of experience, Elmsley stated what his superiors in England would never have admitted: that the effect of the oath requirement was to set up a procedural disability which would prevent Jews from owning land in Upper Canada unless they took a Christian oath. Prior to the arrival of Elmsley, however, no such stand had been openly taken in British North America.

On the contrary, as our story has shown, Jews had been receiving unprecedented treatment as equals in obtaining crown grants of land from the beginning of British settlement in Canada. The very first land grant by the crown in the first British settlement in Canada was to a Jew. John Franks and his partners had received that grant at Halifax on 8 August 1749, and on the same day allotments were also given to Samuel Jacobs and Isaac Solomon. The following year allotments were transferred to Israel Abrahams and Isaac Levy and in 1751 to Abraham Andrews, all of whom became entitled to crown grants by assignment. Crown grants remained common in Nova Scotia. Joseph Jones was given a grant of land on Halifax harbour in 1758. In 1760, 76,500 acres in Yarmouth township were granted to some fifty individuals, including Isaac Levy, David Franks, Benjamin Levy, David Salusbury Franks, and John Franks. When Samuel Jacobs moved to Fort Cumberland, in what was later to be New Brunswick, he obtained a crown grant for 55 acres near the fort on 28 May 1760.[12] In 1765 Joseph Jacobs, a member of the Shearith Israel Congregation in New York, along with Israel and Benjamin Jacobs, shared with others in a patent to 100,000 acres on the Petitcodiac River north of Shuracadie Creek. And in 1784 Joseph Jacobs received a further grant in the township of Gage, Sunbury District, the year the province of New Brunswick was created.[13] Moreover, we know of several Loyalists who were Jews receiving crown grants, including Rachel Myers and her sons, Benjamin and Abraham, and David Goebels.[14] And there were undoubtedly others.[15]

Likewise, in the Old Province of Quebec, no restrictions had applied to Jewish settlers seeking crown grants. "The right of holding Lands," as Samuel Becancour Hart wrote in 1830, "has never been disputed in this Provce to persons of the Jewish faith."[16] Along with his partners Benjamin Price and John Hay, Samuel Jacobs, formerly of Halifax and Fort Cumberland, had received letters patent to a lot under tenure in Quebec on 23 November 1765.[17] Even as late as 1792 John Franks, who had moved on to Quebec, received a crown grant of 200 acres in Hungerford township, Lower Canada.[18] In some parts of the province that later became Upper Canada, crown grants had also been given to Jews without any challenge. For example, by 1786 Lieutenant Governor Patrick Sinclair had given crown grants for lots to Myer Michaels and to several other Jewish traders who were central to the Great Lakes fur trade at Fort Michilimackinac.[19] Myers Solomons was approved for a crown grant in the Cornwall area in 1789, some three years after settling there, but he eventually sold his rights and returned to Montreal.[20]

Once the Constitutional Act of 1791 came into force, however, the barrier was firmly in place. No grants to Jews have been located for the subsequent period. Two individuals who appear to have been Jewish did receive crown grants, but both applicants had been baptized and would have had little difficulty swearing the oaths. John Lawe – whose mother, Rachel Franks, was half-Jewish and whose father, Captain George Lawe, was not – was known to his associates on the frontier as a Jew, but the land board in Newark granted him permission for a town lot in July 1794.[21] John Levy Jacobs was born in 1772 to Samuel Jacobs, a professing Jew, and Marie-Josette Audette, a Roman Catholic. Though commonly known as Levi Jacobs, he applied for a land patent under his formal name and obtained approval for a town lot in Newark on 30 August 1794.[22]

Elmsley's views about the rights of Jews to hold land prevailed for a time because of his position. He was not only chief justice and chairman of the land board but also speaker of the Legislative Council and a member of the Executive Council. When Peter Hunter, the lieutenant governor, left the colony for more than two years, Elmsley, as temporary chairman of the Executive Council, was "probably the most influential man in Upper Canada."[23]

Levy Solomons Jr was hurt by Elmsley's decision. He had been born in Montreal in 1771, the son of Levy Solomons, a member of the important Great Lakes fur trade consortium of the 1760s, and Lizette Loubière. He was circumcised at birth and raised as a Jew in Montreal. After the death of his father in 1792 he opened a tobacco-processing business but it did not prosper, and he left Montreal. "Levy left for Cornwall before I left Montreal," his future brother-in-law, Thomas McCord, wrote in the spring of 1797; "he is engaged in the Distillery business in partnership with a Mr Mckinstry, and I hope will do well – if he is steady I think he may, for he is not extravagant."[24] Although his application for land was refused, Solomons stayed on in Cornwall for two more years. By 1800 he had moved to Albany, where his father had lived fifty years earlier. He married Catherine Manuel in the synagogue in New York in 1801 and became a prosperous tobacco merchant in Albany, manufacturing chocolate, tobacco, and a brand of snuff called Maccaba. He became a citizen of the United States just before he died in Albany in 1823.[25]

Moses Hart,[26] the second Jewish applicant refused by Elmsley, was the eldest son of Aaron Hart, the prosperous Trois-Rivières merchant, and a successful merchant in his own right. In 1797 he had "purchased rights to military lands from discharged soldiers and non-commissioned officers" and, with the assistance of Levy Solomons Jr as agent, applied for patents to those lands. Elmsley, on behalf of the land board, ruled his petition "Not recommended."[27] Hart's case was different from that of Solomons. Solomons had applied for land in his own right, and thus the regulation that required every petitioner for lands to take the usual oaths applied. The oaths were required at the time that the petition was made. According to the usual practice, there was then a lapse of several months while the property was surveyed. When the final letters patent were signed by the lieutenant governor to complete the grant, no additional oaths were required. Because Hart had purchased the rights of others to lands in Upper Canada, those who had actually applied for land by petition had sworn the oaths before Hart's purchase. All Hart had to do was pay for his survey and other fees. He was not required to swear any oaths to obtain his grant. He could not be denied on the ground that he was a Jew, for he was entitled by law to hold land by purchase of others' rights to patents, and no requirement for the "usual Oaths" could bar the way.

Hart was an experienced businessman and did not accept Elmsley's decision. He retained the services of Jacob Farrand of Cornwall. Although Farrand was not a lawyer, he was more than a land agent. He had settled in Cornwall in the 1780s as a Loyalist who had spent over seven years on active duty as a lieutenant with the King's Royal Rangers of New York. He had held a number of government posts and was well known to the land board. In fact, at the time Hart engaged him he was serving as registrar for the counties of Glengarry and Stormont in the Eastern District, which included Cornwall.[28] Farrand was well connected by family ties to the ruling establishment. His first cousin, Robert I.D. Gray, was the member of the assembly for the area, solicitor general, and the treasurer of the Law Society of Upper Canada, as well as a close friend of Elmsley.[29]

Farrand quickly discovered that 11 of the 13 land grants for which certificates had been issued to discharged soldiers had not been settled or located. These certificates were therefore invalid and Hart would have no success with these claims. The two that were located and surveyed, one in the township of Charlottenburgh and the other in the township of Alfred, were claims that could not easily be defeated, however. Farrand drew a new petition for Hart, but one communication in 1798 tells of "my trouble at Niagara in carrying that petition through the Council."[30] Farrand eventually appeared at the land board at the end of August 1799. The board was composed of D.W. Powell and Surveyor General D.W. Smith; Elmsley was not present. Hart's claim to the 200 acres in Alfred was allowed.[31] Moses Hart succeeded in both of his petitions to obtain land patents given on the basis of an assignment of an earlier claim. Interestingly, there is evidence that Levy Solomons Jr assisted Hart financially in pursuing the issue to its conclusion.[32]

Hart's success in obtaining a crown grant by purchasing the rights of others who had already taken the oaths did not resolve the issue of how Jews could directly obtain grants to which they were otherwise entitled, because the state oaths were still a disability. But he had succeeded in showing that Elmsley was wrong in saying that "Jews cannot hold Land in this Province." The way was now open for others.

On 17 February 1804 Isaac Judah obtained letters patent for land in Upper Canada without even applying to the land board. Judah, son of Abraham Judah, was a brother of Dorothea Hart of Trois-Rivières and of Samuel and Uriah Judah. He had been living in Quebec in 1775 when the Americans attacked the city and had joined the British militia in the defeat of the Americans on New Year's Day, 1776. He moved to Montreal shortly thereafter and carried on business as a merchant through the 1780s.[33] By 1792 he was living in Cornwall in a log house on lot 9 at the corner of Sydney and Water Streets.[34] In 1797 he was certified as a former member of Caldwell's militia which had served in the defence of Quebec and thus entitled to receive land in Lower Canada, but he did not take up a grant as the Land Committee rejected Colonel Caldwell's request that his men be exempted from swearing the oaths.[35] He returned to Montreal around 1800. Then in 1803 Judah purchased rights to land in Upper Canada from a person entitled to a patent and sought the approval for the transfer from the Heir and Devisee Commission. A note in the register under claim number 232 for that year, signed by D.W. Smith, indicated that the land was "entered to Isaac Judah and appears to be clear of difficulty."[36]

The position of Moses Jacobs, the third of the applicants refused by Elmsley, appeared to improve once the lieutenant governor, Peter Hunter, began to spend more time in the colony and take a more active part in its affairs. Jacobs had not made a display of his Jewish roots and was apparently not anxious to test his rights.[37] When the American Revolution broke out, he was displaced and he arrived in Kingston in 1793. His application of 30 May 1797 for 200 acres of land was based on his claim to be a Loyalist. When it was deferred, he moved on to Adolphustown, thirty miles west of Kingston, and in July 1798, he applied, with assistance this time, for an assignment of 450 acres of land.[38] No action was taken on this petition either until 11 July 1802, when it was among a number of petitions "not acted upon" that were sent to the lieutenant governor's office for consideration. On 15 July, Hunter declared that "there is no legal impediment to Mr. Jacobs receiving a Grant of the Waste Lands of the Crown." The matter was referred to the Executive Council "when the Petitioner appears in Person, for a single lot subject to the settling Duties."[39] That last phrase, "subject to the settling Duties," had overtones that were unmistakable. Jacobs would have to take the usual oaths as part of these duties. He would have to swear "upon the true Faith of a Christian." The lieutenant governor could still say there was no legal impediment: the substantive law clearly allowed the grant. If Jacobs's conscience would not let him swear the usual oaths and the grant could therefore not be made, that was Jacobs's problem. There is no record that Jacobs ever appeared before the council.

Moses David, the fourth of the Jewish applicants refused by Elmsley, was a natural-born British subject.[40] He had been born in the Old Province of Quebec in 1767, the third son of Lazarus David and Phoebe Samuel. Though his father had died before he was ten and his mother when he was still in his teens, his family was an integral part of the Montreal Jewish community. Not only had his father owned land in the town of Quebec and in Montreal since the 1760s but his older brothers, David and Samuel, were also landowners in Montreal. In 1790 Moses David went to Detroit and volunteered for Sir John Johnson's militia. Three years later he was with the force that stopped General Anthony Wayne at Fort Miami near Detroit. In 1794 he established himself as a merchant in Sandwich, Upper Canada, and built one of the first residences in the area. He remained in the militia, serving under Simcoe as a volunteer in 1796. Elmsley's decision of 1797 that David "belonged to the Lower Province" was therefore not accurate. David had been among the first permanent settlers of Sandwich.

Notwithstanding his long residence in the area, David apparently took Elmsley's reason for his failure to obtain land in Upper Canada as advice. In 1799 he made the long trip to Montreal, and on 18 March he applied on the basis of his military service for a 2000-acre grant in Lower Canada. His application was refused in December on the ground that it was "too late under the present Instructions."[41] In April 1801 he again applied for a land grant in Upper Canada, this time requesting a park lot and forwarding a certificate from the church wardens of Sandwich verifying that his building was already completed. To this petition he received no answer. He applied again on 8 January 1803, but again had no reply.[42]

Unlike Moses Jacobs, Moses David was unwilling to leave the issue unresolved. Perhaps his family's long-time success in the colony and his position as a natural-born subject gave him the confidence to push for his rights. In any case, on 9 March 1803 he sent a prayer for relief to Lieutenant Governor Hunter that forced the governor and his council to face the issue. He set forth the details of his long residence in the area, of his role in founding the township of Sandwich, of his military service, and of his birth in Quebec. He reminded the lieutenant governor that he had still not received any acknowledgment of his 1801 petition. He stated that he understood his application complied with the most recent land regulations, "agreeable to Mr. President Russell's letter to the magistrates of the Western District," and concluded by raising the issue directly. He understood, he said, that his petition had been rejected "under the idea that his religion precludes him from any grant in His Majesty's Colonies."[43]

The lieutenant governor referred David's petition to the Executive Council on 9 May 1803. On the following day, the council, composed of Henry Allcock (Elmsley's successor), Peter Russell, and Aeneas Shaw, considered David's prayer for relief. Notes of the discussion at the meeting have not survived, but the council records indicate David's application was approved on the condition that the church wardens of Sandwich produce a new certificate stating that David's building had been completed on a town lot. The certificate was delivered to the council on 17 May. David was finally given letters patent to 27 acres of land in the township of Sandwich on 20 February 1804.[44] He resided in Sandwich until his death on 27 September 1814.[45]

Somehow, in a way that was not recorded, the Executive Council of Upper Canada had decided to relieve David of the obligation of swearing the oath of abjuration with its Christian form of words. He had been able to apply for and receive a crown grant of land without any disability. On the surface, nothing seemed to have changed. No new statutes or regulations had been passed. The lieutenant governor's instructions from Britain still required that applicants for land swear the usual oaths. Perhaps the council had allowed David to amend the oath of abjuration to the form of "State Oaths for Persons of the Jewish Persuasion" that Carleton had adopted in 1768 and that had been used by John Franks when he was appointed inspector of chimneys. Indeed, section 33 of the Constitutional Act had provided that "all laws statutes and ordinances" of the Old Province of Quebec were to remain in force in the new provinces of Upper and Lower Canada, notwithstanding the division, "except in so far as the same are expressly repealed or varied by this Act." But the Jewish form of state oath used by Franks does not appear to have been authorized by a statute or ordinance and, more to the point, no one seems to have remembered the precedent.

The government's discreet acceptance of Moses David's equal rights was applied to other aspects of the colony's life as well. Prior to 1803 he had been appointed an ensign in the Essex militia of the Western

District, a position that was granted under commission from the crown through its representative, the lieutenant governor. In 1803, the same year that the council determined that he could not be denied the right to receive a land grant from the crown, David was promoted to lieutenant.[46] It appears that he was the first professing Jew in British North America to be appointed an officer in the militia. And he may have been the first Jew to be appointed a commissioned officer in the whole empire, for in Britain itself officers still could receive a commission only upon swearing the state oaths and making and subscribing the declaration against transubstantiation under the Test Act.[47]

There is little doubt that the swearing of the state oaths was a formal requirement for officers in Canada as well. Just before the War of 1812, there was even an attempt to introduce the oath of abjuration as a requirement in Upper Canada for all soldiers in the militia. In February 1812 the administrator of Upper Canada, General Sir Isaac Brock, proposed in the course of his speech from the throne that the Assembly enact such a requirement. Brock's proposal would have barred not only the "many doubtful characters" from the United States thought to be infiltrating the militia but also Jews and Quakers. After some debate, the Assembly defeated the bill in committee on the casting vote of the speaker, Samuel Street.[48]

The instructions to the various governors clearly prevented the appointment of non-Anglicans as officers in the military by the requirement that any person appointed "to hold or exercise any Office" in the province should swear the state oaths and comply with the Test Act.[49] This instruction seems, however, to have been honoured more in the breach than in the observance when it came to military appointments. Somehow, though the records have not been found, Moses David was allowed to obtain his commissions as ensign and as lieutenant without swearing the usual oaths, including the oath of abjuration with its phrase, "upon the true Faith of a Christian." However this was done, the practice was undoubtedly followed again when David was made a captain in the Essex militia in 1807.[50]

In February 1808, Moses David was offered the position of coroner of the Western District. The office was to be filled under a commission granted by Lieutenant Governor Francis Gore. It was a semi-judicial position of the same status as county clerk in Lower Canada. This was the first recorded example of a Jew being appointed by commission to government office in British North America since John Franks's appointment in 1768. It showed how far the government of Upper Canada was willing to go in adopting innovative solutions to allow a person of the Jewish faith to participate in society without swearing the state oaths. The actual commission given to David on 24 February

1808 had been changed from the usual document in one respect. Normally, the governor would state that he was making the appointment "being assured of the Loyalty and Integrity" of the appointee. In this case, the commission read: "being assured of the Loyalty by Bond and Integrity of Moses David." The change meant that the oaths had been waived in this instance, with David filing a bond with the government as security for the performance of his duties.[51] If the intent of the administration was to ensure that Jews, Catholics, Quakers, and other Dissenters could not be office holders, then no change to the state oaths was necessary. But if the intent was to ensure that office holders were loyal, then the state oaths were only one way of determining loyalty. The filing of a bond was an acceptable alternative. The device was a simple one, but it had the effect of making the state oaths unnecessary. The oaths would no longer operate as a disability for Jews, for Quakers, or for others seeking equal rights. Not in Upper Canada at any rate, where the will had existed to find a way to vary the state oaths to conform to the substantive law, even though the oaths were still a mandatory procedure under imperial law.

Never again was there to be any doubt as to the rights of Jews to obtain grants of land from the crown in Upper Canada or to receive and hold at least some civil and military positions.

Moses Jacobs finally got a crown land grant in 1816. In 1815 he had bought a lot in Camden township. The following year, when Jacobs was living in the township of Sophiasburgh, he tried to register his title and discovered that his lot in Camden had also been granted by certificate to someone else and was thus "under double certificate." Jacobs went to York and retained the services of George Ridout, a lawyer. With Ridout's help he applied for and obtained a new lot upon surrendering his certificate for the lot he had purchased previously.[52]

Jacob Franks and James Solomons were each given grants of a building lot at the new British post on Drummond Island in Lake Huron in 1816. Franks had operated as a merchant at Green Bay from about 1794. Although he had no commission, he had played a crucial role in the capture of Mackinac Island from the Americans in July 1812 – the first battle in the war – allowing the British and Canadians to regain control of the Upper Great Lakes and the western fur trade beyond. Franks was a major supplier of equipment for the forces that helped capture the island; Franks himself, at age 44, commanded a detachment of "Canadians or Boatmen" during the attack; there were only four commissioned officers in the invading army of over 850 men. Franks was given his lot to replace a building on Mackinac Island, burned by the Americans after the War of 1812 in retribution for his role in supporting the British.[53] James Solomons was one of the "deserving persons" entitled to a building lot at the new British post on Drummond Island. Solomons intended to use his as a residence for himself and his bride, Kitty, a daughter of Andrew Hays of Montreal.[54] It is likely that other Jewish settlers received grants of crown land as well.[55] In subsequent years, more Jewish settlers came to Upper Canada. Some moved on: Rebecca Franks Kemble,[56] Barnet Lyon,[57] Jacob Jacobs.[58] Some stayed and became a part of the communities in which they lived,[59] including Judith Montgomery who arrived in York from New Brunswick in 1803.[60]

What is apparent is that in the early years of the nineteenth century the governor and his staff were exercising a great deal of discretion in the enforcement of some of the requirements attached to the holding of both land and offices. The governor's instructions in both Upper and Lower Canada continued to require the state oaths and the declaration under the Test Act to be administered to all persons, other than Roman Catholics, "that shall be appointed to hold or exercise any Office, Place of Trust or Profit." But after 1800, the governors in the Canadas, while maintaining these requirements for those holding higher offices, increasingly used their discretion to restrict the definition of office. Commissions to officers in the militia were not treated as appointments to office, particularly during the exigencies of the War of 1812, with the result that large numbers of Dissenters served as officers apparently without being required to "take the Test" and join the Church of England.[61] The same discretion was used in making other appointments by commission, such as that of Moses David as coroner in 1808 or those of the Methodist, John Willson, and the Presbyterian, William Morris, as justices of the peace in 1796 and 1818, respectively.[62] In some cases, the governors appear to have simply narrowed the definition of "office," using their discretion to disregard the Test Act requirements for "unimportant" offices and maintaining the requirements for "important" offices. In other cases, the governors, in their discretion, may have found alternatives to the state oaths and declaration, such as in the bonding formula used for Moses David's appointment to the "important" office of coroner.[63] However, the use of such discretion, which meant that Dissenters and Jews could be treated more or less equally to Anglicans and Catholics, only worked as long as no one objected. An objection, no matter how frivolous, might cause the governor to fall back on the wording of his instructions and to deny offices to all but Anglicans and Roman Catholics. There was still no *right* to be treated equally.

The same use of discretion seems to have prevailed in the Atlantic provinces of British North America, although here Roman Catholics as well as Dissenters and Jews faced the usual disabilities. In 1805, the lieutenant governor of the colony of Newfoundland appointed Simon Solomon, a watchmaker of Jewish origin,[64] to be the first postmaster of the island, located at St John's. Although this was an important post, it was not an appointment to office by commission and it was not necessary for Solomon to swear the oath of abjuration or make the declaration under the Test Act. The appointment was made by the governor, Sir Erasmus Gower, and reported in February 1805 to Francis Freeling, secretary to the General Post Office in London, England. Freeling replied by a letter dated 18 April 1805 approving the appointment. The following year Solomon was appointed by commission as a lieutenant in the Royal Volunteers.[65] Another Maritime example of discretion was the appointment of William Abrahams, identified by his descendants as an English Jew, as justice of the peace in Northumberland County, New Brunswick, on 11 January 1822 – probably without the necessity of complying with the Test Act.[66]

Within a generation in Upper Canada, the conservative members of the Family Compact, the ruling clique that dominated the government of the province, showed a welcoming attitude towards Jewish settlement. "Suppose that there were a congregation of Jews in this town," the attorney general, Henry John Boulton, posited to the members of the assembly in 1831, "would they not be entitled to the protection of this House ... as much as any other sect or denomination?"[67]

13 Beyond the Wilderness: The Jews of Lower Canada, 1791–1831

> What I do not like is that you will be opposed as a Jew. You may go to law, but be assured you will never get a jury in your favour nore [*sic*] a party in the House for you.
>
> Aaron Hart to his son, Moses Hart, 1796[1]

On 20 February 1808, the assembly of the province of Lower Canada resolved by a vote of 21 to 5 "that Ezekiel Hart, Esquire, professing the Jewish Religion, cannot take a seat, nor sit nor vote in this House."[2] This decision was decidedly out of step both with contemporary attitudes towards Jews and other minorities in Upper Canada and with the history of equal treatment of Jews in Lower Canada. Once again the rights of Jews were put to the test in the course of a larger quarrel.

On 2 March 1807, John Lees, one of the two members of the House of Assembly representing Trois-Rivières, had died in office. Ezekiel Hart, the second son of Aaron and Dorothea Hart, had decided to run in the by-election to replace him. It was not the first time a Jew had run for election to the assembly in Lower Canada: Moses Hart, Ezekiel's older brother, had run unsuccessfully for a seat in Sorel (Willam Henry) in 1796.[3] On 11 April 1807 Ezekiel Hart was declared elected over three other candidates, obtaining 59 of the 116 votes cast.[4] Most of Hart's supporters were French Canadians. Yet when he was rebuffed in his attempt to take his seat, it was the French-Canadian members who opposed him.[5] While this affair might on the surface be taken as an example of anti-Semitic attitudes on the part of the majority in Lower Canada, it was in fact an incident in a much broader story: the development of political equality for the large French-Canadian population in English-dominated Lower Canada.

Even though French-Canadian Catholics, who made up well over 90 per cent of the population of the province, had been eligible for appointment to the Legislative Council that assisted the governor in running the affairs of the colony, the majority of those actually appointed to the council were invariably English-speaking Anglicans. This was a subtle method used by the English victors to control the vanquished French-Canadian majority. The Constitutional Act of 1791 had changed the system of government in the colony by providing for the first time for a popularly elected legislative assembly. Although the act did not explicitly set out the powers of the assembly, section 2 indicated that the assembly was to share a legislative function with the appointed Legislative Council, subject always to the right of the governor to disallow any particular legislation. The act provided that the governor was to have power "by and with the advice and consent of the Legislative Council and Assembly to make laws for the peace, welfare and good government" of the province. The composition of the population meant that the majority of members in the first assembly, convened in 1792, were French Canadians; one was even elected speaker, the highest elected office in the province.

But even though French Canadians were invariably in the majority in the assembly (usually some 40 of the 50 members), they were unable to exercise any influence. Under Britain's colonial policy, the governor was not obliged to accept the advice of the assembly or to sign bills it passed into law.[6] The best the assembly could do was to operate as an "official opposition" to the numerically less well represented English party, made up of the five to ten supporters of the governor in the assembly who backed the decisions of the appointed Legislative Council as well as of the governor's small group of advisers. The government supporters were English-speaking and Anglican, save for a few French-Canadian office holders or "place men" like Louis de Salaberry and a few Protestant Dissenters in the assembly.

While the French-Canadian factor made the situation of the government of Lower Canada unique, most of the people governed in the other British North American colonies had generally much in common with the French Canadians of Lower Canada. In all the colonies, the ruling group, composed unapologetically of Anglicans, maintained firm control over the reins of power through the office of the governor and his appointed executive council; the Church of England was the established church, and so entitled to its spiritual and temporal perks; only "loyal" citizens could be appointed to positions of trust or profit. In all the colonies with the possible exception of Nova Scotia and New Brunswick, the majority of the population was not Anglican and therefore did not have civil or political equality with the Anglicans. All the colonies had "radicals" who were to be kept at bay by British establishments using governmental controls.

Though relatively docile for the first dozen or so years, by 1805 the French-Canadian majority in the Lower Canada assembly (composed largely of lawyers and notaries) had begun to attempt to exercise its will. It was rebuffed at every turn. That year a debate arose as to the rights of members of the assembly to be reimbursed for expenses incurred in connection with their work as members. A bill passed by the French-Canadian majority in the assembly, whose members relied on their professional efforts for their income and had no government support, was defeated by the office holders of the Legislative Council with the support of the English minority in the House of Assembly itself. In November 1806 four French-Canadian members of the assembly, led by Pierre-Stanislaus Bédard, a lawyer, launched *Le Canadien*, a journal devoted to popularizing the point of view of the French Canadians. Articles in *Le Canadien* attacked the alliance between the place men and the English members of the assembly and defended the use of legislative privilege as an obstructionist tactic by the majority of the assembly in opposition to the government.[7]

Earlier in the session which denied Hart's right to sit in the House of Assembly, the French-Canadian majority had been defeated in its attempt to bar judges from having seats in the assembly. Sections 20 to 23 of the Constitutional Act had set out qualifications for members of the assembly but had made no specific reference to judges. Although judges were not allowed to hold seats in the British parliament, it served the interests of the governor to allow judges to hold seats and vote in the assembly of Lower Canada. The French-Canadian judges in the assembly usually voted with the English party out of loyalty to the authorities who had appointed them. This issue had simmered for several years and came to a boil just a few days before Hart was barred from his seat.[8] At one point in the session, the assembly in protest passed a resolution providing that judges be "incapable of being elected, or of sitting or of voting in the House of Assembly of any Parliament of this Province." Because judges were already seated in the assembly, it was necessary to pass a bill to unseat them. That bill was duly passed by the assembly but rejected by the Legislative Council.[9]

Ezekiel Hart's election to the assembly in 1807 dropped him into this hornet's nest. The French-Canadian party, frustrated by its constant lack of success in the running conflict with the governing powers, was ready for an issue on which it could win.

Hart had been born in Trois-Rivières in 1770. At the time of his birth, thirty years after the passage of the Plantation Act, the government of the province needed the support of the every loyal English-speaking Jew as it took on the task of ruling a conquered French-Canadian population which vastly outnumbered it. In consequence, officials had adopted a unique, liberal interpretation of the rights of

Jews as set out in that act, an interpretation that was the absolute antithesis of prejudicial action against Jews. The concrete evidence of this policy of liberalization was to be found in the appointment of Hart's father as one of the three chief postal officials of the province, in Eleazar Levy's imperial commission as a notary public, and in the decision of the governor to create a new form of state oath to allow a Jew, John Franks, to receive a commission as chief fire officer in the province.

However, as was customary in the subtle British system, there was no written record to support the civil and political rights and freedoms which Jews had been allowed. While the court system had evolved dramatically during the forty-five years since the conquest, there was still no system of reporting cases that might be relied upon as precedents, as there was in England. Judges' decisions, when given in writing, remained filed on handwritten sheets of paper in the office of the clerk of the relevant court. The British common law system adopted in all the colonies except Quebec relied on the precedent of prior interpretation by officials in similar circumstances, but the civil law system adopted for the colony by the Quebec Act in 1774 relied on a civil code. As a result, by 1800 no one remembered that the authorities in Quebec had consistently followed the precedent of a liberal interpretation of the Plantation Act which allowed Jews equal rights and the ability to amend the oath of abjuration. No one remembered that the Old Province of Quebec had established a special form of "State Oaths for Persons of the Jewish Persuasion" in 1768 as its first precedent. In Lower Canada there were no officials who might have kept a record of these precedents. Without such a record and a legal discipline to find the precedents and point them out to the authorities, the status and rights of Jews had inadvertently come to depend on the will of the majority.

Although a new session of the assembly commenced on 16 April 1807, just five days after Hart's election, he did not rush to Quebec to take his seat for he knew there might well be difficulties. He was confronted by a number of options. One choice – to convert to Christianity and take his seat as a Christian as Samuel Hart had done in Nova Scotia fifteen years earlier – evidently did not appeal to him. A second choice was to swear only the secular oath of office specified by the Constitutional Act. This seemed a logical choice because that act appeared to replace the state oaths with a single oath, even though members of the assembly had continued, as a matter of custom, to swear the state oaths. A third choice was to swear both the secular oath of office specified by the Constitutional Act and the state oaths using the amendment in the Plantation Act for people "professing the

Jewish Religion" which allowed the deletion from the oath of abjuration of the words "upon the true Faith of a Christian." Although Hart may not have been aware that a form of state oaths for "Persons of the Jewish Persuasion" had been introduced in Quebec in 1768, he likely knew of the amendment allowed by the Plantation Act.

During the months between his election in April 1807 and his appearance at Quebec for the session of the assembly that began in January 1808, Hart had done his best to obtain legal opinions to guide his conduct regarding the oaths, but both the opinions he obtained were carefully worded and would not have given him much comfort. The first opinion, received in April 1807 immediately after his election, came from James Reid, who had been Hart's lawyer before he was elevated to the bench in 1805. In Reid's opinion the "distinctions and disabilities respecting the election of Members of Parliament in G. Britain and holding real property there do not extend to this Province in most instances ... and if the disabilities respecting the election of Members of the House of Assembly should hold in this Country as in England, it would never be permitted that a Judge could hold a seat in the House, because he is within the prohibition." The letter concluded: "there can be little doubt on the question you propose – Your right to be elected and sit as a Member of the House I consider to be equal to that of any other Member in it."[10] Reid's opinion had confirmed the current state of Britain's substantive law relating to its North American colonies. Reid had not, however, expressed any opinion on the actual procedure required for swearing oaths as a condition of holding office in Lower Canada or on whether the swearing of oaths in a Christian form was required in all cases within the province.

Towards the end of the year, Hart obtained a second opinion from Sir Vicary Gibbs, England's attorney general, through the assistance of a merchant firm in London that he had dealt with. Dated 24 September 1807, Gibbs's letter stated simply: "I see no legal objection to the eligibility of a Jew who was elected and sits in the House of Assembly after having taken the usual oaths."[11] The last six words were the pitfall. The usual oaths were, of course, the three state oaths, including the oath of abjuration and its phrase "upon the true Faith of a Christian." But Hart seems to have missed that crucial point, and even after his expulsion from the assembly he would write, in May 1808, of the opinion of the "Atty Genl Sir. V. Gibbs which is so positive in my favour."[12]

Armed with these legal opinions but unaware of the "State Oaths for Persons of the Jewish Persuasion," Hart stood at the bar of the House of Assembly on 29 January 1808. He had decided to swear only the secular oath of office, with his head covered according to Jewish practice. According to English law, of which Hart may have been aware, the *manner* of swearing the oath could not be contested as long as the official before whom the oath was sworn deemed it acceptable.[13]

On 1 February Michel-Amable Berthelot Dartigny, member for Quebec County and the one responsible for swearing in new members, reported to the house that when Hart had been sworn the previous Friday, he took the oath of office prescribed by the Constitutional Act, promising allegiance to the sovereign and ending with the words: "So help me God." He had sworn on the Pentateuch, his head covered. He had not sworn the state oaths, including the oath of abjuration. In Berthelot's words, "Ezekiel Hart, Esquire, had taken the Oath but not the Oaths."[14] When Berthelot said these words, members of the English party raised doubts. Jonathan Sewell, attorney general since 1795 and soon to be appointed chief justice of the province, pointed out the unusual omission of the state oaths. Sewell, trained in the British tradition, had scruples regarding Hart's ignoring of the customary oaths and moved "that it is the opinion of this House, that Ezekiel Hart, Esquire, returned to represent the Borough of Three-Rivers, hath not taken the Oath in the customary manner." Sewell's motion was seconded by Judge Pierre-Amable De Bonne and passed without dissent.[15]

Almost two weeks later, on 12 February, Hart petitioned the assembly, asking the house to allow him to take his seat. He confirmed that he had taken the oath prescribed by the Constitutional Act and was therefore entitled to take his seat, but this time he stated that he would "not object to have the Oath re-administered ... in the usual form." On 16 February the house considered Hart's petition and resolved "to enquire into the reasons for which Ezekiel Hart, Esquire, did not take the oath in the customary manner."[16] At this point, the French-Canadian majority, sensing a victory through the possible loss of an English seat, executed a display of legislative power unparalleled since the introduction of the elected assembly in 1792 and, for these reasons, moved to pre-empt the discussion of doubts about the validity of Hart's oath. The proceedings were about to move beyond scruples about the choice of the proper form of oath to the basic question of the right of a Jew to sit in the assembly of Lower Canada.

The main objective of Pierre-Stanislas Bédard, the leader of the French-Canadian party in the assembly, was to reduce the number of seats held by members of the opposing English party. His strategy was to concentrate a direct attack on Hart's right to sit in the assembly. His expectation was that the governor would not come to Hart's defence as much because of Britain's ambiguous undeclared policy on Jewish rights as because the question of expulsion of its members was a matter of the historic privilege of the assembly alone without the intervention of other levels of government.[17] Bédard exploited the doubts in British policy towards Jews, hoping the governor would not feel strongly enough about the issue to intervene. While shrewdly successful in the short term, Bédard's strategy of denying the legitimacy of others would have the long-term effect of aggravating cultural tensions with the resulting destabilization of the rights of the French Canadians themselves. The legal equality that the French Canadians had been granted by the British, while far short of perfect in practice, would be barely able to survive the new conflicts evoked by the Hart episode.

On 17 February the French-Canadian majority, now over the objections of the English party, rescinded the Sewell resolution of 1 February about taking the oath in the customary manner and passed a resolution authorizing the house to hold an inquiry to "receive information from the Members thereof, or any of them, touching their knowledge of the religious profession of Ezekiel Hart, Esquire." After deciding that Hart "is of the Jewish profession of religion," the house set aside 20 February for a debate on the resolution "that Ezekiel Hart, Esquire, professing the Jewish Religion, cannot take a seat, nor sit nor vote in this House."[18]

John Richardson, the member for Montreal West and spokesman for the Executive Council in the assembly,[19] led the defence of Hart's right to be seated in the assembly. During the debate on 20 February, he said that right could be inferred from the Plantation Act of 1740, which had provided that naturalization did not give rights to sit in parliament in England itself but otherwise gave naturalized Jews the rights of natural-born persons. The right of naturalized Jews to sit in a house of assembly in British North America had been confirmed by the law officers of the crown in 1792 and was beyond question. If naturalized Jews had that right, it would be absurd to deny the same right to their children who were natural-born Englishmen. In Richardson's opinion, the other issue – whether a Jew could take the state oaths – had also been decided by the Plantation Act which allowed Jews to amend the oath of abjuration to a form acceptable to them.

Bédard, speaking for the French-Canadian party, favoured the motion to expel Hart. He agreed that there was no problem in a Jew swearing the state oaths as long as the oaths were amended as allowed by the Plantation Act. But his view was that no statute explicitly authorized Jews to sit in the assembly. His position was that the Plantation Act dealt only with naturalized Jews, not natural-born Jews, and because naturalized Jews could have no higher rights than natural-born Jews, it was necessary to note that even in England natural-born

Jews had limited rights. Although Bédard showed some familiarity with English history, his legal reasoning became less tenable as his argument progressed. He explained to the house: "it was well known that before the Jews were driven from England [in 1290], they never enjoyed the rights of a citizen ... that since they were recalled by Oliver Cromwell they had been accorded no new privilege, and that they have remained at the discretion of the King ... That their condition was no better than in other Christian lands; that none accorded them the rights of a citizen; and that this was not rendering them an injustice, since they themselves do not wish to be citizens of any country. That they were dispersed in all countries because they had to be somewhere, but that they considered none of these as their own; that they lived in the land where they could carry on their business and that they only called it 'the land of their residence'; that they were bound by their faith to act thus; that they awaited the Messiah their Prince, and that, while waiting, they could pledge their fidelity to no other Prince than the one for whom they reserved it." From all this Bédard concluded that a Jew born in England or its colonies could have no right to sit in a parliament or an assembly and that a naturalized Jew could have no higher rights than a natural-born Jew.

Bédard knew the words, but he did not understand their significance. He had spoken not only against the rights of Jews but against the tradition of the country and ultimately against his own cultural group. In their own way, French-Canadian Catholics were as vulnerable as Jews. If the free and equal rights of Jews were not legitimate, could not the same reasoning apply to the rights of the Catholic French Canadians? In rebuttal, John Richardson stated that Bédard's reasoning was a sophism, "that it could follow therefrom that the rights of natural born Jewish subjects would thus be reduced to nothing."

When the debate ended, the majority of those present, by a vote of 21 to 5, resolved to exclude Hart because he was a Jew. The vote divided on largely cultural lines, with all the French-Canadian members opposing the seating of Hart as a perceived member of the English party and all the government's supporters rejecting the resolution. How ironic that exactly four days after this backward step in Lower Canada, the lieutenant governor of Upper Canada made the landmark decision that Moses David could file a bond instead of swearing the usual oaths which would have acted as a bar to his acceptance of the office of coroner.

What had happened to Ezekiel Hart was not in accordance with the laws of the province. He had been willing to take – indeed he had taken – the only oath of office legally required, namely, that prescribed by the Constitutional Act, a statute passed by Great Britain itself. He had been willing to swear his oath in whatever manner the assembly required. He had been denied his seat simply because the French-Canadian majority in the assembly had exercised its power arbitrarily to resolve that no Jew could sit in the house.

The resolution excluding Hart undoubtedly embarrassed the governor general, Sir James Craig, because the government party had supported Hart's attempt to be seated. But Bédard had estimated the situation shrewdly: the many inconsistencies in British policies regarding the seating of a Dissenter in an assembly made it difficult for Craig to come to Hart's defence. As the resolution of the assembly dealt with the qualifications of its members, it was doubly difficult for the governor. He could not disallow the resolution, as it was a question of privilege for the assembly alone, not a bill passed by the assembly to be approved by the upper house and submitted to the governor for approval. Short of dissolving the house and calling a new election, the governor's remedies were limited. Hart petitioned the governor general on 29 February, again setting out the facts in detail, but Sir James was not about to assist. Two weeks later, on 14 March, H.W. Ryland, the governor's secretary, officially responded to Hart's petition in a carefully worded sentence: "The Governor ... cannot think it expedient that he should interfere with the proceedings which The House of Assembly has thought proper to adopt in your case."[20] In the face of an objection to a policy of government on religious dissent, the governor was not about to exercise any discretion.

On 27 April, Craig dissolved the house and called a new election. The house had existed for almost four years and an election was required by law. Hart ran again in the election of 17 May 1808. He was again returned along with Joseph Badeaux. When the assembly met, on 10 April 1809, Hart was ready to try again to take his seat, but a new obstacle had appeared. The Executive Council had stated a case for judicial interpretation on the issue of whether a Jew could be sworn on the Pentateuch in taking the oath of office prescribed by the Constitutional Act. On 9 April, Judge Edward Bowen, unaware of the precedent of the use of "State Oaths for Persons of the Jewish Persuasion," handed down the opinion that the commissioners appointed to administer the oath of office to members of the assembly "are bound to administer that Oath in the Customary manner upon the Holy Evangelists, and not otherwise." A Jew, refusing to be so sworn, the judge ruled, might obtain a certificate from the commissioners setting out the facts of his attempt to take the oath according to the dictates of his own conscience. He might then ask the assembly "whether they should not admit the person to take the Oath according to the form of the religion he so professes."[21]

Hart was trapped. Bowen's position was probably contrary to British law which would have allowed Hart to swear an oath of office on the Old Testament.[22] There was no time for an appeal. Hart could hardly obtain the permission of the French-Canadian majority in the assembly to allow him to swear his oath as a Jew so that he could join the opposing English party! When his time came the next day to be sworn, he took the oath of office, this time kissing the "Holy Evangelists" or New Testament, as if he were a Christian, and then he took his seat.[23]

Hart continued to sit and vote in the assembly for several days. Then, on 17 April, the French-Canadian majority of the assembly again started proceedings to have him removed.[24] On 5 May 1809 the house resolved that since Hart professed the Jewish religion, "he cannot sit or vote in this House." For the second time in his political career, Hart was forced to withdraw. The vote was again split on cultural lines except that Thomas Coffin, one of the candidates whom Hart had defeated in the by-election in 1807 but who had been elected to represent Saint-Maurice in June 1808, joined the French party for the vote.[25]

The French party, led by Bédard, was not satisfied by Hart's withdrawal from the assembly. They immediately introduced a bill to ensure that Jews would not run for election to the assembly in the future, but this bill was disallowed by Craig as unconstitutional. Craig's law officers were of the opinion that he did not, however, have grounds to dissolve the house and call yet another election.

At this point, Craig asked his Executive Council for legal advice on the issue. A council committee of the whole reported on 9 May that the assembly had no power of expulsion where the member was legally qualified, as in the case of judges and of Jews who took the oath on the Christian Bible. The committee determined that Jews born in British colonies had the same rights as Jews naturalized under the Plantation Act of 1740 and that these rights had been continued under the Constitutional Act of 1791.[26] The opinion of the committee, chaired by Chief Justice Jonathan Sewell and including two judges among its six other members, must have carried considerable weight with Craig.[27] Even though the committee took pains to emphasize that it was *not* the duty of the governor to call an election on the basis of Hart's unjustified expulsion from the assembly, Craig did dissolve the assembly and call a new election only six days later, on 15 May 1809.

Each time the most senior officials in the colony had been faced with a decision about the legal status of Jews, they had opted for equality. Yet officials in England just as consistently denied that equality when given the opportunity.

Thus, four months later, on 7 September 1809, Lord Castlereagh, the colonial secretary, sent Craig a private dispatch, once again reinforcing the position of the mother country that Jews were not legally equal in Britain itself. Castlereagh noted that the expulsion of Hart was justified, apparently assuming (incorrectly) that the situation in Lower Canada as to eligibility was the same as in Britain. "With regard to the endeavours to expel Mr. Hart for being a Jew," he wrote, "it was obvious that a real Jew could not sit in the Assembly, as he could not take the oath upon the Gospels. [I]t was therefore competant [*sic*] to the Assembly to enquire whether Mr. Hart had complied with all such requisites as might be legally necessary to prove his bona fide conversion to Christianity and that he took the oaths without mental reservation."[28]

Hart again allowed his name to stand as a candidate in the general election of October 1809, but when it appeared he was running third, he withdrew.[29]

The Hart incident, and the French-Canadian party's continuing attempts to bar judges from sitting in the assembly to gain power, had contributed to the deteriorating relations between the French-Canadian party and the governor. And when the new assembly convened, a constitutional crisis ensued, although Hart played no part in it. The new assembly met in January 1810 and quickly passed a bill declaring judges ineligible to sit in the house. When the Legislative Council accepted the bill, but with an amendment protecting Judge De Bonne for the duration of that parliament, the assembly voted a separate resolution barring him. This was beyond its powers, and Craig again dissolved parliament and called yet another election – the third in as many years. In the following weeks Craig, denouncing the "sowers of sedition," seized the press of *Le Canadien*, arrested Bédard and other officials of the paper, filled the streets with armed patrols, and suspended the mail service. When the same French-Canadian members, including Bédard, were re-elected, Craig attempted to rule without calling the assembly into session and pressed the Colonial Office in London to repeal the provisions of the Constitutional Act of 1791 that had allowed an assembly to be created.[30]

The French-Canadian party, in attacking the legitimacy of others, had undermined its own. The concept of limiting the rights of Jews as religious dissenters that the French-Canadian party had initiated in its resolution to expel Hart, could not, in the long run, advance the cause of the French Canadians themselves.

In the next few years a number of related incidents occurred – coincidentally involving other men named Hart. Their effect was to inhibit the progress that Jews had earlier made in obtaining equal rights in Lower Canada.

In 1810, one Theodore Hart had come to Trois-Rivières and applied unsuccessfully to be licensed as a physician. A blood relationship to

the family of Aaron Hart has not been documented, but Theodore
Hart was closely associated with Ezekiel Hart and was apparently
Jewish.[31] Born in Prussia in 1782, he had studied "phisic" in Paris until
the French Revolution drove him to Berlin. He went to live with a
brother in Canterbury in 1797 and "in account of my proficiency in
the french language" was appointed surgeon to one of the prison
hospitals. He left England in 1802 and resided in New York until 1810,
when he came to Lower Canada, in his own words "at the solicitation
of my freinds [sic] at Three Rivers." Upon his arrival he applied for a
licence "to enable me to follow my profession in this country, more
particularly as this is the only means I have of supporting myself."[32]
With one possible exception, there had been no Jewish doctors in
British North America prior to this date, although there was no legal
impediment. Jewish physicians had been recorded in England as well
as in the Thirteen Colonies from the beginning of their settlement in
the seventeenth century. Levi Jacobs, second son of Samuel Jacobs and
Marie-Josette Audette of St Denis, had qualified as a surgeon before
1800, although records of any posts he held in that capacity are not
complete.[33] Jacobs does not appear to have lived as a Jew and he had
been baptized as John Levy Jacobs shortly after his birth in 1772, but
others may well have considered him Jewish.

Theodore Hart's examination in September was a disaster. He did
not have the certificates of all his qualifications. The examiner insulted
him and treated him with an obvious lack of respect. He applied for
a second examination, appealed simultaneously to the governor
asking for a ruling that the certificates he had were satisfactory, and
wrote his friend, Ezekiel Hart, hoping for assistance. He had no more
success on his second examination a few days later. After a lapse of
almost a month he learned that his petition to the governor had been
misdirected, and he was obliged to submit another.[34] Records of what
happened to Theodore Hart after that time are not available, but a
search of the Quebec almanacs indicates that he was never enrolled
as a physician in Lower Canada.[35]

In 1811 Benjamin Hart, the third son of Aaron Hart and younger
brother of Ezekiel, petitioned the governor for having been denied
his civil rights, alleging that he had been excluded from a commission
as an officer in the militia of Trois-Rivières "owing to the fact that he
was a Jew." Although Hart was unable to obtain redress, there may
have been reasons other than his religion for his lack of advancement.
Nathaniel Coffin, the commander of the militia, was the brother of
Thomas Coffin who had been defeated by Hart's brother, Ezekiel, in
the by-election of 1807 and may thus have held a personal resentment
against the younger brother. After all, Coffin had promoted Isaac

Phineas, another Jew, to ensign at about the same time. Even Benjamin Hart admitted that Phineas was "of the same Religious persuasion as your Memorialist," perhaps suggesting that Hart's own lack of advancement was not entirely "owing to the fact that he was a Jew." Many years later, on 11 January 1825, Hart was finally appointed a captain in the Montreal militia.[36]

From 1821 on, Moses Hart had been thwarted in his attempts to obtain a commission in the Trois-Rivières militia for his son, Areli Blake Hart. Finally, on 2 December 1826, the governor's secretary, A.W. Cochran, wrote to Hart explaining that "there are two inseparable objections to your son's getting a Commission the one arising from his Religion and the other his Natural incapacity rendering him an unfit person to hold such a commission."[37] Areli Blake Hart's commanding officer, Lieutenant-Colonel P.D. Courval,[38] was willing to recommend him for a commission in any event and put him on the list of officers to be approved by the adjutant general in Quebec. In June 1827 the adjutant general, Lieutenant-Colonel F. Vassal de Monviel, showed the list to the governor, Lord Dalhousie, who remarked: "Areli Hart is he not one of the family Hart of the Jew religion. [I]f so he cannot hold a commission." De Monviel wrote to Courval, telling him of the governor's words about Hart's lack of capacity and asking for Courval's assistance in replying to this remark as soon as possible. Courval gave de Monviel's letter to Moses Hart in an obvious gesture of support. There the matter rested.[39]

In a sense Dalhousie was following in the footsteps of John Elmsley, the chief justice of Upper Canada who had decided in 1797 that Jews could not hold land in that province. Both had been schooled in England and may not have appreciated the difference between the English and colonial approaches to civil and political rights for Jews. Dalhousie was perhaps also reflecting his personal experience: as a Scottish Presbyterian he had been obliged, as a condition of assuming the office of governor-in-chief, to "subscribe the Test" according to the rites of the Church of England.[40]

Vassal de Monviel was clearly shocked by Dalhousie's remark, however. He had served as adjutant general, the senior officer in the Lower Canada militia, since 1812 and had grown accustomed to winking at the British rules on appointments of Jews as officers in the military. Indeed, by the time of the War of 1812, the practice was already widespread, and almost every known Jewish family was represented in the militia. David David and Samuel David were appointed officers in the Montreal militia by 1807 and 1812 respectively.[41] Ezekiel Hart became an ensign in the Trois-Rivières militia by 1870 and a lieutenant by 1813.[42] Myer Michaels[43] and Isaac Phineas[44] were ensigns in the

Montreal and Trois-Rivières militias, respectively, by 1812. Eleazar Hays – known as Lazarus to his parents, Andrew and Abigail Hays – was quartermaster in the 1st Battalion of the Vaudreuil Division of the Montreal militia during the war.[45] Samuel Seixas, son of Gershom Mendes Seixas of New York's Shearith Israel Congregation, was quartermaster and sergeant in the Montreal militia.[46]

The Canadian colonies had continued to ignore the oath requirement for Jewish officers after the war ended. Ezekiel Hart received a commission as captain in the 1st Battalion of the Trois-Rivières militia in 1816; his brother, Benjamin, was appointed captain in the Montreal militia in 1825. Isaac Phineas received a commission as paymaster of the 2nd Battalion of the Saint-Maurice (Trois-Rivières) militia in 1827; Isaac Valentine received a commission as ensign in the 5th Battalion of the Montreal militia by 1828. Henry Joseph had become a captain in the Berthier militia by 1826.[47]

The new administration of Lower Canada was less welcoming for its Jews in the early years of the nineteenth century than the Old Province of Quebec had been. In 1791 Jews along with Protestant Dissenters had lost that status of equality that had allowed them appointments to offices and places of trust. Jews were facing an increasing number of incidents of prejudice based on their religion.

Reflecting the pattern in other places in which prejudice became more pronounced, it is not entirely surprising to find that during these years the Jewish congregation of Montreal ceased to function on a regular basis and the Jewish population did not increase. Many of the early settlers had died or moved away and their places were not taken by new arrivals. The synagogue in Montreal was no longer used, and it appears that those Jews who sought to maintain the customs of their faith once again looked to the Shearith Israel Congregation of New York.[48] Many were recorded as being in New York for the High Holidays. Between 1804 and 1814 their number included: Ben, Moses, and Alex Hart, three of the four sons of Aaron Hart; Sam Hart, son of Ezekiel Hart, Aaron's fourth son; Charlotte David, widow of Moses David of Sandwich, Upper Canada; Samuel David, Isaac Valentine, and Elkela (Seixas) Solomons of Montreal; "Levy of Canada"; Jacob Wm. Brinley of Kingston and Montreal; and Elizabeth Nathan.[49] During the same period, Lyon Jonas and his family returned from Montreal to New York.[50]

An old man, one of those strangers to the New York Shearith Israel Congregation who appeared at High Holiday services, made a donation in October 1804. The congregation's Sedaka records indicate that three donations were in fact made by Ezekiel Solomons during this period. Solomons, far from his home on Mackinac Island, had returned to the New York congregation after the collapse of the Montreal synagogue. As it turned out, that was the last record that Ezekiel Solomons left.[51]

There is evidence of at least one visit to Lower Canada in October and November 1811 by Gershom Mendes Seixas, hazzan of New York's congregation to minister to his extended flock.[52] According to his notes, Seixas performed four circumcisions: for Eleazar, son of Samuel David, in Montreal; Aaron Uri, son of Benjamin Hart, at Trois-Rivières; Abraham Kitsinger, son of Ezekiel Hart, at Trois-Rivières; and Benjamin Solomon, son of Henry Joseph at Berthier.

Despite the loss of an active synagogue during these less liberal times, some individual families continued to maintain an active Jewish life.

The David family had joined the Harts and the Josephs as the acknowledged leaders of Montreal Jewry during these years. In contrast to many of Lower Canada's early Jewish families, the children of Lazarus and Phoebe David all married Jews, save for the eldest, David David, who remained single. Under the latter's guidance, this extended family made their mark as an independent fur trading enterprise on the Great Lakes. Apart from a link with Quetton St George in York,[53] David David appears to have worked through his brother Moses, who was posted in the Detroit/Sandwich area from about 1791, and through his brother-in-law, Myer Michaels, who had been trading at Michilimackinac from about 1778 and who had married his sister, Frances or "Fanny," in 1793. David and Michaels were formally in partnership for two years from 1793, possibly informally thereafter. He may have relied on his brother Samuel at the headquarters in Montreal, and he may have secured trade goods and sold furs through his brother-in-law, Andrew Hays, the silversmith and merchant who had married his older sister, Abigail or "Brandele," in 1778. The family's fur trade business prospered, with Michaels and David and Samuel David all being elected members of the prestigious Beaver Club, and the business ultimately being sold to the North West Company.[54]

This closely knit family remained observant Jews despite the collapse of formal religious organization in Montreal. We catch two glimpses of Myer Michaels hurrying to Montreal by canoe from Mackinac Island to be with his family for the High Holidays. His brother-in-law, Samuel David, reported in 1802 that Michaels returned from the west on 22 September in time for Rosh Hashonah which began on the twenty-seventh. The following year, Samuel's diary records that "M. Michaels & Others arrived from Mackinac" on 5 September, in time for "Roshashona" on the seventeenth.[55] When David David died in 1824, he left a legacy to the synagogue in New York.[56]

Elizabeth Nathan, another member of Montreal's Jewish community, tried with difficulty to maintain links with synagogues in England.
By her will in 1819, she left £30 Currency "for the support of the
Jewish Sinagogue called Duke's Place in London in England;" but "in
Case should prior to her Decease a Jewish Sinagogue be reestablished
in Montreal then that the said sum or bequest of £30 shall go to and
be paid to the said Sinagogue at Montreal."[57]

The family of Henry and Rachel Joseph was another of the three
or four Jewish families in British North America in this period who
were able to maintain their faith in the absence of a thriving Jewish
community. Henry Joseph was born in England in 1775 and arrived
in Berthier, Lower Canada, about 1790, joining his older brother
Judah who had immigrated at least four years earlier. With Judah until
June 1805 and afterwards by himself, Henry Joseph successfully carried on business as general merchant in Berthier. On 28 September
1803 he married Rachel, the daughter of the late Levy Solomons, the
Montreal fur trader, at Berthier in the absence of a functioning synagogue in Montreal. The ceremony was performed by Barnet Lyon of
nearby Petit Rivière-du-Loup and was witnessed by Joseph's two brothers and their wives, by the bride's mother, brother, and sister who had
come from Montreal, by Lyon's son, and by Solomon Benjamin of
Montreal. As was characteristic of observant Jewish families of the
period, the five of Rachel and Henry Joseph's thirteen children who
married all married Jews. The others remained single. Henry Joseph
died in June 1832 during the cholera epidemic in Montreal.[58]

The much smaller Jewish community at Trois-Rivières had similarly
declined in this period, with few of the Hart, Judah, Phineas, or Lyon
families remaining.[59] By 1824 the High Holiday services for the few
Jews in Montreal were held at the residence of Benjamin Hart,[60] who
had himself moved to Montreal. Despite the continuance of community life among some of those who remained, one Montreal Jew would
write in 1826 that "the old Synagogue ... is now a common store, or
receptacle for all pollution, and in the hands of strangers, to the great
disgrace of our Holy Religion."[61]

Unlike the events of 1808 and 1809 when the French Canadians
had denied Jewish equality, by the 1830s it was French Canadians who
came to the rescue of Lower Canada's Jewish community in its search
for equality. The Lower Canada assembly was still divided into English
and French parties, but the French-Canadian political outlook had
evolved since the debates on Ezekiel Hart's expulsions in 1808 and
1809. To gain political advantage in the debates at that time, the
leaders of the French Canadians had been willing to attack representatives of a disadvantaged religious sect that was seen as an ally of the

British and had allowed the government to act as the group's indignant defender. Twenty years later, however, although the French Canadians were still trying to gain political advantage, their tactics had undergone a significant change. The French-Canadian majority in the assembly had now taken on the role of champion of disadvantaged religious sects against the ruling clique, the Anglican establishment, personified in the appointed Legislative and Executive Councils.

Until the 1830s, for example, only Anglicans, Roman Catholics, and some Presbyterians had the legal right to require their adherents to register vital statistics in Lower Canada. This put Protestant Dissenters at a distinct disadvantage because the rights of dissenting clergy legally to solemnize marriages, administer baptisms, and bury the dead were thereby open to question. In 1825, over the strenuous opposition of the Anglican members of the assembly, the French-Canadian majority passed a bill to give relief to Wesleyan Methodists. The bill was watered down by the Legislative Council in 1827 but still failed to obtain royal assent.[62]

The matter of relief for the Methodists and other dissenting Protestant sects was introduced again at the end of 1828 and supported by the French-Canadian Catholic majority in the assembly. Bills were introduced for the relief of the American Presbyterians at Montreal and for a dissenting congregation of Presbyterians at Quebec, for the relief of Wesleyan Methodists, and for the relief of other Protestant Dissenters. A bill to allow public registers for persons of the Jewish faith was introduced in the assembly at the end of 1828 and passed the following February. It was reserved by the governor, along with the re-enacted Wesleyan Methodist Relief Bill, and both measures failed to receive royal assent. All the relief bills were then re-introduced in 1830 and approved by both the assembly and the Legislative Council.[63]

On 4 December 1828, a "Petition of certain Israelites of the District of Montreal" was presented to Lower Canada's House of Assembly asking for the right to register vital statistics on public registers and for the legal right to hold land for places of burial and for the erection of a place of worship.[64] The petition set out that persons professing the Jewish faith "are by the present laws of the Province of Lower Canada deprived of the benefits of Public Registers to record the Births, Marriages, and Deaths which occur among them." It referred as well to the cloud on the title to the communal cemetery used by Jews in Montreal for the past fifty years, stating that the petitioners were incapable of holding land for a "place of interment for their deceased relations and friends" as they had no religious corporate body.[65]

The assembly, led by its French-Canadian majority, lost little time in attempting to implement the requests of the Jewish petitioners. A bill to allow public registers for persons of the Jewish faith was introduced on 13 December 1828 and was passed by the assembly and Legislative Council the following February. It was however regarded as contentious by the governor, was reserved for the consideration of the British government, and failed to gain approval. The Jews' relief bill was reintroduced by the assembly, again led by its French-Canadian majority, in 1830 and was passed and approved with an amendment by the Legislative Council on 11 March 1830. It was proclaimed in force on 18 January 1831.[66]

Having now addressed equal Jewish civil rights, the French-Canadian majority turned to redressing the balance of Jewish political rights. Three weeks later, on 7 February 1831, Samuel B. Hart, following in the footsteps of his father, Ezekiel, and joined by a large number of "persons professing the Jewish religion," petitioned the assembly, asking that any remaining disabilities of Jews to hold office be removed. He set out the fact that "the disabling Laws of England" had never been introduced into Canada; that "Persons professing the Jewish religion are excluded from office in a manner very public and mortifying"; and that he could not "continue in silence without forfeiting every claim to his own esteem."[67] In a very direct appeal, Samuel B. Hart was asking the elected assembly, with its French-Canadian majority, for help against "the illegal acts of the Colonial Executive" in denying status to the small Jewish group.

The timing of Hart's petition was fortunate because the act allowing the Jewish community to keep registers of vital statistics was just being proclaimed. On 19 March 1831, a bill was presented in the assembly in response to Hart's petition to declare the equality of persons professing the Jewish religion. The bill was passed unanimously by the assembly. It was approved without amendment by the Legislative Council on 29 March, again without dissent, and reserved by the governor at the end of the month for approval by the British government. It secured royal assent on 12 April 1832. The act was a *declaratory* act, passed to resolve doubts that "have arisen whether persons professing the Jewish Religion are by law entitled to many of the privileges enjoyed by the other subjects of His Majesty within this Province." It provided "that all persons professing the Jewish Religion being natural born British subjects inhabiting and residing in this Province, are entitled … to the full rights and privileges of the other subjects of His Majesty."[68]

The Declaratory Act attracted little notice at the time. Lower Canada was the only one of the provinces of British North America to have passed a specific declaration of this nature, but then Lower Canada was the only province to have raised doubts as to the legal status of natural-born Jews as equal citizens in the first place. In that sense, it was an apology by the majority in the assembly. It righted a wrong done to the Jewish minority twenty-five years earlier when the small Jewish community was a casualty in the French Canadians' drive for power. The French-Canadian majority in the assembly had become an ally of the Dissenters in the struggle for the equality of all religious groups.

The Jews of Lower Canada had had their forty years in the wilderness. The equal rights they had enjoyed from the beginning in the Old Province of Quebec that had been questioned since 1791 were now being returned to them – in practice as colonial officials increasingly ignored the governor's instructions, and in law as the French-Canadian majority in the assembly began to champion their cause. Yet questions about the true significance of the Declaratory Act were raised even before its passage. Although the act has been hailed by recent commentators as "the very cornerstone of this country's religious and political freedoms,"[69] it was purely declaratory. It did not amend the state oaths. Nor did it remove the requirement of compliance with the Test Act by taking the Anglican sacrament and subscribing the declaration against transubstantiation. The attitude of the Colonial Office – as represented by the governor of the colony – was still one of enhanced status for Anglicans and mere toleration of others.

A response was certainly required but it could not come from one person or one religious group. It would take a collective effort of the dissenters of British North America, composing overall a large majority of the population, to make their will known to the British authorities. The people of the British colonies in the New World knew that they wanted equality for all religions. As "responsible government" became a reality, that equality became undeniable.

14 Colonial Legislatures and the Demise of the State Oaths and the Declaration, 1820–1860

> You shall also administer or cause to be administered the [State] Oaths mentioned in Our said Commission to all Persons ... that shall be appointed to hold or exercise any Office, Place of Trust or Profit in Our said Province, previous to their entering on the Duties of such Office, and you shall also cause them to make and subscribe to the aforesaid Declaration [against transubstantiation as set out in the Test Act of 1673].
>
> Instructions to Lord Dalhousie as governor-in-chief of Upper and Lower Canada, 13 April 1820, incorporated as standing instructions to the governors of Upper and Lower Canada, 1820–40

By 1822 Laurence Kavanaugh controlled a significant portion of the commerce of Cape Breton Island; at the age of fifty-eight, he had reached his prime as a businessman.[1] He had never been appointed to high office despite his status, but in the elections of November 1820 he had become the first Roman Catholic elected to the Nova Scotia Assembly. On 20 February 1822 he claimed his seat.

It was not unusual for a Roman Catholic to be elected to office in Upper or Lower Canada, but there had been no Catholic members of an assembly in any of Britain's Maritime colonies in North America. At the time of the Quebec Act of 1774, Britain had given French-Canadian Catholics in Lower Canada civil rights equal to those of Protestants, and Catholics had formed the majority in the elected assembly of that province since its introduction in 1792. In Upper Canada as well, Catholic members had been elected to the first assembly in 1792 and one of them, John Macdonnell, had even been chosen speaker. The Constitutional Act of 1791 had provided one simple oath of allegiance, designed to be acceptable to any group, and the instructions to the governors in the provinces of Upper and Lower Canada had enabled Catholics to take seats in the assemblies by omitting any requirement for members to make and subscribe the declaration against transubstantiation.

In the Maritime colonies, however, the requirement of making and subscribing the declaration remained in the governors' instructions long after it had obliged Samuel Hart to become baptized in 1793. Indeed, the instructions to Lord Dalhousie as "Governor in Chief of Nova Scotia and the Islands of St John [Prince Edward Island] and Cape Breton," dated 27 April 1820, had continued to provide that the governor was to cause the state oaths to be administered to, and the declaration to be made and subscribed by, members of the assembly,[2] with the result that not only Jews but Roman Catholics and Protestant Dissenters were "disabled" from becoming members. Thus even though a majority of the population in Newfoundland and Cape Breton was Catholic, there had been no attempt to extend to them the rights offered to their co-religionists in the Canadas.

The enjoyment of equal rights by Roman Catholics in Upper and Lower Canada was a unique situation in British territory. The British government did not allow Catholics in Nova Scotia, New Brunswick, Prince Edward Island, or Newfoundland any greater rights than Catholics had in Britain itself. There, the Roman Catholic Relief Act of 1791 had officially sanctioned public worship by Catholics but the "disabling" requirements for participation in politics or holding office remained in place.

Kavanaugh had waited almost eighteen months after his election before presenting himself to take his seat, a period that had allowed Lieutenant Governor Sir James Kempt time to attempt to negotiate a reduction of the oath requirement with the Colonial Office. Kempt's pro-active role in attempting to accommodate change may have been dictated by the reality that Cape Breton, a separate province ruled by a governor and council from 1784, had an overwhelmingly Catholic population and had been annexed to Nova Scotia in 1820 as an alternative to being granted a separate assembly.[3] Kempt, of Presbyterian origins, had been obliged to take the Anglican sacrament and make the declaration against transubstantiation on assuming the office of lieutenant governor, and appears to have had a particular sensitivity to Kavanaugh's predicament.[4] Now, with Kavanaugh standing before him, the lieutenant governor asked whether he would take the oaths and make and subscribe the declaration. Kavanaugh agreed to take the oaths but not the declaration.[5] Acting in accordance with the instructions he had received, Kempt refused to allow him to take his seat. In a pattern that was becoming all too familiar, Kavanaugh, like Philip Dorland, the Quaker, and Ezekiel Hart, the Jew, was barred from taking his seat because of his refusal to make a declaration contrary to the dictates of his religion.

As Kavanaugh watched from the sidelines, an epic battle began. The elected representatives of the people were ready to fight for the equal society they had come to know. The Old World forces that had kept an empire under British control, doling out tolerance as required, were prepared for a protracted assault. Kavanaugh's predicament occupied the attention of both houses of the Nova Scotia legislature for several days. A majority in the assembly, opposing any restrictions against Roman Catholics, attempted to pass a bill to abolish the declaration against transubstantiation as a prerequisite for office. The Legislative Council refused to pass the assembly's bill. In the message it sent to the assembly, the council agreed that the general emancipation of Catholics from civil disabilities "would not be attended with any evil consequences, but would, on the contrary, tend to preserve that harmony which now so happily prevails among His Majesty's Subjects of all religious denominations in this Province." Nevertheless, the message ran, "His Majesty might not think it decorous in the Legislature to pass a general Act in direct violation of His Majesty's Instructions, without any previous communication with His Majesty's Government on so important a subject." The message concluded with the suggestion that while the council could not support a general bill emancipating Catholics, it would "most willingly concur" in one that admitted Kavanaugh specifically to a seat in the assembly – and added the warning that "the liberal views of the friends of the Roman Catholics might be frustrated by attempting too much for them in the first instance."[6]

The members of the assembly remained adamant in their refusal to do anything less than remove all the disabilities against all Catholics in the province. On 2 March, the assembly therefore responded with a resolution stating that they were "fully aware" that the bill they had passed violated the governor's instructions. A specific bill to admit the member for Cape Breton to his seat had been "duly considered by the House and dismissed." The assembly said it could not be "induced to legislate on terms which are less general than are comprehended in the Bill now before His Majesty's Council."[7] To resolve the impasse, the council asked the assembly to join it in an address to the lieutenant governor requesting him to ascertain whether his instructions could be modified to permit the enactment of a statute emancipating Roman Catholics. The house, refusing any compromise on the principle of equality, declined to join the council "in any Address on the subject."[8]

By the end of the week, the council had nonetheless prepared its own address to the lieutenant governor.[9] It started by acknowledging that Roman Catholics are "excluded from sitting in the Legislature or holding any post under Government, as they cannot conscientiously make the Declaration against Popery and Transubstantiation" required by the governor's instructions. The council went on to agree that restrictions against Catholics may once have been necessary, saying that the "Council are convinced that in the early settlement of this Province it was necessary to confine all such situations and offices to Protestants, in order to secure the exclusion of the French Inhabitants from power who at that time gave too many proofs of their hostility to His Majesty's Government." But that, the address continued, was all in the past; "the situation of the Country is now widely different." The province was largely settled with immigrants from Great Britain, many of whom were Catholics, and "the principles of Religious toleration which prevail so extensively in this Province have been very instrumental in advancing its population and prosperity." As a result, the council asked the lieutenant governor to ascertain from the Colonial Office whether his instructions could be amended "in such manner as to admit Roman Catholics who are willing to take the State Oaths into the Legislature to practice at the Bar and to hold offices under Government without making the Declaration against Popery and Transubstantiation." The view of the council, set out in this address, was that the principles of limited toleration had been instrumental in developing the province and should now be extended. The demand of the elected assembly, however, proceeded from an entirely different principle: the idea of religious equality.

By the time the legislature resumed sitting a year later, Kavanaugh had still not taken his seat although it had been almost three years since his election. In the interval, the Colonial Office had responded that the legislature was given authority to admit Kavanaugh without requiring him to make the declaration against transubstantiation.[10] But there was to be no general emancipation of Roman Catholics. The assembly again debated Kavanaugh's position on 3 April 1823 and again refused to concede defeat. A motion to admit Kavanaugh without referring to the larger question of emancipation was lost on a tie vote. Finally, the house passed a resolution to admit Kavanaugh with the additional promise that it "will, in future, permit Roman Catholics who may be duly elected to take such seat without making the Declaration against Popery and Transubstantiation."[11] This resolution, although it allowed Kavanaugh to take his seat, was of dubious legality because it was a resolution rather than a bill. By choosing to treat the seating of Kavanaugh as a question of privilege, the assembly had avoided putting a bill dispensing with the declaration on transubstantiation in front of the lieutenant governor for his assent because it was clear that such a bill would still have been contrary to his instructions.[12]

Kempt subsequently tried to convince the Colonial Office that article 3 of his instructions should be changed. He argued that "His Majesty having been pleased, in the case of the Member returned for the County of Cape Breton, to dispense with his making the Declaration against Popery and Transubstantiation, I am induced to recommend that the like indulgence be extended to all those who shall in future be elected as Representatives under similar circumstances."[13] The recommendation, which would have permitted Catholics and Protestant Dissenters to be seated in the assembly, was disregarded. The governors of Nova Scotia and Prince Edward Island continued to be instructed to oblige members of the assemblies to make and subscribe the declaration.[14] With the exception of Laurence Kavanaugh, only Anglicans could serve in the assemblies.

The state oaths and the declaration against transubstantiation had been the invention of Britain to meet British concerns. They had eventually been extended to British North America as an instrument of colonial policy. The requirement of making and subscribing the declaration against transubstantiation had been instituted through the governors' instructions from the beginning of British rule in the Maritime colonies for both members of the assembly and office holders and from 1791 in Upper and Lower Canada for office holders. After the use of the state oaths had been declared mandatory throughout the empire by the act of 1766, many of those in the colonial governments had used every opportunity – on an ad hoc basis – to avoid the consequences of the oaths and the declaration and to give relief to those who would otherwise have been disqualified by their enforcement. By 1820, with the British requirements in no way diminished, the colonies were no longer satisfied with relying on official discretion to avoid the state oaths and the declaration, and thereby exempt non-Anglicans from their operation on an individual basis, and had begun to agitate for the direct abolition of the oaths and the declaration.

In 1828 the parliament of Great Britain passed the Sacramental Tests Repeal Act amending the Test Act of 1673 so that it no longer operated to exclude Protestant Dissenters from office in England. The amended act was carefully worded such that it would continue to create a disability for Roman Catholics and Jews. The act repealed only so much of the Test Act as linked the making of the declaration against transubstantiation to the taking of a sacrament according to the rites of the Church of England. In this way Protestant Dissenters could make and subscribe the declaration without being obliged to be baptized as Anglicans. Roman Catholics could not, of course, make the declaration against transubstantiation because it was a denial of a central tenet of their faith. Finally, the act of 1828 introduced a new declaration requiring office holders to swear not to use any influence they might possess to "injure or weaken" the Church of England. However this new declaration continued to disable Jews in England because the words "upon the true faith of a Christian" were included in the body of the declaration. The only benefit of the act as far as Jews in England were concerned was that naval and military officers below the ranks of rear admiral and major-general and persons engaged in customs or the post office were expressly exempted from the necessity of making a declaration.[15]

The next year parliament gave Catholics complete civil and political equality with Protestants in England under the Roman Catholic Relief Act (1829). Those British North American colonies that had not already granted equality to Catholics now proceeded to do so with despatch in accordance with the instructions of the Colonial Office. In 1830, Nova Scotia, Prince Edward Island, and New Brunswick all passed Catholic emancipation acts which essentially adopted the imperial statute.[16]

Newfoundland was in a different position from the other colonies because it had no assembly but was still ruled by a governor sent from Britain. Unfortunately for Roman Catholics on the island, the law officers of the crown gave the opinion that the Roman Catholic Relief Act passed in Britain in 1829 did not apply to Newfoundland "and that consequently the Roman Catholic Inhabitants of it must remain under all the Civil disabilities which had been enforced on them by the King's Instructions to the Governors until those Instructions shall have been rescinded by new ones under the Great Seal or by an Act of Parliament passed expressly for that purpose." In the face of "considerable irritation and angry feeling" manifested by Roman Catholics in Newfoundland, Lord Goderich, the colonial secretary, was pressed to concede to the acting governor of the island in May 1832 that under the new commission and instructions being issued to Sir Thomas Cochrane as governor, Roman Catholics resident in Newfoundland would be relieved "from all the Civil disabilities to which they were previously subject."[17]

Roman Catholic relief whether by statute or by the instructions to the governor did not amount to a general repeal of the requirements for swearing the state oaths or making the declaration against transubstantiation as set out in the Test Act of 1673. Roman Catholic relief amounted to a removal of the Test Act requirements for Catholics and an amended oath of office that would not be objectionable to them. The impediments for Jews remained.

Jamaica was the first of Britain's American colonies to attempt to remove the disabilities for Jews which were linked to the state oaths. Between 1826 and 1830 it passed three statutes giving relief to Jews, but British officials prevented each in turn from coming into effect. The first was "An Act to entitle Jews born within the ligence of the King to the rights and privileges of other natural born subjects." It provided for an amendment to the state oaths for Jews as well as exempting Jews from the requirement of making the declaration under the Test Act. This act passed the assembly and the council and was assented to on 22 December 1826, but it was subsequently disallowed by the Colonial Office. In 1828 the assembly passed a more limited act which would allow Jews to take the benefit of alteration of the oath of abjuration allowed under the Plantation Act. This attempt was also disallowed. Two years later the assembly passed a third act, this time "repealing the clauses disabling Jews from being elected members of the Corporation of Kingston and for removing all doubts as to their right of enjoying all the other privileges and advantages of His Majesty's other natural born subjects." Again the act was disallowed.[18]

In 1831 Jamaica passed a fourth statute for the relief of its Jewish minority, amending only the wording of the oath of abjuration.[19] The statute was passed by the assembly on 2 November and by the council on 3 November. The act was signed into law by the governor, apparently without reference to his instructions, even though the new act was in direct conflict with the imperial act of 1766, which had required that the form of oath of abjuration used in Britain be the one used in "his Majesty's Dominions, and no other." The act had apparently been passed to take account of the situation of Alexander Bravo, who had been appointed magistrate and assistant judge of the Court of Common Pleas for the parish of Clarendon on 27 October 1831 and who had been elected to the assembly but had not yet taken his seat.[20] Once the act was signed, Bravo became the first Jew to take a seat in an assembly in any English jurisdiction.

Prince Edward Island, perhaps inadvertently, became the second of the British American colonies to remove one of the disabilities for Jews, even though no Jews were known to be living on the island at the time. In 1830 the legislature passed a bill to abolish the state oaths entirely as a requirement for voting in elections or serving as a member of the assembly. It provided instead secular oaths for both voters and members of the assembly. The act was given assent by the governor on 6 February 1832. The requirement that colonial officials subscribe to the declaration under the terms of the Test Act remained in the governor's instructions, however, so that in fact no Jew could assume any office or place of trust, even as member of the assembly.[21]

Upper Canada was next to challenge the state oaths and declaration requirements for holding public office. A bill had been introduced in its assembly on 31 January 1831 to remove the last legal barriers to public office for Jews, Quakers, and other Dissenters. The bill passed the following year as "An Act to dispense with the necessity of taking certain Oaths and making certain Declarations in the cases therein mentioned; and also to render it unnecessary to receive the Sacrament of the Lord's Supper as a qualification for offices or for other temporal purposes." The Upper Canada Oaths Act received royal assent on 13 February 1833.[22] By this act, Upper Canada did not merely amend the imperial act of 1766 by replacing the state oaths, but it became the first of the British colonies in America to dispense with the declaration against transubstantiation and the requirement of taking the sacrament according to the rites of the Church of England.[23] The state oaths and the declaration were henceforth not to be required in Upper Canada for appointments "to any office in this Province, Civil or Military," for any person becoming "a Mayor or other Officer or Member of any Corporation therein,"[24] or for persons admitted or called as barristers or attorneys.

Instead, section 1 of the act provided a secular oath of allegiance for those assuming those positions: "I, A.B. do sincerely promise and swear that I will be faithful and bear true Allegiance to His Majesty King William, (or the Reigning Sovereign for the time being,) as lawful Soverign [sic] of the United Kingdom of Great Britain and Ireland and of this Province dependent on, and belonging to the said Kingdom, and that I will defend Him to the utmost of my power against all traitorous conspiracies or attempts whatsoever which shall be made against His Person, Crown or Dignity; and that I will do my utmost endeavour to disclose and make known to His Majesty, His Heirs or Successors, all treasons or traitorous conspiracies and attempts which I shall know to be against Him ar any of them; and all this I do swear without any equivocation, mental evasion or secret reservation, and renouncing all pardons and dispensations from any person or power whatsoever to the contrary. – So help me God." The act did not mention a secular oath for members of the assembly because that matter had been covered by the Constitutional Act.

Even though Upper Canada had previously found ways to appoint Jews and Dissenters to public office – by relying on the governor's discretion in waiving the declaration requirement for "unimportant" offices or by accepting a bond in lieu of the state oaths and declaration, as when Moses David was appointed coroner by commission in 1808 – all such restrictions were now removed by legislation. Instructions to governors continued to require the state oaths and the declaration as a condition of being appointed to office,[25] although that portion of the instructions was contrary to the Upper Canada Oaths Act. In the event, the instructions were treated as superseded except in the area of appointment of legislative and executive councillors which remained – at least for a few years – a royal prerogative not affected by the statute.

It may be more than coincidence that two Jews interested in careers in the civil service, George Benjamin and John Joseph, came to Upper Canada shortly after the passage of the Oaths Act in 1833.

George Benjamin of Belleville single-handedly tested almost all the political rights available in British North America on behalf of Jews. Born Moses Cohen in 1799 to a family of strong Jewish commitment in Brighton, England, Benjamin had arrived in Toronto, Upper Canada, in 1834 with his fourteen-year-old Jewish wife, Isabella Jacobs of New Orleans, and a new baby. His brother had challenged the restrictive system in England during the debates on the Great Reform Bill of 1832 through his *Brighton Guardian*. Two of his brothers-in-law had set precedents in England in holding elective and appointed offices. From his position as publisher and editor of the *Belleville Intelligencer*, which he founded in August 1834, Benjamin set out on a career that would bring him many of the offices that had been denied to Jews and others in British jurisdictions for centuries. His election as clerk of Thurlow township in 1836 made him the first Jew elected to municipal office in British North America. He was an officer in the militia during the 1837 Rebellion. By 1846 he had also served as clerk of Belleville, received commissions as a notary public, obtained an appointment as registrar of deeds for Hastings County, and been appointed to a number of other offices. He was elected warden of Victoria District in 1847 and warden of Hastings County in 1851. In 1850 he had been elected reeve of Hungerford township in Hastings, becoming the first Jewish reeve of a Canadian municipality. In 1854 he was elected chairman of the Belleville School Board. In October 1856, at the peak of his career, Benjamin was elected to the legislature of the province of Canada in the by-election for North Hastings, Canada West. When he took his oath of office in February 1857, he became the first Jew seated in a legislature in British North America. Before his retirement in 1863, he was offered a position as minister of the crown in the cabinet of John Sandfield Macdonald.[26]

Although Benjamin was not an observant Jew and lived in much the same manner as his Christian neighbours, neither was he a Christian. He maintained some tenuous links with his religion as had the Marranos of the past. In spite of outward appearances, the fact that

Benjamin was a Jew was well known to his contemporaries and did nothing to diminish his exceptional popularity. Like Samuel Hart in Nova Scotia years earlier, he was a casualty of his own efforts. His valiant attempts to win equality resulted in precedents for others but personal tragedy for himself. While he died in poverty, almost forgotten, his achievements stand to the credit of all who value the struggle for civil and political equality.

John Joseph, described as "a Jewish English civil servant,"[27] arrived in Upper Canada in December 1835 as the civil secretary to the new lieutenant governor, Sir Francis Bond Head.[28] Joseph, who had served as private secretary to William Wilberforce and as a clerk in the Colonial Office in England, was recalled by William Lyon Mackenzie as "an awkward and loutish lad who opened the door and handed a chair."[29] Doomed to remain in a menial position in the British government because of his religion, in 1833 he joined a number of other Jews "earnestly desirous to obtain enfranchisement" in petitioning a member of parliament for the removal of disabilities.[30] By 1835 it was clear that the British government was taking no action to remove disabilities for potential Jewish office holders and Joseph decided to come to Upper Canada, where similar disabilities had been removed two years earlier.

In Upper Canada Joseph was not actively involved in Jewish life and quickly became part of the local social establishment through a close friendship he formed with the chief justice, John Beverley Robinson. In July 1837 he married Anne Elizabeth, daughter of Christopher Hagerman, attorney general of the province. He remained Head's secretary during the rebellion of 1837 and for a short period he continued as secretary to his successor, Sir George Arthur. After the death of Joseph's wife in June 1838, Arthur arranged for him to be transferred to the clerkship of the Legislative Council, a position he held until it disappeared with the Act of Union in 1840. He later served as the clerk of the Executive Council of the province of Canada from 1847 until his death in 1851.

In Lower Canada, despite the flexible practice of the early governor, Guy Carleton, Jews had been effectively excluded from civil offices or places of trust from 1791 until 1832 when the Colonial Office secured royal assent to the declaratory act passed by the assembly the previous year. Despite that act's statement that Jews should have the same rights and privileges as the king's other natural-born subjects, the state oaths remained in place, and a question remained as to whether the Declaratory Act of 1832 would be accepted as overriding the necessity for taking the state oaths and making the declaration against transubstantiation under the Test Act.

The matter of becoming a lawyer in Lower Canada illustrates the issue. On 30 November 1824, Ezekiel Hart's son, Aaron Ezekiel Hart, had completed his training as a "Barrister, Advocate, Proctor, Solicitor and Counsel" in Lower Canada,[31] becoming the first lawyer of the Jewish faith in British North America.[32] One of the requirements for being granted a commission in Lower Canada was that the applicant swear the oath of abjuration. The younger Hart, obviously aware of the debates in the Lower Canada Assembly fifteen years earlier, swore the standard oath "upon the true Faith of a Christian" along with the rest of his colleagues.[33] Some years later, however, Aaron Philip Hart, a professing Jew and son of Benjamin Hart, who was admitted to the practice of law in Lower Canada on 28 December 1830,[34] and Eleazar David David, also a professing Jew, who was admitted to practice in 1832,[35] do not appear to have been required to swear the oath of abjuration in the Christian form.

The death of George IV in 1830 meant that all commissions issued by the deceased king came to an end unless reissued. A printed circular was therefore sent to a number of citizens in the province asking whether they were qualified to be appointed as commissioners of the peace. Samuel Becancour Hart, eldest son of Ezekiel Hart, received the circular in Trois-Rivières and responded on 28 July 1830 that he had "no objections to act as a magistrate for this district and can qualify as such." On 19 October, however, the secretary to the administrator, then Sir James Kempt, wrote to Hart advising him that Kempt intended to omit Hart's name because "a person professing the Jewish Faith cannot take the Oath of Qualification and consequently ought not to be included in the Commission."[36] This created a potential crisis for the Jews of Lower Canada in their relationship with the administration of the colony. Once again, the state oaths were being used by high officials in the province to bar Jews from positions to which they were entitled by law.

It was in fact this incident that had prompted Samuel B. Hart and a large number of "persons professing the Jewish religion" to petition the Lower Canada Assembly the following February, asking that any remaining disabilities of Jews to hold office be removed, asking the elected assembly, with its French-Canadian majority, for help against "the illegal acts of the Colonial Executive" in denying status to Jews. In response to Hart's petition of 7 February, a bill to declare the equality of Jews was presented in the assembly on 19 March 1831 and was passed unanimously by both the assembly and the council. After being reserved by the governor for approval by the British government, the act (commonly called the Declaratory Act of 1832) secured royal assent a year later, on 12 April 1832.[37]

What was becoming clear as the terrible memory of the expulsion of Ezekiel Hart from the assembly receded was that the Jews of Lower Canada increasingly owed their equality to the French Canadians rather than to the British. It had been the French-Canadian leaders of the militia who had tried to assist Areli Blake Hart when his promotion was denied by Dalhousie. It was the French-Canadian majority in the assembly who had passed a special act declaring the equality of Jews in order to overcome the governor's objection to Samuel B. Hart's appointment as a justice of the peace. When government officials blocked their way, Jews began to turn to the French Canadians for help, and they were not disappointed.

Even before the act of 1832 was in force, the government changed its position and appointed a Jew as justice of the peace, notwithstanding the decision of 1830 regarding Samuel B. Hart. On 31 December 1831, nine months after the Declaratory Act had been passed but ten weeks before it received royal assent, Eleazar David David was made a justice of the peace.[38] David's appointment manifested a clear change in policy, resulting from the government's acceptance of the Declaratory Act in response to the assembly's initiative.

More serious questions about the exact meaning of the Declaratory Act of 1832 were raised soon after it had obtained royal assent. On 24 April 1833, a new list of candidates for the office of justice of the peace was prepared by the governor-in-chief's office. It included the names of Samuel B. Hart, Benjamin Hart, and Moses Judah Hays of Montreal. Even though no change in the governor's instructions had been made (or would be for some years), the opinion of the attorney general, Charles Richard Ogden, was that "as all doubts had been removed by the Act, he had thought fit to name the Jewish men from Montreal."[39] Ironically, questions about the meaning of the act were raised by Aaron Philip Hart, Benjamin's son, rather than by any official of the province. On 31 May 1833 he advised his father and Moses Judah Hays that he was "decidedly convinced that persons professing the Jewish faith cannot take the Oath of Abjuration necessary to be taken by the Justices of the Peace until some legislative enactment be made, providing for the omission in the Abjuration Oath of the words in question" and that the act of 1832 "has not in any way provided for the omission of the words 'upon the true faith of a Christian' in taking the oath of abjuration by Jews of the province."[40] Benjamin Hart and Moses Judah Hays therefore withdrew their names, citing Aaron Philip's legal opinion as justification.[41]

Even though Aaron Philip Hart was a young and inexperienced lawyer,[42] his legal opinion was forwarded to the governor who sent it to the Colonial Office for comment. The attorney general, responding to the doubts, retreated to the letter of the law – the usual response to any challenge to an appointment that had not been made strictly according to the rules. He changed his opinion and accepted the withdrawals. Once Benjamin Hart and Moses Judah Hays decided to refuse to accept a commission as justice of the peace, Benjamin wrote to his nephew, Samuel B. Hart, advising him to refuse as well. Samuel did not accept his uncle's advice. "My answer was," Hart recalled, "that I refused this method of proceeding being persuaded that the law was in my favour."[43]

Nevertheless, Samuel B. Hart could not take office as a justice of the peace until he had sworn his oaths before one of the commissioners appointed by the province to administer them. Hart applied to two of the three English-speaking commissioners to take his oaths, but, being aware of the controversy, they refused to do so and advised him that the third would refuse as well. Hart then applied to Joseph Badeaux, the French-Canadian commissioner. Rather than being confronted by his cousin's opinion as adopted by the attorney general, Hart swore his oaths, and in the oath of abjuration he made an alteration (as allowed by the Plantation Act), substituting the words "upon the true faith of a Jew." Badeaux was satisfied, took the oaths on 28 August 1833, and five days later certified that Hart had sworn his oaths "conformably to the Laws of the said Province of Lower Canada."[44] This was the very form of oath that the government of Quebec had authorized "for Persons of the Jewish Persuasion" in 1768 at the time that John Franks had received his commission as overseer of chimneys. Badeaux clearly took the position that Jews had had equal rights to hold office since the 1760s. In that case, the Declaratory Act of 1832, rather than being the cornerstone of this country's religious and political freedoms, merely removed any lingering doubts as to the long-standing existing status of the Jews.

Two months later, in October 1833, Joseph-Rémi Vallières de St-Réal, the resident judge at Trois-Rivières, was brought into the dispute because of obstacles raised by English-speaking members of the administration. About a month after his appointment, according to Samuel B. Hart's account, the sheriff of Trois-Rivières, "called upon Judge Vallières to enquire of him what other obstacle in his opinion existed to prevent me from taking my seat." The judge gave his opinion that the religious form of oath of abjuration was "not according to Law," presumably because a secular form of oath was all that was required. He therefore concluded that "there was no obstacle whatever" to Hart's taking up his office. Under these circumstances the attorney general was obliged to qualify his position and agree that Jews could alter the oath of abjuration and take office. Samuel B. Hart, formally sworn into office on 28 August 1833, formally took his seat on the Bench of the Court of Quarter Sessions on the following 21 October.[45]

To resolve once and for all the issue raised by Aaron Philip Hart, the governor-in-chief, Lord Aylmer, sent a message to the House of Assembly on 8 February 1834 setting out the circumstances and asking whether an amendment to the law regarding oaths was necessary fully to remove disabilities for Jews.[46] The house referred the issue to a special five-member committee chaired by Dr René-Joseph Kimber of Trois-Rivières. The other four members were Louis-Théodore Besserer, Frédéric-Auguste Quesnel, Pierre Bureau, and Jean-François-Joseph Duval. Quesnel and Duval were the only lawyers on the committee; Duval, later chief justice of Quebec, was probably the author of the committee's report.[47]

The Kimber committee completed its work in less than three weeks and dealt decisively with the issue. Aaron Philip Hart was not called as a witness, although his opinion of 31 May 1833 was appended to the committee's report. Nor did the committee call for opinions of the law officers of the crown. Of the four witnesses called to speak, three were brothers, the sons of Ezekiel Hart, namely: Aaron Ezekiel Hart, who appeared on 17 February; Adolphus Mordecai Hart, a student at law, who appeared on 18 February; and the eldest, Samuel B. Hart, who appeared on 20 February. They spoke eloquently in support of the existing law allowing Jewish candidates for office to alter the oath of abjuration. Aaron Ezekiel could not resist attacking his first cousin, Aaron Philip, as the source of the problem. "To return to the question, by whom has that Statute [of 1832] been miscon-strued?" he asked the committee. "By a young man who has scarcely been admitted but two years to the practice of the Law, and who is far from being celebrated for the consistency of his opinions, or for the solidity of his judgment, he having been of a diametrically opposed opinion but a short time ago."[48] Moses Judah Hays was the fourth witness. His testimony on 25 February was brief and when the mem-bers of the committee were satisfied that he had relied on the opinion of Aaron Philip Hart in refusing his appointment and had not sought any other legal advice, he was asked no further questions.[49]

The committee reported to the assembly on 28 February.[50] It con-cluded that Jews had the right to amend the oath of abjuration by deleting the words "upon the true Faith of a Christian" whenever necessary, that that right had existed from the time of the Plantation Act for both naturalized and natural-born Jews, that the act of 1832 was merely a declaratory act passed to remove doubts and did not add anything to the rights of Jews which already existed, and that no further amendments were necessary to any legislation regarding oaths because Jews in Lower Canada suffered no disabilities. The committee noted "with regret that two persons professing the Jewish faith alone made any objection to the existing law, and put their own interpretation upon the Statute." The assembly accepted the Kimber committee's report without objection.[51]

Benjamin Hart and Moses Judah Hays were finally appointed justices of the peace on 13 April 1837.[52] They had not needed a declaration of their rights to achieve those offices. The Jews of Lower Canada had had thirty years of complete equality prior to 1791. There had followed forty years when that equality was challenged. Although they had enjoyed freedoms earlier than their co-religionists in most other jurisdictions only to lose some of them, the way was now clear. The had finally been officially declared to be equal to other British subjects in the province.

Notwithstanding the changes to the state oaths in Upper and Lower Canada, Prince Edward Island, and Jamaica, officials in Britain continued to refuse to allow the colonies to abolish the state oaths by legislation, citing the requirement of the imperial act of 1766 that the form of the oath of abjuration used in Britain had to be used in the rest of the empire. Nova Scotia took the next step in the battle to abolish the oaths. Its Catholic Emancipation Act had replaced the three state oaths and the declaration against transubstantiation with a single, simple oath of allegiance for Roman Catholics. Protestants, however, were still required to swear the oaths, take the sacrament, and make the declaration in the old way. This gave rise to a distinction between persons of different religions which the president of the Legislative Council, T.B. Robie, declared to exert "an injurious influence," tending to "excite party feelings by bringing into notice Religious differences of opinion in affairs merely secular."[53]

Between 1836 and 1838 the Nova Scotia Assembly made the abolition of the state oaths "a favourite measure" and tried three times to enact legislation. On the first two occasions the Legislative Council refused to pass the legislation; on the third attempt the council passed the bill, but the governor refused to assent to it. In desperation, the assembly and council addressed the Colonial Office, asking for a definitive ruling on a draft bill to replace the state oaths with new forms rather than with a single secular oath. The address explained that the "invidious distinction between the Oaths now required from your Majesty's Protestant and Roman Catholic Subjects tends only to perpetuate religious differences, and, if persisted in, might call into activity hostile and angry feelings, now happily forgotten, whose revival would be an evil of the greatest magnitude to the people of this Colony."[54] The new forms of oath suggested in the draft bill appear to have been intended to assist Protestant Dissenters. They had clearly not been drawn up with Jews in mind, for the new oath of abjuration was still to conclude with the words "upon the true Faith of a Christian."

Meanwhile, in Britain itself, the drive to emancipate Jews had moved ahead after the Roman Catholic Relief Act in 1829 only to grind to a halt shortly thereafter. A bill "to repeal the civil disabilities affecting British born subjects professing the Jewish religion" had been introduced into the House of Commons in 1830 but was defeated. Three more times, in 1833, 1834, and 1836, similar bills were passed by the Commons but defeated in the Lords. In 1837, when parliament exempted Quakers, Moravians, and Separatists from the disabilities imposed by the state oaths and the declaration, as all three regarded swearing in any form as contrary to their faith, an amendment that the bill be extended to Jews was defeated in the House of Commons.[55] Typically, the arguments against the bill were similar to that put forward by the archbishop of Canterbury in 1834, namely that the advocates of relief for Jews "refer to the removal of the Catholic disabilities as a precedent, but the cases of the Catholics and the Jews were perfectly distinct, for the former, though differing from Protestants upon some important points of doctrine, were still Christians, whilst that latter disbelieved the divine essence of the founder of our religion." To this argument could be added Lord Malmsbury's suggestion that "it would be a most extraordinary and improper thing for a Christian community to be placed in the situation to look up to their lawgivers as persons who considered their saviour to be an impostor."[56]

It was against this background that the Nova Scotia petition for the revision of the state oaths and the abolition of the declaration reached the desk of the colonial secretary, Lord Glenelg, in May 1838. Even though the proposed legislation would not be extended to Jews, Glenelg was aware that his approval of such a change for Nova Scotia might be considered a precedent for changes in England and elsewhere in the empire and that any change in the oaths "will encounter the censures with which it can hardly fail to be attended."[57] To avoid the broader question, Glenelg narrowed the issue to a single point of law: "whether the Acts of Parliament on this subject are not binding on the Govt. and in force in British North America." He referred the question to the law officers of the crown, who reported that by the imperial act of 1766: "the form of the Oath of abjuration was fixed not only for Great Britain & Ireland, but *for the rest of HM Dominions.* The form has since been altered so far as relates to Roman Catholics but not as to Protestants – & therefore, however reasonable may be the views of the Provincial Legislature, we are compelled to state it as our opinion that the act to which we have referred prevents H M from assenting to any proposal (not sanctioned by the Imperial Parliament) for altering the form of Oath."[58]

The opinion could have noted that the British parliament had already relieved not only Catholics but Quakers, Moravians, and Separatists from disabilities they had faced. Even more of a departure, the Colonial Office had previously accepted alterations of the state oaths for Jews by colonial legislatures in Jamaica, Prince Edward Island, and Upper and Lower Canada, contrary to the imperial act of 1766. Finally, in some quarters, there was legal opinion that the imperial state oaths had no application in British North America. This opinion had been followed by the Old Province of Quebec in 1768 when it had refused to accept the act of 1766 at face value and had amended the oath of abjuration to accommodate persons of the Jewish persuasion. While there is no evidence that the Kimber committee knew about the 1768 decision, it had adopted the same opinion in 1834.

There was one other issue that should have been dealt with in the opinion of the law officers. Although the requirements in the Test Act linking the sacrament and the declaration against transubstantiation had been altered by the legislation of 1828, removing disabilities for Protestant Dissenters in Britain, Upper Canada was the only colony in British North America to have followed suit. Indeed its legislation of 1833 repealed all the Test Act requirements for everyone, thereby removing the related disabilities from Jews as well as Dissenters. Nevertheless, the requirements of the Test Act remained – though minimally adhered to – in the colonies because they continued to be a part of the governors' instructions. It was not until after the rebellions of 1837 in Upper and Lower Canada that the Test Act requirements were removed from those instructions.

The instructions to Lord Durham as governor-in-chief of Nova Scotia, issued on 10 February 1838, still required the state oaths to be sworn by members of the assembly, councillors, and other officers but did not require the making or subscribing of the declaration or taking of the sacrament by anyone. From that date, all disabilities had been removed from Dissenters and Roman Catholics, though not from Jews, in Nova Scotia. In Prince Edward Island, where the state oaths requirement had been removed by legislation in 1830, Durham's instructions, by removing the Test Act requirements as well, should have effectively removed all disabilities from Protestants, Catholics, and Jews from February 1838. Contrary to expectations, however, the governor's instructions maintained the state oaths notwithstanding the colonial statute. Newfoundland followed the practice in Nova Scotia and New Brunswick by removing the requirement for the declaration in the late 1830s and the requirement for the state oaths about ten years later.[59]

Durham's instructions as governor-in-chief in both Upper and Lower Canada, dated 2 April 1838, stated that the standing instructions to previous governors, "are in many respects obsolete & inapplicable to the present condition of the said Province of Upper Canada & have in certain respects been superseded by Statutes" and that therefore Durham was "to conform to and abide by the said standing Instructions but so far only as the same are not obsolete, or have not been superseded by any such Statute as aforesaid or as the same may not be found to be inapplicable to the present state of affairs in our said Province."[60] The state oaths and the declaration had been superseded by statute in Upper Canada. The Kimber committee had found, in effect, that the state oaths and the declaration were "inapplicable to the present state of affairs" in Lower Canada.

What had confronted British North Americans until this time was an administrative structure rooted in England at the time when the nobility and gentry had been given their land and the benefits that grew from it in return for accepting a responsibility to go to war if necessary and to sacrifice all to uphold the nation. It was these few (who had most to lose in a war) on whom the monarch could depend for loyalty. The rigid class system in England, with the loyalty of the upper class to the monarch as well as to the Church of England, cemented the link between church and state.

As the colonial period developed, the monarch needed an administrative technique which would guarantee British North America's loyalty during Britain's colonial expansion and wars. The new colonists, who were needed to administer a largely non-English population, were given their share in the bounty of the expanding colonial world. But British interests dictated that a mechanism had to be found which would ensure absolute loyalty to the mother country from colonial officials who were not drawn from the English upper classes. The mechanism chosen was the extension to the colonies of statutory requirements which meant, in essence, that colonial officials were required to be members of the Church of England, thereby reinforcing the administrative structure religiously and socially. Colonials, anxious to emulate the aristocracy in England with its privileges, joined the Church of England and thus obtained the social caste that it provided, and the world of administrative plums was thereby open to them. The price was exacted when the call to arms was heard as was seen in their dedicated and loyal participation in the military at times of war and rebellion.

The colonials who became the new aristocracy in the New World did not have the familial and landed connections to their positions which were common in Britain. It was the newer administrative structure which gave them their positions. They enjoyed the benefits, and many identified with and sought to emulate the English gentry. Families went back and forth to England with some regularity; the fashions were from the continent; and colonial society was a somewhat closed circle much like that in England. Horsemanship, with its historic connection to the cavalry, was a social necessity for this class. They followed the principle of *noblesse oblige*. The official class in the colonies, like the upper class in England, was prepared to defend the empire out of a sense of duty, whether that duty was simply to "king and country," whether it arose from an Anglican need "to do your duty in that state of life into which it has pleased God to call you," or whether it was a duty of the privileged class to support the constituted government which was obviously supportive of its worldly goods.[61]

The difference in British North America was that the administrative structure was based on Britain's realistic goal of having a ruling class it could control. This "establishment" class was created through a religious test. In British North America any able person could enter the circle if they converted to the Church of England. Although society was more open than in Britain, it still featured central control and privileges for those in the administrative or official class.

This administrative structure caused anger and discontent because its workings were often secretive and it had not been created by public laws. The requirements for holding office were often unknown or obscure to the population. If wishing to advance, a person who was not a member of the ruling Church of England minority came up against inexplicable hurdles in his desire to share equally in the fruits to be found in full participation in building the nation. This resentment against the new administrative class that had emerged eventually led to rebellion.

Stewart Derbishire, the operative who reported to Lord Durham in 1838 about the grievances that had led to rebellion in Lower Canada, was struck by the long-standing equality that had been given to Roman Catholics. He found that the French Canadians "laboured under no practical grievances; and that their condition, social and political, was an enviable one, as compared with all other people on the face of the globe." He noted that "the freedom of the person, of political opinion, and of the press have been secured to the habitan [*sic*] by equal laws impartially administered." In view of this lack of practical grievances, he felt he had "totally failed as yet in search of a … practical ill in the condition of a people referable to the form of administration of the Government." He concluded that there was "no cause of discontent *other than an official class*."[62] The meaningful offices were still only available by appointment and a majority of the legislative and executive councillors were always the governor's supporters, leaving the

French in Lower Canada as well as non-Anglican Protestants and others in both Upper and Lower Canada anxious for a more open system.

The resentment provoked by this administrative structure in both Upper and Lower Canada led to the many efforts to displace the British rules. The resulting changes eventually came to be the law of the land based on a new philosophy that a nation could grow and flourish without one homogeneous ruling class. This new philosophy was at the root of Canadian identity.

Once firmly established, Britain's colonies had sought to remove by law the inequalities and disabilities which imperial legislation (particularly the Test Act and the act of 1766) created for non-Anglicans who sought to participate in the public life of their country. Over time, colonial legislation and practice had allowed considerable deviation from the strict letter of the law. However, the British government, in the person of the colonial secretary, considered the restrictions inherent in the state oaths and the Test Act provisions to be an important instrument of colonial policy. As a general rule, Britain showed a reluctance to make changes. Advances proceeded on a case by case basis so long as no one objected. The maintenance of these restrictions was firmly reiterated in the instructions to successive governors.

The emancipation of the Jews in Nova Scotia, New Brunswick, and Prince Edward Island was to be achieved not because of any public interest in the Jews, but because the public disliked the distinction between loyal Roman Catholic and Protestant subjects caused by the state oaths. The people of the individual colonies of British North America persisted in their quest be free of laws based on religious distinctions. It should be stressed that while individuals who suffered the effects of the laws were not content to let such issues slide, the struggle for equality enlisted many people and was not pursued only by the minorities affected. Britain was not prepared to allow precedents to be established in the colonies which might be used in England. Despite changes during the 1820s and 1830s, it attempted to prevent further changes in the state oaths by the colonies. By 1838, therefore, the equality of Jews, particularly in the provinces of Nova Scotia and New Brunswick, was not yet complete.

The first test of responsible government in the new united province of Canada revolved around the state oaths, which, if retained, would maintain the "official class" which Derbishire had identified as the major cause of discontent leading to rebellion in Upper and Lower Canada. However, the state oaths were disregarded as a condition of holding office in the new province from the time of its formation in 1841, largely because their continued use was incompatible with responsible government.[63]

The issue had, indeed, surfaced well before the rebellion. Even after the Upper Canada Oaths Act of 1833 provided a secular oath of allegiance for all offices and abolished the use of the sacramental tests, the instructions to the governor nevertheless continued to require the old form of the oath of abjuration "upon the true Faith of a Christian" for all the same offices. Such were the instructions carried by Sir Francis Bond Head when he arrived in Upper Canada as lieutenant governor in January 1836. After summoning his new Executive Council, he was required to "administer to each of the Members the several Oaths, and subscribe to the Declaration therein required."[64] In February 1836, when Robert Baldwin was appointed to the council, he refused to take the oaths, nominally because he did not agree that Protestants should continue to swear a religious form of oath not required of Catholics.[65] But the deeper reason for his refusal was based upon his concept of responsible government.

While the Oaths Act of 1833 had applied to any person "appointed to any office in this Province," it applied only to appointments made under authority of a statute not to prerogative appointments made by the governor as representative of the crown. Baldwin's concept of responsible government dictated that the authority to swear oaths came not from the crown's prerogatives but from the crown acting on the advice of the representatives of a majority in the assembly as embodied in the Oaths Act. Head acquiesced in Baldwin's refusal, and he and two other men joined the Executive Council, swearing only the oath of allegiance specified in the Oaths Act.[66] Within a month, however, Baldwin and the rest of the executive councillors resigned over Head's refusal to accept the principle that he could act solely on the advice of an executive council responsible to a majority in an elected assembly.

That new principle was tested again in May 1841 when Lord Sydenham, governor general of the province of Canada, invited Robert Baldwin to join his Executive Council and to form a government chosen from among the majority elected to the first assembly of the new province. The Act of Union of 1840 specified a secular oath of allegiance – identical in wording to that in the Constitutional Act of 1791 – for members of the new House of Assembly and Legislative Council. But there was, as yet, no general oaths act for the united province, comparable to that for Upper Canada in 1833, and as yet no legislation that specified the form of oath for these new executive councillors. Relying on his instructions as governor, Sydenham asked Baldwin to take the state oaths. Baldwin refused to take the oath of supremacy, because it was not a secular oath and because he knew that Sydenham's prerogatives as governor were now to be superseded by the will of the legislature under the system of responsible government. Sydenham accepted Baldwin's position, and without consulting the Colonial Office allowed him to take office after swearing only the oath of allegiance.[67]

The incident called for the law officers in England to recognize the new situation in the united province of Canada as different from the decision made two years before. In 1839 the law officers of the crown in Britain had responded to bids by Nova Scotia's assembly and legislative council to alter the state oaths by colonial legislation by stating that they saw no ground for altering or modifying their previous opinion and that the legislature clearly had no power to alter the form of the oath of abjuration.[68]

Now Sydenham and the law officers of the crown in Canada were about to offer a contrary opinion based on the new status of a responsibly elected government, not subject to the governor's prerogative powers. Sydenham asked his solicitors general for Canada East and Canada West for their opinions on whether he should have dispensed with the state oaths in Baldwin's case. The solicitor general for Canada West, Baldwin himself, decided simply that the "oaths referred to do not in my opinion apply to the Colonies and are not therefore in force in this Province. Neither the Royal Commission nor the Royal Instructions can legally enforce an oath not required by law." Charles D. Day, the solicitor general for Canada East, although he was Baldwin's political opponent, agreed that the act of 1766 requiring the oath of abjuration did "not extend to the Colonies." Day's opinion did differ from Baldwin's in one important respect. Baldwin believed that the governor general could not therefore use the discretion allowed him in his instructions to require the state oaths. Day, however, believed that the governor's instructions, not imperial laws, governed the oath requirements and that Sydenham's instructions therefore gave him the discretion to dispense with or require the state oaths.[69]

Sydenham next consulted the imperial law officers to obtain their confirmation of his action in allowing Baldwin to assume office having sworn only the oath of allegiance. By 1841 there were new law officers in England and, faced with a fait accompli, they agreed that "it was not imperative on Lord Sydenham to administer he oath, but that he might do so if he thought fit."[70] Thus, the law officers essentially upheld Day's opinion over Baldwin's. The imperial act of 1766 was no longer the legal basis for requiring the state oaths in the colonies, but if his instructions were so worded, the governor would have the discretion to waive the state oaths and substitute an oath of allegiance.

The focus of the battle over the use of the oaths had moved dramatically from imperial legislation to the royal prerogative as embodied in the instructions to the governors. Ever since the instructions given on 2 April 1838 to Lord Durham as governor-in-chief of the Canadas those instructions had acknowledged that the governor was entitled to exercise prerogatives provided that they "had not been superseded by any Statute made and enacted by Us or by Our said Royal Predecessors either with the advice and consent of Parliament or with the advice and consent of Our said Province of Upper Canada."[71] Imperial laws regarding the oaths were no longer to apply to the colonies, and if no laws regarding oaths had yet been passed by the colonial legislature itself, then the prerogative power of the crown, as expressed in the governor's instructions, would fill the void – but only until such time as the legislatures passed such laws.

The rule however was clear: in the future Lord Sydenham or his successors might still be able to exercise prerogative power in requiring oaths of office not specified by statute, but in so doing they would be obliged to rely on the advice of their duly elected ministers. The legal barrier the colonies had hitherto faced with their legislation to abolish the state oaths had finally been breached.

The oaths requirement had now been dealt with in the Canadas and Prince Edward Island. However in Nova Scotia and New Brunswick the prerogative power of the crown, as expressed in the instructions, had the force of law, with the governor, following the opinion of the law officers, having discretion to modify the state oaths only if his instructions were so worded. In the Maritime provinces the instructions with respect to oath requirements had always been worded much more restrictively than those in the Canadas and allowed virtually no discretion. Thus Durham's instructions as governor-in-chief of Nova Scotia in 1838 did not include a discretionary clause and the instructions given to Sir Charles Bagot as governor general of New Brunswick on 7 October 1843, for example, repeated these instructions: namely, that he cause the state oaths to be administered to all "Persons who hold any Office or place of trust or profit in Our said Province, without the doing of all of which, you are not to admit any person whatever into any Public Office, nor suffer those who may have been already admitted to continue therein."[72]

The continuation of the oaths requirement in New Brunswick meant that the most significant Jewish community in British North America after those in the united province of Canada remained disabled from participation in public life. This community, which was now composed of ten or twelve extended Jewish families, had been established in Northumberland County early in the nineteenth century.[73] In 1814 Michael Samuel[74] had come to Chatham, later joined by his brother-in-law, John Joseph.[75] In 1819 the firm of Joseph &

Samuel opened a general store, their partnership being dissolved in 1834, just before Joseph's death. The business grew with a branch in Newcastle run by Michael's brother Jacob,[76] and another in Dalhousie run by a nephew, Jonah.[77] Michael Samuel's brother Joseph had arrived in Chatham with his Jewish wife, Phoebe, and his family, by 1824.[78] He, too, was a merchant, first on his own and later in association with his son Solomon and with Morden S. Levy, possibly a nephew.[79] Other members of this community included Simon Aaron,[80] Michael Samuel Jr,[81] Morris Joseph,[82] and Joseph Levy.[83] By 1870 this community had dispersed,[84] but during the time that it existed in northeastern New Brunswick, it played its part in the struggle for equality.

In the elections in Northumberland County in 1842–3 Jews were barred from voting only if challenged by any candidate. If so challenged, they would have had to swear the state oaths as a condition of voting. Joseph Samuel had been accused of using his influence in the election in favour of Alexander Rankin and John Ambrose Street against John Williston.[85] Immediately after the election of Rankin and Street, the New Brunswick Assembly enfranchised its Jews by enacting that electors and members of the assembly swear a simple oath of allegiance in place of the state oaths.[86]

Three years later, in April 1846, New Brunswick petitioned the crown to abolish the state oaths as did Nova Scotia. This time, the latter's petition, unlike its earlier petitions of 1836–8, no longer requested an oath that could be sworn only by Christians.[87] Both colonies asked simply that the state oaths be repealed and replaced with a single secular oath. The New Brunswick petition sounded the death knell of the state oaths. The assembly had been unanimous in endorsing the request for abolition of the oaths, noting that "Your Majesty had been graciously pleased to abolish the customary State Oaths in other parts of Your Majesty's Dominions." The petition continued: "We need not present for Your Majesty's gracious consideration the reasons which induce us to make this request, as your Royal Mind must be well informed as to the controversies which some of the present Oaths are calculated to perpetuate among different classes of Your Majesty's Subjects in this Province, whose lives and property are not considered valuable from the position of allegiance in which they stand to Your Majesty and the Throne of the realm."[88] The Colonial Office responded with uncharacteristic despatch. Within two months, the secretary of state for the colonies, William Gladstone, had replied that the instructions to all colonial governors would be amended: the state oaths would be replaced with a single oath of allegiance.[89] In 1857, the appointment of Morden S. Levy as a justice of the peace for Kent County in New Brunswick would show that the new order was in place.[90]

The small observant Jewish community on the Miramichi in New Brunswick atrophied either because of intermarriage or because its members died unmarried for want of Jewish partners or returned to England. But the community – the Samuels, the Levys, the Aarons, the Josephs – had helped to leave an important legacy. They had remained true to their religion and had been welcomed by their neighbours. The laws had been changed to allow them to participate fully as citizens in their community. They were not merely tolerated: they were equal.

Another barrier – though it touched only a few – to equal participation in government in the British North American colonies was the continuing requirement, even after the 1840s, that the governor of each colony take the state oaths upon assuming office, unless he was a Catholic, in which case he could take the simple oath of allegiance.[91] In 1858 the act of 1766 was again amended in England by the Jewish Relief Act, which allowed the state oaths to be replaced by a single oath of allegiance. Thereafter the instructions to the governors were to be amended as well. From that date, even the office of governor in British North America was open to Jews as well as to others.[92]

Although most of the disabilities that individuals had faced were now in the past, the Church of England, by virtue of its establishment, still retained extraordinary privileges. These were now to be abolished. On 5 June 1851, Joseph Curran Morrison, the member for York West, moved in the legislature of the province of Canada to bring in a bill to repeal the imperial laws pertaining to rectories in the province.[93] The bill had originated among those opposed to the right of the Church of England to be the established church of Upper and Lower Canada and to use public funds to promote that church's objectives. The bill went well beyond the intention of those who simply opposed the power of the established church. Though the last three of the act's four sections actually dealt with abolishing rectories, the first section read like a declaration of rights: "the free enjoyment of religious expression and worship, without discrimination or preference, so as the same be not made an excuse for acts of licentiousness, or a justification of practices inconsistent with the peace and safety of the province, is by the constitution and laws of this Province allowed to all Her Majesty's subjects within the same."[94]

There was no doubt as to the legislature's intent in approving the statute. As Morrison said during the debate on 24 July: "Very few, indeed, argue in favour of a state religion in Canada, peopled as it is with persons from all creeds and from all nations, and equally entitled to the favour and protection of the Government."[95] The establishment of the Church of England elsewhere in British North America was also repealed in subsequent years.[96]

On 1 November 1855, members of the Jewish community of Montreal met in a densely packed room, ostensibly to celebrate the election of David Salomons as lord mayor of London, England, but actually to congratulate themselves on having won equal rights in Canada. They keynote speaker, Abraham de Sola, the celebrated spiritual leader of Montreal's Portuguese Jewish Congregation,[97] reminded his listeners that the government of Canada had been saner and more impartial towards its people than had the government in Great Britain. He reviewed the long but successful struggle to end the use of religious oaths as a tool of British policy. "In this great happy and enlightened colony," he explained, "the doors of Parliament, the temples of culture and dignified public office are open to all." De Sola concluded his remarks by recalling the restrictions of the Old World that had driven his listeners and their forebears to the shores of the New World. "No more yellow badges!" he exclaimed.[98] "No more Ghetto; no more Judenstrasse; no more civil disabilities; no more religious tests. The Jews wish to hold their heads as other men do, as God has created them. They want to be the equals of their fellow citizens of other creeds."[99]

Each of the British North American colonies had confronted the question of how to comply with the imperial statute of 1766 that stipulated a Protestant form of oath as a requirement for enfranchisement, landholding, and public office. By the middle of the nineteenth century each colony had been able to adopt a secular form of oath. As a result, Jews and others were fully equal under the law in British North America, not merely tolerated. By 1851 all of the provinces had also established freedom of religion.

Table 5
Removal of Disabilities for Religious Minorities in British North America by 1867

	Quebec/ Lower Canada	Upper Canada	Nova Scotia	New Brunswick	Prince Edward Island	Newfoundland	Vancouver Island	British Columbia
Guarantee of toleration (Liberty of conscience; right of public worship)	To all from outset, 1763: Treaty of Paris	To all from outset, 1791: Constitutional Act	To all from outset, 1749	To all but Catholics from outset, 1784: to all from 1830: 11 Geo. IV, c. 7 (NB)	To all but Catholics from outset, 1784; to all from 1830: 11 Geo. IV, c. 8 (PEI)	To all but Catholics from outset, 1762; to all from 1784	To all from outset, 1849	To all from outset, 1858
Able to sit in assembly (abolition of last of state oaths or declaration)	1791: Constitutional Act, s. 29	1791: Constitutional Act, s. 29	Decision of Colonial Office, 1846	1843, 6 Vict., c. 44 (NB)	Durham's instructions, 6 February 1838	All but Jews and Quakers from outset, 1833; all from 1848	Decision of Assembly, 1861	Ordinance of governor, 1859
Abolition of state oaths (as a condition of holding offices, places of trust)	Protestant Dissenters, 1763; Jews, 1763; French-Canadian Catholics, 1763; all Catholics, 1791	Roman Catholics, 1791; Jews and Protestant Dissenters, 1833: 3 Will. IV, c. 13 (UC)	Decision of Colonial Office, 1846	Decision of Colonial Office, 1846	1830: 11 Geo. IV, c. 8 (PEI)	19 July 1848: Le Marchant's instructions	1858: by interpretation of 21 & 22 Vict., c. 49 (Britain)	Ordinance of governor, 1859

Abolition of sacramental tests	For French-Canadian Catholics, 1774; for all Catholics, 1791: Constitutional Act; for all, Durham's instructions, 2 April 1838	For Roman Catholics from outset, 1791: Constitutional Act; for all, 1833: 3 Will. IV, c. 13 (UC)	For Lawrence Kavanaugh alone, governor's instructions, 1823; for all, Durham's instructions, 10 February 1838	Durham's instructions, 10 February 1838	Durham's instructions, 6 February 1838	Cochrane's instructions, 26 July 1832	From outset	From outset, 1858
Establishment of Church of England repealed	Rectories Act, 1851: Statutes of Canada, 14 Vict., c. 75	Rectories Act, 1851; Statutes of Canada, 14 Vict., c. 75	1851: Revised Statutes of Nova Scotia, c. 170	No statute; by evolution	1879: 42 Vict., c. 19 (PEI)	Not located	No establishment	No establishment
General equality for religious minorities	Roman Catholics, 1774: Quebec Act, 14 Geo. III, c. 83; Jews, 1832: Declaratory Act, 1 Will IV, c. 57 (LC)	Roman Catholics from outset, 1791	Roman Catholic Relief Act, 1830: 11 Geo. IV, c. 1 (NS)	Roman Catholic Relief Act, 1830: 11 Geo. IV, c. 7 (NB)	Roman Catholic Relief Act, 1830: 11 Geo. IV, c. 8 (PEI)	Roman Catholics, 1832, decision of Colonial Office	Not located	Not located

15 The Last "Little Spot"

It is intolerable to suppose that this little spot will permit such a stigma to attach to it, as that of being the last refuge of religious persecution.

Victoria Gazette, 5 March 1860

The first meeting of the second House of Assembly of Vancouver Island on 1 March 1860 took place in one of the five new government buildings across the bay from the town of Victoria.[1] The lobby was filled to overflowing; the gallery of the chamber was packed with more than twenty women. The people at the opening of the assembly should have expected that something unusual was about to happen. After all, controversy had dogged almost all the events leading up to it. The newspapers called the building a "Court House" and, indeed, it had been built as a court house. A separate contractor was to erect a matching structure to the west for the assembly. But the previous August, that contractor, a man named Herman Rolant, had abandoned the project when it was only partly finished.[2] Thus, while the court house neared completion, the assembly building had been left "in statu quo, the contractor having levanted, the mechanics employed, minus their dues."[3] As the date for the opening of the assembly approached, the government decided to use the court house for the assembly and let the courts occupy the assembly building when it was completed.[4] The buildings were unusual by contemporary standards. They were built of square timber frame, the spaces in between being filled with bricks. One architect described them as "of an ornamental character,"[5] but the editor of one of the newspapers called them "something between a Dutch toy and a Chinese Pagoda,"[6] and the people in town, recalling how the frames looked before they were filled in with brick, would always call them "the birdcages."[7]

Across James Bay from the government buildings, past the store fronts on Yates Street leading up from the harbour, even a casual glance would show that no part of the town was more than two years old. The streets were unpaved, the buildings were of wood, and many were hastily constructed. Victoria was a frontier town perched on the southern end of Vancouver Island. The settlement had mushroomed around the Hudson's Bay Company's Fort Victoria two years before as a result of the discovery of gold on the Fraser and Thompson rivers in the new mainland colony of British Columbia. The population had exploded from 500 to 5,000 for a brief moment in the spring and summer of 1858 but had now dropped back to about to about 1,500.[8] Victoria had few British subjects. There were an unusual number of Americans in the town, some of them black, who had arrived by way of San Francisco. Most people, however, had red or yellow skin and spoke with accents and in languages not common in Great Britain.[9] According to the account of I.J. Benjamin, a Romanian Jewish merchant who travelled through Victoria in 1861, the Indians alone outnumbered the whites in town by more than two to one.[10]

At the opening of the assembly, however, everyone spoke English and most of the colony's population was not represented. Nor had most voted in the recent election. Those who had voted, who had been elected, and, indeed, who were present that day were British subjects born or naturalized in England or its colonies. Although Indians and Chinese made up the overwhelming majority of the populace, virtually none of them had had the right to vote in the recent elections. Nor had Americans been entitled to vote unless they could establish status as British subjects. An exception had been made for American blacks who had not been accepted as citizens in the United States. Under the Franchise Act, passed by the assembly of Vancouver Island in 1859, a potential voter was disqualified if he had "taken the oath of allegiance to, or become a citizen of, a foreign state or nation, unless three months previously to the time at which he may claim to be registered in the lists of voters, he shall have taken the oath of allegiance to Her Majesty."[11] This act was used to extend the franchise to American blacks but not American whites.

On the floor of the assembly, ten of the thirteen newly elected members sat clustered around two long tables places diagonally so that the clerk could sit between them.[12] The chair on the bench at the front of the room was occupied by the eleventh member, the newly chosen speaker, Dr John Sebastian Helmcken, who had been elected to represent Esquimalt County and was the son-in-law of the governor, James Douglas.[13] The two remaining members were in San Francisco and would not be joining the assembly for another week or two.[14] At the time appointed for swearing the oath of office and beginning the session, Helmcken rose, stood before the clerk, placed his hand on the Bible, and swore his allegiance declaring his loyalty to the queen, concluding with the words: "I make this declaration upon the true faith of a Christian." The attorney general, George Hunter Cary,[15] and William John Macdonald of Sooke District each took the oath in the same manner.

The next member to be sworn, Selim Franklin of Victoria, awaited his turn. Unlike the others, he was a Jew and could not swear the same oath. Franklin had been born in Liverpool and had arrived in San Francisco in 1849, just at the start of the California gold rush. He had been successful as a storekeeper until fire claimed his establishment, and in 1851 he became an auctioneer and land agent. He arrived in Victoria in 1858, shortly after the discovery of gold in British Columbia, brought his older brother Lumley up from San Francisco, and set up business as Franklin and Company, auctioneers, at the foot of Yates Street. As the only British-born auctioneer in the two colonies, he had been appointed by Governor Douglas in 1859 as the first government auctioneer in British Columbia and Vancouver Island.[16] He was regarded, with some deference, as "silver tongued Franklin."[17]

Franklin and his brother were by no means the only Jews in town. By 1860 Victoria had the second largest Jewish population of any town or city in British North America. The core Jewish population, made up of at least 50 or 60 families with a membership of about 200 (most of whom had arrived by way of San Francisco), formed at least 10 per cent of Victoria's non-Asian/non-native population of 1,500.[18] The Jews of Victoria were numerous enough to have organized themselves for High Holiday services in September 1858, to have established a cemetery by 1859, and to have formally established the "First Victoria Hebrew Benevolent Society" in May of the same year.[19] According to I.J. Benjamin's somewhat exaggerated account of Victoria in February 1861, the Jewish community had an impact out of proportion to its numbers:

About a hundred Jews live here ... The beginnings of the city of Victoria are really due to the Jews. For, no matter how many persons streamed to the island at the outbreak of the gold-fever, they scattered again, for the most part, to the four corners of the world when their disillusion followed too quickly. The Jews, however, held their ground, set up tents for residence and booths for shops; for they soon realized that this place had a great commercial future. This was to be deducted, easily enough, from the situation of the island, which lies between the Sandwich Islands [Hawaii], California and China.[20]

Two years earlier, in 1859, after the assembly had passed an act to incorporate the First Victoria Hebrew Benevolent Society, its inaugural fund-raising ball had been well supported by the public at large.[21] By 1862, a congregation was organized and a year later, in September 1863, it occupied its new synagogue building.[22]

According to John Sebastian Helmcken, after the gold rush started in 1858, Victoria's population "had completely changed, being now composed of Americans – of adopted ones in whole or in part – Jews in large numbers, but it must be said in fairness, that they did not complicate matters, but were on the side of law and order – of course with some exceptions."[23] It was not just the gold rush that had brought Jews to Victoria. The Hudson's Bay Company's legal monopoly of the West Coast fur trade had just come to an end, and about three dozen "Indian traders" obtained trade licences in Victoria to take advantage of the new opportunity. According to recent research, roughly two-thirds of them were Jewish.[24] They included William and Amelia Copperman, Lewis Levy, Abraham Martin and Abraham Israel, Morris Dobrin, Julius Seitz, Wolfe Cahn, Abraham Frankel, Nathan Solomon, Aaron Oldenberg, Leopold Blum, Lewis Goldstone, Samuel Myers, W. Baranski, Meier and John Malowanski, Moses Phillips, John Jacob Hart, Morris Moss, and the five Shirpser brothers. While several of these ran "Indian stores" and operated as wholesale fur buyers in Victoria, a number, such as the Shirpsers, Hart & Phillips, Moss, and Meier Malowanski (with his Croatian partner, Vincent Baranovich) operated trading schooners that ventured up the coast into Indian territory previously considered the preserve of the Hudson's Bay Company through its trade at the company's post, Fort Simpson. The Victoria traders were so successful that by 1863, it was reported by the Hudson's Bay Company that natives would no longer bring their furs to the fort. At that point, the company purchased a trading sloop and stationed it at Fort Simpson to compete with the independent fur traders, but its monopoly had ended and it became only one of several trading enterprises.

Some of Victoria's Jewish community were British subjects and had therefore probably voted in the election. Franklin's co-religionists were no doubt following his career with great interest. Franklin had won the second of Victoria Town's two seats, running behind George Hunter Cary but narrowly edging out Amor De Cosmos, the mercurial editor and publisher of the *British Colonist*.[25] Franklin had every reason to feel confident as he rose from his seat and strode up to the clerk to take his turn being sworn. Two years earlier, long after most of its colonies had dealt with the issue, Britain had amended the oath required for members of parliament, allowing practising Jews to sit in the House of Commons. A year before Douglas had proclaimed the Oaths Act for the mainland colony of British Columbia. That act confirmed that the alterations to the oaths allowed to be made by Roman Catholics, Quakers, and Jews in Great Britain were to be allowed in the colony of British Columbia as well.[26] Douglas's commission and instructions as governor of Vancouver Island in 1851 had not referred to either the oath of abjuration or the other state oaths but had ordered that, when summoning assemblies, persons elected "shall before their sitting, take the oath of allegiance."[27] Nor had the assembly of the colony of Vancouver Island passed any legislation on this matter. That morning, at the suggestion of the chief justice, David Cameron,[28] Franklin had taken his oath of office in a private ceremony, omitting the words "and I make this declaration upon the true faith of a Christian."[29] Cameron was not only chief justice but the brother-in-law of Douglas, so Franklin's oath ceremony appeared to have been given the blessing of the colonial authorities.

In the assembly Franklin took his oath of office in public, again omitting the words "upon the true faith of a Christian." Suddenly, Alfred Penderell Waddington,[30] a member for Victoria District, announced that he was obliged to object "merely in order to secure obedience to the law," and he pointed out that Franklin had not taken the usual form of oath.[31] Waddington, born in London in 1801, had lived in France, done a stint as a prosperous grocery merchant in San Francisco, lived in Victoria since 1858, and now served as one of two members who opposed the government party.[32] While there was a possibility that Waddington's objection was prompted by his self-described role as an opposition member, his action bordered on a personal attack on another member. Franklin sat down and the remaining seven members took their oaths of office in the usual form. Waddington rose again and reminded the speaker that Franklin had not complied with the law. The speaker thereupon asked Franklin to withdraw.

Franklin left the chamber amid confusion. There were several suggestions by the remaining members as to what to do next. The speaker suggested that the British act of 1858 extended to the colony and thus needed only a resolution to implement it. Henry Crease, also representing Victoria District, suggested that Franklin himself might help them avoid the problem if he were willing to swear the usual oath as well as the one he had already sworn.[33]

Helmcken called Franklin back into the room and asked him whether he would "take the oath in the form prescribed by law." The speaker thereby added a new dimension to the issue: it was one thing to refer to "the usual oath" but quite another to refer to "the form prescribed by law" because no form of oath had yet been specified by law in Vancouver Island. Could Helmcken have understood the implication of what he was asking? Could he have known that many years before, in another colony of British North America, another Jewish elected representative by the name of Ezekiel Hart had adopted the very tactic he was suggesting, that of swearing a Christian oath that would not bind his conscience but would permit him to take his seat? Could he have known that Samuel Hart had become an Anglican in order to take his seat in the assembly of Nova Scotia and that George Benjamin attempted to appear to be an Anglican in Canada West in order to gain acceptance? Could he have known of the many Catholics, Presbyterians, Lutherans, and other Protestant Dissenters, in addition to Jews, who had become Anglicans in British North America in order to hold office? Could he have known that the Church of England had become a "flag of convenience" for those who would otherwise suffer from "disabilities"?

Franklin, whose reply was recorded by the *British Colonist*, answered: "Mr. Speaker, having received a peremptory order to withdraw, I accordingly withdraw, as in duty bound. I took the oaths this morning, and those now proffered to me, and I claim my seat to sit and vote as a member of this House." Helmcken did not feel Franklin had answered his question, and asked it again. Franklin, "under considerable excitement," repeated the same answer. There was an outburst of debate, each member giving his opinion, none conclusive. Finally the speaker faced Franklin a third time. "Does the new member decline taking the oath?" he asked. Franklin stood his ground. He said that he had already taken the oath twice and that he "declined any other." Then he left the house.[34]

The next day, 2 March, the house met again. John Coles of Saanich moved, seconded by George Hunter Cary, that Franklin "shall take his seat in the House of Assembly." At this point Franklin entered the house and was proceeding to take his seat when the speaker requested that he withdraw. The debate occupied the rest of the day's business. There was considerable confusion about what the law really was. The attorney general felt that there was no requirement for a Christian form of oath according to local law and that the law of Great Britain applied, in particular the law passed in 1858 that had changed the oath to allow Jews to sit in the imperial parliament. A number of the members disagreed. Henry Crease was a London barrister who had left England only two years before. He echoed Lord North's views on the Test Act in stating that he considered "that the oath lay at the very foundation of our common law and could not be evaded."[35] The motion that Franklin be allowed to take his seat was then put to a vote but was defeated by six to three. A new motion, that a committee be appointed to report to the house "on what disabilities (if any) attach to British Subjects becoming Members of this House," was then carried.[36] Franklin returned again on 5 March and was about to take his seat when the speaker again asked him to withdraw.[37] The debate continued after his departure.

The *Victoria Gazette* saw the events as religious intolerance pure and simple – the question being "the propriety of admitting a Jew to a seat in our Colonial Legislature." The *Gazette* saw a disregard of the oaths as a solution, regardless of any legal complexities, saying that "it is utterly absurd to object to any man's religious opinions unless they interfere with his civil duties – and it cannot be asserted that a Jew's do. It is much more probable that a Roman Catholic's might, yet he is admitted without hesitation." "In all countries," the *Gazette* noted, "Jews are admitted to the same political rights as Christians; in England herself and in all her colonies the same." The article concluded that it was "intolerable to suppose that this little spot will permit such a stigma to attach to it, as that of being the last refuge of religious persecution."[38]

When the house next met, on 7 March, the committee on disabilities reported that "the only disabilities affecting the right of British subjects to sit & vote in the House are their failure to take the oath of allegiance, otherwise of fidelity, as prescribed by Her Majesty's order in Council, and the disabilities imposed by the Franchise Act of 1859."[39] None of these required Franklin to swear "on the true faith of a Christian" in order to take his seat. The challenge to his rights seemed to have ended, but Waddington returned to the charge with a motion that accused Franklin of trying to secure a seat "in a manner highly derogatory to the purity, dignity and honor of this Honorable House, and altogether unbecoming ... and through the connivance of Chief Justice Cameron, by administering and aiding in proffering an oath contrary to the form prescribed by Statute."[40] Waddington would later be described by a contemporary as one who was "prompt to delude himself on any matter of which he makes a hobby."[41] And by this time it was becoming clear that Waddington was seeking by whatever means to have Franklin condemned for any conduct that would make him unfit to serve as a member. He would then be unseated and replaced by the candidate with the next highest vote total in the Victoria Town elections: namely, Amor De Cosmos, Waddington's ally in opposition to the government.

Even though one of the other members was willing to second Waddington's motion, everyone else found it "objectionable in the language" and Waddington was forced to withdraw it. A compromise resolution was then passed, one whose wording attacked the government and its supporters, without attacking Franklin personally. A committee was to be appointed "to institute a thorough examination into the manner in which the first oath was administered to Mr. Selim Franklin & how this faulty form of oath was laid before him."[42]

Once again a colony of British North America had declined to take a step that might have resulted in a Jew being persecuted or merely tolerated in order to affirm the country's commitment to equality. John Franks, Moses David, Ezekiel Hart, Samuel B. Hart, and many others had been challenged by rules that would have made them less free. Each in his own way had met the challenge, and the country had been better for it. Now it was Franklin's turn. John Coles moved again that Franklin be allowed to take his seat. The speaker ruled the motion was no longer necessary because there was no longer any disability. Even Waddington agreed, telling the house that that there was nothing to stop Franklin from taking his seat "but his own feelings on the subject."[43]

When the house resumed sitting on 12 March, with Franklin in his seat, Waddington attempted a different tactic to have Franklin's place declared vacant. He now presented a petition from De Cosmos against the return of Franklin for Victoria Town. The petition was not based on faulty oaths but upon irregularities in voting. The election had given Franklin 106 votes to De Cosmos's 91, but 18 of Franklin's votes were cast by blacks who, De Cosmos alleged, should not have been entitled to vote. Once again, however, it was clear that this was an attack on the government rather than on Franklin himself.

Over fifty black families, many of them runaway slaves, had taken refuge in Victoria on the eve of the civil war in the United States. They had received an unaccustomed warm welcome in the uncrowded frontier society to the north. In 1857 the United States Supreme Court had decided in the infamous Dred Scott case that Negro slaves could not become citizens of the United States simply by living in a "free" area.[44] George Hunter Cary has been given the credit for the decision that gave the blacks the right to vote in Victoria. Douglas, at Cary's urging, decided that if Negroes were not citizens of the United States they were not citizens of any country and therefore had no citizenship to renounce. As immigrants without a country, they might be admitted as British subjects by simply subscribing to an oath of allegiance to the queen and by proving three months' residence. It was common knowledge that those blacks who voted had voted as a block for Cary and Franklin.[45] De Cosmos protested through the columns of his newspaper, later saying that the "Yankee blacks" were "bogus voters" and should not have been counted.[46]

At the end of the day Franklin was still in his seat, but the committee on the faulty oath had yet to report and a decision on De Cosmos's challenge had yet to be made.

This entire scene had been played before. The setting and characters differed somewhat from past performances, but the script was much the same. More than anything, it was the epic quality that made this scene part of the same drama as those that had gone before. Could this have been happening in 1860, over a century after the landmark debate in the British House of Commons about the naturalization of Jews that had since been successfully resolved in the colonies? All the other English-speaking jurisdictions had developed comprehensive systems that allowed Jews equal civil and political rights. Still, some of the elements of Franklin's situation were signs of the times, a reminder that the political rights of Jews and other minorities in British North America and elsewhere were yet recently acquired.

There had been enormous strides made in the acceptance of the political equality of Jews in the half-century since Ezekiel Hart had been ordered to withdraw from the Lower Canada Assembly. In 1843 Henry Hague Judah was elected in a by-election to represent Champlain in the Legislative Assembly of the new province of Canada. Although Judah was of Jewish descent, the evidence is that he was not himself Jewish.[47] Samuel C. Benjamin, an observant Jew, was elected to Montreal's City Council in 1849;[48] William Hyman, a co-religionist, was elected first mayor of the township of Cape Rosier in the Gaspé in 1858.[49] In October 1856, George Benjamin was elected to the parliament of Canada representing North Hastings. When he took his oath of office in February 1857, he became the first Jew seated in a legislature in British North America.

Even in Great Britain, Jews had now been granted political equality. In 1858, with the passage of the Jewish Relief Act, England's first Jewish member of the House of Commons, Baron Lionel de Rothschild, was finally allowed to take his seat, eleven years after he had been first elected. The Jewish Disabilities Removal Act of 1845 allowed David Salomons to be elected alderman for the city of London in 1847 and lord mayor in 1855.[50]

Selim Franklin was a practising Jew and a member of the Jewish community in Victoria. Because of the precedents, he could not long be denied his seat. On 17 March 1860 the committee on the faulty oath reported. Its decision was that the oath administered to Franklin by the chief justice had been offered him in good faith.[51] Attached to the report was a 13-page memorandum from Cameron himself, tabled for the record "to prevent any misconception in future."[52] The document provided a scholarly review of the law relating to oaths of office. Cameron reviewed the origin of England's oath requirements and noted that those oaths had "the effect of disenfranchising a great many conscientious persons" – Nonconformists, Quakers, Roman Catholics, and others of differing beliefs who were "thereby deprived of their civil rights." However, he continued, "these disabilities are all now matters of history, Act after Act of relief having been passed by Parliament, until the whole were finally done away with, by the passing of the 21 & 22 Victa. Chap 49 entituled 'An Act to provide for the relief of Her Majesty's subjects professing the Jewish religion'" in 1858.

Cameron noted the effect of the Plantation Act of 1740 in allowing naturalized Jews in the British colonies to amend the oath of abjuration. He noted that that act had been expanded to allow the same rights to Jews born in England. He concluded that the law of England did indeed apply to the colony of Vancouver Island, that that law included the Jewish Relief Act of 1858 allowing Jewish persons to sit in parliament and to modify any oath of office by omitting the words "upon the true Faith of a Christian," and that another act, passed on the same day,[53] consolidated the three usual oaths taken by Protestants into one oath "inflicting civil disability on none, yet varying in its words to suit the religious belief, and bind the consciences of all Her Majesty's Subjects, whether Protestant or Catholic, Quaker, or Jew."

By the end of June, the assembly of the colony would put the matter to rest by passing, with Franklin's supporting vote, an Oaths Act providing for the administering to members of the house, the same oath as in the House of Commons of the imperial parliament.[54] De Cosmos's challenge to Franklin's election became bogged down in the Elections Committee because he had changed his name from Smith, but Franklin was formally declared elected by the committee on 24 July, more than four months after he been allowed to take his seat.[55]

In the end, it had taken the new colony of Vancouver Island only ten days to reach the same decisions that the other colonies of British North America had arrived at over longer periods of time. There would be other "little spots" at other times where minorities would be denied civil and political rights, but the rule had been established. Jews were to be equal in this new nation. Vancouver Island was no exception.[56]

16 From Toleration to Equality

> Where equality is the law of the land, there is no privileged class. Liberty precludes the idea of *toleration*, and the majority, no matter how large, have no right to claim any merit for leaving the minority undisturbed in the enjoyment of equal rights.
>
> Isaac Leeser, *Philadelphia Gazette*, 12 December 1839[1]

Toleration had been the new idea of the seventeenth century. At the outset of the era of colonial expansion, most countries were geographic entities that had a national religion and were composed primarily of a single nationality or culture. Full rights of citizenship belonged only to those of that dominant religion, language, or culture.[2] Those who were not of that culture, if they were even allowed to live in the countries of Europe, were merely tolerated, and their rights were severely circumscribed. Toleration acts were passed to allow some dissenting sects liberty of conscience and the right to worship publicly without penalty as well as the exercise of limited rights. However, the acts dealt not with equality but with domination of one group over others. While offering a few rights to Nonconformists, toleration in fact entrenched the rights of the dominant culture. In Britain the jurisprudence defining tolerance began with the Toleration Act of 1689.

Equality, the declared ideal of the American and French revolutions, became the new idea of the eighteenth and nineteenth centuries. Those in the Americas adopted a new philosophy. As Thomas Paine remarked, they saw that toleration is not the opposite of intolerance but its counterfeit – that both are despotisms. They understood that toleration or tolerance offers only privileges, not rights, and that privileges can be withdrawn. In 1790 the French Jews noted that the United States had rejected the word "tolerance" for its constitution, "as a term tending to compromise individual liberty and to sacrifice certain classes of men to other classes," and concluded that "to tolerate is, in fact, to suffer that which you could, if you wished, prevent and prohibit."

Notwithstanding these theories, it took many years for the ideal of equality to approach realization in both France and the United States. The spirit of equality evident in the early phases of the French Revolution was quickly reversed during the Napoleonic era. And even though the American Declaration of Independence proclaimed that "all men are created equal" and the first amendment to the constitution effectively separated church and state in the federal sphere, many years were to pass before the individual American states (which had the real responsibility for allowing rights) were willing to remove the privileges of the dominant religions or the disabilities of minority groups and so did not conform to the lofty ideals of the Declaration of Independence until much later.

In British North America the pattern was different. Equality was not proclaimed as an ideal in any founding document. Instead, it grew from a series of small steps which put those colonies on a swift and relentless course towards acceptance of the principle that all citizens, whatever their creed or origin, were equally entitled to the favours and protection of the government.

Equality for all was by no means the premise underlying the British government's initial method for administering its colonies, however. Faced with the prospect of using its limited population and resources to control a large and far-flung empire populated overwhelmingly by people who were foreign in culture, Britain sought to ensure that key positions in colonial governments remained in the hands of individuals whose loyalty could be depended upon. To this end, an ambiguous system of disabilities prevented those who did not share the established religion of Britain itself from assuming offices and places of trust. On occasion others were allowed to share in government if it would enhance Britain's interests and so long as they were not perceived as a threat to those interests or no one complained. However, it was the British government's policy for its colonies that allowing "outsiders" to share in government would in no respect undermine the role of the Church of England as the established church or the privileges granted to its adherents.

It was therefore an astonishing departure when, after 1760, Britain sought to ensure the loyalty of the 70,000 French-Canadian Catholics in Quebec by giving them not only freedom of religion but also virtual civil and political equality with Anglicans. This policy, which applied to French-Canadian Catholics but not to other Catholics, was enshrined in the Quebec Act of 1774 and maintained in the Constitutional Act of 1791 (when it was expanded to include other Catholics as well) at a time when neither Britain itself nor any of its other colonies allowed Catholics such equality. Catholics in Britain would not obtain equal rights until the Roman Catholic Relief Act of 1829.

Britain's treatment of Protestant Dissenters in its colonies was complex and inconsistent. Dissenters were often encouraged to settle in the colonies by offers of land, but they were not offered civil and political rights equal to those of the Anglicans, and in some instances rights given to Dissenters in early times were taken away later when the Colonial Office consolidated its control in the colonies. Although Protestant Dissenters in Quebec were given virtual equality with Anglicans from 1763, that equality was withdrawn under the Constitutional Act of 1791 which created the new colonies of Upper and Lower Canada and was not reinstated until the 1830s. In the Maritime colonies of British North America, where the settlement of German Protestants had originally been solicited, neither Protestant Dissenters nor Catholics were allowed rights equal to those of the Anglicans until the 1840s.

Despite the law in England, the colonists of British North America, most of whom were not followers of the Church of England, believed that equality was the only philosophy that would work in the New World. Elected representatives who sat in colonial legislatures continued to champion the rights of their neighbours, frequently against the wishes of the British government. Examples multiplied as time progressed. In 1786, the New Brunswick Assembly passed an act giving relief to Quakers by allowing them to declare and affirm instead of swear an oath, if "required on any lawful occasion to take an oath." The French-Canadian majority in the House of Assembly of Lower Canada gave equal rights to Quakers at its first session in 1793 and in the 1820s repeatedly passed bills to give equality to Protestant Dissenters even though the Colonial Office refused to allow the bills to become law. In the 1820s the Nova Scotia House of Assembly repeatedly resolved – against the wishes of the Colonial Office – to allow Roman Catholics the right to sit in the Assembly.

It was not until 1830 that Britain itself had removed all the restrictions that had denied equality to most Protestant Dissenters and Catholics in that country. It was only after these changes in Britain that the British government ceased to support restrictions on the civil and political rights of Protestant Dissenters and Catholics in the Maritime colonies and Protestant Dissenters in Upper and Lower Canada.

Within this subtle system of control in the colonies, Jews had a special status from the beginning. In the early years of the eighteenth century the British had realized that the Jews would be an asset in their trading competition with other imperial powers. The Plantation

Act of 1740 thus offered Jews certain rights which were not available to them elsewhere as well as the possibility of exemption from some of the disabilities that other non-Anglicans faced. Official encouragement of Jewish settlement followed.

Jews were freely given government land in the original allotment when Halifax was founded in 1749 even though in Britain itself their right to be landholders was severely restricted. Although Jews had previously been recorded as landholders in some of the Thirteen Colonies, these grants of land in Halifax directly from the crown to John Franks, Samuel Jacobs, Isaac Solomon, and others were unprecedented. The existence of a Jewish cemetery on crown land in Halifax was also unusual.

By 1768 John Franks had been given the right to hold high government office by commission in the Old Province of Quebec, long before any similar instances in the United States or in England. The governor, Guy Carleton, made it plain that Franks was not to be an exceptional case by creating a general form of official "State Oaths for Persons of the Jewish Persuasion" in the form recommended by the Plantation Act. When Moses David was appointed coroner in Upper Canada by commission in 1808, the lieutenant governor, Francis Gore, while apparently unaware of the exemption for Jews in the Plantation Act, allowed David to dispense with the usual state oaths and Test Act requirements for holding office and to file a bond instead.

These unprecedented incidents of the equal treatment of Jews, rather than being isolated stories, illustrated the policy. On at least three occasions subsequent to its passage in 1740, legal authorities gave written decisions confirming that the Plantation Act provided the basis for the equal rights of Jews. That act, while applying nominally to Jews and foreign Protestants who were naturalized in the colonies, was thereby determined to apply to Jews and others who were born in the colonies as well. (Conversely, the effect of the American Revolution for the Jews in the Thirteen Colonies was to remove that legal equality which had been provided by the Plantation Act.) Over the 127 years after its passage, the act's legal interpretation was the basis of the equality of Jews as citizens. In 1809, a committee of the Executive Council of Lower Canada, led by Chief Justice Jonathan Sewell, confirmed that Ezekiel Hart could not be prevented from being seated in the assembly because of the rights he had been granted as a Jew under the Plantation Act.

To clarify the precedents and remove the doubts its own House of Assembly had raised twenty-five years earlier, Lower Canada's Declaratory Act of 1832 provided that Jews in the province were entitled "to the full rights and privileges of the other subjects of His Majesty." Two years later a committee of the Lower Canada Assembly led by René-Joseph Kimber determined that no further specific amendment to the province's oath legislation was necessary to give Jews equal access to office because the equality of Jews stemmed from the Plantation Act.

In 1861, Chief Justice David Cameron of Vancouver Island determined that Selim Franklin could not be barred from taking his seat in the assembly by reason of the requirement of any oath or declaration to the contrary because his equal rights as a Jew stemmed from the Plantation Act.

By 1867, any ambiguities in the Plantation Act had been unequivocally resolved, and the act was established by legal authority as the basis of Jewish equality in British North America since 1740. There had been incidents in which Jews had not been treated equally by British officials, such as the requirement that Samuel Hart become an Anglican so that he could be seated in the Nova Scotia Assembly in 1793, the reported suggestion of Lord Dalhousie in 1827 that Moses Hart's son, as a Jew, could not hold a commission in the militia, and the dictum of Chief Justice John Elmsley in 1798 that Jews could not hold land in Upper Canada. However, the evidence is that whenever an instance of unequal treatment was directly challenged, the equal rights of Jews were upheld. So it was when Moses David successfully appealed Elmsley's decision to the Executive Council in 1803.

Reflecting this legal equality, even though they formed a small percentage of the population,[3] Jews in British North America had joined with the rest of their fellow colonists in building a country where equality rather than mere toleration was the governing philosophy. By 1867 Jews had had a fair share of elected politicians; one of them, George Benjamin, had been asked to serve in the highest political capacity – to hold office in the cabinet of John Sandfield Macdonald. Benjamin's life could be seen as a microcosm of the struggle for equal civil and political rights. He had understood the unprecedented nature of Canadian equality and had personally tested the challenge Jews had faced for centuries – the denial of opportunity caused by a society based on one established religion or culture. He had found the freedom to take his place among the peoples of Canada, holding almost every public office during his lifetime, participating in the building of a nation "upon the eternal foundations of justice."

In 1851 the province of Canada, with the passage of the Rectories Act, had put persons of all religions on an equal footing by removing the official status of the Church of England in that province. Before the act's passage, the Church of England had been the official church and thus the followers of other religions had second-class status. With its passage, the Church of England was disestablished in the Canadas and lost its special rights. J.C. Morrison stated the government's position when he introduced the bill in the house: "Very few, indeed, argue in favour of a state religion in Canada, peopled as it is with persons from all creeds and from all nations, and equally entitled to the favour and protection of the Government." Shortly afterward, the Church of England lost its special status in the other colonies of British North America.

The equality that existed by 1867 was not perfect, but it was advanced for its time. The removal of political and civil disabilities did not mean the end of discrimination or of inequality, but by 1867 the provinces of British North America had made some strides towards acknowledging the legal equality of different races as well as religions. There were still deplorable instances of racial inequality and many doors would remain closed to religious and racial minorities for another hundred years, but the removal of disabilities and the legal recognition of diversity could only have given encouragement to those seeking out a new land. Blacks, aboriginals, and women, for example, had all made advances.

The enslavement of blacks in British North America had ended thirty years before slaves were emancipated in the United States in 1865.[4] In this respect as in many others, Upper Canada had led the way with an act that ended slavery for practical purposes in 1793.[5] The province's common schools acts, beginning in 1850, gave blacks as well as Catholics the legal right to their own separate schools supported by public money.[6] As a result, Upper Canada became the haven for slaves escaping slavery in the United States on the "underground railroad." The colony of Vancouver Island, which had welcomed American fugitive slaves and given them rights to vote in 1861, had the distinction of having the first person of colour to be elected to public office in a North American city when Mifflin Wistair Gibbs was elected to Victoria's City Council in 1866.[7]

Native Indians, too, had moved from the United States to British North America, seeking freedom. Shortly after the American Revolution the Iroquois nation resettled in Upper Canada on a tract of nearly three million acres stretching six miles on either side of the Grand River. Similarly, there was nothing approaching gender equality in British North America by 1867. But while the settled areas still allowed rights only to those women who had no husbands,[8] a rough equality existed for women on the frontier.[9]

In this new land, the legal framework of religious equality was in place by 1867. British North America had already become a unique kind of multicultural nation where the legal, political, and civil equality of all its citizens predominated – a society with egalitarian goals based on a long view of historical freedoms where one cultural group would not be "promoted" at the expense of others.[10] The meaning of "equality" would continue to evolve over the next century, building on the legal underpinning already in place. The inequality based on the prominence of the old establishment would survive many years more, but it, too, would eventually be superseded.

Canada's heritage is founded on a series of laws that deny the concept of one élite homogeneous group dominating society with others merely tolerated. Peopled by those of many cultures and religions who were dissatisfied with the lack of freedom and equality of opportunity in their countries of origin, Canada grew to become a new kind of society that offered equality to its citizens earlier than both its mother country and other colonies. The tradition of respect for the right of every individual to define him/herself within the context of a free and equal society is the essence of our nationality.

Ezekiel Solomons, Chapman Abraham, and their partners, as well as John Franks, Moses David, George Benjamin, Esther Brandau, Elizabeth Nathan, Ezekiel Hart, Samuel B. Hart, Selim Franklin, and all the others, had forged the way in a new land, helping creating a country with people of other religions, races, and nationalities, a country in which all peoples could work together as equals.

The message went back to the Old World that this was a good place to settle. For the Jews, the search had been completed. Soon more would arrive in their thousands, knowing they would be putting down roots for their children in a land where there was equal opportunity.

Epilogue

Fond land that held my hopes when hope could thrill!
Your memory is as bright, as life is sweet,
Dear as the prayer that childhood's lips repeat.
Your beauty and your grandeur haunt me still.
Home of intrepid thought and dauntless will!
Where zeal and aspiration strive to meet,
And eager patriotic pulses beat
To plan what eager purpose must fulfil.

Dear land of promise, Empire of the free!
You symbol all that consecrates the earth,
The truth of loyalty, the pride of worth,
The garnered fruitage of prosperity
And all that strengthens peace and harmony
Linked with the parent lands that gave you birth.

"Canada," a sonnet by Isidore Gordon Ascher, c. 1867[1]

Throughout our history the idea of a nationhood based on a concept of racial purity or a homogeneous grouping of people was repeatedly rejected by Canadians. Canada joined other nations in fighting to defend itself from the epitome of that concept during the Second World War. The depth of Canada's commitment was shown by the fact that one in nine Canadians voluntarily joined the war effort.

The concept of a country whose inhabitants belong to a single "pure" group is now being challenged throughout the world. There are still some struggling to maintain the dominance of one race or culture, blinding themselves to the reality that in the boundary-free world of the future, cultural or ethnic divisiveness based on historical geographic isolation can no longer be sustained.

In a world where there are no longer any real geographic barriers and where communication is immediate, Canada's experiment in bridging the old and new concepts of nationhood is becoming even more relevant. The idea of a "multicultural" nation that respected the equality of each of its citizens planted its roots in British North America during the eighteenth and nineteenth centuries. It grew, despite the existing official mindset which reflected the experience in Britain at the time, to become the fact of everyday life and law in evidence in Canada today.

The same story had been repeated for all peoples, again and again, from coast to coast, each time with a similar conclusion. Rights had been tested by minorities, found to be theirs, and had become the law of the land. These were the pathfinders who searched out the land, found that it was good, and passed on the word. Josiah Henson, the runaway slave whose story was the model for Harriet Beecher Stowe's *Uncle Tom's Cabin*, wrote of his arrival in Upper Canada in 1830: "It was the 28th of October, 1830, in the morning, when my feet first touched the Canada shore. I threw myself on the ground, rolled in the sand, seized handfuls of it and kissed them, and danced around, till, in the eyes of several who were present, I passed for a madman.[2]

Canada's people had all come from someplace else, from distant corners of the earth. They wore all manner of costume: some wore robes, some clothes, some skins. They wore hats of beaver, of knitted wool, of cloth. Some dressed in bright colours, some in drab, some were indistinguishable from the shades of the forest. They came in all sizes and shapes, and at all ages. Their shades of skin ranged from red through yellow and white to black. They came by all manner of transport – some crowded into small ships, some in carriages or carts, some on the backs of animals, some on foot.

The land was big enough for all. It was a land of impassable stands of timber, of mountain ranges that concealed fertile valleys, of great expanses of fresh water and of oceans teeming with fish, of natural waterways, of huge arable tracts. It was a land of wilderness, of abundant wild life, of rock outcroppings that held a store of natural wealth. It was a land of winters that were at once harsh, silent, and majestic. In short, it was a vast land of great beauty.

Perhaps it was the land itself that was the bond – a land whose vastness could be seen as a challenge instead of a threat. Those who had come to search out the land had found a need to search out others in the common struggle to create a place to stand amid the bounty of the country in the face of great natural obstacles. They found a unity in their diversity. They found that each could draw strength from the other, that the whole was somehow much greater than the sum of its parts.

They had come to search out a land but had founded a country. The land they shared seemed smaller because of the common threads that held it together. Its regions demanded separate consideration, but the country's integrity lay in its common bonds. Never before had countries been built of so many cultures and creeds – none with a clear enough mandate to make its own the official culture. It was a country that would need a positive co-operative effort to help its inhabitants speak to each other, to learn to respect the rights of others, to define themselves within the context of a free and equal society. There would still be hurdles to overcome. Despite the laws, there would still be inequalities to be addressed. The removal of disabilities still did not give equal opportunity to all, nor did it remove discrimination between people. Education and good will would be needed to ensure that all Canadians, old and new, understood the strength of the values that evolved as the heritage of the country. Canada would be a nation in its own right as long as its peoples would continue to be equally entitled to the favour and protection of the government. It was a nation which placed its rights upon "the eternal foundations of justice."

It was a model for the world to come.

Table 6
Jews and the Development of Civil and Political Rights before 1867 (jurisdiction of first known instance **highlighted**)

Right allowed	England	British North America		Thirteen Colonies	United States
		First Instance	Second Instance	To 1774	From 1775
Legal residence	December 1655	1749	—	**1654, New York**	—
Public worship	**1673**	c. 1752, Nova Scotia	—	1682, New York	—
Oath on Pentateuch	1680	1752, Nova Scotia	—	**1658, Rhode Island**	—
To sue and be sued	1697	1752, Nova Scotia	—	**1658, Rhode Island**	—
Leave bequests for religious purposes	1846: 9 & 10 Vict., c. 59	1819, Lower Canada: Elizabeth Lyons	31/12/1824, Lower Canada: David David	**18/4/1737, New York: Rachel Luis**	—
Citizenship by naturalization	1826: 6 Geo. IV, c. 67	**1740: 13 Geo. II, c. 7**	—	**1740: 13 Geo. II, c. 7**	—
Purchase land without disability	after 1830	8/2/1750, Halifax: Israel Abrahams	18/4/1750, Nova Scotia: Isaac Levy	**15/7/1661, New York: Asser Levy (Leevi)**	—
Allotment of land by government	after 1830	**8/1749, Halifax: John Franks**	8/1749, Halifax: Samuel Jacobs, Isaac Solomon	—	—
Crown or government patents	after 1830	8/1/1760, Nova Scotia: John Franks, David S. Franks et al.	28/5/1760, Fort Cumberland [NB], Samuel Jacobs	**1757, Virginia: Michael Israel**	—
Serve on a jury		**1755, Nova Scotia: Napthali Hart Jr., Nathan Nathans**	1760, Nova Scotia: Joseph Jones		
Hold government office (no commission)		28/3/1763, Quebec: Aaron Hart, postmaster, Trois-Rivières	2/1805, Newfoundland: Simon Solomon, postmaster, St John's	**1703, South Carolina: Simon Valentine, commissioner in charge of guard, Charleston**	

Hold government office by commission	after 1828: 9 Geo. IV, c. 17	**18/11/1768, Quebec: John Franks, chief fire official**	24/2/1808, Upper Canada: Moses David, coroner	—	1778, Georgia: Moses Sheftall, commissioner of issues
Serve in military	1689	1775, Quebec: John Franks, Isaac Judah	1793, Upper Canada: Moses David	1754, New York: Isaac Myers, Michael Franks	—
Officers in military	1809, Joshua Montefiore, captain	1803, Upper Canada: Moses David, ensign/lieutenant	1807 (1808), Lower Canada: David David, lieutenant	—	**5/1778: David S. Franks, major**
Lawyer	**23/1/1770: Joseph Abrahams, solicitor;** 30/1/1833, Francis Goldsmid, barrister	30/11/1824, Lower Canada: Aaron Ezekiel Hart, barrister & solicitor	28/12/1830, Lower Canada: Aaron Philip Hart, barrister & solicitor	—	1778, Pennsylvania: Moses Levy
Notary public (imperial)	**24/6/1737: Ralph Schomberg**	24/12/1766, Lower Canada: Eleazar Levy	—	8/5/1772, Rhode Island: Napthali Hart	—
Notary public (local)	**24/6/1737: Ralph Schomberg**	18/2/1836, Upper Canada: George Benjamin	1840, Lower Canada: Myer Solomons	—	7/2/1789, Pennsylvania: Isaac Franks
Justice of peace, Lower Canada	—	**31/12/1831: Eleazar David David**	28/8/1833: Samuel Becancour Hart	—	—
Justice of peace, other areas	—	1856, Upper Canada: George Benjamin	27/3/1857, New Brunswick: Morden S. Levy	**1768, Georgia: James Lucena (possibly); see below, p. 259**	1806, South Carolina: Lyon Levy
Exercise franchise without challenge	1867	**1789, Nova Scotia: 29 Geo. III, c. 1**	1810, New Brunswick: 50 Geo. III, c. 36		
Abolition of state oaths	1858	**12/4/1832, Lower Canada: 1 Will. IV, c. 57**	13/2/1833, Upper Canada: 3 Will. IV, c. 13		

Table 6 (continued)

Right allowed	England	British North America		Thirteen Colonies	United States
		First Instance	Second Instance	To 1774	From 1775
Chief constable	1835, David Salomons, sheriff of London, 5 & 6 Will. IV, c. 28	1845, Montreal & District: Moses Judah Hays, chief commissioner of police			
Election to municipal office, not seated	1814, Brighton: Hyam Lewis				
Election to municipal office, seated	1822, Brighton: Hyam Lewis	4/1/1836, Upper Canada: George Benjamin, clerk Thurlow township			
Election to office in municipal corporation, not seated	12/1835, City of London: David Salomons				
Election to office in municipal corporation, seated	1847, City of London: David Salomons	2/2/1847, Canada West: George Benjamin, warden, Hastings County	1849, Canada East: Samuel C. Benjamin, alderman, Montreal		
Election to legislature, not seated	1847, Baron Lionel de Rothschild	5/3/1793, Nova Scotia: Samuel Hart, Liverpool	1807, Lower Canada: Ezekiel Hart, Trois-Rivières		11/1/1775, South Carolina: Francis Salvador, provincial congress
Election to legislature, seated	8/1858, Baron Lionel de Rothschild	26/2/1857, Canada: George Benjamin, North Hastings	3/1860, Vancouver Island: Selim Franklin, Victoria City	—	
Invitation to Privy Council (cabinet)	10/11/1871 George Jessel Solicitor General	21/5/1862, Canada: George Benjamin			

Notes

ABBREVIATIONS

AJA   American Jewish Archives
AJHS   American Jewish Historical Society Archives
AJHSP *American Jewish Historical Society Publications*
ANQ-M Archives nationales du Québec – Montréal
AO   Archives of Ontario
ASTR   Archives du Séminaire de Trois-Rivières
BCARS British Columbia Archives and Records Service
CJA   Canadian Jewish Archives
DCB   *Dictionary of Canadian Biography*
JHSET *Jewish Historical Society of England Transactions*
NA   National Archives of Canada
PANB   Provincial Archives of New Brunswick
PANS   Public Archives of Nova Scotia
PRO   Public Record Office, London

PREFACE

1 Kohler, "Civil Status of the Jews in Colonial New York," 90. Kohler, a New York lawyer with a postgraduate degree in history, presented his paper to the fifth annual meeting of the American Jewish Historical Society at Baltimore, 27 and 28 January 1897.

2 The plaque was presented to the Mackinac Island State Park Commission by the Jewish Historical Society of Michigan on 31 May 1964. The information on the plaque was confirmed by Resolution 121 of the Senate of the state of Michigan on 28 May 1964: "Memorializing Michigan's First Jewish Settler and the Jewish Historical Society of Michigan."

3 From 1761 when Solomons arrived at Fort Michilimackinac until 1791 when the Constitutional Act was passed by the British parliament, the area later to be known as "Michigan" was British North American territory. Although legally ceded to the United States of America in 1796 as

a result of Jay's Treaty, the area continued to function as part of British North America until 1805 when the United States Congress established the Michigan Territory and took steps to set up its administration.

4 The same observation can be made about a number of the other central figures in this book including three of the four other members of the consortium – Chapman Abraham, Benjamin Lyon, and Gershon Levy – as well as Eleazar Levy, Hyam Myers, John Franks, Levy Solomons Jr, Moses David, Samuel B. Hart, Elizabeth Nathan, Selim Franklin, and others. The *Dictionary's* offices maintain probably Canada's largest collection of biographical research files on eighteenth- and nineteenth-century individuals, most of whom are not the subject of separate biographies in the *Dictionary.*

5 B.G. Sack's *The History of the Jews in Canada: From the Earliest Beginnings to the Present Day, volume I* appeared in Yiddish in Montreal's *Jewish Daily Eagle* in 1911, in an English version in the *Canadian Jewish Chronicle* in 1925, and in book form in 1945. Benjamin Gutl Sack (1889–1969) made an enormous contribution in the face of tremendous obstacles. When he did his research, in the days before microfilm and photocopiers, primary sources were scarce and inaccessible. Moreover, he had no formal academic training and his mobility had been severely restricted by muscular dystrophy since childhood. His book remains the standard work on pre-Confederation Jewish history, even though subsequent research has raised questions about the reliability of many of his conclusions. Denis Vaugeois has assessed Sack's book as "a general survey of uneven historical value": "Aaron Hart," *DCB* 4: 333. In his *Les Juifs et la Nouvelle-France* (p. 112), Vaugeois expressed his frustration that contemporary scholars continue to base their histories on inaccuracies in Sack's research: "La question est vraiment troublante: une liste de noms cités avec une régularité étonnante mais dont la plupart ne sont jamais mentionnés dans les documents connus de l'époque."

6 Michael Bliss, "Privatizing the Mind: The Sundering of Canadian History, the Sundering of Canada," *Journal of Canadian Studies* 26 (winter 1991–92): 7, 16.

7 *Colonial Advocate* (York), 12 June 1828.

8 Three years after Max Kohler called for an authoritative review of the legal status of the Jews in England and America during colonial period, Henry Strauss Quixano Henriques started his remarkable series of articles on the "Jews and the English Law," published in the *Jewish Quarterly Review,* republished as a book under the same title in 1908. Henriques's work was authoritative and has not been challenged since its publication. To date, no one has attempted a similar study with respect to Canada or the United States. Particularly notable among the Canadian books that touch on the subject are: Arthur Brodey's unpublished thesis, "Political and Civil Status of Jews in Canada" (1933), a booklet by

David Rome published in 1982 under the title "Samuel Becancour Hart and 1832." Finally, John Garner's *The Franchise and Politics in British North America*, published in 1969, provides well-researched background, although it is limited to the subject of the franchise. It is worth noting that Canadians seem to have produced more studies of Jewish rights than the Americans.

9 Indeed, there is evidence that it was the hope of the imperial authorities that, in the words of one member of the British House of Commons of the day, nothing "will contribute more towards the conversion of the Jews than that of freeing them from all manner of persecution, and empowering, and even inviting them to become purchasers of land estates." Robert Nugent, 7 May 1753, in Hansard, *The Parliamentary History of England*, XIV: *1747–1753*, 1383.

10 Because of the focus of the book on the development of equality, some of the details of the lives of these previously unknown individuals have had to be placed in the notes. The genealogies of the Jewish families who came to British North America during this period have been compiled by the authors and will be published as a separate volume under the title, "Who Was Who in Canadian Jewry, 1749–1840."

11 The royal instructions to colonial governors which contained many of the rules relating to these rights were personal to each governor: they were almost never made public, and rather than being copied or recorded at some central registry in the colony, these documents usually left the colony along with the governor's other private papers when his term expired.

12 In early times, this was done through the law. Today, the law provides equal access, although subtle inequalities persist in our society.

13 By 1743, two years before the British captured the French fortress at Louisbourg for the first time, a report from Nova Scotia prepared for the British government stated that the "Principal Town in this Province is Annapolis": M. Bladen, R. Plumer, Jas. Brudenell, and B. Keene, "An Account of Nova Scotia in 1743," *Nova Scotia Historical Society Collections* 1(1878): 106–7. Because this was the location of the garrison, as well as of the two or three families who had settled there, it may have included Jews as well.

Aaron Gershom, whose name may suggest Jewish ancestry, was a soldier in the Rhode Island militia and was at Annapolis in the spring of 1747 when he deserted along with most of his company: see *The Muster Rolls of Three Companies Enlisted by the Colony of Rhode Island in May 1746, for an Expedition Against Canada Proposed by Great Britain* (Rhode Island: Society of Colonial Wars 1915).

There may also have been Jewish settlers with the British garrison at Louisbourg on Cape Breton Island, captured from the French in 1745 and returned to France in the summer of 1749 when the British occupants of the fortress were carried by ship down to join the settlers at Halifax. Samuel Jacobs, possibly Canada's first permanent Jewish settler, was likely located at Annapolis before 1745 and at Louisbourg during the British occupation: see pp. 73–4.

PROLOGUE

1 Hansard, *The Parliamentary History of England* (hereafter *Hansard*), XIV: *1747–1753*, 1391.

2 *Hansard*, XV: *1753–1765*, 162. For biographical accounts of Vernon, see Namier and Brooke, *House of Commons*, III: *1754–1790*, 583, and Michener, *The Caribbean*, 332–5. Vernon's early successes against the Spaniards in the Carribean were overshadowed by his loss of the British fleet in an unsuccessful attempt to take Cartagena in 1742. A contemporary account of Vernon's defeat, possibly by a veteran of Cartagena, was bitter about Vernon's reliance on past victories ("True Account of Admiral Vernon's Conduct at Cartagena," private collection):

While Vernon sate all glorious,
From the Spaniard's late defeat,
And his crew with shouts victorious,
Drank success to England's fleet ...
I, by twenty sail attended
Did this Spanish town affright,
Nothing then its wealth defended,
But my orders not to fight ...

3 *Hansard*, XIV: *1747–1753*, 1381. Isham, a Tory, had represented Northamptonshire in the house since 1737: Namier and Brooke, *House of Commons*, II: *1715–1754*, 668.

4 A parliamentary oaths act, passed in 1677 as 30 Car. II stat. 2, c. 1, required members of the House of Commons and the House of Lords, prior to sitting or voting to make a declaration under oath in words "commonly understood by *English* Protestants," professing that certain Roman Catholic practices "are superstitious and idolatrous." While the act did not strictly apply a religious test for Protestant Dissenters, it created some doubt as to whether those who were not "*English* Protestants" could make the declaration. The Act of Union of 1707 provided relief from any such doubt in the case of the forty-five members of the House of Commons, many Presbyterian, entitled to be elected from Scotland. During the eighteenth century, Protestant Dissenters were elected to the house in isolated circumstances, and, after 1727, slightly more often because of acts passed annually indemnifying those office holders who failed to make the required declaration. The effect of the indemnity acts was to make office holding a privilege that could be terminated rather than a right.

5 *Hansard,* XIV: *1747–1753,* 1381.

6 The Jews Naturalization Act – 26 Geo. II, c. 26 (1753) – was passed on 22 May 1753 and received royal assent on 7 June.

7 *Hansard,* XV: *1753–1765,* 161.

8 Ibid., 160.

9 As set out by Sir Roger Newdigate, ibid., 131–4. Newdigate in fact opposed repeal of the act.

10 Ibid., 139–40. This argument had been developed by Sir Edmund Isham in opposing the original passage of the naturalization bill in the debate in the Commons on 7 May 1753 (*Hansard,* XIV: *1747–1753,* 1381): by allowing Jews to purchase and hold land estates, "we are giving the lie to all the prophecies in the New Testament, and endeavouring to invalidate one of the strongest proofs of the Christian religion. By those prophecies they are to remain dispersed: they are to remain without any fixed habitation, until they acknowledge Christ to be the Messiah, and then they are to be gathered together from all corners of the earth, and to be restored to their native land."

11 This was the accepted contemporary opinion: see the remarks to the house during the debate on the naturalization bill in May: ibid., XIV: *1747–1753,* 1371 (William Northey), 1377–8 (Lord Dupplin), and 1413 (Horace Walpole).

12 Nicholas Fazakerley, MP for Preston, ibid., 1411.

13 Ibid., 1379–83. Before their expulsion in 1290, the Jews were used extensively as money lenders by the king and his court because, unlike Christians, they were not subjet to the laws of the church prohibiting "usury" or lending at interest. The money provided was so important to the realm that laws were designed to regulate the interest chargeable by Jews rather than to prohibit it: see, for example, the remarks of Sir John Barnard, ibid., 1390–1. During the economic upheaval in the last quarter of the thirteenth century, defaults on loans to Jews were widespread, and because they frequently were required to retain lands held as security for loans, Jews were widely perceived as substantial owners of English lands.

14 Ibid., 1388–9. Barnard, a London merchant, supported the Whig government. Of Quaker parentage, he had joined the Church of England as a young man. He had represented London since 1722. Namier and Brooke, *House of Commons,* II: *1715–1754,* 49.

15 *Hansard,* XV: *1753–1765,* 123.

16 Ibid., XIV: *1747–1765,* 1389.

17 There are references to Jews living in England during the period of the "expulsion." See, for example, Hyamson, *The Sephardim of England,* 1–13.

18 This is the conclusion of Henry Strauss Quixano Henriques in his seminal work, *The Jews and the English Law.* See, for example, his chapter, "The Civil Rights of English Jews," 177–220, at 178.

19 For a detailed discussion of the issues, see ibid., 229–40, 234–5. See also Samuel, "A List of Persons Endenized and Naturalized," 112–13.

20 *Hansard*, XIV: *1747–1753*, 1415. Walpole, third son of Robert Walpole, was elected to the Commons at the age of 23 in 1741, but did not follow in his father's footsteps. He retained his independence from his father's Whig connections; he was a writer and chronicler rather than a career politician. He was, in his own words, "a person who loves to write history better than to act in it." See Namier and Brooke, *House of Commons*, III: *1715–1754*, 595–7.

21 A full account of the issue can be found in Henriques, *The Jews and the English Law*, 241–5, and Hollander, "Naturalization of Jews in the American Colonies," 104–17.

22 Born an Irish Catholic in 1709, Robert Nugent had come to London in 1730, joined the Church of England about 1732, and was elected to Parliament in 1741. Horace Walpole wrote of him shortly thereafter: "This modest Irish converted Catholic stallion does talk a prodigious deal of nonsense in behalf of English liberty." He remained in the Commons until 1784 and died in Dublin in 1788, having returned to the Roman Catholic faith. See Namier and Brooke, *House of Commons*, II: *1715–1754*, 302–3.

23 *Hansard*, XV: *1753–1765*, 136.

24 Great Britain, *Journals of the House of Commons*, 26 (17 June 1750–6 April 1754), 132.

25 As quoted in Hollander, "Naturalization of Jews in the American Colonies," 106. Dr Henry Sacheverell, an Anglican cleric, was tried for preaching ultra-Tory sermons in February/March 1710 during the reign of Queen Anne. His convictions further endeared him to the people and aided the Tory cause by causing a popular outcry that the Church of England was in danger, thereby helping to defeat the Whig government. The reference to King James is to James II, whose autocratic and pro-Catholic policies led to his abdication in 1688.

26 A reference to Holland as the place of origin of potential immigrant Jews: see Henriques, *The Jews and the English Law*, 243.

27 Sir Roger Newdigate, *Hansard*, XV: *1753–1765*, 133.

28 Ibid., 152.

29 Henriques, *The Jews and the English Law*, 244.

30 Ibid., 245. The repeal of the Jews Naturalization Act received royal assent on 20 December 1753 and was published as 27 Geo. II, c. 1 (1754).

31 *Hansard*, XV: *1753–1765*, 129.

32 Dashwood, a Tory, had represented Oxfordshire since 1740; Edward Harley, a courtesy lord, had been elected as a Tory in 1747: Namier and Brooke, *House of Commons*, II: *1715–1754*, 300–1, 586.

33 *Hansard* (xv: *1753–1765*, 162–3) notes that the motion for the repeal of the Plantation Act "occasioned a great deal of debate." Unfortunately, it was not actually recorded in *Hansard.*

34 Hollander, "Naturalization of Jews in the American Colonies," 108. Hollander was able to piece together some extracts from the debate from biographies of participants and their contemporaries. William Pitt, at this time paymaster general to the armed forces, was to be prime minister, first as leader of the majority Whig party in the Commons (1756–61) and later as the first earl of Chatham (1766–8): Namier and Brooke, *House of Commons,* iii: 290–9.

35 *Hansard,* xv: *1753–1765,* 102.

36 Speaking in the House of Commons for the repeal of the Jews Naturalization Act, Sir George Lyttelton made it clear how much church and state were still connected in the England of 1753: "It is the misfortune of all the Roman Catholic countries that there the church and the state, the civil power and the hierarchy, have separate interests, and are continually at variance one with the other. It is our happiness that here they form but one system. While this harmony lasts, whatever hurts the church, hurts the state; whatever weakens the credit of the governors of the church, takes away from the civil power a part of its strength, and shakes the whole constitution." Ibid., 130.

CHAPTER ONE

1 Petition of French Jews to the National Assembly of the French Republic, 29 January 1790, quoted in Kohler, "Phases in the History of Religious Liberty in America, with Special Reference to the Jews," 57–8.

2 Hansard, *The Parliamentary History of England* (hereafter *Hansard*), xiv: *1747–1753,* 1415.

3 Henriques, *The Jews and the English Law,* 164–6; *Hansard,* v: *1688–1702,* 444–5.

4 Henriques, *The Jews and the English Law,* 191–4.

5 Ibid., 192. The statutes were 55 Hen. III (1271) and the Statute de Iudaismo. They were first printed in Tovey's *Anglia Iudaica* in 1738. See also the note by Humphrey Tindal, vicar of Wellington, in *Hansard,* xiv: *1747–1753,* 1365–8.

6 Henriques, *The Jews and the English Law,* 63–5. According to *Black's Law Dictionary,* a "villein" was attached to a manor, substantially in the condition of a slave who performed base or servile work as the lord's property and was bound to do all such services as the lord commanded; "villeinage" was a servile tenure passed from generation to generation. According to Henriques (pp. 188–9), a number of court cases tried as late as 1684 relied on the laws of England before Jews were expelled

and treated the status of Jews in the manner of villeinage based on the king's direct rights over them. Henriques, however, disagrees (pp. 63–5) that Jews were ever the king's villeins as they were usually described before 1290 as "the King's bondmen." To remove any doubts, Jews were specifically excluded from the status of villeinage in 1846 by the Religious Disabilities Act.

7 *Hansard*, XIV: *1747–1753*, 1399.

8 Henriques, *The Jews and the English Law*, 192–3. See, for example, Blunt, *History of the Jews in England* (1830), introduction, v, and 119–27.

9 According to *Black's Law Dictionary*, a *privilegium* was a special constitution by which the Roman emperor conferred an irregular right or obligation on an individual.

10 Rex *v.* Bosworth (1739), 2 *Strange* 1112–14.

11 Henriques, *The Jews and the English Law*, 201.

12 This type of restriction might help to explain the attractiveness to Jews of newer occupations such as distiller, chemist, and optometrist which were based on scientific discoveries and were not subject to the restrictions of older craft guilds or the qualifications imposed by cities upon those who desired to carry on the retail trade. Other non-restricted industries that might have been equally attractive would have included finance, international trade, and trade in newer commodities such as fur, as well as home industries such as garment-making.

13 Grimwade, "Anglo-Jewish Silver," 121–3.

14 Ibid., 120, 125. There is no doubt of Hart's Jewish commitment: he was treasurer of the Hambro Synagogue in 1807 and 1808.

15 Arthur G. Grimwade, *London Goldsmiths, 1697–1837: Their Marks and Their Lives* (2nd ed; London: Faber and Faber 1982), 723.

16 Shaftesley, "Jews in English Regular Freemasonry, 1717–1860," 165, 188; Keith Neal, *Great Britain's Gunmakers, 1540–1740* (London 1986), 444–7. According to Turner Kirkland, principal of Dixie Gun Works, Union City, Tennessee, "it is authenticated that Segalas was Jewish."

17 The Act of Supremacy, 1 Eliz., c. 1 (1558), and the Act of Uniformity, 1 Eliz., c. 2 (1558).

18 John Locke, *Epistola de Tolerantia* [A Letter on Toleration] (Oxford: Clarendon Press 1968), 60, 65. This work, written during Locke's exile in the Netherlands, was first published in Latin in 1689.

19 The Toleration Act, 1 Will. & Mary, c. 18 (1689).

20 Henriques, *The Jews and the English Law*, 164.

21 Ibid., 158–72. The Roman Catholic religion became offically tolerated in England by the Roman Catholic Relief Act of 1791 (31 Geo. III, c. 32), though the remaining disabilities were not removed until 1829. Toleration was extended to Quakers by the Places of Religious Worship Act of 1812 (52 Geo. III, c. 155) and to Unitarians in 1813 (53 Geo.

III, c. 160). A bill designed to remove remaining Jewish disabilities had passed the House of Commons in 1841 but was rejected by the Lords, 98 votes to 64. Jews in England were finally brought within the Toleration Act in 1845 and 1846 by the Jewish Disabilities Removal Act (8 & 9 Vict., c. 52) and the Religious Disabilities Act (9 & 10 Vict., c. 59).

22 Henriques, *The Jews and the English Law*, 149–50.

23 Locke, *Letter on Toleration*, 145.

24 Da Costa *v.* De Paz (1744), *Ambler's* 228, 1 *Dickens* 258, and 2 *Swanstons* 487 et seq. See Henriques, *The Jews and the English Law*, 19–22.

25 Henriques, *The Jews and the English Law*, 22.

26 Ibid., 229–40.

27 24 Geo. III, sess. 2, c. 16 (1784).

28 Henriques, *The Jews and the English Law*, 177–220. The full Coke quotation (p. 186) is: "All infidels are in law *perpetui inimici*, perpetual enemies (for the law presumes not that they will be converted, that being *remota potentia*, a remote possibility), for between them, as with the devils, whose subjects they be, and the Christian there is a perpetual hostility, and can be no peace." In November 1689, Mr Hampton Jr, in supporting a special tax on the Jews, had echoed Coke's sentiment, telling the House of Commons: "I hear some of these Jews are naturalized, but I would know how they come to be naturalized? If a Jew kill a man, or a man a Jew, he will be hanged. There is a great deal of difference betwixt being subject to the laws, and enjoying the benefit of the laws." *Hansard*, V: *1688–1702*, 444–5.

29 *Hansard*, 7 May 1753, XIV: *1747–1753*, 142–5.

30 Henriques, *The Jews and the English Law*, 186–91.

31 *Hansard*, 27 November 1753, XV: *1753–1765*, 155.

32 Naturalization Amendment Act, 6 Geo. IV, c. 67 (1825), altering and amending 7 Jac. I, c. 2 (1608).

33 The Corporation Act, 13 Car. II, c. 1, s. 2 (1661).

34 The Test Act, 25 Car. II, c. 2 (1673). See also Henriques, *The Jews and the English Law*, 140, 247–9. According to *Black's Law Dictionary*, the term "recusant" applied only to Roman Catholics in England, describing a person who did not join his proper Anglican parish.

35 The Test Act and the Corporation Act were repealed by the Sacramental Tests Repeal Act, 9 Geo. IV, c. 17 (1828). The new form of declaration required was as follows: I, *A.B.*, do solemnly and sincerely in the presence of God profess, testify, and declare, upon the true faith of a Christian, That I will never exercise any power, authority, or influence which I may possess by virtue of the office of — — — to injure or weaken the Protestant Church as it is by law established in England, or to disturb the said Church or the said Bishops and Clergy of the said Church in the possession of any rights or privileges to which such

Church or the said Bishops or Clergy are or may be by law entitled. See
also Henriques, *The Jews and the English Law,* 162.

36 The Roman Catholic Relief Act, 10 Geo. IV, c. 7 (1829).

37 Henriques, *The Jews and the English Law,* 247–51.

38 Ibid., 255–6.

39 Ibid., 254–6.

40 13 & 14 Will. III, c. 6 (1701).

41 The state oaths are printed in full as an appendix to Garner, *Franchise
in British North America,* 215–16.

42 The form of the oath of abjuration specified by the act of 1701 was
altered several times during the reign of Queen Anne: 1 Anne, c. 22,
s. 1 (1701); 5 Anne, c. 8 (1706); 6 Anne, c. 7, s. 20 (1707); 6 Anne,
c. 14 (1707); 8 Anne, c. 15 (1709); and once during the reign of
George I in 1714: 1 Geo. I, c. 13, s. 2. It was modified slightly for the
last time in 1766: 6 Geo. III, c. 53, on the death of the Old Pretender.

43 Emphasis added. According to Henriques (*The Jews and the English Law,*
224–5), a Jesuit named Garnet had previously written *A Treatise on Equivocation* that set down that a man, "when called upon, as he thinks
unjustly, to make a declaration or take an oath, may lawfully equivocate
by using ambiguous words or by reserving mentally a sense of the words
used different from that actually expressed" – by figuratively crossing his
fingers – as long as he does not so bring his true faith towards God into
doubt. The concluding words of the oath were designed to counter this
argument.

44 9 Geo. I, c. 24 (1722).

45 10 Geo. I, c. 4 (1723), An Act for explaining and Amending an Act of
the last Session of Parliament, Intituled, An Act to oblige all Persons,
being Papists, in that part of Great Britain called Scotland, and all persons in Great Britain, refusing or neglecting to take the Oaths appointed for the Security of His Majesty's Person and Government, by several
Acts herein mentioned, to Register their Names and Real Estates, and
for enlarging the Time for taking the said Oaths, and making such Registers, and for allowing farther Time for the Enrolment of Deeds or
Wills made by Papists, which have been omitted to be enrolled, pursuant to an Act of the Third Year of His Majesty's Reign; and also for
giving Relief to Protestant Lessees.

46 Picciotto, *Sketches of Anglo-Jewish History,* 66.

47 The words of the act were: "And whereas the following Words are contained in the latter Part of the Oath of Abjuration, viz. (Upon the true
Faith of a Christian) be it further Enacted by the Authority aforesaid,
That whenever any of his Majesty's Subjects, professing the Jewish Religion, shall present himself to take the said Oath of Abjuration, in pursuance of the above recited Act, or of this present Act, the said Words

(Upon the true Faith of a Christian) shall be omitted out of the said Oath in administering the same to such Person, and the taking [of] the said Oath by such Person professing the Jewish religion, without the Words aforesaid, in like manner as Jews are admitted to be sworn to give Evidence in Courts of Justice, shall be deemed to be a sufficient taking of the Abjuration Oath within the meaning of this and the said recited Act."

48 Henriques, *The Jews and the English Law,* 203. For the precise operation of the indemnity acts, see The King *v.* Parry (1811) and In the Matter of Stevenson (1823): Henriques, "The Political Rights of English Jews," 326.

49 Similar acts continued to be passed annually thereafter until 1868 when the Promissory Oaths Act was enacted.

50 Henriques, *The Jews and the English Law,* 267–301.

51 Roth, "Jews in the Defence of Britain," 10–12. Samuel, "Anglo-Jewish Notaries and Scriveners," 118–19, confirms Schomberg's baptism. Schomberg's journal contains several pages of notes as well as a plan of Quebec in the hand of Wolfe himself: Roth, "Challenge to Jewish History," 12.

52 Samuel, "Anglo-Jewish Notaries and Scriveners," 156–7.

53 Montefiore was reported to have obtained a commission as a captain and, later, to have been present at the capture of Martinique and Guadeloupe in 1809. The circumstances of his compliance with the state oaths and the Test Act at the time of his appointment have not, however, been verified: Roth, "Jews in the Defence of Britain," 18–19. He resigned his commission in 1812 and moved to the United States: Samuel, "Anglo-Jewish Notaries and Scriveners," 143–6.

54 Roth, "Jews in the Defence of Britain," 18–19. Jewish soldiers, however, have been documented in England by 1689: ibid., 12.

55 Stanley, *Canada Invaded, 1775–1776,* 13.

CHAPTER TWO

1 Quoted in Hühner, "The Jews of South Carolina," 41–2.

2 The state-sponsored inquisition or sacred tribunal had been established in Spain in 1480 and in Portugal in 1536. The purpose of the inquisition was to find secret Jews or Marranos among the "New Christians" who had been forcibly converted to Catholicism, to convict them, and to punish them by expulsion and confiscation of property or by public burning at the stake. (For a discussion, see Cecil Roth, *The Spanish Inquisition* [New York: Norton 1964], 208–26.) Antonio José da Silva, the illustrious poet and dramatist born in Rio de Janeiro in 1705, was the last known Jew to die at the stake under Portuguese rule. The inquisition in Lisbon convicted him of Judaizing, of being a secret Jew, and

he, along with his wife and his mother, was burned at the stake on 19 October 1739: Kohut, "Martyrs of the Inquisition in South America," 135–50. In May 1768 King José I renewed the laws affecting New Christians and Marranos but provided that they were to be punished by deportation and confiscation of property rather than by being burned at the stake. The inquisition in Portugal was not formally ended until 1821. Spain was equally harsh in punishing suspected Jews found in its colonies. The inquisition in Lima, in the Spanish colony of Peru, arrested and imprisoned Francisco Moyen of Potosí as a suspected Jew. The warrant for Moyen's arrest was issued on 14 May 1749. After nearly twelve years' imprisonment, Moyen was exiled from Peru, shipped to Spain, and finally perished off Cape Horn: Kohut, "Martyrs of the Inquisition," 151–9.

3 Roth, "Challenge to Jewish History," 34.

4 Mendelssohn, "Jewish Pioneers of South Africa," 180–1, 183, 203–4.

5 Donovan, "The Gradis Collection and the Interpretation of Jewish History at Louisbourg," note 22, citing Raymond Mentzer, "Marranos of Southern France in the Early Sixteenth Century," *Jewish Quarterly Review* 72(1982): 304–5.

6 Donovan identifies the Rodrigue family of Louisbourg, merchant correspondents of the Gradis family, as of Jewish descent: ibid., 10–11.

7 Ibid., citing France, Archives Nationales, Section Outre-Mer, G², vol. 196, dossier 107, 27 September 1718.

8 Sack, *History of the Jews in Canada*, 22–4.

9 Donovan, "The Gradis Collection and the Interpretation of Jewish History at Louisbourg," 10. The authors have located some other examples of Jews in the eighteenth century signing by a crossed mark.

10 Ibid., 10–11.

11 Mendelssohn, "Jewish Pioneers of South Africa," 184; Roth, "Challenge to Jewish History," 16.

12 Wolf, "American Elements in the Resettlement," 80.

13 Hartog, *The History of St. Eustatius*, 56. The privilege was granted by the States General of the Netherlands in response to a petition from the Jewish community of Amsterdam. The Jews of St Eustatius were also exempted from service in the civil guard or militia on Saturdays. However, the same author states (*The Jews and St. Eustatius*, 10) that "on St Eustatius, [Jews] were not allowed to be members of the Guard, a regulation prompted by practical motives, as on Saturdays they could do no service for religious reasons." On Curaçao, Jews formed a separate corps of the civil guard.

14 Although no accurate population statistics of Jews exist for this period, the available evidence shows that on the eve of the American Revolution, Curaçao had a Jewish population of about 2,000 souls and

St Eustatius, about 350. St Maarten so had a sizeable, if smaller, Jewish population. All three colonies had synagogues by the middle of the eighteenth century: Hartog, *The Jews and St Eustatius*, 11, 16 (n. 14). See also Moses Burak and Malcolm Stern, *Jewish History of the Caribbean* (American Airlines [c. 1980]). This large population may have been a result of the decision to permit Jews expelled from Bohemia, reported in volume 55 of the *Gentleman's Magazine* to number 46,000, to settle in Dutch territories: Samuel Oppenheim, "The Expulsion of the Jews from Bohemia, 1744–1745, and the Action of the English Jews Thereon," AJHS, P–255, Oppenheim Collection, box 35, file 13. In contrast, there were about 2,500 Jews in the Thirteen Colonies in 1775: Marcus, "The Jew and the American Revolution," 103.

15 Hyamson, *The Sephardim of England*, 150.

16 Michener, *The Caribbean*, 204.

17 Samuel, "Review of the Jewish Colonists of Barbados, 1680," 8 and summary. Samuel's calculation should be considered authoritative as it was based on detailed research rather than reliance on a list of apparently Jewish names. Samuel notes at the outset that "it is impossible to answer adequately the momentous question 'What have her Jews done for England?' without analysing the history of those early Jewish pioneers whose activities were a factor – and in some instances, perhaps, a vital one – in the development of the trade, communications and civilization of the British Colonies during the seventeenth and eighteenth centuries." See also May Lumsden, *The Barbados American Connection* (London: Macmillan 1988), 4–6.

18 The authors are indebted to Edward Challenger for this information.

19 The remaining English-speaking Jewish community large enough to support a synagogue was of course in London itself. This information comes from a verse by Daniel Levi de Barrios, *Historia de la Gran Bretana* [1688], 55–6, quoted in Bethencourt, "Notes on the Spanish and Portuguese Jews in the United States, Guiana, and the Dutch and British West Indies during the Seventeenth and Eighteenth Centuries," 38:

Ya, en seis ciudades anglas, se publica
luz de seis juntas de Israël sagradas;
tres en Nieves, London, Iamaica;
Quarta y quinta en dos partes de Barbadas;
Sexta en Madras Patân se vérifica.

The translation reads:

Already there has been news in six English cities
of the existence of six sacred Jewish communities;
Three in Nevis, London, Jamaica;
The fourth and fifth in two parts of Barbados;
The sixth among our Madras countrymen is being verified.

20 Wolf, "American Elements in the Resettlement, 80.

21 Reproduced in ibid., 82–6. The original document, in the British
Museum, Egerton MSS, vol. 2395, no. 8, is undated and does not spec-
ify any location on "the Wilde Cust." Wolf's conclusions on these issues
are convincing.

22 The document is reproduced in Wolf, "American Elements in Resettlement," 94–5.

23 Hollander, "Documents Relating to the Departure of the Jews from Suri-
nam in 1675," 8–29. The population estimate is at page 13. The docu-
ments were copied from the Colonial Papers in the Public Record
Office. Despite the proclaimed departure, by 1792 the population of
Surinam included 2,000 whites, of which one-half were Jews: Lebowich,
"Jews in Surinam," 169.

24 There appear to have been Jews at some Hudson's Bay posts from time
to time. Ferdinand Jacobs, the most notable of them, was of Jewish
ancestry and probably of Jewish birth. He joined the company in 1732
at about nineteen years of age and spent his seven-year apprenticeship
in the fur trade as a bookkeeper at Prince of Wales's Fort on the
Churchill River. He assumed increasing responsibility in the company's
trade, becoming chief factor at the fort in 1752, a position he retained
until 1762 when he become chief factor of York Factory. He retired to
England in 1775. He died in London in November 1783 and was
buried in the cemetery of the Anglican parish of St Sepulchre, West
Ham. According to company records, he was a supporter of the Church
of England. His son, Samuel, was christened as an infant by the surgeon
at Churchill on 22 February 1756. However, Jacobs's Jewish origin
seems to have been apparent on the frontier. Jenny, one of his children,
was later described as "the daughter of a Governor called Jacobs (a Jew)
she had also a Jewish countenance and disposition": Chiel, "Manitoba
Jewish History," 57–60. See also Smith, "Ferdinand Jacobs," DCB 4: 383–
4.

25 The Royal Proclamation of 1 November 1697, translated from the
Dutch, appears in Sack, History of the Jews in Canada, 47–8. In 1926 de
la Penha's heirs petitioned the Privy Council in England to have their
title to the territory verified: Sack, 48–9. See also Montreal Star, 6 November 1926, Montreal Gazette, 17 April 1935.

26 Barnett, "Correspondence of the Mahamad of the Spanish and Portuguese Congregation," 3–4 and note 6.

27 Law No 61 (M.L.). Davis, "Notes on the Jews in Barbados," 133. See
also Friedenwald, "Jews in the British West Indies," 45 et seq. An exception regarding the use of the courts by Jews for personal injury actions
was apparently added in 1675. In 1681, the English government
directed "the Governor to require the legislature [of the island] to pass

an act that such Hebrews as are naturalized and reside at Barbados shall and may be freely admitted to give their testimony in the courts of judicature in such manner and form as their religion permits and such as the Governor, Council and Assembly shall allow of and also to enjoy the full benefit of their naturalization according to His Majesty's letters patent." Notwithstanding the direction, the government of Barbados does not appear to have further expanded Jews' rights to testify as witnesses: "Barbados; Laws pertaining to Jews," AJHS, P–255, Oppenheim Collection, box 18, file 5.

28 Judah, "The Jews' Tribute in Jamaica," 158–9. See also Friedenwald, "Jews in the British West Indies," 55–7, and appendixes XIV and XV.

29 Friedenwald, "Jews in the British West Indies," 57. The instructions to John Gregory, president of the council of Jamaica in the absence of the governor, on 18 March 1736, specified "that you do not for the future give your consent to any act or acts to be passed in the assembly of our said island whereby any tax shall be imposed on the said Jews as Jews only, over and above what is laid on the rest of our subjects there." The instructions to the new governor, Edward Trelawney, on 12 January 1738 were strengthened further: see Labaree, ed., *Royal Instructions to British Governors*, 1: 149.

30 PRO, Colonial Office, no. 1015, 27 June 1707, Sunderland's Report to H.R.H. on Acts of Bermuda "not yet approved or disallowed by your Majesty" including "An Act allowing an Imposition on all Jews and Reported Jews trading in these colonies" as follows: "This Act passed 12 years ago, and tho there has been no complaints against it, it will be much in Your Majesty's power by leaving it as probationary to repeal it if just cause should be at any time hereafter offered." *Calendar of British State Papers*, XXIII: *America and West Indies, 1706–June 1708*, edited by Cecil Headlam (London: His Majesty's Stationery Office 1916), 488–9.

31 McKinley, *Suffrage Franchise in the Thirteen Colonies*, 475–6. The restrictions in Pennsylvania, South Carolina, and Rhode Island, although legislative provisions exclusively in favour of Christians, did not specifically exclude Jews as did the New York resolution of 1737. See also Garner, *Franchise in British North America*, 146. A survey of advances in civil rights for Jews in the Thirteen Colonies before the Revolution is in Morris, "Civil Liberties and the Jewish Tradition in Early America," 20–39.

32 The subject of "freedom of the city" in New York is covered in Kohler, "Civil Status of the Jews in Colonial New York," 99–103. Kohler lists the names of 52 Jewish citizens granted "freedom of the city" between 1687 and 1769.

33 The King *v.* Moses Gomez, Hayman Levi, Daniel Gomez, Isaac Gomez, Naphtali Hart Myers, Hayman Myers, and Asher Myers (21 October 1756), New York County Court House, Office of the Clerk of the New

York Supreme Court, Archives, Minute Book of the New York Supreme Court of Judicature, 308. The evidence appears in the prosecutor's file, New York Historical Society, Kempe Papers, BSW 2. See also Godfrey and Godfrey, "The King vs. Gomez and Others," 397–407. The "two strange Jews" were probably Chapman Abraham and Levy Solomons.

34 Ian A. Hunter, "The Shape of the Devil: The Salem Witch Trials of 1692," *Law Society Gazette* 27(1993): 60.

35 Hershkowitz, *Wills of Early New York Jews*, 51.

36 See pp. 23–4.

37 De Sola Pool, *An Old Faith in a New World*, 39. See also Kohler, "Civil Status of the Jews in Colonial New York," 93–6.

38 Quoted in Kohler, "Civil Status of the Jews in Colonial New York," 93.

39 As quoted in Hühner, "The Jews of South Carolina," 41–2.

40 Reznikoff and Engelman, *The Jews of Charleston*, 3–4.

41 The text of the act is printed in Elzas, *The Jews of South Carolina from Earliest Times to the Present Day*, 20–1 and appendix A. Notwithstanding this wording, there is no evidence to support the conclusion that the Jewish religion was not legally tolerated.

42 Hollander, "Civil Status of the Jews in Maryland," 33–44. See also Marcus, *Early American Jewry*, 2: 520; Hartogensis, "Early Jewish Settlers of Baltimore," 191–5.

43 Wolf, "American Elements in the Resettlement," 77.

44 Thorpe, comp., *The Federal and State Constitutions*, 6: 3212.

45 Although the new restrictions were only occasionally enforced, they remained on the statute books until 1783: McKinley, *Suffrage Franchise in the Thirteen Colonies*, 451–3. In 1762 the Superior Court of Rhode Island refused the privilege of freemanship to two Jews on the grounds that "it appears that the free and quiet enjoyment of the Christian religion and a desire of propagating the same were the principal views with which this colony was settled, and by a law made and passed in the year 1663, no person who does not profess the Christian religion can be admitted free of this colony": Kohler, "The Jews in Newport," 71.

46 Gutstein, *The Jews of Newport*, 42.

47 McKinley, *Suffrage Franchise in the Thirteen Colonies*, 451.

48 Thorpe, comp., *The Federal and State Constitutions*, 5: 3071–2.

49 Ibid., 3076 et seq.

50 "The Charter of Georgia, 1732," ibid., 2: 773–4.

51 An Act for the Making Aliens Free of this part of the Province, passed 4 November 1704, in Thomas Cooper and David J. McCord, eds., *The Statutes at Large of South Carolina* (10 vols; Columbia SC: A.J. Johnston, 1838–41), 2, no. 228, 251–5.

52 McKinley, *Suffrage Franchise in the Thirteen Colonies*, 138–9.

53 Ibid., 475.

54 Elzas, *A Century of Judaism in South Carolina*, 5.

55 New York, Legislative Council, *Journal*, vol. 1, 15 November 1727, 560. See also Daniel Nunez da Costa, AJHS, P–255, Oppenheim Collection, box 2, file 65.

56 *The Colonial Laws of New York from the Year 1664 to the Revolution* (Albany: James B. Lyon 1894), 2: 418–19, c. 508 (25 November 1727).

57 Goodman, *American Overture*, 199; Allen D. Candler, comp., *The Colonial Records of the State of Georgia* (26 vols; New York: AMS Press 1904–14), 17: 190.

58 Thorpe, comp., *The Federal and State Constitutions*, 5: 3071–2, 3076 et seq.

59 The Navigation Acts were 12 Car. II, c. 18 (1660) and 13 Car. II, c. 14 (1661).

60 The most complete treatment of this subject is Samuel, "A List of Persons Endenized and Naturalized," 111–44. Samuel lists 283 possible Jewish recipients of letters of denization between 1660 and 1740: a percentage of these cannot be positively identified as Jewish. Only five of the names listed have a North American address, all in New York. The listing is apparently only partial. For example, a copy of a petition for denization dated 1712 lists Nathan Simson, Samuel Levy, Moses Levy, Moses Michaells, Moses Hart, and Mordica Nathan, all Jewish merchants who had lived in New York with their families for many years. The petition was officially recommended for approval although the letters of denization have not yet been located: copy of petition and recommendation in AJHS, P–255, Oppenheim Collection, Nathan Simson file. As to the later period, lists of persons endenized and naturalized, 1740–1761 are in the PRO, Colonial Office, Colonies General, Entry Books, series 1, CO 324, vols. 59 and 66; see also Hollander, "Naturalization of Jews in the American Colonies," 103–17.

61 Elzas, *The Jews of South Carolina*, 20–1 and appendix A.

62 See p. 59.

63 "The Frame of Government of the Province of Pennsylvania," 7 November 1696, in Thorpe, comp., *The Federal and State Constitutions*, 5: 3075; Peter A. Winkel, "Naturalizations, Province of New Jersey, 1747–1775," *Genealogical Magazine of New Jersey* 65(1990): 1 et seq.

64 The original resolution is in New York, General Assembly, *Journal*, 1737, 711–12.

65 See William Smith Jr, "The History of the Province of New-York" (continuation), *New York Historical Society Collections* (1826), 36–41 (first published in 1757), and William Dunlap, *History of the New Netherlands, Province of New York, and State of New York* (2 vols.; New York: Carter & Thorp 1839), 1: 318. Ironically, Smith and and his son successfully defended the board or junto of New York's Shearith Israel Congregation against criminal charges of assault in 1756: Godfrey and Godfrey,

"The King vs. Moses Gomez," 397–407. The son would be chief justice of Quebec from 1786 to 1793.

66 McKinley, *Suffrage Franchise in the Thirteen Colonies,* 214–15. It would not be until 1777, when the first constitution of the state of New York was adopted, that that state would be the first in the Thirteen Colonies to put Jews on a footing of absolute equality with other citizens: Kohler, "Civil Status of the Jews in Colonial New York." See also Samuel Oppenheim, "The Supposed Disenfranchisement of the Jews of New York after the Contested Election for Representatives in 1737: A History," an unpublished paper presented to the American Jewish Historical Society Conference in Washington, 5 May 1923, AJHS, P–255, Oppenheim Collection, box 34, file 9.

CHAPTER THREE

1 Hansard, *The Parliamentary History of England* (hereafter *Hansard*), XIV: *1747–1753,* 1376.
2 The Plantation Act, 13 Geo. II, c. 7 (1740).
3 *Hansard,* 27 November 1753, XV: *1753–1765,* 158.
4 Ibid., 7 May 1753, XIV: *1747–1753,* 1415–16, 1397, 1401.
5 Ibid., 1391.
6 Ibid., 15 November 1753, XV: *1753–1765,* 98, and 7 May 1753, XIV: *1747–1753,* 1409.
7 Ibid., XIV: *1747–1753,* 1401–2.
8 Ibid., 1415 and 1391.
9 Ibid., 1386.
10 Ibid., 15 November 1753, XV: *1753–1765,* 103, 102.
11 The walls of the synagogue of the Honen Dalim Congregation, built in 1738, still stand: see Hartog, *The Jews and St. Eustatius.* See also Barka, *Archeology of the Jewish Settlement Honen Dalim, St. Eustatius* and Garrett and Grode, "Gravestone Inscriptions, St. Eustatius, N.A., 1686–1930."
12 Hartog, *The History of St. Eustatius,* 38–45.
13 The diversion of Admiral Rodney's fleet to St Eustatius over a period of four months would allow the French Caribbean fleet to go to the assistance of the Americans in Virginia to join in the final defeat of the British in the American Revolution. Clearly the capture of the island was important. Ibid., 88, 95.
14 Rodney to General Cunningham, governor of Barbados, 17 February 1781, quoted in F. Edler, "The Dutch Republic and the American Revolution," *Studies in History and Political Science* 29 (no. 2, 1911), 184, cited in Burak, "Moses Myers of Norfolk," 23.
15 Hartog, *The History of St. Eustatius,* 84–93. Dutch and American merchants were also expelled, but were allowed to retain their household

goods; French merchants were transported to Martinique and Guadeloupe with their possessions in co-operation with the French navy.

16 *Hansard,* 27 November 1753, XV: *1753–1765,* 158. It is no wonder that the Jewish contribution to Britain's American colonies has remained relatively unknown.

17 See Samuel, "A List of Persons Endenized and Naturalized," 111–44. Although section 5 of the Plantation Act required the secretary of each colony to transmit to London annually "a true and perfect list" of persons naturalized within the colony under the provisions of the act during the previous year so that the information would be available "for publick View and Inspection" and provided a penalty for non-compliance of £50 "for every Neglect or Omission," the provision does not appear to have been enforced. The secretaries of New Jersey, for example, never sent any lists, although several hundred persons were naturalized in that colony under the act: Peter A. Winkel, "Naturalizations, Province of New Jersey," *Genealogical Magazine of New Jersey* 65(1990): 1–2.

18 A "James Lucena" was naturalized by vote of the Rhode Island assembly in December 1760: John R. Bartlet, *Records of the Colony of Rhode Island and Providence Plantations in New England, 1636–1792* (10 vols.; Providence RI 1856–65), 6: 262 and 267. Cecil Roth found convincing evidence that Lucena was of Jewish descent and had fled the Portuguese inquisition, coming to Rhode Island shortly after 1755, moving to Savannah by 1767, and returning to Portugal by 1783. No evidence however has been found that he was a professing Jew. Roth, "Some Jewish Loyalists," 93–6.

19 For Lopez, see Gutstein, *The Jews of Newport,* 158–62; for Elizer, see Samuel, "A List of Persons Endenized and Naturalized," 132.

20 The full text of section 6 reads: "Provided always, and it is hereby further enacted That no Person who shall become a natural born Subject of this Kingdom by virtue of this Act, shall be of the Privy Council or a Member of either House of Parliament, or capable of taking, having or enjoying any Office or Place of Trust within the Kingdoms of Great Britain or Ireland, either Civil or Military, or of having, accepting, or taking any Grant from the Crown to himself or to any other in trust for him, of any Lands, Tenements, or Hereditaments within the Kingdoms of Great Britain or Ireland; any Thing hereinbefore contained to the contrary thereof in any wise notwithstanding." The words respecting the exclusion of naturalized persons from holding offices or taking grants from the crown "within the Kingdoms of Great Britain or Ireland" had first appeared in 1700 in the statute 12 Will. III, c. 2. They were not aimed specifically at Jews; according to Sir William Blackstone (*Commentaries on the Laws of England* [13th ed.; London 1800], 374), the original statute "was passed from a jealousy of King William's partiality to foreigners."

21 This argument would be put forward in 1834 by Aaron Ezekiel Hart, Lower Canada's first Jewish lawyer, before a committee studying the rights of Jews: see p. 203.

22 An Act to explain Two Acts of Parliament, One of the Thirteenth Year of the Reign of His late Majesty, for naturalizing such Foreign Protestants, and others, as are settled, or shall settle, in any of His Majesty's Colonies in America; and the other of the Second Year of the Reign of His present Majesty, for naturalizing such Foreign Protestants as have served or shall serve, as Officers or Soldiers in His Majesty's Royal American Regiment, or as Engineers, in America, 13 Geo. III, c. 25 (1773). The right to become a member "of the Privy Council or a Member of either House of Parliament," referred to in section 6 of the Plantation Act, was not included in the 1773 act.

23 The text of section 3 read: "And whereas the following Words are contained in the latter Part of the Oath of Abjuration, videlicet, (upon the true Faith of a Christian): And whereas the People professing the Jewish Religion may thereby be prevented from receiving the Benefit of this Act: Be it further enacted by the Authority aforesaid, That whenever any Person professing the Jewish Religion shall present himself to take the said Oath of Abjuration in pursuance of this Act, the said words (upon the true Faith of a Christian) shall be omitted out of the said Oath in administering the same to such Person, and the taking and subscribing the said Oath by such Person, professing the Jewish Religion, without the Words aforesaid, and the other Oaths appointed by the said Act in like manner as Jews were permitted to take the Oath of Abjuration, by an Act made in the tenth year of the Reign of His late Majesty King George the First [10 Geo. I, c. 4 (1723)]."

24 Montefiore defined royal colonies as "Provincial establishments, the constitutions of which depend on the respective commissions issued by the crown to the governors, and the instructions which usually accompany those commissions under whose authority provincial assemblies are constituted, and empowered to make local ordinances not repugnant to the laws of England": see Montefiore, *A Commercial Dictionary.*

25 As the medium through which the Mother Country implemented its policies, the commission and instructions issued to the governors of the royal colonies are the most important constitutional documents in British colonial history prior to the introduction of responsible government in the 1840s. The instructions were normally prepared in England after some negotiation between the governor designate and officials of the Colonial Office and were taken by the new governor to the colony. While the commission was usually published in the colony, the instructions as a rule were treated as secret orders and not made known even to the governor's appointed council. During the seventeenth and

eighteenth centuries, the instructions became longer and more mandatory. In 1752 the instructions were thoroughly revised: see Andrews,
"Introduction" to "List of Commissions, Instructions, and Additional
Instructions issued to the Royal Governors and Others in America,"
395–8.

26 See p. 44.

27 See Stern, *First American Jewish Families*, 170; Hühner, "Asser Levy of
New Amsterdam," 22; Kohler, "Civil Status of the Jews in Colonial New
York," 100; Reznikoff and Engelman, *The Jews of Charleston*, 6–7; Elzas,
Leaves from My Historical Scrapbook, 4.

28 McKinley, *Suffrage Franchise in the Thirteen Colonies*, 138–9; Thomas
Cooper and David J. McCord, eds., *The Statutes at Large of South Carolina*
(10 vols; Columbia SC: A.J. Johnston 1838–41), 1: 232.

29 Labaree, ed., *Royal Instructions to British Governors*, 1: 40–1.

30 Remarks of Thomas Prowse, MP, in the British House of Commons, *Hansard*, 27 November 1753, XV: *1753–1765*, 139.

CHAPTER FOUR

1 Quoted in Max Savelle, *The Foundations of American Civilization: A History
of Colonial America* (New York: Henry Holt 1942), 560.

2 The likely place of the meeting is suggested by Solomon da Costa's
letter from that place to Thomas Hill, secretary to the Board of Trade,
on 12 December 1748. According to Edgar Roy Samuel, da Costa's residence and counting-house had moved to that address in 1742: see
"Anglo-Jewish Notaries and Scriveners," 121. The day of the meeting is
suggested by the fact that da Costa received the letter from Hill on Saturday, 10 December, but could not reply at once "by reasons of the day
[being the Sabbath]; and also because it was necessary to shew it to my
Associates, and consult with them the answer." da Costa to Hill,
12 December 1748, in Elzas, ed., *Documents Relative to Jews in South Carolina*, 14–15.

3 *Journal of the Commissioners for Trade and Plantations*, 8: 357 (8 December
1748) and 358 (13 December 1748). The Board of Trade, which functioned from 1695 to 1784, was constituted as "the Lords Commissioners
for promoting the Trade of our Kingdom and for Inspecting and Im-
proving our Plantations in America and elsewhere."

4 The committee's mandate also included relief for the sick and poor at
home: Barnett, "Jacob de Castro Sarmento," 90–1. The efforts of the
committee were partly directed towards the establishment of a Jewish
hospital (Beth Holim) because it was acknowledged that "the Poor at
present often want the common necessaries of life" and because the
food in the public hospitals was not kosher.

5 Ibid., 90–1. According to James Picciotto (*Sketches of Anglo-Jewish History*, 144), writing in 1875 on the basis of his research in the records of the Spanish and Portuguese Jews' Congregation, "the totality of the Hebrew population" in London in 1733 was about 2,000: "There were perhaps 150 to 200 families that might be considered rich, about two-thirds of which belonged to the Spanish and Portuguese Congregation. Then we should find at most as many families engaged in small retail trade, and finally we should see a floating mass, at least five times as numerous as the other two classes together, consisting of hucksters, hawkers, journey-men, and others, either verging on pauperism or steeped hopelessly in its abyss."

6 Newman, "Expulsion of the Jews from Prague," 30–41.

7 The fact that the Bohemian refugees were of the Ashkenazic or German tradition and that the establishment of the London Jewish community was of the Sephardic or Spanish/Portuguese tradition is not without sig-nificance and should be the subject of a separate inquiry. The prepon-derance of Ashkenazic Jews over Sephardic Jews in North America dates from the approximate time of the expulsion of the Jews from Bohemia.

8 Samuel Oppenheim, "The Expulsion of the Jews from Bohemia, 1744–1745, and the Action of the English Jews Thereon," AJHS, P–255, Oppen-heim Collection, box 35, file 13. By the time the decrees were revoked in 1748, the Jewish population of Bohemia had been reduced by half.

9 Sir Edmund Isham, House of Commons, 7 May 1753, Hansard, *The Par-liamentary History of England*, XIV: *1747–1753*, 1379–83.

10 A biography of Solomon da Costa Athias or Attias (1696–1769) is to be found in Samuel, "Anglo-Jewish Notaries and Scriveners," 120–3 and 156–7.

11 Joseph Salvador (sometimes referred to as Joseph Jessrun Rodrigues) (1716–1786) was again parnas of Bevis Marks in 1751, 1755, and 1765. He later achieved importance as chief financial adviser to the third Earl of Bute during his term as prime minister in 1763 and 1764. Woolf states that he led the Jewish community's effort to secure passage of the Jews Naturalization Act in 1753 and was the (anonymous) author of sev-eral pamphlets in support of the act during the agitation for its repeal. See Woolf, "Joseph Salvador," 104 et seq.; also Elzas, *Joseph Salvador*, and Barnett, "Jacob de Castro Sarmento," 90–1.

12 Benjamin Mendes da Costa (1704–1764), one of the largest holders of Bank of England stock, was born in Holland. He was listed as a "stew-ard" of the public hospital. See Barnett, "Diplomatic Aspects of the Sephardic Influx," 216–17; *The Jewish Encyclopedia*, 4: 290–1; "Jewish Obituaries from the Gentleman's Magazine," 39; Picciotto, *Sketches of Anglo-Jewish History*, 89, 95, 155; Barnett, "Jacob de Castro Sarmento," 91 and 100, n. 87.

13 Marcus, *Early American Jewry*, 2: 520, suggests there was "a handful" of Jews in Baltimore in this period. Hartogensis ("Early Jewish Settlers of Baltimore") suggests something less than that.

14 Dyer, "First Chapter of New York Jewish History," 43–6.

15 Asser Levy purchased a lot at auction on 15 July 1661 and took possession on 1 May 1662: Rosendale, "An Early Ownership of Real Estate in Albany, New York by a Jewish Trader."

16 Grinstein, *Rise of the Jewish Community of New York*, appendix 1, 469. The "Jewish" population of New York was somewhat larger than indicated, because Grinstein counts only members of New York's Shearith Israel Congregation and their families and does not include Jews who were not affiliated with the synagogue.

17 The authors are indebted to Bernard Kusnitz of Newport for making the results of his extensive research available to them. See also Gutstein, *The Jews of Newport*, 48–57.

18 Edwin Wolf II and Maxwell Whiteman, *The History of the Jews of Philadelphia from Colonial Times to the Age of Jackson* (Philadelphia: Jewish Publication Society of America 1957), 30–2.

19 Marcus, *Early American Jewry*, 2: 5–6.

20 Reznikoff and Engelman, *The Jews of Charleston*.

21 Ibid., 67; and Hühner, "Jews of Georgia in Colonial Times," 66–9.

22 Reznikoff and Engelman, *The Jews of Charleston*, 76–9; see also Jones, "The Settlement of the Jews in Georgia," 5–12, and Abrahams, "Some Notes on the Early History of the Sheftalls of Georgia," 167–86.

23 Goodman, *American Overture*, 190, 193–5. This conclusion is based on a letter from one of the Jewish settlers in Georgia to a correspondent in Germany, published in Plaut, "Two Notes on the History of the Jews in America," 580–1. The letter of 12 February 1738 states in part: "Es koennen nicht mehr, als zwo Familien, Judenteutsch. Ob sie von den Herren Trustees werden Freyheit bekommen eine Synagogue zu bauen, wissen sie selbst noch nicht ..." ["We still don't know whether the two German Jewish families will obtain permission from the Trustees to build a synagogue, they themselves don't know yet ..."].

24 Labaree, ed., *Royal Instructions to British Governors*, 2: 494.

25 Letter of James Topham, Marblehead, Mass., 19 August 1774, to an unidentified correspondent in Newport, Rhode Island: "Sir. Noing you to be a most noble Spirited Gentleman, I give my self the liberty, to inclose a few lines to you, in behalf of this Young man, how he has been Brought up a Jew how he is left destitute of Friends and Seeing him so shamefully abused, by being Stoned through the Street, because he is a Jew. I have Advised him to go to Newport, where I hope he will meet with better Treatment." *M & S Rare Books Catalogue* (Weston MA, 1986), 27, item 263.

26 Georgia's oath of abjuration requirement would also have been amended by the Plantation Act, but it was an unlikely choice for a further colonization attempt after the apparent failure of the first settlement.

27 Petition of James Peyn, 17 November 1747, in Munro, ed., *Acts of the Privy Council of England, Colonial Series*, 4: 33. An earlier version of Peyn's petition had been considered by the Board of Trade on 26 October 1747: *Journal of the Commissioners for Trade and Plantations*, 8: 263 (8 December 1747).

28 Ibid., 264 (17 December 1747) and 265 (22 December 1747). In 1771 Joshua Sharpe would handle Eleazar Levy's appeal to the Privy Council: see pp. 99–100.

29 Petition of John Hamilton, 22 March 1748, in Munro, ed., *Acts of the Privy Council of England, Colonial Series*, 4: 60–1.

30 *Journal of the Commissioners for Trade and Plantations*, 8: 281, 324, 328, 329, and 333 (June-July 1748). Reprinted in Elzas, ed., *Documents Relative to Jews in South Carolina*, 1–15.

31 Ibid., 8: 281 (5, 6, and 8 July 1748) and 357 (8 December 1748).

32 Ibid., 8: 358 (13 December 1748); reprinted in Elzas, ed., *Documents Relative to Jews in South Carolina*, 14. In fact, the first land patent given to a Jew in the Thirteen Colonies of which there is a record was not granted until 1757 in Albemarle County, Virginia: Hühner, "Jews of Virginia," 90.

33 Marcus, *Early American Jewry*, 2: 281.

CHAPTER FIVE

1 Fergusson, "Jewish Communities in Nova Scotia," 45. Fergusson, who was Nova Scotia's provincial archivist for many years, based this conclusion on a study of the ship lists of settlers who came with Cornwallis.

2 Akins, *Halifax City*, 3–22. Akins lists 2,576 passengers. The original ship lists, as transcribed and indexed by the Public Archives of Nova Scotia, list 2,391 passengers.

3 In 1730, an Isaac Solomons of Boston was recorded as having donated £10 towards the construction of a new building for the Shearith Israel Congregation of New York: "Earliest Minute Book, Congregation Shearith Israel, 1728–60," 24. Isaac Solomon, tobacconist, was one of two trustees who purchased land in Boston in 1734/5 for use as a burying ground for "the Jewish nation": Friedenwald, "Early Jews in Boston," 153. Isaac Solomon was probably the same person as the Isaac Solomons whose proposed marriage to Mary Todd in Boston in 1733 was forbidden by the clergy: Hühner, "Jews of New England," 81. In 1749 Solomon was listed as being indebted to the New York congregation: "Earliest Minute Book, Congregation Shearith Israel, 1728–60," 60.

4 John Franks, who was probably unmarried when he arrived in Halifax (see below, note 15) but married shortly thereafter, clearly had a number of connections with Philadelphia. His first wife, Elizabeth, seems to have had family links with the city for she moved there from Halifax in 1758. After winding up his business in Halifax by 1760 Franks also returned there briefly, where he married for a second time (to Appolonia Seymore) in June 1760: Ball *v.* Franks, 1760, PANS, RG 37, vol. 8; Petition of John Franks, 10 August 1768, NA, RG 1, L3L, 42874; *Pennsylvania Archives* 2(1876): 107 and 8(1878): 95. Another piece of evidence for the Philadelphia connection is a reference years later to Franks's eldest son, David, who is described on "one of his visits to Philadelphia, where his near relations resided": Rosenbach, "Documents Relative to Major David S. Franks," 157.

5 Memorial University of Newfoundland, Maritime History Archive, Samuel Jacobs file. See also Vaugeois, "Samuel Jacobs," *DCB* 4: 384–6, and Mann, "The Jew of St Denis."

6 According to Akins, *Halifax City,* 3, prior to formal settlement in 1749, the governor of the colony of Nova Scotia "resided at Annapolis Royal, a small fortified post, with a garrison of two or three hundred regular troops, and was, in great measure, dependent on New England for his necessary supplies."

7 Cornwallis to the Board of Trade, 24 July 1749, PANS, RG 1, vol. 35, doc. 2, 1.

8 Cornwallis to the Board of Trade, 22 June 1749, ibid., doc. 1, 2.

9 Cornwallis to the Board of Trade, 20 August 1749, ibid., doc. 5, 2. We are indebted to Allan E. Marble of Halifax for sharing the summaries of his research on the first settlers of Halifax in 1749. He has concluded that the Louisbourg garrison consisted of about 2,000 people, military and civilian. They were transferred to Halifax by 24 July 1749 and encouraged to remain.

10 Picciotto, *Sketches of Anglo-Jewish History,* 145. Picciotto's account was based on his research into the records of the Spanish and Portuguese Jews' Congregation.

11 Cornwallis to the Board of Trade, 20 August 1749, and 24 July 1749, PANS, RG 1, vol. 35, doc. 5, 3 and 2, and doc. 2, 3.

12 Cornwallis to the Board of Trade, 20 August 1749, ibid., doc. 5, 3.

13 See pp. 66–8.

14 Franks's son (born 1 March 1750) was to be named David Salusbury Franks. His middle name may have been chosen because the official responsible for the granting and allocation of lots in 1749 was the Hon. John Salusbury, a member of Cornwallis's first council. It would have been fitting for John Franks, as a Jew and the first recipient of a lot in Halifax, to name his child after the official responsible for his status as

a landholder: Godfrey and Godfrey, "Who Was Who in Canada," Franks II.

15 Provincial Crown Records Centre, Halifax, Halifax Allotment, book 1, John Franks, Robert Barnstable, and Will Culbert, lot A 1, Collier's Division; Samuel Jacobs, lot A 14, Collier's Division; Isaac Solomon, lot B4, Callender's Division. According to Allan Marble's research, only 419 of the 606 heads of families allotted land on 8 August had come with Cornwallis. The other 187 heads of families, including the Jewish ones, had arrived in Halifax from elsewhere. See also Akins, *Halifax City*, 13: "at a Council held on the 1st of August, it was resolved that on Tuesday following, the 8th of August, all heads of families who were settlers, should assemble at seven o'clock with the overseers, and single men should form themselves into families, four to each family, and each family should choose one to draw for them." On the basis of this information, John Franks was single in August 1749 and Samuel Jacobs and Isaac Solomon were married.

16 Israel Abrahams was in Halifax by February 1750: Provincial Crown Records Centre, Halifax, Halifax Allotment, book 1, 25. He had carried on business in partnership with Nathan Nathans in Newport, although the business had failed by 1745: Marcus, ed., *American Jewry: Documents*, 325–6. In Halifax, he carried on business in a partnership with his brother and Joseph Jones. There is a possibility that Israel Abrahams may have been related to Abraham Abrahams "whose parentage is not known" and who was appointed both notary public and scrivener in London in 1764: Samuel, "Anglo-Jewish Notaries and Scriveners," 131–2, 157.

17 After arriving in Halifax by 1750, Nathan Nathans (d. 1778) formed a partnership with Isaac Levy in a retail shop until the latter's death in March 1751. He then carried on business in partnership with Naphtali Hart Jr from 17 October 1751 to 4 May 1754 under the name Nathans & Hart: Naphtali Hart and Isaac Hart *v.* Naphtali Hart Jr and Nathan Nathans, 1761, PANS, RG 37, vol. 10; Naphtali Hart Jr *v.* Nathan Nathans, 1761, PANS, RG 37, vol. 11, and Hart *v.* Nathans, 1768, PANS, RG 39, C, vol. 7. A copy of the Nathans & Hart partnership agreement appears as an exhibit in Hart *v.* Nathans (1761). Dissolution of the parntership was published in the *Halifax Gazette* of 11 May 1754.

18 Isaac Levy, born in Cucksam, Germany, was likely in Halifax in 1749. His death in March 1751 was the first recorded death of a Jew in Halifax. A bachelor, he left his estate to his sister in Cucksam: Halifax County Court of Probate, Isaac Levy estate. He may have been the Isaac Levy who was naturalized in New York between June 1740 and June 1741: Samuel, "A List of Persons Endenized and Naturalized," 125,

no. 304. That Isaac Levy was granted freedom of the city in New York on 1 November 1740: Kohler, "Civil Status of the Jews in Colonial New York," 102.

19 Nathan Levy (d. 1787) arrived in Halifax by 1751 and carried on business as a trader and shopkeeper: Deeds from Francis Elliott to Nathan Levy, 30 December 1751, and "from Nathan Levy of the Town of Halifax to Ireal [*sic*] Abrahams of the same place," 29 January 1752, Halifax County Registry of Deeds, book 2, 408–9.

20 Joseph Jones (d. 1771) and his wife Judith (d. 1767) were in Halifax by April 1750: Jones *v.* Trider, 1750, PANS, RG 37, vol. 1. They also had two daughters, Rebecca and Phoebe.

21 Isaac Judah, who signed his name in Hebrew (Yitzhak ben Moshe) as well as in English in witnessing Isaac Levy's will, was in Halifax by March 1750: Halifax County Court of Probate, Isaac Levy estate. He may have been the Isaac Judah who contributed to the fund for the building of a wall at the Shearith Israel Cemetery, in New York in 1737: De Sola Pool, *Portraits Etched in Stone*, 28–9. In Halifax, Judah carried on business in partnership with Hector Campbell as Judah & Campbell until the spring of 1752 when debt overtook them. He was put in "His Majesty's Jail in Halifax" for a short time as a result of his debts "for want of goods Chattels or Estate": Catherwood *v.* Judah & Campbell, 1751, PANS, RG 37, vol. 1. Judah is recorded to have had a family of nine: Gutstein, *The Jews of Newport*, 136.

22 See pp. 43–4.

23 Halifax County Court of Probate, Isaac Levy estate.

24 Abraham Andrews mortgage to Israel Abrahams, 1752, Halifax County Registry of Deeds, book 2, 72.

25 Emanuel Abrahams *v.* Mordecai Jones, 1753, PANS, RG 37, vol. 2A; Webb and Ewer *v.* John Franks, 1752, PANS, RG 39, C, vol. 1.

26 PANS, RG 39, Records of the Supreme Court, series C, and RG 37, Inferior Court of Common Pleas, 1750–7. The contrast with Barbados is striking: in 1679 the Jews had formed 10 per cent of the population of Bridgetown and yet were not allowed to use the courts for mercantile purposes: see above, 000.

27 Nathan Nathans and Naphtali Hart Jr were jurors in the Inferior Court in March 1755: Fairweather *v.* Jones, PANS, RG 39, C, vol. 2. Joseph Jones was a juror in the Supreme Court in 1760: Franks *v.* Ball, RG 37, vol. 9. Nathan Levy was a juror in the Inferior Court in 1762: Jeffery *v.* Jones and Robertson, RG 39, C, vol. 4, and RG 37, vol. 15. Mordecai Jones was a grand juror in the Supreme Court in 1763 and again in 1768: RG 37, vol. 15 and vol. 21B. Mordecai Jones had been called as a petit juror at the time of his death in 1770: RG 37, vol. 22A.

28 Akins, *Halifax City,* 246–61.

29 Fergusson, "Jewish Communities in Nova Scotia," 47. On 2 November
1758, a committee of the Nova Scotia Assembly and Council acknowledged that a Jewish cemetery had existed for some time when it recommended that the land set aside as "the Jews' burying ground" be used
"as a site for a Workhouse." The burying ground was probably included
in the Halifax allotment under the names of a trustee or trustees: this
was the practice followed by Oglethorpe in the allotment in Savannah,
Georgia, in 1733, where, similarly, a Jewish cemetery existed from that
date, although no documentary proof of an actual allotment for one
could be found in 1770, when Georgia's Legislative Council investi-
gated the issue: Goodman, *American Overture,* 196–7. Further research
in the office of the Halifax County Registry of Deeds may provide the
actual location of the Jewish burying ground. The possibility that lot A1,
Collier's Division, which went to John Franks, Robert Barnstable, and
Will Culbert, was the burying ground should not be discounted, particularly as that allotment was made to three persons rather than to the
four required by resolution of the governor's council on 1 August.

30 Stern, *First American Jewish Families,* 4 (Abrahams I). See also De Sola
Pool, *Portraits Etched in Stone,* 86–7 (Abraham I. Abrahams).

31 Israel Abrahams *v.* Jacobs, 1752, PANS, RG 37, vol. 1A, 1749–53, no 39.
As Jacobs had obtained an allotment by himself in 1749, however, he
must have satisfied the authorities at that time that he was the head of
a family.

32 Stern, *First American Jewish Families,* 12 (Andrews II).

33 The evidence for the relationship of Judith Jones and the Abrahams is
circumstantial. Her husband, Joseph, carried on business in partnership
with Israel and Emanuel Abrahams in Halifax from 1752 to 1754: Deed
from Richard Gibbons and others to Joshua Mauger, Halifax County
Registry of Deeds, book 2, 411. After her death in New York on 26 February 1767 (Congregation Shearith Israel, New York, Register, 1759–
1834, f. 32), Joseph deeded valuable property, including the residence
of their son, Mordecai, near Jones Wharf in Halifax, to the minor children of Abraham Isaac Abrahams on 12 April 1768 for the nominal
sum of ten shillings and "for the love and affection that Joseph Jones
hath and beareth for Isaac Abrahams and Rachel Abrahams son and
daughter of the said Abraham I. Abrahams": Joseph Jones to Abraham
I. Abrahams, Halifax County Registry of Deeds, book 11, 2325–31.

34 Stern, *First American Jewish Families,* 4.

35 Israel Abrahams *v.* Abraham Andrews, 1753, PANS, RG 37, vol. 2. Either
Andrews's first wife was a sister of the Abrahams, or Emanuel Abrahams's wife and Abraham Andrews's wife were sisters. Andrews and his
first wife had a child named Rachel, born in Boston, 22 February 1753;

she later married Solomon Woolf and died in Charleston, South Carolina, in 1835: Stern, *First American Jewish Families*, 12 (Andrews II). Emanuel Abrahams, whose will was probated in Charleston on 3 December 1802, left the residue of his estate to "my dear niece," Rachel Andrews Woolf: Charleston County Library, Charleston, SC, Court File, book 28, 354–5.

36 Hart's position as an observant Jew is borne out by his subsequent conduct. Following his return to Newport, he married Shepran, a Jewish woman. His son, Nathan, was circumcised by Abraham I. Abrahams in Newport on 18 May 1768: "Registry of Circumcisions by Abm. I. Abrahams," 154, item 39. Hart became a leader of the Nephutse Israel Congregation in Newport. He was one of nine members of the congregation who signed a mortgage to cover the construction costs of the synagogue building. He was likely a member of the congregation's junto or board: see Marcus, ed., *American Jewry: Documents*, 88.

37 Akins, *Halifax City*, 256.

38 "Solomons from Halifax" was recorded to have made a donation to the Sedaka Fund at Shearith Israel, New York, 14 October 1755: AJHS, P–255, Oppenheim Collection, box 23, book 4. Solomon was in the synagogue on the Day of Atonement, 15 October 1755, and was a witness to an incident that gave rise to a criminal charge laid by Solomon Hays against all seven elders of the congregation. He later appeared as a witness at the trial in New York in October 1756: The King *v.* Gomez et al., New York Historical Society, Kempe Papers, BSW 2. His son, Gedaliah, was circumcised at New York on 2 November 1758: "Registry of Circumcisions by Abm. I. Abrahams," 151, item 9. He was again listed as a member of the Shearith Israel Congregation in 1759: "Earliest Minute Book, Shearith Israel Congregation, 1728–60," 79.

39 Franks's first two children, David Salusbury (born 1 March 1750) and Elizebeth (born 20 May 1752), were both baptized in Halifax: Holder, comp., *Baptisms, Marriages and Burials, 1749–1768, St. Paul's Church*, 28 and 41.

40 Minutes, Shearith Israel Congregation, Montreal, NA, MG 8, G 67; also Marcus, ed., *American Jewry: Documents*, 106–14.

41 See p. 65.

42 Judah sold his only real estate in Halifax to Israel Abrahams in January 1752: Halifax County Registry of Deeds, book 2, 74. No records have been found to indicate that he was in Halifax after 1752. He returned to Newport: Gutstein, *The Jews of Newport*, 136.

43 See above, note 36. At the end of 1772, Hart left Newport and moved his family to the West Indies, settling on the Dutch island of St Eustatius in February 1773: see Stern, *First American Jewish Families*, 99 (Hart VII), and Naphtali Hart Jr to Aaron Lopez, 12 March 1773, in Marcus,

ed., *American Jewry: Documents*, 420–1. Hart may have been the "NAPTHALY HART, a literate person, born in the Province of Rhode Island in America" who was given the right to practise as a notary in England on 8 May 1772: see Samuel, "Anglo-Jewish Notaries and Scriveners," 138–40.

44 In December 1751, Abraham Andrews mortgaged lot B 15, Callender's Division, to Israel Abrahams to secure a loan of "one hundred pounds and interest": Halifax County Registry of Deeds, book 2, 72. This lot was included in the property Israel Abrahams and his partners later lost to Joshua Mauger: see note 45. It is not known whether Andrews was entitled to redeem his lot. He was still in Halifax in March 1756: Jones *v.* Gerrish, 1756, PANS, RG 39, C, vol. 2. Andrews subsequently moved to New York and carried on business as a shopkeeper, becoming naturalized on 22 April 1762: Samuel, "A List of Persons Endenized and Naturalized," 131, no. 540. On 2 July 1761, he had married Nelly, the widow of Israel Abrahams (who had drowned), in New York. According to the synagogue register, "Mr Abm. I. Abrahams give the Kidusim in that ocation"– in other words, the reception, which commenced with the blessing of the wine, was sponsored by Abraham Isaac Abrahams: Congregation Shearith Israel, New York, Register, 1759–1834, f. 74. Andrews subsequently moved to Charleston with his family: Stern, *First American Jewish Families*, 12 (Andrews II).

45 Joseph Jones, Israel Abrahams, and Emanuel Abrahams carried on business in partnership in Halifax from 1752 to 1754: Deed from Abrahams, Jones, and Abrahams in company to Joshua Mauger, and others, "Trustees Appointed by the said Company's Creditors," 1 March 1752; also Deed from Richard Gibbons and others, "Creditors and Trustees together with Joshua Mauger," to Mauger, 6 March 1755, both in Halifax County Registry of Deeds, book 2, 408–10, 411. The second deed transfers all the property of Israel Abrahams, Emanuel Abrahams, and Joseph Jones as "Traders & late also Copartners in Trade" to Joshua Mauger, one of their creditors. Other property owned by Joseph and Mordecai Jones was sold by the sheriff on 31 January 1755 pursuant to a judgment obtained against the Jones by Nathans & Hart: Halifax County Registry of Deeds, book 2, 411.

46 We know Israel Abrahams had drowned by mid-1761 because of his widow's remarriage, although it is not known whether he was still living in Halifax at the time of his death. Emanuel Abrahams had returned to New York by 1756 and carried on business as a distiller and tobacconist, at first in partnership with his brother, Abraham I. Abrahams, and after July 1757 as a sole proprietorship. He was operating a store on Stone Street in 1758: AJHS, P–255, Oppenheim Collection, Emanuel Abrahams file. He was granted the "freedom of the city" in New York on 4 January 1757 and entitled to carry on retail trade within its boundaries: Kohler,

"Civil Status of the Jews in Colonial New York," 102. He died in Charleston in 1802. See also p. 268n35.

47 The quotation is from a letter by the Rev. John Breynton, rector of St Paul's Anglican Church in Halifax, 8 December 1755. The population was still 1,300 in 1766. Hill, "History of St Paul's Church I," 40, 46.

48 When settlement moved across to Fort Cumberland in what later became New Brunswick, Jacobs was there by 1758 and had one of the first land patents in the area. On 28 May 1760 he obtained a crown grant for 55 acres near the fort in Westmoreland county: PANB, RS 686, vol. A, no 130. He would follow the British to Quebec.

49 John Franks lost a judgment for over £400 in 1752: Webb and Ewer v. Franks, PANS, RG 39, C, vol. 1. Advertisements of his imminent departure appeared in the Halifax Gazette on 13 April 1752, 9 March 1754, and 4 May 1754. On 19 August 1757 he wrote from Halifax to John Kide in Philadelphia that he was intending to store all his cargo as he could "not Sell Any thing at Present to My Liking" and that the "Expedition Causes a Great Stagnation here": Historical Society of Pennsylvania, Stauffer Collection, vol. 8, 590. See also Ball v. Franks, 1760, and Franks v. Ball, 1760, PANS, RG 37, vols. 8 and 9.

50 Fergusson, "Jewish Communities in Nova Scotia," 47.

51 Garner, Franchise in British North America, 146.

52 Holder, comp., Baptisms, Marriages and Burials, St. Paul's Church, 103, item 3344. Levy had moved to Chester by 1768: Deed from Webber to Levy, 21 December 1768: Lunenberg County Registry of Deeds, book 1, 315 (1768). After the death of his first wife on 3 July 1771, he married Susannah Tufts, daughter of Gershom Tufts of Chester: PANS, MG 4, vol. 13, 390(2) and section 2, 17. He died insolvent in Chester in May 1787: Nova-Scotia Gazette, 19 June 1787; Deed of Susannah Levy, administrator to the estate of Nathan Levy, to Caspar Wollenhaupt, 9 September 1789, Lunenberg County Registry of Deeds, book 3, 531 (1793). See also genealogical chart 202 (Levy family), PANS, T.B. Smith Collection, MG 1, vol. 843; H.D. Levy, History of Sherwood (1953), 40ff., in PANS, Library; and PANS, mfm w589 (White family).

53 Naphtali Hart Jr v. Nathan Nathans, 1761: PANS, RG 37, vol. 11, and Hart v. Nathans, 1768, PANS, RG 39, C, vol. 7. Nathans was shown as a debtor of Joseph Jones at the time of Jones's death in September 1771: a note in the estate file made by Jones's executors in 1773 notes that Nathans was "no good for the money": Halifax County Court of Probate, Joseph Jones estate, file J 29.

54 Nathans died in Halifax on 19 November 1778 and was buried in the cemetery of St Paul's Anglican Church: PANS, Stayner Collection.

55 Provincial Crown Records Centre, Halifax, Halifax Allotment, book 1, 124 (1758). Joseph Jones continued to own his half-interest in the wharf which was sometimes known as "Jones' Wharfe": Deed from executors

of Joseph Jones estate to Thomas Cochran, September 1774, Halifax County Registry of Deeds, book 14, 232 (1774), and book 7, 147 (1765).

56 Wood *v.* Joseph Jones, May 1760. The case was not proceeded with in the courts: PANS, RG 37, vol. 8

57 Congregation Shearith Israel, New York, Register, 1759-1834, f. 32; charitable donations by Jones to the Sedaka Fund are recorded in 1763, 1764, and 1765: AJHS, P–255, Oppenheim Collection, box 23, books 1 and 5.

58 Return to Jury Notice, June 1770, PANS, RG 37, vol. 22A.

59 AJHS, P–255, Oppenheim Collection, box 23, book 6.

60 Jones *v.* Pigott, 1768, PANS, RG 39, C, vol. 7; Halifax County Registry of Deeds, book 5, 277 (1762), and book 8, 20 (1766); Joseph Jones estate, will probated 20 September 1771, Halifax County Court of Probate, file J29; David Jones *v.* Elizabeth Jones, 1772, PANS, RG 39, C, box 10.

61 David Jones estate, 1782, Halifax County Court of Probate, file J25.

62 Wenham *v.* Joseph Jones, 1759, PANS, RG 39, C, vol. 3. Nahum Israel may have been a member of the Abrahams family. According to Stern, a son of Abraham Isaac Abrahams named Emanuel (1776–1839) was known as "Menachem Israel": Stern, *First American Jewish Families,* 4 (Abrahams I). Nahum is a short form of Menachem.

63 Roth, "Some Jewish Loyalists," 98–103. According to a suit filed against him in 1771, he was a yeoman and mason who no longer lived in Nova Scotia: Buttar and Bird *v.* Decosta, PANS, RG 39, C, vol. 9. He may have been the Isaac Da Costa Jr (1746–1809) of Charleston: Stern, *First American Jewish Families,* 44 (Da Costa I). See also p. 124.

64 Isaacs Abrahams (1756–1813) was living in Halifax as a trader in 1786: Buckle *v.* Isaac Abrahams, PANS, RG 39, C, vol. 42; Stern, *First American Jewish Families,* 4 (Abrahams I). The farm and house on the beach near Jones Wharf that Joseph Jones had deeded in 1768 to Isaac and Rachel, the children of Abraham I. Abrahms (see note 33), remained in the family and were rented out to tenants: Abrahams *v.* Scott, 1788, PANS, RG 39, C, box 48. Myer Myers, a cousin of Isaac Abrahams (their mothers being sisters) and the son of Hyam Myers of Montreal and New York, was also known to be living in Halifax as a trader although he left suddenly in 1786 and died in Haiti in 1791: R. *v.* Myers, 1786, PANS, RG 39, C, vol. 45; also Stern, *First American Jewish Families,* 218 (Myers II) and 179 (Louzada).

65 See pp. 145–52.

66 Jacob Calnek (1745–1831) married Rosina Wolf (1753–1822) in 1771 at Arolsen, in the Anspach [now Ansbach] principality, Germany. Both were "of Jewish descent," according to their grandson, W.A. Calnek, and

from a review of their family genealogy it appears likely that they were married in a Jewish ceremony. Jacob Calnek came to Nova Scotia in 1775 in aid of the British during the American Revolution as quartermaster of the 1st battalion of the Anspach Regiment. He decided to stay, settling near Annapolis in 1783: Calnek family, PANS, RG 1, vol. 369, doc. 42, 346. His wife joined him with four children the following year. They both died in Granville, Nova Scotia. Of their six children, three did not marry; the remainder married Christians: see Calnek, *History of the County of Annapolis*, 485–7.

67 Solomon Jacobs (c. 1755–99), a Halifax constable, was in Halifax by 1785. His marriage and the births of his children were recorded in St Paul's Anglican Church. PANS, RG 39, C, box 1, "A List of Constables" and Stayner Collection.

68 According to R.G. Dun's credit ledgers, in the period between 1810 and 1850 there were only three Jewish merchants in Halifax, namely, Isaac and Alexander Levi and Aaron Moses, all of whom were recorded between 1813 and 1817: Tulchinsky, *Taking Root*, 84. A "Mrs. Isaac Levy of Halifax" was noted as present in New York in August 1820 as godmother at the circumcision of Abraham, son of Myer Bar Abraham and his wife Rebecca: Congregation Shearith Israel, New York, Register, 1759–1834.

CHAPTER SIX

1 Francis Maseres to Fowler Walker, 30 March 1768, in Wallace, ed., *Maseres Letters*, 71–3.

2 Much of the description of these events is taken from Alexander Henry's *Travels & Adventures in Canada and the Indian Territories*. Written more than forty years after the incident, this is the most detailed account of the Indian uprising at Michilmackinac in 1763. It was edited by David A. Armour and published in 1971 under the title, *Attack at Michilmackinac, 1763*. The citations to Henry's *Travels* that follow refer to Armour's edition. As Henry recalled it, the weather on the day of the massacre was "sultry" (p 49); that night at dusk, "a shower of rain having begun to fall" (p 55). Henry's recollection of dates is almost accurate; for example, he gave the date of the massacre as 4 June (p 48), but as Armour notes contemporary accounts give the date of 2 June.

3 This house was used by Solomons and his partner, Gershon Levy, prior to his purchase of the Parant/Chaboillez house in 1765. Solomons had hidden in the house facing the central square or parade ground of the fort immediately to the north of his own. The authors are indebted to Dr Donald Heldman, director of archeology of the Mackinac Island

State Park Commission, for his assistance in identifying the location of Solomons's rented house as the easternmost house in the south/south-west rowhouse, immediately beside the fort's gate. On the larger house purchased in 1765, see the original notarial act in the record book of "Cardin, Notaire Royal," at 21–2, confirming sale of a trader's house at Fort Michilimackinac from Pierre Parant and Marianne Chaboillez to "Ezechiel Solomon" and "Levy" on 29 June 1765: William L. Clements Library, Gage Papers. An English translation of the notarial act is in Halchin, *Excavations at Fort Michilimackinac*, 38. We cannot positively identify "Levy" as Gershon Levy, but the evidence leaves little doubt. See also Heldman, "Michigan's First Jewish Settlers," *Journal of New World Archeology* 6(1986): 21–33.

4 "Cote" was likely Gabriel Cotté: Ruth R. Jarvis, "Gabriel Cotté," *DCB* 4: 171.

5 Declaration sworn by Ezekiel Solomons before Daniel Disney, town major, at Montreal, 14 August 1763, in "Henry Gladwin Papers," 667.

6 Ibid.

7 Letter from John Thurman to John Sargent, 3 September 1760, in AJHS, P–255, Oppenheim Collection, Gershon Levy file.

8 "Ordinance Regarding Trade to the Upper Country," 1 April 1761, Public Archives of Canada, *Report*, 1918, 43.

9 Unfortunately, the records of passports to the Upper Country, issued by Gage to traders pursuant to his ordinance, have not been located. In consequence, one can only examine probabilities. While no English traders had been allowed to go to the Upper Country until after Gage's ordinance, Alexander Henry, James Stanley Goddard, and Ezekiel Solomons were all at Michilimackinac by September of that year: David A. Armour, "Alexander Henry," *DCB* 6: 316–19, and David Roberts, "William Grant," *DCB* 5: 368. An editor's note in the *Collections* of the State Historical Society of Wisconsin [18(1908): 254] says: "Ezekiel Solomon went up in the summer of 1761 from Montreal to Mackinac, to enter the fur trade." Henry, in his *Travels*, notes that he arrived at Michilimackinac in September but does not suggest he was the first. Armour's suggestion (*DCB* 6: 319) that in the spring of 1761, Henry was the second Englishman (after Henry Bostwick) to obtain a passport is supported only by the dates of *engagements* or private contracts to carry goods not by evidence of passports actually issued by Gage. The listing in E.-Z. Massicotte, "Répertoire des engagements pour l'ouest conservés dans les Archives judiciaires de Montréal (1670–1778)," Archives nationales du Québec, *Rapport*, 1932–3, 245–304, shows contracts for Henry and Bostwick in July 1761 but not for Solomons, even though he did journey to the Upper Country at the same time.

10 In 1900, Lewis Solomon recalled that his grandfather, Ezekiel Solomons, was born in Berlin: Osborne, "The Migration of Voyageurs from Drummond Island to Penetanguishene in 1828," 126–37.

11 James Stanley Goddard was associated with William Grant and Forrest Oakes in the fur trade at Michilimackinac from September 1761: David Roberts, "William Grant," *DCB* 5: 368. He was engaged in the western fur trade as late as 1778 when he retired to Montreal.

12 Henry, *Travels*, 29–31.

13 Ibid., 45, 48. Armour states that there were only four English merchants at the post: Solomons, Henry, Bostwick, and Tracy.

14 David A. Armour, "Madjeckewiss," *DCB* 5: 567–8.

15 Henry, *Travels*, 61. Henry says seventy of the ninety in the garrison were slaughtered, but Armour's research indicates that of the thirty-five soldiers in the garrison, sixteen were killed and two wounded in the massacre and five more were killed later in the month while prisoners of the Indians.

16 Gage to the earl of Egremont, 28 August 1763, NA, MG 11, CO 42, series Q, vol. 1, 210.

17 Henry, *Travels*, 61–4. According to Henry (pp. 68–9), the Chippewa actually did eat one of the soldiers they had killed.

18 Etherington, L'Arbre Croche, to Charles Langlade, Jr., Michilimackinac, 1 July 1763; also Etherington, Michilimackinac, to Henry Gladwin, 18 July 1763, State Historical Society of Wisconsin, *Collections* 18(1908): 254–5, 225–6.

19 "Mr Ezekiel Solomons and Mr Henry Bostwick were taken by the Ottawa, and after the peace, carried down to Montreal, and there ransomed": Henry, *Travels*, 69. Rabbi Arthur Chiel has written an account of this incident ("The Ransom of Ezekiel") but it offers no documentation and thus cannot be given much weight as evidence. A more likely version of the events, in a letter written on 28 August 1763 by Gage to the earl of Egremont, indicates that Solomons and the British force were ransomed only in the sense that Gage gave presents to the Ottawa who escorted them to Montreal: NA, MG 11, CO 42, series Q, vol. 1, 210. He wrote that the Chippewa made an agreement with the Ottawa "that the Post should not be established, but the officers, soldiers and British Traders should pass down to Montreal in safety. A nation of Ottawas undertook to escort Them, and after arming the Prisoners, recovering & saving from the Plunder of the Enemy, a very large Quantity of Pelletry & other Effects belonging to the Traders, They escorted the whole down to this Place. I thought it very proper to reward them for this service, and have given Them the presents usualy [*sic*] made to the Indians, on occasion of some signal Service, and They are returned back very well satisfied."

20 Gershon Levy, the son of a New York merchant, Moses Levy, was likely born in New York: John Blackwood to Samuel Jacobs, 12 May 1785, and Jacobs to Messrs Grant & Blackwood, 18 May 1785, NA, Samuel Jacobs Papers, 3132–2c and vol. 4, Letterbook, 154–5. He was a practising Jew, for he was listed as a member of New York's congregation in 1759: "Earliest Minute Book, Congregation Shearith Israel, 1720–1760," 79. Gershon Levy was the brother of Isaac Levy, the Montreal merchant, and his sister, Bilah Abigail, had married Jacob Franks, the prominent New York merchant and father of John Franks.

21 Henry, *Travels*, 69. Henry records (*Travels*, 72) that on 7 June two large canoes from Montreal appeared with "goods consigned to a Mr Levy." The canoes were seized and the goods confiscated.

22 On 17 August 1763, Ezekiel Solomons gave evidence in a Montreal court that Levy had signed a note for £1,200 to J.-B. Proulx on 12 July, Proulx having threatened to take Levy's furs if he would not acknowledge this debt which Solomons said was not yet due: case against "Sieur Gershon Levy, et son associé, Sieur Solomon," brought by Proulx in the Chambre des milices, Montreal, 17 and 23 August 1763, NA, MG 8, E 6, vol. 4; photocopy in CJA, Levy Solomons file.

23 "A Short Journal of the Siege of Detroit, May 7–20 1763": Detroit Public Library, Burton Historical Collection, John Porteous Papers; "Journal of Robert Rogers," Detroit, 8 August 1763, in Corey, ed., *Papers of Sir William Johnson*, 13: 293.

24 Robert Davers, the 5th baronet of Rushbrook, had arrived in Detroit on 1 December 1761, seeking, according to one observer, "the most savage and uncultivated spots." Still in the area during Pontiac's uprising, he was killed by the Indians on 6 May 1763 on the St Clair River, one of the first casualties in the uprising: Harry Kelsey, "Sir Robert Davers," *DCB* 3: 166–7. He was apparently well known to Chapman Abraham: see p. 277n27.

25 "Lieut James McDonald to George Croghan giving an Account of all Transactions at Detroit from the 6th of May to the 12th. July, 1763," in Corey, ed., *Papers of Sir William Johnson*, 10: 736–44.

26 The will of Chapman Abraham (c. 1723–1783), signed 10 March 1783 and probated 11 April 1783, left a portion of the residue of his estate "to my Dear Brothers Solomon Abraham and Hart Abraham of Plimouth in Great Britain": ANQ-M, CM1–1, no. 8. Abraham arrived in New York from Holland by 1756. He was first recorded in Detroit in 1762: see Katz, "Chapman Abraham," 81–6. He married Elizabeth (Betsy) Judah in 1781. The original of their marriage contract or ketubah of 18 July 1781 is in the possession of Barton Myers III; it describes Chapman as "Kaufman ben Avraham Hacohen" – Kaufman, son of Abraham Cohen. See also Irving I. Katz, "Ketubah of Detroit's First Jewish Settler,"

Detroit Jewish News, 9 March 1973; copy in AJA, Chapman Abraham news-print file. Katz suggests Abraham was born in Germany. On the Abrahams who settled in Plymouth, see V.D. Lipman, "The Plymouth Aliens List, 1748 and 1803," Jewish Historical Society of England, *Miscellanies*, part 6 (1962): 194.

27 In a letter to his close friend, Abraham, on 19 February 1763. James Sterling writes tongue in cheek: "Damned Jew: I thought you should act like a Christian since Sir Robert Baptised you; but I find you are still a Jew by mistrusting your best friends, do you think that because you have been absent a little while that has forgotten you or is unwilling to serve you?": William L. Clements Library, James Sterling Letterbook, 1761–1765, 100; copy in AJA, Chapman Abraham correspondence file. See also "James Sterling," *DCB* 4: 722.

28 "Henry Gladwin Papers," 642–3. See also Katz, "Chapman Abraham."

29 John Heckewelder, "History, Manners and Customs of the Indian Nations," 257–8. Also see Heineman, "The Startling Experience of a Jewish Trader," 31–5. In 1933 Stephen Vincent Benet published a story based on the incident, "Jacob and the Indians," in *Tales before Midnight*, reprinted in the *Saturday Evening Post*, 14 May 1958.

30 McDonald to Croghan, 12 July 1763, in Corey, ed., *Papers of Sir William Johnson*, 10: 741.

31 Levy Andrew Levy, based in Fort Pitt was an associate of the Lancaster group composed of Joseph Simon, Bernard and Michael Gratz of Philadelphia, William Trent, Edward Ward, Michael Croughan, and others for trading in furs in the Illinois country: William Vincent Byars, "The Gratz Papers," 7; Rosenbloom, *Biographical Dictionary*, 93. While Levy was captured during the Indian uprising, and was released shortly thereafter, the partnership suffered a loss of £85,916 "in sundry Goods Ware's and Merchandize" as well as the loss of most of their servants and factors who were put to death by the Indians. The Six Nations Indians subsequently made restitution to the partnership by the grant of a large tract of land on the north side of the Ohio River up to the southern boundary of Pennsylvania: copy of "Petition of the Traders of 1763 to the King's Council of Virginia, Fort Pitt, September, 1775," private collection.

32 Levy Solomons (1730–1792), whose Hebrew name was Uri, was likely the Dutch Jew at Albany known as "Levi" as there is ample evidence that he was commonly known as "Mr Levy." He was referred to as "Mr: Levi" by his legal counsellor, Francis Maseres, in 1768: Wallace, ed., *Maseres Letters*, 73. An entry in the Minutes of the Shearith Israel Congregation of Montreal, 26th Nissan 5539 [12 April 1779], refers to Levy Solomons, the parnas, as "Mr Levy": NA, MG 8, G 67; see also Marcus, ed., *American Jewry: Documents*, 111–12. Mary Solomons, his daughter,

signed her name as "Mary Levy" prior to her marriage to Jacob Franks
in 1816: note on reverse of letter from Jacob Franks to John Lawe, 9
January 1816, State Historical Society of Wisconsin, John Lawe Papers,
box 1, item 2157. Mary's sister, Rachel Solomons, was also known as
Rachel Levy; she married Henry Joseph on 28 September 1803 as
"Rachel Solomons," yet Samuel David, a member of the Montreal community, noted on 28 September 1803, "Henry Joseph married to
Rachel Levy": Journal of Samuel David, NA, MG 24, I.13. In the winter
of 1814–15, Jacob Franks was referring to Mary Solomons and her
younger sister Jessy when he stated that "I am boarding with the Miss
Levys where I am very well off": Franks to Lawe, State Historical Society
of Wisconsin, *Collections* 19 (1910): 369. Also, Rebecca Franks Kemble
referred to Rachel Solomons Joseph in writing to her brother, Jacob
Franks, that "the Levy family and myself are friends": Kemble to Franks,
May 1807, John Lawe Papers, State Historical Society of Wisconsin,
box 1, item 2192.

Levy Solomons was in Montreal by 1763: Dunn, "Lucius Levy Solomons," *DCB* 4: 718–19. Solomons was recorded at the synagogue in
New York in 1756 and 1759 to 1764 inclusive and is described in 1762
as "of Albany": Congregation Shearith Israel, Offering Book, 1752–
1797. Notwithstanding Dunn's suggestion that Solomons's full name
was Lucius Levy Solomons, there appears to be no evidence to support
the suggestion. He did, however, have a grandson of that name (1803–
30) who lived in Albany: "Levy Solomons His Book Albany Septr 2^d
1806," AJA, Lucius Solomon Collection. Nor is there any evidence of a
blood relationship with Ezekiel Solomons, despite the suggestion of
Irving I. Katz in *The Beth El Story,* 4.

33 "A List of Traders Names and their Servants killed and taken and their
Losses by the Present Indian War," William Trent, Fort Pitt, 5 September, 1763: NA, MG 13, WO 34/40, f. 709 (mfm C–12843, B–2658).

34 Benjamin Lyon (d. 1806) was in business as a fur trader in Albany and
Oswego as early as 1757, as a partner with Gershon Levy as "Lyons Levy
& Company" and with Levy and Chapman Abraham as Gershon Levy &
Company: NA, Samuel Jacobs Papers, MG 19, A 2, series 3, vol. 4, Letter-
book, 154, and AJHS, P–255, Oppenheim Collection, Gershon Levy file.

35 "Memorial of Isaac Levi of Quebec, Merchant, and Levy Solomons, Benjamin Lyon, Gershon Levi, Ezekiel Solomons, and Chapman Abraham
of Quebec, late Merchants and Copartners, to the Honourable Guy Carleton," NA, series S, 13, 83–83b.

36 Godfrey and Godfrey, "The King vs. Gomez and Others," 397–407.

37 Notice in the *New York Gazette or The New York Post Boy,* 1–15 May,
12 June, and 10 July 1758: AJHS, P–255, Oppenheim Collection, Gershon Levy file.

38 In 1785 Samuel Jacobs stated that "I hold Gershon Levy's note sign'd
for himself & Compy. – The Company Concern was Messrs Lyons Levy
& Chapman which I now find difficult to prove tho' I am quite certain
of it": Jacobs to Messrs Grant & Blackwood, 18 May 1785, NA, Samuel
Jacobs Papers, Letterbook, 154; see also AJHS, P–255, Oppenheim Collection, Gershon Levy file.

39 See, for example, the notice published by "Heyman Mayers" at New
York, in *Weyman's New York Gazette*, 16 and 30 July 1759, to the effect
that bills of exchange amounting to £400, drawn by the paymaster of
the 44th Regiment in favour of Gershon Levy or Levy & Company, but
not yet endorsed by Levy, were "stolen at Oswego." See also notes in
AJHS, P–255, Oppenheim Collection, Gershon Levy file.

40 See, for example, Henry Nelles, Niagara, to Sir William Johnson, 8 May
1760: Corey, ed., *Papers of Sir William Johnson*, 10: 145. Moreover, in an
earlier volume of the papers, reference is made to a certificate, since
destroyed, by John Fitzgerald dated 5 April 1762 regarding a dispute at
Niagara "between Jean Baptist De Couagne, Indian Interpreter, and
Levy Solomon, sutler": 3: 671.

41 Ibid., 10: 145. Nelles reported he had been ordered to give "two pipe
Tomohawks" to Indian warriors which he "borrowed from Levi the Sutler, and since I cannot get them made I must pay for them."

42 "Memorial of Isaac Levi et al.," NA, series s, 83–83b.

43 AJHS, P–255, Oppenheim Collection, Gershon Levy file, referring to letter
from John Thurman, New York, to John Sargent, London, 3 September
1760, extracted from Thurman's letterbooks. It is Oppenheim who noted
that the "Jew traders" referred to were Gershon Levy and his partners.

44 Alexander Mackenzie, a Quebec merchant, was Jacobs's partner during
1761. About a year later he had joined his brother William in partnership.

45 This conclusion is based on a letter to Jacobs from Myers at Montreal,
4 October 1770. "As I am here at Present, I am sorry to acquaint you
through the Law Suit subsisting between us my Friend has counter-
manded his Orders for me for Goods from England. I spoke to Mr Levy
& he seems Ignorant & pretends to know nothing about it. Therefore I
beg you would immediately send me what Papers you have Concerning
the Company to convince them how Innocent I am in the Affair. Likewise to shew it is all owing to their doings. I will do the utmost in my
Power to satisfy you as soon as lays in my Power": NA, Samuel Jacobs
Papers, MG 19, A 2, series 3, vol. 10, 743.

46 Petition of Jacobs to Murray, [1762], ibid., vol. 7, 9–11; printed in Marcus, ed., *Early American Jewry: Documents*, 363–4.

47 "Memorial of Isaac Levi et al.," NA, series s, 83–83b; "Report by B.
Roberts to the Earl of Dorchester, on Micilamacanong, 1767," NA,
MG 23, A 1, series 1, vol. 6, 267 et seq.

48 Francis Maseres to Fowler Walker, 30 March 1768, in Wallace, ed., *Maseres Letters,* 71–3.

49 Evidence of Ezekiel Solomons, The case against "Sieur Gershon Levy, et son associé, Sieur Solomon" brought by J.-B. Proulx, in the Chambre des milices, Montreal, 17 and 23 August 1763: NA, MG 8, E 6, vol. 4; photocopy in CJA, Levy Solomons file. The location of Fort Dauphin was determined by Ernest Voorhis: *Historic Forts and Trading Posts of the French Regime and of the English Fur Trading Companies* (Ottawa: Department of the Interior 1930), 58. On 9 December 1761 Gershon Levy had entered into an *engagement* with one Pierre Bertrand to carry trade goods to the Rivière Saumon as far as the post of "Lhegachy:" ANQ-M, Étude Simonet. Harry W. Duckworth believes Lhegachy to have been Oswegatchie (Ogdensburg, New York).

50 Ibid. For example, Proulx brought his claim against Gershon Levy and Ezekiel Solomons for £1,200 in the Montreal court on 18 August 1763, while Proulx and Levy were still in Michilimackinac and Solomons had been back in Montreal following his ransom for only a few days. On 23 August the court ordered that the proceedings must await the return of Proulx to Montreal.

51 "Memorial of Indian Traders" to Gage, 30 December 1763, in Corey, ed., *Papers of Sir William Johnson,* 10: 992–3. The memorial was signed by the principals of Howard Bostwick & Chinn, by James Stanly [*sic*] Goddard and Forrest Oakes for Goddard, Grant & Oakes, and by Holmes and Memsen [Morrison?] as well as by "Gorsen Levy."

52 Their share made up less than 10 per cent of the total of all beaver sent by traders, however: "Return of the Trade at Michilimacinac, 1767," NA, William Legge Dartmouth Papers, MG 23, A 1, series 1, vol. 6, 267ff; copy in CJA, Gershon Levy file. No documents have been located to indicated any activity by Gershon Levy & Company at Detroit in this period.

53 "Memorial of Isaac Levi et al," NA, series S, 83–83b.

54 Burt, *Old Province of Quebec,* 104.

55 Petition of Jacobs to Murray [1762], requesting the governor to grant an order securing the goods of Gershon Levy & Co. of Montreal in favour of Samuel Jacobs and Alexander Mackenzie to cover a debt of about £1,460: NA, MG 19, A 2, series 3, vol. 7, 9–11; printed in Marcus, ed., *American Jewry: Documents,* 363–4.

56 Petition dated 17 November 1767: NA, MG 11, CO 42, series Q, vol. 5–1, 248–50.

57 Carleton to the earl of Shelbourne, 21 November 1767: ibid., 245–7.

58 "Memorial of Isaac Levi et al.," NA, series S, endorsement, 6210, "Read 8 Feby 1768, withdrawn."

59 No records relating to Gershon Levy have been found after 8 February 1768, the date when the consortium withdrew its petition. In a letter

dated 27 September 1763, Hayman Levy of New York wrote of "the late Gershon Levy": NA, Amherst Papers, WO 34, vol. 91, 275ff. See also Vaugeois, *Les Juifs et la Nouvelle-France*, 102–3, n. 44: "De plus il n'y a aucune trace de lui après cette date [27 September 1763] dans les documents que nous avons consultés, à l'exception de la fameuse petition de 1768."

60 Twenty years later Jacobs was still trying to collect the debt owed him: Jacobs to Messrs Grant & Blackwood, 18 May 1785, NA, Samuel Jacobs Papers, MG 19, A 2, series 3, vol. 4, Letterbook, 154.

61 Chapman Abraham died at Montreal between 10 March and 7 April 1783: a notarial copy of his will, signed 10 March 1783 and probated 11 April 1783 is on file at ANQ-M, CM1–1, no. 8. See also Marcus, ed., *American Jewry: Documents*, 431–5, for typescript of will and household inventory.

62 Benjamin Lyon had a house at Fort Michilimackinac during the 1770s and returned periodically to Montreal where he was a member of the Shearith Israel Congregation: his 1770 fur trade licence is in NA, RG 4, B 28, vol. 112, 811–18. Lyon appears to have conducted substantial business on behalf of Aaron Hart of Trois-Rivières during the 1770s. A claim filed by Hart on 5 October 1776 states that of £1,568.4.5 in trade debts owing, £347.8.3 was owed by "Benjamin Lyons & Co.": ASTR, Fonds Hart, N–G–3. In July 1779, when the post at Mackinac Island was reorganized to protect "the safety of the Upper Country" by creating a self-governing fur trade company known as the "General Store," Lyon and Ezekiel Solomons were among its associates: in 1780 Lyon and other Mackinac merchants suffered serious loss and petitioned Haldimand for indemnification: NA, series B, vol. 97, I, 203 and II, 577; published in *Michigan Pioneer Collections* 10(1886): 605–7, 9(1886): 658, and 13(1888): 56–7. In January 1784 his goods at Berthier were seized by the sheriff at the suit of Levy Solomons: Samuel Judah to Aaron Hart, 26 January 1784, ASTR, Fonds Hart, J–I–a.13.

63 Levy Solomons died on 18 May 1792, aged about 62 or 63 years: "Levy Solomons His Book Albany Septr 2^d 1806," AJA, Lucius Solomon Collection. See also "Items Relating to the Solomons Family, New York," 376.

64 There has been no record located to confirm Ezekiel Solomons's death or burial, although the likelihood is that he died in 1804–5, probably in New York: see pp. 184–5.

CHAPTER SEVEN

1 Manuscript notes made by the Reverend Gershom Mendes Seixas, 13 January 1783, on *The Constitutions of the Several Independent States of America; The Declaration of Independence; The Articles of Confederation between the Said States; The Treaties between His Most Christian Majesty and the United States of America*, 84, Rosenbach Library, Philadelphia.

2 NA, RG 68, vol. 89, Commissions and Letters Patent, vol. 1 (1764–75), 209. The same document, without Franks's oath of office, is in NA, MG 11, CO 42, vol. 29, f. 25–6. The original form of the oath for Jews is in the NA, RG 1, E 11, vol. 1.

3 The only known precedent of a Jew being appointed to office in the American colonies was the case of Simon Valentine: see p. 59. Valentine was among 19 individuals "appointed commissioners to take charge of the town guard and patrol in Charles Town": "Simon Valentijn," in Elzas, *Leaves from My Historical Scrapbook*, 4. However, this position does not appear to have been created by "commission" or appointment by the sovereign, but was rather a position of constable, chosen from among volunteers.

4 The Plantation Act allowed a "Person professing the Jewish Religion" to alter the oath of abjuration by deleting the words "upon the true Faith of a Christian." This provision was stated to apply "in order to intitle such person to the Benefit of being naturalized by virtue of this Act," but it was open to the interpretation that it applied in other situations.

5 See chapter 10, for a fuller discussion of this issue.

6 Burt, *Old Province of Quebec*, 103–4. See also Hilda M. Neatby, *Quebec: The Revolutionary Age, 1760–1791* (Toronto: McClelland and Stewart 1966).

7 Burt, *Old Province of Quebec*, 1, 104; NA, MG 11, CO 42, series Q, vol. 2, 332–6.

8 The treaty is printed in Kennedy, ed., *Statutes, Treaties and Documents*, 31–5.

9 "Instructions to Governor Murray, 1 December 1763," ibid., 43–52. See also Justice William Renwick Riddell, "Pre-Assembly Legislatures in British Canada," *Transactions of the Royal Society of Canada* 12(1918): 109–34.

10 Burt, *Old Province of Quebec*, 86–7. François Mounier, a French Protestant merchant, had settled in Quebec by 1750, although he was barely tolerated by the French government: *DCB* 3: 477–8. Hector T. Cramahé was also a Huguenot, as was William Hey, the new chief justice, who came to Quebec in 1766 and joined the council: *DCB* 4: 787–92 and 348–50, respectively.

11 "Ordinance Establishing Civil Courts, 1764," in Kennedy, ed., *Statutes, Treaties and Documents*, 52–5.

12 An interesting piece of evidence on this point is a pamphlet published in New York in 1760 which is the English translation of the service held by the Shearith Israel Congregation on 23 October, the day appointed "for a General Thanksgiving ... for the Reducing of *Canada*": *AJHSP* 37 (1926).

13 Vaugeois, *Les Juifs et la Nouvelle-France*, 119–22.

14 Petition of Jacobs to the governor of Quebec, 22 March 1762, War Office Records, Amherst Papers, Letters from the Commanders-in

Chief, New York, to the Governor of Quebec, 1760–1763, NA, MG 13, WO 34, vol. 3 (mfm C–12837).

15 Jacobs was buried in Quebec on 5 August 1786: ANQ-Q, Anglican Cathedral at Quebec, Parish Register. See Vaugeois, "Samuel Jacobs," *DCB* 4: 384–6; Mann, "The Jew of St Denis," 85–9.

16 His headstone, originally in the Alexander Street Cemetery in Trois-Rivières, states that his full name was Aaron Philip Hart and he was born in 1726 and died in 1800: memorandum of Gustavus N. Hart, 1941, "respecting the reburial on Wednesday, the 27th October, 1909, in the Cemetery of the Congregation of Spanish and Portuguese Jews, at Montreal, of remains brought by Mr. and Mrs. Alfred Belasco, from the Jewish Cemeteries at Three Rivers," CJA, year files, 1796, Hart Genealogy. According to Stern, however (*First American Jewish Families*, 95), he was born 16 August 1724. Hart and his wife, Dorothea Judah, headed one of the very few strictly observant Jewish families in eighteenth-century British North America although he does not appear to have joined or supported the Jewish congregation in Montreal, maintaining instead contacts with the Jewish community in New York. See Vaugeois, "Aaron Hart," *DCB* 4: 331–3; Douville, *Aaron Hart: récit historique;* Marcus, *Early American Jewry,* 1: 218–89; ASTR, Fonds Hart.

17 Isaac Levy (1706–1777) was in Quebec by January 1760: Deposition of Isaac Levy, 25 November 1766, NA, MG 23, I 13, Joshua Sharpe Papers, vol. 1, 211–12. He was the son of Moses Levy of New York, a brother of Gershon Levy, and a brother-in-law of Jacob Franks, the New York merchant: Stern, *First American Jewish Families,* 154 (Levy I(1)). Levy and Aaron Hart were partners in New York and then moved to Canada where the partnership was dissolved in 1761. Levy was in Montreal until about 1770 when he returned to New York: AJHS, P–255, Oppenheim Collection, box 5, Aaron Hart file, and box 10, Isaac Levy files.

18 "Memorial of Isaac Levi et al," 8 February 1768, NA, series S, 83–83b.

19 See the references in Corey, ed., *Papers of Sir William Johnson,* 3: 671 ("Levy Solomon, sutler") and 10: 145 ("Levi the Sutler").

20 NA, MG 11, CO 42, series Q, vol. 2, 332–6.

21 Benjamin Sack's list of Jews who arrived either "with Amherst" or "in the years immediately following the capitulation of Montreal" includes Aaron Hart, Lazarus David, Levy Solomons, Ezekiel Solomons, Simon Levy or Simon Levi, Samuel Jacobs, Eleazar Levy, David Salesby [Salusbury] Franks, and Andrew Hays. The list also includes individuals who appear to have arrived substantially later: Samuel Judah, Uriah Judah, Jacob and David Franks, Abraham Franks, Elias Seixas, Myers Solomons, and Moses Hart, Aaron's brother. *History of the Jews in Canada,* 51–4. Unfortunately, Sack cites no authority for his information: Sack's list also includes a number of individuals who Denis Vaugeois suggests may

not be Jewish at all – Hananiel Garcia, Emanuel de Cordova, Isaac de Miranda, Uriel Moresco, and Jacob de Maurera: *Les Juifs et la Nouvelle-France*, 107–14.

22 John Franks was in Quebec by 1761 and was carrying on business in the partnership of Franks & King in Quebec in June 1761: Petition of John Franks, 10 August 1768, NA, RG 1, L3L, vol. 87, 42874; Historical Society of Pennsylvania, Gratz Papers, case 16, box 11, John Franks file. See also p. 265n4.

23 In a petition of 2 April 1792, Elias Solomon (1699–1800) stated that he had been "an inhabitant of Quebec upwards of thirty-two years" and bore arms in defence of Quebec in the winter of 1775–6: NA, RG 1, L3L, vol. 185, 88740–1.

24 Lazarus David (1734–1776) had emigrated from Wales in 1761 and was in Quebec by 1763. In 1768 he moved to Montreal. On 26 March 1767, he had purchased a 72 by 54 foot lot on Notre-Dame Street on which there was a stone house of 35 feet frontage: NA, MG 24, L 3, vol. 36, 23003–7. He was married to Phoebe Samuel who had been born in New England.

25 Eleazar Levy (c. 1716–1811) arrived in Quebec from New York in May 1760 and established a store in Montreal by 1763: Petition of Eleazar Levy to the earl of Dartmouth, 1774, NA, MG 11, CO 42, vol. 33, 67; reprinted in Marcus, ed., *American Jewry: Documents*, 227–32.

26 Hyam Myers came to live at Eleazar Levy's house in Quebec in the spring of 1763: Vaugeois, *Les Juifs et la Nouvelle-France*, 128–9.

27 Ibid., 124: "Aaron" who worked for Samuel Jacobs. Jacobs's letter to "Mr Aaron" on 30 November 1761 is from NA, MG 19, A 2, series 3, vol. 8, 57; reprinted in Marcus, *Early American Jewry*, 1: 210.

28 Levy Simons purchased a house and lot in Montreal on 5 November 1763: ANQ-M, CN1–308, vol. 11, no. 1977. See also Vaugeois, *Les Juifs et la Nouvelle-France*, 129.

29 Elias Henry, late of Sheffield, was in New York by 1758. His partnership with Hart Aaron and Jacob Cohen was recorded as being insolvent by June 1761. He made Sedaka offerings to New York's Shearith Israel Congregation in 1763 (described as "Elias Henry of Montreal") and again in 1765 and 1766: AJHS, P–255, Oppenheim Collection, box 23.

30 Levy Michaels (c. 1723–1815) of New York had married Rachel Hays in 1759 against the wishes of her father, Judah Hays, a wealthy New York Jewish merchant. He died in July 1764, cutting his daughter out of his will. The Michaels emigrated to Montreal about 1764: Marcus, ed., *American Jewry: Documents*, 12–14, 89, and 227–32. See also Congregation Shearith Israel, New York, Register, 1759–1834, ff. 6, 10, 19, 28, 32, and 67.

31 Andrew Hays (1742–1835) was living at 15 rue Saint-Jacques in Montreal in 1763: Rome, comp., "The Hays Family," 237. Hays was a son of Solomon and Gitlah Hays of New York. His father, a Sephardic Jew probably born in Holland about 1710, had settled in New York with his

family by 1725. Solomon Hays had been licensed as a schohet or supplier of kosher meat by David Mendez Machado, the hazan or spiritual
leader of New York's Shearith Israel Congregation, in 1736: Phillips,
"Family History of the Reverend David Mendez Machado," 48. The
family had a running dispute with the New York congregation which
led to Solomon Hays being "excommunicated" by the synagogue: see
Godfrey and Godfrey, "The King vs. Gomez and Others."

32 An official document recorded that during the "Trinity Term, 1765"
[22 May to 12 June] "Monr. Godett Pet[ioned] to the Judge desiring to
be excused serving as a juror according to sumons [sic]. Monk to speak
to Mr. Walker about naming Jews." While no further record indicates
the decision made, another document in the same file records that
John Franks had already been summoned as a grand juror during the
Hilary Term, on 23 January 1765: "Miscellaneous records of the
[Grand Jury] of Quebec, 1765," NA, RG 4, B 16, vol. 34. The authors
are indebted to Patricia Kennedy of the National Archives for uncover-
ing the information in this file as "a little Chanukah gift" in 1993. Myer
Michaels served as a juror in the Illinois district of the Old Province of
Quebec in 1787: see C.W. Alvord, ed., *Cahokia Records, 1778–1790*
(Springfield: Illinois State Historical Society Library 1907), 28.

33 "Enterprising and audacious, and without doubt favoured by that policy
of protection by which the English granted the conquerors and their
friends advantages persistently refused to the former French colonists,
the Jews knew how to obtain various official or lucrative appointments."
Malchelosse, "Les Juifs dans l'histoire canadienne," 179–80.

34 Petition to Governor James Murray by Benjamin Price et al., 15 July
1765, NA, RG 1, L3L, vol. 160, 78536–8; Letters Patent to Benjamin
Price et al., 23 November 1765, NA, RG 68, liber A, 258–62; List of All
Lots Granted under Tenure, 25 November 1765, NA, RG 1, L3L, vol. 8,
2366.

35 A circular order by the governor, Ralph Burton, of 23 August 1763,
advises that "His Excellency has thought fit to establish a Post Office in
Canada, under the direction of Mr. Finlay, residing at Quebec and for
the accommodation of the public, a post office has been established by
the said gentleman in the Town of Trois-Rivières." A proclamation by
the governor elaborated that Finlay "has opened a post office in this
town of Trois-Rivières in the house of Mr Hart, merchant: "Military
Government of Canada: Trois-Rivières 1760–1764," Public Archives of
Canada, *Report*, 143–4.

36 See Ian K. Steele, "Hugh Finlay," *DCB* 5: 314–19.

37 Haldimand to Gage, 29 July 1764, as quoted in Marcel Trudel, *Le
Régime militaire dans le Gouvernement des Trois-Rivières* (Trois-Rivières: Édi-
tions du Bien Public 1952), 76; also Vaugeois, *Les Juifs et la Nouvelle-
France*, 119.

38 According to Sack (*History of the Jews in Canada*, 51), Hart was a "commissary officer," "one of the officers" who rode by the side of General Amherst and was "a member of his staff" when Amherst and his army rode triumphantly through the gates of Montreal following the city's surrender on 8 September 1760. The suggestion that Hart was an officer in the regular army is not supported by any known documentary reference, and would, if substantiated, be the first example of a professing Jew being an officer in the British army. Denis Vaugeois (*Les Juifs et la Nouvelle-France*, 107–19) concludes that Hart could not have been an officer in the British army and that the the army had no such position as "commissary officer." Vaugeois, who refers to Sack's book as "a general survey of uneven historical value" ("Aaron Hart," *DCB* 4: 333) may have been too harsh in his conclusion, as the British army is known to have had uniformed "Commissary Staff" in the eighteenth century (see, e.g., "James Sterling," *DCB* 4: 722). Further research is necessary to determine whether Hart may have been a non-commissioned officer on the commissary staff in view of his role as provisioner to the army.

39 This information comes from Malchelosse, "Les Juifs dans l'histoire canadienne," 180, but no reference is cited there.

40 There is a copy of Eleazar Levy's appointment in NA, RG 68, liber C, part B, Imperial Commissions, 24 December 1766: 31–2; Deposition of Eleazar Levy, 24 November 1766, is in NA, MG 23, I 13, Joshua Sharpe Papers, vol. 1, 185–6.

41 Levy is not included in the Tableau de l'ordre des notaires – the list of notaries who practised in the the province of Quebec. His notarial records, while theoretically public documents, are not held by the ANQ or by any known repository in the state of New York to which he moved in 1772.

42 See pp. 30–1.

43 Despite an exhaustive search, we have found no evidence on whether Levy took the oaths.

44 NA, MG 21, British Museum Add. MSS 35915, vol. 337, 139–54; copies of the appellant's and respondents' cases in Levy *u* Robertson et al. are to be found in Add. MSS 15491, at 25–40 and 41–58 respectively; Records of Levy *u* Burton in the William L. Clements Library, Gage Papers, and NA, series Q, vol. 10, 95–111. Copies of documents in the case from the files of Levy's lawyer are in NA, MG 23, I 13, Joshua Sharpe Papers, vol. 1, 220–308. See also Burt, *Old Province of Quebec*, 96–7; and Rome, comp., "On the Early Harts – Their Contemporaries, pt. 5," 1–15.

45 "Memorials to the Continental Congress," 26 August 1779, and in 1783, published in *AJHSP* 2 (1894): 123–7. Levy died impoverished in New

York in 1811: Eleazar Levy to Aaron Hart, 8 March 1797 and 25 August 1799, ASTR, Fonds Hart, J–A–6; Letters of Administration of the Estate of Eleazar Levy, 22 February 1811, New York County Surrogate's Court, liber 17, 324.

46 Sack states that "Uriah Judah ... was Prothonotary of Three Rivers": *History of the Jews in Canada*, 58. Although the court records in Trois-Rivières or in the ANQ provide no evidence that Judah held any judicial office, Sack's comment has been repeated by others.

47 Meeting of the Governor's Council, 27 June 1765, together with appendices including "The humble Petition of the poor unhappy Sufferers by fire ...," 7 June 1765: NA, RG 1, E 1, vol. B, 23–35 (mfm C–85). See also Hilda Neatby, "Benjamin Price," *DCB* 3: 541–2. Price was one of two commissioners sent by the council to report on the fire.

48 NA, RG 1, E 1, vol. C, 33–8. (mfm C–85).

49 Meeting of the Governor's Council, 18 April 1768, NA, RG 1, E 1, vol. C, 13 (mfm C–85) 13. No link has been established with John Labatt, the brewer.

50 The additional commissions and oaths of office for Franks are in NA, RG 68, vol. 89, Commissions and Letters Patent, vol. 1 (1764–75): 210–11; the same documents, without Franks's oath of office, are in NA, MG 11, CO 42, vol. 29, ff. 25–6. Franks continued to hold his offices until after 1778: a report by him on the state of houses in Quebec is dated 27 August 1778: NA, S series index.

51 See p. 228n12.

52 Moses David was appointed coroner of the western district of Upper Canada by commission on 24 February 1808: NA, RG 68, liber D, 13.

53 Cramahé to Dartmouth, 13 December 1773, in Shortt and Doughty, eds., *Documents, 1759–1791*, 1: 491–2.

54 Ibid., 493–4.

55 See Seixas, manuscript notes, on *The Constitutions of the Several Independent States of America ...*, Rosenbach Library, Philadelphia.

56 Seixas's position was made permanent in 1769, and he remained the congregation's spiritual leader for over fifty years, save for the years of the American Revolution which he spent in Philadelphia. He died in New York in 1816. See Phillips, "The Levy and Seixas Families," 208; also De Sola Pool, *An Old Faith in a New World*, 167–74, and De Sola Pool, *Portraits Etched in Stone*, 345–55.

57 Jewish settlers who are known to have arrived in Quebec between 1768 and 1774 include: Solomon Myers Cohen (1768); Simon Nathans (1768–9); Moses Hart, brother of Aaron (1768–9); Simon Levi (1769); Isaac, Uriah, and Elizabeth Judah (c. 1770); and Heineman Pines or Phineas (1773).

CHAPTER EIGHT

1 Chapman Abrams [*sic*], Montreal, to William Edgar, Detroit, 30 June
 1776, photocopy in AJA, Chapman Abraham(s) correspondence file.
2 The words are from a report by Carleton, 1 May 1775, NA, MG 11,
 series A, vol. 11, 170, 173. An extensive report of the incident was published in London in 1776 by Francis Maseres: see *Additional Papers Concerning The Province Of Quebeck: Being An Appendix To the Book entitled "An
 Account of the Proceedings of the British and other Protestant Inhabitants of the
 Province Of Quebeck in North America, in order to obtain a House of Assembly
 in that Province"*, 155–69; quoted in Rome, comp., "David Salesby Franks
 in Montreal," 94–100.
3 The Quebec Act, 14 Geo. III, c. 83 (1774).
4 Stanley, *Canada Invaded, 1775–1776*, 12–20.
5 Ibid., 18.
6 The Solomons incident was documented by Carleton on 4 May 1775:
 NA, MG 11, series A, vol. 11, 171–2. See also Rome, comp., "The Partners: Ezekiel Solomons," 38, and Stanley, *Canada Invaded, 1775–1776*,
 12.
7 Edgar Andrew Collard, "Throwing a Statue down a Well," *Montreal
 Gazette*, 3 December 1945, presents a detailed account of the incident,
 apparently based on original research. Quoted in Rome, comp., "The
 Partners: Ezekiel Solomons," 35–7. Franks's own account of the incident
 is found in Maseres, *Additional Papers Concerning Quebeck*.
8 Pierre Tousignant and Madeleine Dionne-Tousignant, "François-Marie
 Picoté de Belestre," *DCB* 4: 633–6.
9 This particular account of the incident accompanied Franks's letter to
 the newly inaugurated president, George Washington, on 12 May 1789:
 Straus, "New Light on David S. Franks," 101–8.
10 Ibid.
11 Rome, comp., "David Salesby Franks: American," 101–5; Rosenbach,
 "Documents Relative to Major David S. Franks," 157.
12 For Franks's subsequent career, see Straus, "New Light on David S.
 Franks," 101–8; H. Friedenwald, "Jews Mentioned in the Journal of the
 Continental Congress," *AJHSP* 1 (1892): 76, 82, 84–5; Hühner, "Some
 Notes on David S. Franks," 165–8. Franks, ironically, became the first
 recorded Jewish officer by commission in the new United States,
 although it is not known whether he considered himself Jewish as he
 had been baptized at birth. By May 1778 he was a major; by January
 1779, a lieutenant colonel; and by 1785, a colonel.
13 Notes by a descendant of Samuel Judah, who was in Montreal at the
 time, record "enormous sums of Continental money, received by Mr.
 Judah, for clothing and provisions given him to the Army – not a dollar

of which was ever redeemed by the Government": AJHS, P-78, Judah Family file.

14 See p. 90.

15 McCord Museum, Thomas McCord Papers, 0209, item M8972; Godfrey and Godfrey, "Who Was Who in Canadian Jewry" (Franks I).

16 The details of Solomons's experience are found in "Memorial of Levy Solomons of Montreal in the Province of Quebec, Merchant To the United States of America in Congress assembled November 15th 1784," National Archives of the United States, Continental Congress Papers, no. 35, 149a; photocopy in AJA, Levy Solomons file; typescript in NA, MG 23, B 3, file 1.

17 Aaron Hart to "Col. James Livingston before Quebec," 4 January 1776: British Museum Add. MSS 21731, ff. 250, 253.

18 Stanley, *Canada Invaded, 1775–1776*, 42, 55–6.

19 NA, MG 19, A 2, series 3, Samuel Jacobs Papers, vol. 6, 4–5 (dated in English, 23 October 1775) and vol. 2, 3316–6a (n.d.). Volume 6 also contains a typescript of an extract of a letter from Jacob R. Marcus of the Hebrew Union College, Cincinnati, to the archivist, saying that the "Hebrew script materials" from the Jacobs Papers are "a personal diary for the month of October, 1775, and recount Jacobs' reaction to the coming of the American troops, under Montgomery no doubt, to his town of St Denis. Unfortunately, though the script is Hebrew, the language is phonetic English and it is almost impossible to create a text. I have one expert philologist working on it now, after another had already put two weeks on it. We have ten to fifteen per cent of the text, not enough to really help us in any detail. Apparently Jacobs was a British patriot and the peasants around him were toasting 'Congress and Liberty.'" The code has still not been unscrambled. In 1986, in a letter to the authors (18 August 1986), Dr Marcus advised that the "text employs the Hebrew script to write the English which Samuel Jacobs spoke. They are practically indecipherable because of his accent. I have turned these letters over, in the course of years, to three scholarly men of great linguistic skills. They could do practically nothing with them, although we managed to get a few ideas. Jacobs was watching his neighbours and intended to report them to the British authorities; the peasants were sympathetic, apparently, to the advancing Americans. Let me give you one example of the difficulties. The word 'sir' turns out to be his version of the English 'third.'"

20 Hazen to Jacobs, 28 March 1776, NA, MG 19, A 2, series 3, Samuel Jacobs Papers, vol. 14, 1524. Moses Hazen is not known to be of Jewish origin, although the French pronunciation of his name has provoked that suggestion from some historians: see Stanley, *Canada Invaded, 1775–1776*, 28, and Allan S. Everest, "Moses Hazen," *DCB* 5, 412–15, footnotes on file at the DCB office, Toronto.

21 Petition of John Franks, 10 October 1792, NA, RG 1, L3L, vol. 87, 42879–80.

22 Petition of Elias Solomon, 2 April 1792, ibid., vol. 185, 88740–1. Solomon nevertheless testified that he bore arms in defence of Quebec in the winter of 1775–6. Although Solomon was likely Jewish, his origins have not been conclusively established and he had no clear affiliation with the Jewish community. It is known, however, that he had a business relationship with Samuel Jacobs; that in 1779 Jacobs sent his son Samuel to be educated by Solomon in Quebec: NA, MG 19, A 2, series 3, Samuel Jacobs Papers, vols. 18 and 20, and Letterbook, vol. 3; that Solomon was not English-born and was naturalized in 1761: Memorial of Elias Solomon to Alured Clarke, 3 March 1792, NA, series Q, s58–1, 231–9; and that Solomon was not buried in the Anglican cemetery as was his wife but in the Protestant cemetery which might more readily have accepted burials of those who had not been baptized: ANQ-Q, Protestant Church records.

23 Petition by Colonel Henry Caldwell and Others, NA, RG 1, L3L, vol. 52, 26644.

24 Stanley, *Canada Invaded, 1775–1776*, 99–103.

25 Rome, "Hyam Myers," 41–5; Samuel, "A List of Persons Endenized and Naturalized," 131; "Earliest Minute Book, Congregation Shearith Israel, 1728–1760," 60–1, 213; Vaugeois, *Les Juifs et la Nouvelle-France*, 126–9; George Allsopp to Samuel Jacobs, 31 January 1769, NA, MG 19, A 2, series 3, Samuel Jacobs Papers, vol. 10, 448–9, "Mr Myers is at Three Rivers or Montreal on his way to New York." Myers died in August 1801, either in New York or Norfolk, Virginia: Stern, *First American Jewish Families*, 218 (Myers II).

26 Moses Jacob Burak, "Moses Myers of Norfolk," MA thesis, University of Richmond, Virginia, August 1954, 17, 19, 20; copy in Old Dominion University Archives, Barton Myers Collection. Myers's name appears in the muster roll of Captain Joel Pratt's Company of the 2nd Battalion from 28 June to 13 October 1775, with the note that he was sick in hospital. His service apparently was over by the end of the year, and he returned to mercantile pursuits. He died in 1835.

27 Sack, *History of the Jews in Canada*, 1:62.

28 Myers's petition to the "Honorable Council of the State of Massachusetts Bay," 13 July 1778, Massachusetts Archives, book 168, 444–4a.

29 "The Declaration of Hyam Myers, lately come from Boston. Intelligence," 12 September 1778, British Museum, Add. MSS 21844, 22.

30 See pp. 86–8.

31 "I have allso to acquaint you that I have ones more purchased Mr Mansfield's house [in Detroit] formerly my Property. as I shall set off in a few days from here with a Cargo of Goods for your place": Chapman

Abraham to William Edgar, Detroit, 30 June 1776, photocopy in AJA, Chapman Abrahams correspondence file; location of original not indicated but shown as page "524."

32 Abraham was "one of those who had the honour of repelling the Rebels at Long Point, who with an effrontery peculiar only to themselves had formed the design of taking this city": Memorial of Chapman Abraham, 11 August 1778, NA, MG 21, series B, Haldimand Papers, vol. 217, 7–9.

33 Aaron Hart's bill to "Mr Chapman Abrahams" includes a item for "Cash Lent to you 17 Novr to go to Montreal £2/5/0"; the account was one of the "Debts owing to Aaron Hart" sworn at Quebec, 5 October 1776, ASTR, Fonds Hart, N–G–3.

34 According to Abraham's memorial to Haldimand of 11 August 1778, NA, MG 21, series B, Haldimand Papers, vol. 217, 7–9, he was "one of a party that was detached from Quebec to surprize Mr. Arnold's men, just before that town was invaded by the Rebels," and he "turned out a volunteer when the Rebels were defeated at Three Rivers."

35 Chapman Abrams [sic] to William Edgar, 30 June 1776, photocopy in AJA, Chapman Abrahams correspondence file.

36 Ibid.

CHAPTER NINE

1 Minutes, Shearith Israel Congregation, Montreal, NA, MG 8, G 67, vol. 2; published in Marcus, ed., American Jewry: Documents, 109. Citations in this chapter are from Marcus.

2 According to tradition the congregation was organized in 1768, but the earliest located written reference to that year as the date of its organization is a newspaper account 125 years later: "The Spanish and Portuguese Jews of Montreal, Shearith Israel – An Interesting and Venerable Record: Their 125th Anniversary Today," Montreal Daily Star, 30 December 1893.

3 While visiting rabbis made occasional appearances, none of the North American synagogues had a rabbi in regular attendance until the middle of the nineteenth century. As long as there was a minyan, no specially trained minister was required to lead a Jewish religious service. It was usual for the larger congregations to have a hazzan or cantor to lead the services, although even he was a layman – one with a good voice but with no special training. In the eighteenth century, a rabbi was "ordained" by other rabbis because of his familiarity with legal traditions not because of his knowledge of theology. He was an official of the community rather than of the synagogue. His duties were legal (interpreter of Jewish religious law) and judicial (head of the beth din

or Jewish court) rather than pastoral. See Grinstein, *Rise of the Jewish Community of New York*, 81–4.

The lack of ordained rabbis did present problems on some matters: for example, if a member of a community required a divorce. In 1814, Moses Hart wanted a divorce from his estranged wife, Sarah, and sought, through a cousin in London, an opinion from Dr Solomon Hirschell, the chief rabbi of London and head of the rabbinic court at the Bevis Marks Synagogue. The opinion as transmitted by his cousin was as follows: "Dr. Hirschel [*sic*] thinks it necessary to inform Mr. Moses Hart that his request can in no Way be complied with as in order to form a Divorce a written parchment must be framed in the presence of the Husband under the immediate Eye of a Person properly qualified as a Rauf [rav or rabbi] or a beth din with out wich together with all the minutie thereto attended the Get [ritual divorce] would not be Legal & the woman neaver be freed to marry anney other man. it is true a Get Can be framed & be sent to the Womman thro a messenger propperly appointed by Regular authority but the presence of the man at the time of writing is quite Indispensible. Mr Hart has therefore no other resource but to go to Some Place where there is a congregation and proper officers where such a Ceremony may be duly executed": G. & H. Joel to Moses Hart, 3 August 1814, ASTR, Fonds Hart, P–A–35.

4 Certificate of Barnet Lyons dated February 1817 as to circumcision of Levy Solomons, son of Levy Solomons, on 23 December 1771, in Montreal, by Hyam Myers, "conformable to the Jewish ritual": Thomas McCord Papers, 0209, Solomon Family, McCord Museum, item M8972.

5 This incident is discussed in Phillips, "Family History of the Reverend David Mendez Machado," 55–6.

6 The decision to build a synagogue appears to have been made prior to Lazarus David's death on 22 October 1776 although the formal establishment of the congregation did not occur until later. The minutes on the 25th of Ellul 5538 [17 September 1778] state that "the congregation met to elect a parnass and a gabay in the room of Mr. David Franks and Mr. Ezekiel Solomons." Marcus, ed., *American Jewry: Documents*, 106.

7 It is unlikely that this David Franks is David Salusbury Franks, who had by his own account, left the province with the American army in June 1776. It is possible that the reference was to David Franks of Philadelphia, a son of Jacob Franks, and a brother of Abraham Franks and John Franks, members of the Montreal congregation. According to Sack (*History of the Jews in Canada*, 69), David Franks "used from time to time to visit Montreal where he would often remain for a considerable length of time and show the keenest interest in the affairs of the community." Sack provides no source for this information however.

Although a Loyalist, this David Franks was not forced to leave Philadelphia until after a resolution of the executive council of Pennsylvania, passed 6 October 1780: Wolf and Whiteman, *History of the Jews of Philadelphia*, 91. A third possibility, entirely speculative, is that the David, son of Abraham, who signed the minutes of the Shearith Israel Congregation in Hebrew was a son of Abraham Franks and was the person indicated.

8 The records of the congregation locate the synagogue "in St. James Street, Montreal": Marcus, ed., *American Jewry: Documents*, 106. Sack (*History of the Jews in Canada*, 60) states that "the synagogue was situated on Notre-Dame Street near the site of the present Court House" but cites no authority although he refers to a tablet "placed by the Numismatic and Antiquarian Society" to mark the site. We do know that Lazarus David did own property fronting Notre-Dame Street close to the area where St James once met Notre-Dame. Records show that on 26 March 1767, he purchased a lot on Notre-Dame Street with a frontage of 42 feet and a depth of 54 feet and a stone house of 35 feet frontage: NA, MG 24, L 3, vol. 36, 23003–7. It is not clear whether this lot was donated to the synagogue by the David family, or whether the David family simply allowed the synagogue to be built on land it owned. Sack (*History of the Jews in Canada*, 60) states that the synagogue was erected in 1777 on "land which was donated by David David (born in Montreal 1764; died 1824) who inherited it from his father, Lazarus David." The statement is not supported by documentation, and as David David had just reached his twelfth birthday at the time of his father's death, it is unlikely he would have donated the land unless a prior arrangement had been made with his father. There is evidence, however, that the lot was still owned by the David family fifty years later; in a pamphlet dated 24 July 1826, Benjamin Hart wrote that "the old Synagogue in the possession of the Executors of the late David David, Esqr. is now a common store, or receptacle for all pollution, and in the hands of strangers, to the great disgrace of our Holy Religion": copy of pamphlet in ASTR, Fonds Hart, A–H–3.

9 Marcus, ed., *American Jewry: Documents*, 113.

10 Jacob Raphael Cohen (c. 1738–1811) is believed to have been born on the Barbary Coast but was educated in London where he became a mohel or ritual circumciser: Rome, "Jacob Raphael Cohen," *DCB* 5: 193–4.

11 Sack, "A Suit at Law Involving the First Jewish Minister in Canada," 181–6, citing records of the Quebec Court of Appeal in the case of Jacob Cohen *v.* Levy Solomons, [decision 1784], NA, series Q, vol. 33–1, 17–30.

12 Heineman Pines or Phineas (died c. 1799) was in Quebec by 1774 and operated a potash manufacturing plant at Petit Rivière-du-Loup (near

Trois-Rivières) from about 1780. His main business relationship was
with Messrs Grant and Blackwood at Quebec and in 1790 his properties
were seized and sold to cover his trading debts. He was active in the
Hebrew Congregation of Montreal as the records show him as a signa-
tory to the by-laws in 1779, a contributor towards the purchase of a
Torah scroll in 1779, and a contributor to the purchase of land for the
Jewish cemetery in 1798. See Rome, comp., "Heineman Pines," 47–8;
Pines to William Dummer Powell, 21 April 1780, and Pines to Grant
and Blackwood, 26 May 1783, private collection; *Quebec Gazette*, 13 January 1791; Minutes, Shearith Israel Congregation, Montreal, NA, MG 8, G
67, vol. 2.

13 Barnet Lyons (or Lyon) was possibly the brother of Benjamin Lyon (or
Lyons) and was in Montreal by 1769 and in Petit Rivière-du-Loup by
1803. Godfrey and Godfrey, "Who Was Who in Canadian Jewry."

14 Membership in the congregation was limited to males who had attained
twenty-one years of age or were married and had a child. "Subscribers,"
who had contributed to the building of the synagogue as well as their
oldest adult sons had a double vote "for ever": Marcus, ed., *American
Jewry: Documents*, 108. A comparison of the members' names in the congregation's minute book of the time with genealogical information
shows that 6 were bachelors, 7 had Jewish wives, 6 had Christian wives,
and the marital status of 4 was not known. Those married to Christians
were Ezekiel Solomons (Louise Dubois), Heineman Pines (Elizabeth
Holmes), John Franks (Appolonia Seymore or Seymour), Barnet Lyons
(Françoise Davis), Uriah Judah (Mary Gibbon), and David Franks (Margaret Evans). See Godfrey and Godfrey, "Who Was Who in Canadian
Jewry."

15 Delisle, "Register of Protestant Marriages Deaths and Births, 5 October,
1766 to 5 September, 1787 [Montreal]," lxxxi. The following christen-
ings are also recorded: Samuel Solomon, born 26 July 1773, baptized
26 September 1773; Joseph Solomon, born 1 June 1774, baptized
10 July 1774; Mary Solomon, born 26 September 1774, baptized
26 October 1774 (probably not their child); Ezekiel Solomon, born
16 July 1775, baptized 20 July 1775; William Solomon, born 28 May
1777, baptized 18 June 1777; Elizabeth Solomon, born 3 September
1778, baptized 9 September 1778. See also Gundry, *The Zacheus Patterson Descendants*, 221–33, especially chart of the Solomons family at 233.

16 See E.-Z. Massicotte, "Répertoire des engagements pour l'ouest conservés dans les Archives Judiciaires de Montréal (1670–1778)," *Archives
nationales du Québec, Rapport*, 1932–3, 297–300.

17 George Sutherland's Journal, 31 January 1780, and Report at Glouces-
ter House, 18 April 1781, Hudson's Bay Company Archives, B.211/a/1
and B.78/a/6. Solomons was in partnership with Alexander Shaw in the

Nipigon trade until about 1783. This information on Solomons's activities was kindly supplied by Harry W. Duckworth.

18 Marcus, ed., *American Jewry: Documents*, 106, 107.

19 Ibid., 107. The congregation unanimously determined "that no man or boy, whomsoever shall be, after sixty days from this date, be buried in the burying place of this congregation unless circumcised."

20 Ibid.

21 Notwithstanding Sack's assertion (*History of the Jews in Canada*, 60) that the name Shearith Israel was chosen for the Montreal congregation in 1768, the earliest documentary reference located using the name is Benjamin Hart's *To the Israelites of the Province of Lower-Canada*, 24 July 1826, ASTR, Fonds Hart, A–H–3. In 1779, Jacob Raphael Cohen referred to it as "K K Montreal." The letters "K.K." for *Kahal Kadosh* or holy congregation were commonly applied to Jewish congregations in the eighteenth century. [Jacob Raphael Cohen], "Mikveh Israel Jewish Congregation, Register of Births Deaths and Marriages, 1776–1834," Historical Society of Pennsylvania, entry of 2 December 1779 recording the death of Moses Joseph Pines, "Belonging to the K K of Montreal."

22 Phillips, "The Congregation Shearith Israel," 129–30.

23 Marcus, ed., *American Jewry: Documents*, 111–12, 113; "Memorial of Levy Solomons of Montreal in the Province of Quebec, Merchant To the United States of America in Congress assembled November 15th 1784," National Archives of the United States, Continental Congress Papers, no. 35, f. 149a; photocopy in AJA, Levy Solomons file; typescript in NA, MG 23, B 3, file 1.

24 Sack, "A Suit at Law Involving the First Jewish Minister in Canada," 181–6.

25 De Sola Pool, *An Old Faith in a New World*, 170.

26 In 1846, ten years after the re-establishment of the Montreal congregation, any potential further confusion of names with the Shearith Israel Congregation of New York was ended by the formal renaming of the Montreal congregation as "The Corporation of the Portuguese Jews of Montreal" under the statute of the Province of Canada, 9 Vict., c. 96.

27 Marcus, *Early American Jewry*, 1: 273. Marcus supports his thesis by reference to a petition by Jews and others in Quebec seeking a "House of Representatives with the power to lay taxes and duties and for a constitution and government on … fixed and liberal principles." However, the complete wording of the passage in the 1784 petition for a House of Assembly cited by Marcus is as follows: "And be Graciously pleased to Secure to them, a Constitution and Government, on such fixed, and liberal Principles, as may promote the desire Your Affectionate Subjects of this Province have, of rendering this Mutilated Colony, a bright Gem in the Imperial Crown of Great Britain": Petition for House of Assembly, Shortt and Doughty, eds., *Documents, 1759–1791*, 2: 743 and 745.

28 John Franks may also have been motivated to impeach Solomons to reinforce his own loyalty. He had fought with the British militia against the Americans at Quebec, but his son, David Salusbury Franks, had departed with the retreating American troops in 1776.

29 De Sola Pool, *An Old Faith in a New World*, 167–74. See also De Sola Pool, *Portraits Etched in Stone*, 345–55.

30 See Seixas, manuscript notes, on *The Constitutions of the Several Independent States of America...*, Rosenbach Library, Philadelphia.

31 Ibid. Article 22 of Delaware's constitution required a Christian oath of office. Article 35 of the Maryland constitution required "a declaration of belief in the Christian religion" as a condition of holding any state office. Article 40 of the Pennsylvania constitution also required a Christian declaration as a condition of office. Seixas's marginal notes with respect to Massachusetts have unfortunately been torn off the page, but article 1 of chapter 6 of that state's constitution provided that any person elected to the offices of governor, lieutenant-governor, councillor, senator, or representative, before assuming office, was required to subscribe to a declaration that "I believe in the Christian religion, and have a firm persuasion of its truth." Article 32 of the North Carolina constitution denied public office to individuals unable to affirm the "truth of the Protestant religion" or the "divine authority" of the New Testament. In December 1809 the Assembly of North Carolina nonetheless unanimously decided that this provision did not bar Jacob Henry, a Jew who had been elected to the assembly, from taking his seat.

32 Ibid. See articles 6 and 19 of the New Jersey constitution; articles 3, 12, and 13 of the South Carolina constitution; and article 6 of the Georgia constitution.

33 Ibid., 84.

34 Virginia's act, originally passed in 1785, is printed in *Revised Code of Virginia* (c. 1900), vol. 1, 41. See also Kohler, "Phases in the History of Religious Liberty in America, with Special Reference to Jews."

35 Petition for House of Assembly, 24 November 1784, in Shortt and Doughty, eds., *Documents, 1759–1791*, 2: 742–52. Jewish signatories included Elias Solomon and Hyam Myers from Quebec, Aaron Hart, Moses Hart, and Ezekiel Hart from Trois-Rivières, and John Franks, Abraham Hart, David David, Levy Michaels, Isaac Hart Abrams, Uriah Judah, Isaac Judah, and Samuel Judah from Montreal.

36 Marcus, ed., *American Jewry: Documents*, 113.

37 Godfrey and Godfrey, "Who Was Who in Canadian Jewry," (Judah I). Earlier residence in Montreal by Abraham Judah and his wife is likely. A sampler made in Montreal by their daughter Elizabeth at about eight years of age in 1771 is the oldest surviving Canadian sampler; it is in the custody of the Gershon & Rebecca Fenster Museum in Tulsa, Oklahoma.

38 Marcus, ed., *American Jewry: Documents*, 113.

39 Samuel Judah to Aaron Hart, 4 October 1784, ASTR, Fonds Hart, J–A–
13; *New York Gazette & Weekly Mercury*, 2 September 1784; AJHS, P–255,
Oppenheim Collection, box 8, Abraham Judah file.

40 Letter written by a descendant, AJHS, P–78, Judah Family file.

41 Stern, *First American Jewish Families*, 141 (Judah II(1)). The marriage
agreement of Samuel Judah and Elizabeth, daughter of Aaron Cohen,
in London, England, 27 March 1775, was recorded in New York
County, liber 45, and Conveyances, 482–6; copy in AJHS, P–255, Oppenheim Collection, Samuel Judah file, box 9, no. 7. This Samuel Judah
(c. 1725–1789) is not to be confused with a merchant of the same
name (1728–19 October 1781) who was in New York by 1760, was married to Jessy Jonas, and was an elder of that city's Shearith Israel Congregation: see Stern, *First American Jewish Families*, 139 (Judah I(1)).

42 Rome, comp., "Samuel Judah," 126–31.

43 Samuel Judah appears to have conducted a substantial business during
his early years in Quebec on behalf of his wealthy brother-in-law: according to a claim filed by Aaron Hart in Quebec on 5 October 1776, he
was owed 40 trade debts amounting to £1568.4.5 currency at that date,
of which £958.0.1 was owed by Samuel Judah. The account was subsequently marked "paid": ASTR, Fonds Hart, N–G–3.

44 On Levy Solomons, see p. 277n32. When Aaron Hart died in 1800, the
inventory of his estate disclosed a large amount of unredeemable notes
in Continental currency: Vaugeois, "Aaron Hart," *DCB* 4: 332.

45 Samuel Judah to David Franks, 9 June 1776, Historical Society of Pennsylvania, Tench Coxe Papers.

46 Samuel Judah file, AJHS, P–255, Oppenheim Collection, box 9, no. 7.

47 Stern, *First American Jewish Families*, 141 (Judah II(1)). A grandson of
Samuel Judah, another Samuel, moved to Vincennes, Indiana, where,
before he reached the age of 30, he was elected a member of the state
legislature. A letter of Benjamin Hart of Montreal citing this fact as
example of the state of Jewish rights in the United States was used as a
basis for material in Francis Henry Goldsmid, *The Arguments Advanced
against the Enfranchisement of the Jews* (2nd ed; London 1833): see *AJHSP*
12(1904): 263–4.

48 Godfrey and Godfrey, "Who Was Who in Canadian Jewry," (Judah I).

49 See NA, MG 19, A 2, series 3, Samuel Jacobs Papers, vol. 10: 448–9
(George Allsopp to Samuel Jacobs, 31 January 1769); vol. 10, 743
(Hyam Myers to Jacobs, 4 October 1770); vol. 21, 2865 (Robert Russell
to Jacobs, 24 March 1773); and vol. 22, 2973 (Russell to Jacobs, 19 February 1784). In this last letter, Russell says: "In answer to your last I
have to inform you that I have only recovered the debt due by Mr.
Myers (whereof I have paid you £20)."

50 Myer Myers, St Thomas, to Moses Myers, New York, 8 November 1784, Old Dominion University Archives, Barton Myers Collection, item 206; "I hope this will find you safe returned from Quebec, and that you left our dear Parents Injoying health, in company with our dear Sister. I am unhappy I can't mention dear Jake, it is useless to grieve. The Lord's will must be obeyed." Jacob Myers had been born in New York on 24 June 1762: Stern, *First American Jewish Families*, 218 (Myers II); he was circumcised in New York on 2 July 1762: "Registry of Circumcisions by Abm. I. Abrahams," 152, item 14. Belle or Bilah Myers was born on 28 February 1764. Stern states that her birth is the first known birth of a Jewish child in Quebec.

51 Burak, "Moses Myers of Norfolk," 20–8, citing F. Edler, "The Dutch Republic and the American Revolution" *Studies in History and Political Science* 29 (no. 2, 1911), 42–3, 57, 62, 181–4. A petition to the Continental Congress in March 1784 referred to Moses Myers's "Sufferings in St. Eustatia [*sic*] in Person and Property on Account of his Attachment to his Country": ibid., 24, citing Isaac Moses to Thomas Mifflin, president of the Continental Congress, New York, 10 March 1784, National Archives of the United States, Continental Congress Papers, no. 46, ff. 375 and 378.

52 Moses Myers [to Samuel Myers], 30 August 1784, Old Dominion University Archives, Barton Myers Collection, item 205.

53 Myer Myers, St Thomas, to Moses Myers, New York, 8 November 1784, ibid., item 206. Rachel Louzada Myers died in New York on 28 February 1790; Hyam Myers died in August 1801, in New York or Norfolk, Va: Stern, *First American Jewish Families*, 179 (Louzada) and 218 (Myers II).

54 The evidence for the relationship of Abraham and Aaron rests on the former's role as a witness to the signature of Elizabeth Hart, widow of Henry Hart, also a brother of Aaron Hart, at Kingsbury, New York on 26 December 1788: Administration Papers, 1787–1823, Washington County, Register of Deeds, Fort Edward, New York. See also Aaron Hart to Ezekiel Hart, c/o Alex Zuntz, New York, 1793, McCord Museum, Early Hart Papers, M18653.

55 In the summer of 1780, Solomons's furs had been seized at the request of Alexander Ellice & Co. acting on behalf of his creditors: "Account of 14 Packs Peltries belonging to The Estate of Ezek^l Solomon Seized upon by Edwd. Wm. Gray Esqr. Sheriff – at the request of Alex^r. Ellice & Co. as acting Trustees for said Estate ... dated St. Maries 3d. Augt. 1780" together with "Account of 28 Packs of Furs & Peltries Seized upon by Edwd. Wm. Gray, Esqr. [n.d.]," Private collection. By 1781 Solomons was officially declared bankrupt: *Quebec Gazette*, 23 and 30 August 1781.

56 See pp. 145–52.

57 According to Cecil Roth: see "Some Jewish Loyalists," 98–103. See also p. 80.

58 Benjamin and Abraham Myers obtained a grant of 100 acres (lot 62, Gagetown) on 14 July 1784. Rachel Myers (c. 1735–1801) obtained a grant of 32 acres (lot 11, Grimross Neck, Gagetown) in May 1786: PANB, RS 686, vol. A, grant 98, and vol. 1, grant 41. See also the petitions in the PANB of Rachel Myers, 25 August 1785 (mfm F1027) and 24 June 1786 (mfm F1031), as well as of Benjamin Myers, 24 July 1786 (mfm F1031). Another petition of Rachel Myers (3 April 1781; NA, MG 24, B 1, doc. 3427) gives information on Benjamin's service in the militia. Other background information appears in Marcus, ed., *American Jewry: Documents*, 273–4.

59 Widows and single women who had reached majority were entitled to the exercise of property rights; the property of a married woman was legally held by her husband.

60 After her return to the United States, another of Rachel Myers's sons, Mordecai, was wounded at the Battle of Crysler's Farm while serving with the invading American forces as a captain with the 13th Pennsylvania Infantry during the War of 1812. He later became a member of the New York legislature (1831–4) and, later still, mayor of Schenectady: Adler and Connolly, *From Ararat to Suburbia*, 4–5. While at the scene of battle in 1813 he wrote to a more literate correspondent: "Sum must spill there blud and others there ink. I expect to be amongst the former and I hop you are amongst the latter." "Extracts from the Note Books of Rev. J.J. Lyons," 346–7. As to Judith Montgomery, see p. 322n60.

61 Koven, *Weaving the Past into the Present*, 65–8.

62 Stern, *First American Jewish Families*, 106 (Hays (4)); letter of Abigail Hays (a first cousin of Barrak) in New York to her mother, Hetty Hays, 1 May 1783 ("Barrak and his Wife Jack and Solomon is going to Quebeck"): Westchester County Historical Society, Pleasantville, NY, Hays Family Papers, box 1, item 1.25. See also Rome, comp., "Barrak Hays," 241. The suggestion of Max Kohler ("Jewish Factors in the Settlement of the West," *AJHSP* 16[1907], 27) that Barrak Hays was a lieutenant in the Loyalist Scouts is in error: Solis-Cohen "Barrak Hays: Controversial Loyalist," 55; and Memorial of Barrak Hays, 4 August 1783, NA, MG 21, series B, Haldimand Papers, vol. 13, 335–6, in which Hays described himself as having been appointed "an officer of guides" by New York's Governor Clinton.

63 On 30 July 1769 a general meeting of the congregation adjudged that Solomon Hays and his sons Barrak and Andrew, along with three other individuals, had "Acted in Opposition, and tending to subvert the Laws & Rules made for the Good order and Support of our Congregation" and that if they did not make "Satisfactory Concessions to the Parnasim

& assistants" within one month, then their names shall be Eraised from the List of Yaheedim and not be intitled to any benefits or Rights in this Congregation." In response Barrak Hays sued the officials of the congregation, and the case came to court in October of 1772: Solis-Cohen, "Barrak Hays: Controversial Loyalist," 54–7.

64 His son, Solomon Hays, agreed on 4 March 1794, to go to the Upper Country for a term of three years as apprentice to Grant Campion & Co. of Montreal: Marcus, ed., *American Jewry: Documents*, 464–5.

65 AJHS, P–255, Oppenheim Collection, box 8, file 47, noting an unclaimed letter in the post office for "Lion Jonas," as published in the *New York Gazette or the Weekly Post Boy*, 25 July 1765, and an advertisement in the *New York Gazette and Weekly Mercury*, 27 December 1773. For a published later advertisement, see Friedenwald, "Some Newspaper Advertisments of the Eighteenth Century," 58–9.

66 Petition of Sarah Jacobs, 13 January 1802, NA, RG 1, L3L, vol. 112, 55215. She signed her name in Hebrew. Lyon and Sarah Jonas had two sons, Lyon who was 31 and Abram or Abraham who was 27 by April 1800: Declaration of Lyon Jonas, 29 April 1800, NA, RG 1, L3L, vol. 112, 55213–14. His declaration before James McGill, JP, was not made "on the Holy Evangelists" as was usually the case.

67 Certificate as to Lyon Jonas, 4 June 1777, ibid., vol. 112, 55209.

68 According to a descendant of the Seixas family, from the dissolution of the New York congregation in August 1776 until the arrival of the Rev. Jacob Raphael Cohen in 1783 the synagogue was closed except for being opened occasionally by Lyon Jonas, who was described as a leader of the Tory party: Phillips, "The Congregation Shearith Israel," 129–30.

69 "Lyon Jonas, Furrier, Living in St. Paul's Street, opposite Mr. St. Dezier," advertised the goods in his Montreal shop in the *Quebec Gazette*, 6 November 1783: Rome, comp. "Lyon Jonas," 49.

70 The minutes of Shearith Israel Congregation of 21 June 1784 record that a book of the congregation which Lyon Jonas had kept during the war was formally transferred to the congregation: De Sola Pool, *An Old Faith in a New World*, 281. "Minute Book, Congregation Shearith Israel, 1760–86," 156–9. No record has been located indicating that Jonas attended the synagogue after that time.

71 AJHS, P–255, Oppenheim Collection, box 8, file 47.

72 Memorial of Sundry Inhabitants of Montreal, 1794, NA, RG 1, L3L, vol. 135, 66351–3; Minutes, Shearith Israel Congregation, February 1798, Montreal, NA, MG 8, G 67, vol. 2.

73 NA, RG 1, L3L, vol. 112, 55209; vol. 2, 527; vol. 74, 5159 and 5166.

74 De Sola Pool, *An Old Faith in a New World*, 347–8. Lyon Jonas died at the age of 86 in February 1817: Congregation Shearith Israel, New York, Register, 1759–1834, f. 69.

75 William D. Reid, *The Loyalists in Ontario* (Lambertville NJ: Hunterden House 1973), 231 and 312.

76 According to oral evidence gathered in the late 1950s from descendants of original settlers in Cornwall Township by Marion MacRae for her work with Anthony Adamson in connection with the restoration of Upper Canada Village near Morrisburg, a Jewish family whose surname was Moses were Loyalists who had come from New York state and had anglicized their name by changing it to "Moss." Another Jewish family named Solomons was said to have lived on the adjoining lot. This oral history is confirmed by the record. By 1786 Myers Solomons was located on the east half of lot 25, 2nd concession, Upper Canada Land Book, Cornwall Township, and was approved for a grant in 1789: AO, RG 1, series A–IV, vol. 8, 54; Sergeant Samuel Moss of the King's Royal Rangers of New York occupied the adjoining lot, the west half of lot 24, 2nd concession, and obtained letters patent on 22 May 1797: no. A 44, Ontario, Ministry of Government Services, Official Documents Office. See also "Plan of the Town of Cornwall in the District of Lunenburg Conveyed in The Years 1784, 1785, 1786 & 1787 ... with the Proprietors Names Inserted on the Lots," mfm 6784, Ontario, Ministry of Natural Resources, Survey Records Office, and "Plan of Part of the New Settlements on the North Bank of the South-West Branch of the River S. Lawrence," by Patrick McNiff, 1 November 1786, OA, SR 11081.

77 Moses Jacobs may have left Massachusetts under other circumstances because that area was not known for its toleration at the time: see p. 263n25. It is likely that he is the Moses Jacobs listed in Census A, Rhode Island, as living in Kent in 1790: Rosenbloom, *Biographical Dictionary*, 74.

78 See pp. 158–65 for the story of Jacobs's petitions for land. His death was reported in the *Kingston Chronicle*, 5 September 1823, 3, col. 3.

79 31 Geo III, c. 31 (1791).

CHAPTER TEN

1 Hansard, *The Parliamentary Debates* (hereafter *Hansard*), 1787, vol. 2, 28 March 1787, 112.

2 Namier and Brooke, *House of Commons, 1754–1790*, 2: 72–3.

3 Beaufoy's speech is reported in *Hansard*, 1787, vol. 2, 28 March 1787, 70–107.

4 The petition was published as "The Case of the Protestant Dissenters, with Reference to the Corporation and Test Acts," in *Gentleman's Magazine* (London) (March 1787), 237–40.

5 *Hansard*, 92–101 passim.

6 Ibid., 108–14 passim. North (1732–92) was born Frederick North, son of Francis, first Earl of Guilford. He entered the House of Commons at the first general election after he came of age and rose to become first minister at 37 in 1770, remaining in the position until 1782, a period that covered the loss of Britain's American colonies: Namier and Brooke, *House of Commons, 1754–1790*, 3: 204–12.

7 Besides the Thirteen Colonies, Britain's American empire in 1763 included Quebec, Nova Scotia, Newfoundland, Florida East, Florida West, Jamaica, Barbados, Bermuda, the Leeward Islands (Antigua, Montserrat, St Christopher's, and Nevis), Grenada and the Grenadines (including the colonies of Dominica, St Vincent, and Tobago and Territories depending, or the Windward Isles). St John's Island (Prince Edward Island) became a separate colony in 1769.

8 Cornwallis's instructions as governor-in-chief of Nova Scotia, 2 May 1749, NA, MG 40, B 13, pt 2.

9 Britain's other Catholic colonies acquired by treaty in 1763, Grenada and East and West Florida, also received exceptional treatment: all three were initially exempted from the Test Act requirements. Although Grenada was given an assembly in 1769, the experiment was unsuccessful, and the provision for the assembly was revoked and the Test Act imposed in 1771. Both East and West Florida were retaken by Spain in 1781 and given to it by treaty in 1783: see Labaree, ed., *Royal Instructions to British Governors*, 1: 18–19, 40–1, 96–9, 433–4, 497.

10 Shortt and Doughty, eds., *Documents, 1759–1791*, 1: 181–205. Compare with usual requirement in other colonies: Labaree, ed., *Royal Instructions to British Governors*, 1: 36–7, 40–1.

11 See, for example, the instructions to Guy Carleton as governor of Quebec in 1768 and in 1786: Shortt and Doughty, eds., *Documents, 1759–1791*, at 1: 301–24 and 2: 816–37, respectively.

12 "Military Government of Canada: Trois-Rivières 1760–1764," Public Archives of Canada, *Report*, 1918, 143–4.

13 6 Geo III, c. 53, ss. 1 and 2 (1766). According the Montefiore, *A Commercial Dictionary* ("Plantations"), "By stat. 7 and 8 Will. c. 22, all laws, bye-laws, usages and customs, which shall be in practice in any of the plantations, repugnant to any law made or to be made in this kingdom relative to the said plantations, shall be utterly void and of none effect."

14 In North Carolina, for example, on 20 November 1771, the new governor of the colony sent a message to the assembly advising that "His Majesty, by his Royal Instructions having Commanded me to Administer, or cause to be administered, to the Members and Officers of His Majesty's Council, and to the Members of the Assembly, and to all Officers whatsoever throughout this Province the Several Oaths appointed by Acts of Parliament to be taken to Government; and it appearing that the Oath

of Abjuration, as altered by an Act of the 6th year of His Majesty's Reign [1766] hath never yet been in use in this Province, I have thought proper to accompany this Message with a Copy thereof to the end that it may be Administered Accordingly." William L. Saunders, ed., *The Colonial Records of North Carolina* (Raleigh NC: P.M. Hale, Printer to the State, 1890), 9: 137–8.

15 Garner, *Franchise in British North America*, 146; McKinley, *The Suffrage Franchise in the Thirteen Colonies*, 476.

16 Goodman, *American Overture*, 199, refers to three "Jewish names" among those appointed to high office in Georgia: Moses Nunes who was appointed "searcher of the Port of Savannah" on 9 June 1768; David Emanuel who was installed as justice of the peace for St George Parish in 1766; and James Lucena who was appointed justice of the peace in Christ Church Parish in 1773. All three swore a Christian oath. A parchment document giving the original Georgia oaths and a list of office holders with their dates of appointment was later published: George White, comp., "Georgia Roll," *Historical Collections of Georgia* (New York: Rudney & Russell 1854), 38–41. This Moses Nunes may not have been the same person as the Moses Nunez who was the son of Dr Samuel Nunez: Stern, *First American Jewish Families*, 234. David Emanuel, of Jewish descent, became the sixth governor of the state of Georgia in 1801; he may have been a Presbyterian: Hühner, "First Jew to Hold the Office of Governor." On James Lucena, see p. 259n18.

17 In 1757, Nova Scotia's council resolved that "no Popish recusant" could vote in the election for the assembly and authorized the use of the state oaths and the declaration against transubstantiation to enforce the exclusion. A Nova Scotia bill of 1780 to enfranchise Roman Catholics was disallowed in 1782 by the Colonial Office because it was more liberal than the British Relief Act of 1778 which dealt only with ending prosecutions of "Popish Bishops," imprisonment for life for "Papists" who keep schools, and the disabilities that had prevented Catholics from holding land. An act of the Nova Scotia Assembly passed in 1789 was finally approved by the Colonial Office, allowing Roman Catholics to vote: Moir, ed., *Church and State in Canada*, 64–5.

18 Ibid. According to Moir, voting for Roman Catholics and Jews in Prince Edward Island was restricted by a council minute of 1773 requiring the swearing of the state oaths, but a provincial statute of 1780 to the same effect was disallowed on a technicality. Catholics obtained no relief in Prince Edward Island until a general emancipation act was passed in 1830. Jews continued to be restricted by the state oaths after that time.

19 Ibid., 65. According to the *Journal* of the House of Assembly of New Brunswick, 1786, 18, the house went into committee of the whole to consider the sheriff's return for the County of Westmoreland and

decided that "the French votes as stated by the Sheriff were not legal and that therefore Charles Dixon, Esq was duly elected"; PANB, mfm F4. An act effectively restoring the vote to Roman Catholics in New Brunswick was passed in 1810.

20 "Report of the Special Committee to whom was referred the Message of His Excellency the Governor in Chief, of the 8th February, 1834, relating to the Act 1st Will. IV. Cap. 57, intituled, "An Act to declare persons professing the Jewish Religion, entitled to all the Rights and Privileges of the Other Subjects of His Majesty in this Province'," Lower Canada, House of Assembly, *Journal*, 1834, appendix G.g.

21 The oath specified for Catholics by section 7 of the Quebec Act read: "I, A.B., do sincerely promise and swear, That I will be faithful and bear true Allegiance to His Majesty King GEORGE, and him will defend to the utmost of my Power, against all traitorous Conspiracies, and Attempts whatsoever, which shall be made against His Person, Crown and Dignity; and I will do my utmost Endeavour to disclose and make known to His Majesty, His Heirs and Successors, all Treasons, and traitorous Conspiracies, and Attempts, which I shall know to be made against Him, or any of Them; and all this I do swear without any Equivocation, mental Evasion, or secret Reservation, and renouncing all Pardons and Dispensations from any Power or Person whomsoever to the Contrary. – So Help Me GOD."

22 Even after the Quebec Act, the instructions to the governors of the province still required an appointee to the governor's council, who was not a Canadian "professing the religion of the Church of Rome" to swear the state oaths and make and subscribe the declaration against transubstantiation: see section 3 of the instructions to Carleton, 3 January 1775, to Haldimand, 15 April 1778, and to Carleton, 23 August 1786: Shortt and Doughty, eds., *Documents 1759–1791*, 2: 595–6, 697, 817. Thus, Anglicans and French-Canadian Roman Catholics were eligible to be members of the council, while Dissenters such as Presbyterians, Irish and Scottish Roman Catholics, and Jews were not. This provision perhaps explains William Grant's action in converting from Roman Catholicism to the Church of England before his appointment to the council in 1777. When the instructions to Lord Dorchester as governor-in-chief in 1791 relieved all Catholics from the necessity of making and subscribing the declaration against transubstantiation, Grant was no longer obliged to remain an Anglican to hold office. This perhaps explains Grant's apparent reversion to Catholic practices late in life: see David Roberts, *DCB*, 5: 367–76.

23 Labaree, ed., *Royal Instructions to British Governors*, 1: 40–1.

24 See pp. 56–7.

25 "Report of the Special Committee to whom was referred the Message of His Excellency the Governor in Chief, of the 8th February, 1834, relating to the Act 1st Will. IV. Cap. 57, intituled, 'An Act to declare persons professing the Jewish Religion, entitled to all the Rights and Privileges of the other Subjects of His Majesty in this Province,'" Lower Canada, House of Assembly, *Journal*, 1834, appendix G.g.

26 13 Geo. III, c. 25 (1773).

27 Cornwallis's instructions, 2 May 1749, NA, MG 40, B 13, pt. 2.

28 32 Geo II, c. 5 (1758) (Nova Scotia).

29 Carleton's instructions as governor of Quebec in 1768 replicated word for word those given to Cornwallis: Shortt and Doughty, eds., *Documents 1759–1791*, 1: 312–13. In Prince Edward Island the Church of England was established by 43 Geo. III, c. 6 (1802); in New Brunswick by 26 Geo. III, c. 4 (1786); in Quebec in the Quebec Act, 14 Geo. III, c. 83, ss. 5 and 6 (1774).

30 Labaree, ed., *Royal Instructions to British Governors*, 2: 482–3 and 494.

31 During 1755–6, some 6000 people, (about one-half of the Acadian population) who refused to take the unqualified oath of allegiance to the British monarch were expelled from Nova Scotia. Many of the remainder deserted their farms to seek refuge in New Brunswick and Prince Edward Island. Some of those expelled settled in Louisiana which was then French territory. For a good documentary background of the expulsion, see Moir, ed., *Church and State in Canada*, 21–31.

32 Labaree, ed., *Royal Instructions to British Governors*, 2: 494.

33 Ibid.

34 D.W. Prowse, *A History of Newfoundland from the English Colonial and Foreign Records* (London: Macmillan 1895; reprinted Belleville: Mika Studio 1972), 363–5.

35 According to the census of winter inhabitants of St John's taken in 1815, there were 8,531 Roman Catholics and 3,343 Protestants: ibid., 701. In the rest of the island, Protestants were the majority: by one account, in 1825 there were 60,000 inhabitants of the island of whom 25,000 were Catholics: M.F. Howley, "The Roman Catholic Church in Newfoundland," *A History of the Churches in Newfoundland: A Supplement to A History of Newfoundland* (London: Macmillan 1895; reprinted Belleville: Mika Studio 1972), 29.

36 See p. 195.

37 Kennedy, ed., *Statutes, Treaties and Documents*, 32, 137–40.

38 For the instructions given to Dorchester of 25 August 1787: Shortt and Doughty, eds., *Documents, 1759–1791*, 2: 838–40. The text of the first amendment of the United States constitution begins: "Congress shall make no law respecting an establishment of religion, or prohibiting the

free exercise thereof." Although Britain appeared to adopt a qualified concept of "free exercise" for British North America, it diverged from the United States which prohibited "establishment" at the federal level. The "Protestant Church of England" remained established as the official church as was made clear by sections 20 and 24 to 29 of Dorchester's instructions.

39 The legal precedents, because they were not published, were rarely known to the public. Even historians are only beginning to review the court records of the period. See, for example, Evelyn Kolish, "Some Aspects of Civil Litigation in Lower Canada, 1785–1825: Towards the Use of Court Records for Canadian Social History," *Canadian Historical Review* 70 (September 1989): 337–65.

40 Shortt and Doughty, eds., *Documents, 1759–91*, 2: 742.

CHAPTER ELEVEN

1 NA, MG 40, D 13, pt 4.

2 The information on St Paul's Church used in this sketch draws on two articles by the Reverend George W. Hill published by the Nova Scotia Historical Society in the 1870s and the recent book of J. Philip McAleer, *A Pictorial History of St. Paul's Anglican Church, Halifax, Nova Scotia.*

3 There is a tradition that this organ was intended for a Roman Catholic chapel in South America but was seized from a Spanish ship and brought to Halifax as a prize: Hill, "History of St Paul's I," 45.

4 "The bishop of Nova Scotia, whose chief residence was in Halifax, attended St Paul's Church, but it is manifest that he did so as a parishioner, and not as entitled by virtue of his office." He was assessed as a parishioner and required to pay pew rent. Hill, "History of St Paul's II," 88.

5 McAleer, *Pictorial History,* 63. According to one account – which may apply to this period – "The Communion Table stood against the southern wall, with a low railing before it. The pulpit – a three decker – was a little to the west of the centre aisle. On either side – east and west – were square pews for the officers of the army and navy. On either side of the centre aisle, in front of the Communion Table, were the pews for the Governor, the Admiral and the Bishop. The Governor's pew was a miniature drawing room. It was square, furnished with tables, a desk, chairs, etc. The Admiral's pew was equally comfortable. Both were upholstered in crimson. The Bishop's pew was upholstered in blue." The governor's pew had been decorated in 1786: Hill, "History of St. Paul's II," 75.

6 Hill, "History of St Paul's II," 80–1. Commenting on the union of church and state created by the establishment of the Church of

England in Nova Scotia, Hill says that "this very position legally bestowed did more to injure the interests of the Church of England than anyone unacquainted with its constitution and its relations can conceive."

7 St Paul's Church Baptismal Record, Anglican Diocesan Centre, Halifax: "Bapt'd March 17 [1793] Mr. Samuel Hart, Merchant, an Adult."

8 *The Book of Common Prayer, and Administration of the Sacraments and other Rites and Ceremonies of the Church, According to the Use of the Church of England* (Oxford: T. Wright and W. Gill 1775).

9 The writ for the election had been issued 22 January 1793 and returned 20 March 1793. Hart's election actually took place on 4 March 1793 as he was acclaimed and declared elected at that time: Fergusson, ed., *Diary of Simeon Perkins*, entry of 4 March 1793.

10 On the official policy of conversion of non-Anglicans, see pp. 59–60. The royal instructions to Lieutenant Governor John Parr on 25 August 1787 showed that this policy was still a priority in Nova Scotia. The governor was "to take especial Care that God Almighty be devoutly and duly served throughout your government, that the Lord's Day be duly Kept, and that the Services and Prayers appointed by and according to the Book of Common Prayer be publickly and solemnly read and performed throughout the year": NA, MG 40, D 13, pt 4.

11 Stern, *First American Jewish Families*, 100 (Hart XII); Godfrey and Godfrey, "Who Was Who in Canadian Jewry," Hart I. This Hart family was not related to the family of Aaron Hart of Trois-Rivières.

12 "Items Relating to the Seixas Family, New York," 350; "Items Relating to the Jews of Newport," 181; "Items Relating to the Newport Synagogue," 404, 407–9; Gutstein, *The Jews of Newport*, 92–3.

13 A Samuel Hart, described as a son of Moses Hart, died in Barbados in October 1773, although he is said to come from New York not Newport: Rosenbloom, *Biographical Dictionary*, 55. Nevertheless Samuel Hart of Newport was likely in Barbados at this time because on 21 June 1773, Samuel Hart and his nephew Samuel received instructions to go to Barbados as agents of Jacob Rodrigues Rivera & Aaron Lopez: Lopez Papers, Newport Historical Society. However, there was a Samuel Hart alive in Newport after 1773 – presumably the younger Samuel.

14 Hühner, "Jews Interested in Privateering in America," 166–7, citing *Acts and Resolves of Rhode Island*.

15 Scott, comp., *Rivington's New York Newspaper*, 2 December 1780, 3; Jacob Hart's application for government assistance, London, 11 November 1783: NA, Audit Office, 12/100, ff. 18 and 23. The Audit Board was "perfectly convinced of the Loyalty of this old man and his family" and acknowledged that "a Brother of Mr. Hart's was murdered for his Loyalty." The decision concluded: "There is another Circumstance which

we take notice of because it had weight with us in considering this Family as deserving Objects of the bounty of Government. We found that they were so considered at New York & that the old Man & his Son [Moses] had seperate Allowances there[.] from our Knowledge of Sir Guy Carlton [*sic*] & his Mention to save the Public Money we draw this Inference from it that they must have been meritorious Loyalists."

16 Naphtali Hart Jr had gone to St Eustatius with his family in February 1773: Hart to Aaron Lopez, 12 March 1773, in Marcus, ed., *American Jewry: Documents*, 420–1. He died between 12 December 1793 and 27 November 1796: see Emanuel, *Jews of the Netherlands Antilles*, 1050–2. Hannah Hart died 25 November 1779: Register, 1759–1834, Congregation Shearith Israel, New York, f. 53. Isaac Hart's family and their in-laws, the Pollocks, went to St Eustatius: Roth, "Some Jewish Loyalists," 91. There are today families named "Hart" and "Pollock" living at Dieppe Bay on St Kitts, twelve miles across the Caribbean from St Eustatius. Abraham Hart had returned to London by 1765: AJHS, P–255, Oppenheim Collection, box 5, file 20; Naphtali Hart died in Newport on 22 August 1786: "Items Relating to the Seixas Family, New York," 350.

17 Hart's will of 14 November 1793 gives his wife's background: Halifax County Court of Probate, Samuel Hart estate, H–42, 1810.

18 Roth, "Some Jewish Loyalists," 88–9.

19 Godfrey and Godfrey, "Who Was Who in Canadian Jewry," Hart I(2). Also, petitions of Jacob (11 November 1783), Esther (5 December 1784), and Moses Hart (11 July 1785) for government assistance: NA, Audit Office, London, 12/100, ff. 18 and 22, and 12/101, ff. 163 and 161, 223–4.

20 "The Hart Family of Newport," 86–90.

21 Joseph Kirkham *v.* Samuel Hart, 1785, PANS, RG 39, C, vol. 37; also, Sutherland, "Samuel Hart," *DCB* 5: 409–10.

22 The purchase was made from John Turner on 15 December 1786: Halifax County Registry of Deeds, book 24, p–10. This property was Hart's major asset at the time of his death in October 1810: Halifax County Court of Probate, Samuel Hart estate, file H–42.

23 See David Franks *v.* Samuel Hart, 1788, PANS, RG 39, C, vol. 51.

24 Hill, "History of St Paul's," I: 53–4, II: 69.

25 See pp. 79–80.

26 Fergusson, ed., *Diary of Simeon Perkins*, xxxii–xxxiii. See also Rome, comp., "The First to Sit?" 156–8.

27 Kennedy, ed., *Statutes, Treaties and Documents*, 7.

28 Garner, *Franchise in British North America*, 146. Interestingly, the 1775 bill "was designed for the sole benefit of the Jews since the bill, by retaining the Declaration against Transubstantiation, intended to continue to disfranchise Roman Catholics." Garner suggests that the

"Assembly's singular interest in the Jews" may have been an accommodation for Joshua Mauger, "a wealthy English Jew." Garner's assertion of Mauger's religious background is not documented in his work and appears contrary to other accounts. According to David Rome, "on the level of documented history, Mauger was no Jew": "Mauger," 22. See also Donald F. Chard, "Joshua Mauger," *DCB* 4: 525–9. The Maugers appear to have been a Huguenot family, but "Jewish ancestry" cannot be ruled out.

29 29 Geo. III, c. 1, s. 1 (Nova Scotia).

30 "We are of opinion," the law officers said on 6 July 1792, "that Persons born out of your Majesty's Ligience who have been naturalized by any special Act of the British Parliament, or come within the act of the 13th of his late Majesty, Chapter 7 for naturalizing foreigners generally in your Majesty's colonies in America are capable of voting for, or being elected members of the Assembly of Lower Canada." The opinion was rendered in response to a petition dated 3 March 1792 by 43 inhabitants of the town of Quebec, all natives of Europe naturalized under the Plantation Act, advising that doubts had arisen whether, under the Constitutional Act, they would be able "to enjoy all the privileges of His Majesty's natural born subjects," including the right of being "capable of voting at an election of a member to serve in the Assembly, or of being elected at any such election": quotations from Brodey, "Status of Jews in Canada," 231–9. See also Doughty and McArthur, eds., *Documents, 1791–1818*, 107.

31 Commission to John Wentworth as lieutenant governor of Nova Scotia, 13 January 1792, and commission to Sir Guy Carleton as governor-in-chief of Nova Scotia, 27 April 1786: NA, MG 40, D 12, pt 2, 302–3, and 270–99.

32 Individual instructions to Wentworth as lieutenant governor may never have been issued as he was to follow Dorchester's instructions. Instructions to Wentworth are not in the National Archives or the Nova Scotia Archives; nor do they appear to be in the relevant entry books in the Public Record Office. It is possible, of course, that Wentworth merely took his instructions with him on his return to England, as they were his personal property.

33 Instructions to Lord Dorchester as governor-in-chief of Nova Scotia and the Island of St John and Cape Breton, 23 August 1786: NA, MG 40, D 13, pt 4.

34 Goeb, "The Maritime Jewish Community," 14. We have been unable to verify this information. Moses Montagu Hart, son of Samuel and Rebecca, was baptized at St Paul's Anglican Church on 1 September 1793, having apparently been born during the summer: Anglican Diocesan Centre, Halifax, St Paul's Church Baptismal Record.

35 Moses Hart was buried at London's Great Synagogue on 12 November
   1825: Burial Register of the Great Synagogue, London, 1823–37, 1 E
   141, f. 48.
36 Sutherland, "Samuel Hart," *DCB* 5: 410. See also Halifax *Weekly Chronicle*, 3 November 1809; *Nova-Scotia Royal Gazette*, 10 October 1810; Halifax County Court of Probate, Samuel Hart estate, file H-42.
37 The colonial administration was zealous in enforcing the establishment
   of the Church of England in Upper Canada. For example, the first Marriage Act of the province of Upper Canada, passed in 1793 (33 Geo.
   III, c. 5), authorized only ministers of the Church of England to solemnize marriages "according to the form prescribed by the Church of
   England." While the act did not affect the marriages of Roman Catholics (who were permitted marriage by priests) or Jews and Quakers
   (who did not require a minister to perform a marriage ceremony), it
   meant that marriages of Protestant Dissenters were not valid. In 1798
   the Upper Canada legislature passed an act (38 Geo. III) to authorize
   ministers of the Church of Scotland and Calvinists and Lutherans to solemnize marriages and to validate marriages of those three denominations previously solemnized. In 1818 the legislature validated marriages
   of other denominations which had been outside the Marriage Act since
   1791 (59 Geo III, c. 15) but did not authorize ministers of other
   denominations to perform marriages. Methodists, who had come to
   Canada from the United States and who were becoming the largest religious group in the province numerically, were not brought into the Marriage Act until an amendment which was passed in 1829 and received
   royal assent in January 1831 (11 Geo IV, c. 36). See also Moir, ed.,
   Church and State in Canada, 140–9.
38 There was some concern among Catholics after 1791 that they would
   not have the right to set up an episcopal organization in Upper Canada
   where one had not existed before. The Quebec Act had granted the
   clergy of the Roman Catholic Church in Quebec the right to "hold,
   receive, and enjoy, their accustomed Dues and Rights," a provision confirmed by the Constitutional Act. However, some ambiguity was created
   by the order in Dorchester's instructions as governor of Upper Canada
   "that no Episcopal or Vicarial Powers be Exercised within Our said Province by any Person professing the Religion of the Church of Rome but
   such only as are essentially and indispensably necessary to the free Exercise of the Romish Religion and in those Cases not without a License
   and Permission from you": Doughty and McArthur, eds, *Documents 1791–
   1818*, 43. Finally, in April 1807, Alexander McDonell, a Catholic priest,
   was sent to the lieutenant governor of Upper Canada on behalf of
   Bishop Joseph-Octave Plessis of Quebec, the senior representative of the
   Catholic Church in Canada, to request permission for the establishment

of ecclesiastical jurisdiction in Upper Canada. McDonell wrote Plessis that he was not optimistic, saying "yet after all I do not by any means flatter myself with hopes that the Governor & Council will decide upon the matter until it be referred home, & instructions received relative thereto." Four months later McDonell reported to Plessis "that his Excellency is extremely well disposed to favor your Lordship's plans respecting the Catholic Religion in this Province, & will have no objection to the Residence of a Person invested with Episcopal powers in Kingston or any other part of the Province where your Lordship may be pleased to appoint." McDonell to Plessis, 16 April and 8 August 1807, Archives de l'Archediocèse de Québec, Plessis Papers, Haut-Canada, III-14 and III-17.

39 Instructions to Lord Dorchester as governor of Lower Canada, 16 September 1791, section 2: Doughty and McArthur, eds., *Documents, 1791–1818*, 13–14. His instructions as governor of Upper Canada on the same day are virtually identical.

40 Ibid., section 4.

41 Ibid., section 3.

42 The oath required the defence of the king "to the utmost of my power against all traitorous conspiracies," an undertaking that implied personal combatant service repugnant to Quakers. It might be thought that Dorland, who had been a lieutenant in Cuyler's Corps of Associated Loyalists, might have had little difficulty with that concept. However, his brother, Thomas Dorland, had been disowned by the Society of Friends for taking up arms with the Associated Loyalist troops during the Revolution and this may have influenced Dorland's position in 1792. See Dorland, *Quakers in Canada*, 22–3; "Grants of Crown Lands in Upper Canada, 1787–1791," Archives of Ontario, *Report*, 1928, 148, 167–9; Robert Lochiel Fraser, "Thomas Dorland," *DCB* 6: 214–16.

43 "Journal and Proceedings of the House of Assembly of the Province of Upper Canada, 1792," Archives of Ontario, *Report*, 1909, 3–4.

44 Ibid., 4.

45 Upper Canada Oaths Act, 3 Will. IV, c. 13 (1833). Still, Quakers were allowed to affirm instead of swear in almost all other situations, a right that was even extended by statute to Mennonites and Tunkers in 1809. The act allowed "every Menonist or Tunker, in any case in which an Oath is required by Law to make his or her Affirmation or Declaration in the same manner and form as a Quaker by the Laws now in force is allowed to do."

46 After passage of 26 Geo. III, c. 19 (1786) (New Brunswick), Quakers were permitted to make an affirmation in the following words: "I, A.B. do solemnly, sincerely, and truly declare and affirm." The affirmation was declared by the statute "to be of the same force and effect in all

cases where by Law an Oath shall be required, as if such Quaker had taken an Oath in the usual form."

47 An Act for granting Indulgences to the People called Quakers, 33 Geo. III, c. 4 (1793) (Lower Canada), allowed Quakers to affirm instead of swear oaths as well as to be excused from military service upon payment of a levy.

48 See Instructions to Lord Dorchester as governor of Lower Canada, 16 September 1791, and Instructions to Lord Dorchester as governor of Upper Canada, 16 September 1791, in Doughty and McArthur, eds., *Documents, 1791–1818*, 13–32 (Lower Canada), 33–48 (Upper Canada). Compare Shortt and Doughty, eds., *Documents, 1759–1791*, 2: 838–40.

49 Doughty and McArthur, eds., *Documents, 1791–1818*, at 14 and 34 respectively. The texts of the oath of abjuration and the declaration on transubstantiation administered to non-Catholic senior officials in the province of Upper Canada from 9 July 1792 to 13 February 1833 are in NA, RG 1, E 11, vol. 4:

"I A.B. do solemnly and sincerely declare that I do believe in my conscience, that not any of the descendants of the person who pretended to be Prince of Wales during the life of the late King James the Second … hath any right, or title whatsoever, to the Crown of this realm or any other the dominions thereunto belonging … And I do make this recognition, acknowledgement, abjuration, renounciation [*sic*] and promise, heartily, willingly, and truly upon the true faith of a CHRISTIAN. – So help me GOD."

"I A.B. do declare that I do believe that there is not any transubstantiation in the Sacrament of the Lord's Supper or in the elements of bread and wine at or after the consecration thereof by any person whatsoever."

A different form of oath was to be sworn by judges upon their appointment to the high courts, concluding with the words "as God help you and all Saints." This oath was last used in 1829. The original judge's oath on parchment is in NA, RG 1, E 11, vol. 12.

50 The expression is from the "Petition for House of Assembly," dated 24 November 1784, Shortt and Doughty, eds., *Documents, 1759–1791*, 2: 743, and 745 as follows: "And be Graciously pleased to Secure to them, a Constitution and Government, on such fixed, and liberal Principles, as may promote the desire Your Affectionate Subjects of this Province have, of rendering this Mutilated Colony, a bright Gem in the Imperial Crown of Great Britain."

51 Royalist France ceased to be a threat to Britain's control of Quebec with the French Revolution of 1789, but the British authorities continued to fear invasion by revolutionary France: see Greenwood, *Legacies of Fear*.

52 The declaration required for applications for crown land by Loyalists and others was different from that under the Test Act and posed no difficulty to Dissenters or Jews. The additional instructions to Governor

Frederick Haldimand, 16 July 1783, contained a requirement that applicants for land in Quebec should swear "the oaths required by law" and subscribe a declaration in the following form (Shortt and Doughty, eds., *Documents, 1759–1791,* 2: 731): "I, A.B. do promise and declare that I will maintain and defend to the utmost of my power the Authority of the King in his Parliament as the Supreme Legislature of this Province." The same wording is found in section 42 of the instructions to Dorchester of 23 August 1786 (ibid., 831), and again in section 35 of each set of instructions to Dorchester as governor of the provinces of Lower and Upper Canada on 16 September 1791: Doughty and McArthur, eds., *Documents, 1791–1818,* 22, 42.

53 The case of Lawrence Kavanaugh in Nova Scotia in 1821 was an exception: see pp. 194–5.

54 The National Assembly of the Republic of France granted full civil rights to Jews on 27 September 1791, although those rights were sharply curtailed by Napoleon in 1806. The constitution of the United States of America, as noted, contained a declaration that no religious test should ever be required as a qualification to any office or public trust, and its first amendment provided that "Congress shall make no law respecting an establishment of religion, or prohibiting the free exercise thereof."

55 The disabilities of non-Anglican Protestants in this period by virtue of the enforcement of the Test Act deserves further study. Three Scotsmen who came to Upper Canada by about 1800 would provide an interesting beginning.

●William Allan (c. 1770–1853), born in Scotland, arrived in Montreal in 1787 and in Niagara the following year. His biography indicates "his family background is obscure" but it is likely that he was a Presbyterian. He joined St James Anglican Church in York shortly after 1800 and became one of the most prolific office holders in the colony: "William Allan," *DCB* 8: 4–13; Edith G. Firth, ed., *The Town of York, 1815–1834* (Toronto: The Champlain Society/University of Toronto Press 1966), 50–1.

●John Strachan (1778–1867), born in Aberdeen, had studied at St Andrews University before coming to the Kingston at the end of 1799. In 1802 he applied to be appointed minister of the Presbyterian "Scotch Church" on St Gabriel Street in Montreal. Upon being passed over, he subsequently confirmed his adherence to the Church of England, rising to become the first bishop of Toronto as well as a holder of many high government offices: G.M. Craig, "John Strachan," *DCB* 9: 751–76; Moir, ed., *Church and State in Canada,* 63–4.

●William Morris (1786–1858), another Scottish Presbyterian, arrived in Upper Canada with his family in 1801, championed the rights of Presbyterians as their chief lay spokesman, but was not appointed to high office because he could not comply with the Test Act. He was able to take the non-sectarian oath of office in the Constitutional Act upon his election as a member of the Upper Canada Assembly for Perth in 1820. He was apparently not required to take the sacrament as dictated by the Test Act upon his appointment as justice of the peace in 1818 or upon his appointment as lieutenant-colonel of the 2nd Regiment of Carleton militia in 1822. He supported the government party in the assembly but, according to his biographer, "never entered the charmed circle of the Family Compact whose members held official portfolios." Harry J. Bridgman, "William Morris," *DCB* 7: 638–42.

CHAPTER TWELVE

1 Quoted in Moir, ed., *Church and State in Canada*, 143–5.
2 Petition of Levy Solomons, 23 October 1797, NA, RG 1, L3, bundle S4/25; "Upper Canada Land Book D, 1797–1798," Archives of Ontario, *Report*, 1931, 109.
3 "Upper Canada Land Book D, 1797–1798," Archives of Ontario, *Report*, 1931, 104–14.
4 Petition of Moses Hart, 30 October 1797, NA, RG 1, L3, bundle H4/107; ibid., 109.
5 The phrase, "proving ground," came into use in the mid-eighteenth century to describe the area kept clear so that barrels of guns could be "proofed" or tested to see if they conformed to the regulations of gunmakers' companies. Today, it also has a more figurative meaning as "a place for scientific testing and experiment, hence a practical test for something."
6 Petition of Moses David, 31 July 1797, NA, RG 1, L3, bundle D6/23–23f; Petition of Moses Jacobs, 30 May 1797, NA, RG 1, L3, bundle J10/35–35f.
7 Rosendale, "An Early Ownership of Real Estate in Albany, New York by a Jewish Trader."
8 On 9 January 1797, when he had been in office scarcely a month, Elmsley participated in a land board decision on his own petition that had awarded him 5000 acres as an interim measure until the secretary of state could rule on "the propriety of obtaining His Majesty's permission to grant the Chief Justice such a proportion of land as may be deemed adequate to his rank": "Upper Canada Land Book D, 1797–1798," Archives of Ontario, *Report*, 1931, 79–80, 82.
9 Edith G. Firth, "John Elmsley," *DCB* 5: 303–5. See also Firth, ed., *Town of York, 1793–1815*, 36, 42, and 91–2.
10 See pp. 16–17. Also, Kohler, "Civil Status of the Jews in Colonial New York," 81–106, and Brodey, "Status of Jews in Canada."
11 *A Proclamation to such as are desirous to settle on the lands of the Crown in the Province of Upper Canada; by His Excellency John Graves Simcoe, Esquire;*

Lieutenant Governor and Commander in Chief of the said Province, 7 February 1792: reprinted in Archives of Ontario, *Report*, 1906. The instructions to governors are found in Shortt and Doughty, eds., *Documents, 1759–1791*, 2: 731, 831, and Doughty and McArthur, eds., *Documents, 1791–1818*, 42. Note, however, that in Lower Canada an additional instruction to Dorchester (18 November 1783) exempted Quakers from swearing the oaths as a condition of applying for land grants; they were able to make a declaration instead: "Lower Canada, Instructions to Governors, 1791–1839," Public Archives of Canada, *Report*, 1905, 26.

12 See chapter 5. The records of land grants are in the Provincial Crown Records Centre, Halifax, and the Public Archives of New Brunswick.

13 Nova Scotia Grant Book 6, 466–7, and Nova Scotia Grant Book 13 (old), 120, Provincial Crown Records Centre, Halifax; PANB, RS 108, F1031 (1786).

14 See 124–5.

15 For example, Barnard Moses, an inhabitant of Charleston, SC, was stranded in New York in 1783 with other Loyalists. Finding himself banished from his home, and his property confiscated, he petitioned "to go to Nova Scotia and receive some encouragement like others": Petition of Barnard Moses to Sir Guy Carleton, New York, 8/9 June 1783, in *Report on American Manuscripts in the Royal Institution of Great Britain* (Hereford: Anthony Brothers 1909), 4: 135.

16 Petition of Samuel Becancour Hart to the King, 5 November 1830, NA, RG 4, A–1, vol. 351 (1831), 96–8.

17 See pp. 97–8.

18 Petition of John Franks, 1792, NA, RG 1, L3L, vol. 87, 42872–81.

19 "Register of the Post of Michilimackinac *begun & opened* by James Gruet, Notary, June 1st 1785," Mackinac County Court House, Michigan. Myer Michaels (1760–1815) was the son of Levy Michaels and Rachel Hays of Montreal and a member of the Shearith Israel Congregation: Minutes, Shearith Israel Congregation, Montreal, NA, MG 8, G 7, vol. 2.

20 Myers Solomons was described as a Jewish resident of Montreal in the 1760s by Benjamin Sack in his *History of the Jews in Canada*, 53, although no evidence is cited in support of this statement. However, the records show that in 1773 he married Sarah Combs in a Protestant ceremony in Montreal: Delisle, "Register of Protestant Marriages Deaths and Births, 5 October, 1766 to 5 September, 1787 [Montreal]," Public Archives of Canada, *Report*, 1885. By 1786 Solomons was located on the east half of lot 25, 2nd concession, township of Cornwall. In 1789 he received approval for this land grant: AO, RG 1, Series A–IV, vol. 8, 54. Solomons was one of two early Jewish settlers in the township, the other being his neighbour, Samuel Moss: see pp. 125–6.

21 Petition of John Lawe, NA, RG 1, L3, bundle L Misc., 1788–95, vol. 306, 66a-b. Lawe was baptized on 26 December 1779, three weeks after his

birth on 6 December: see "Copy of the Register of the Parish of Montreal," Public Archives of Canada, *Report*, 1868, lxxxix. He was involved in the fur trade in the Upper Great Lakes with his uncle, Jacob Franks: Godfrey, "Jacob Franks," *DCB* 7: 328–9. After being appointed a judge in 1831 and elected to the Legislative Assembly of the Wisconsin Territory in 1835, Lawe became a supporter of the Roman Catholic Church. He was converted to Catholicism just before his death in Green Bay on 11 February 1846. An anguished account of his loss from Protestantism, written by the Rev. Jeremiah Porter of Massachusetts on 20 December 1845, noted that "Mr. Lawe I am told was by education and birth a Jew." See Jeanne Kay, "John Lawe, Green Bay Trader," *Wisconsin Magazine of History* 64 (1980): 26–7.

22 Petition of John Levy Jacobs, ibid., bundles I-J Misc., 1788–95, vol. 266, 15–15a.

23 Firth, ed., *Town of York, 1793–1815*, 42n.

24 Thomas McCord, Dublin, to Jacques Terroux, London, 14 June 1797, McCord Museum, Montreal, Thomas McCord Papers, 0207, item 4405. Jacques Terroux was a half-brother of Levy Solomons Jr. Thomas McCord (1750–1824) and Sarah Solomons (1769/70–1812) were married in London, England, on 27 November 1798: certificate M8442 (item 200) and letter of Sarah Solomons to "my dear brother," Jacques Terroux, 27 November 1798 (item 4411) are in the Thomas McCord Papers. Notwithstanding his mother's religion, there is no doubt that Levy Solomons Jr, was Jewish: "Entre nous, il est trop Juif," McCord wrote in the letter to Terroux cited above, suggesting that Levy Solomons tried too hard to be Jewish.

25 For biographical data on Levy Solomons Jr, see ibid., 0209; "Items Relating to the Solomons Family, New York," 376–9; "Levy Solomons His Book Albany Septr 2^d 1806," AJA, Lucius Solomon Collection. The naturalization certificates of Levy Solomons Jr and his wife, dated 25 March 1823, are in AJA, Lucius Solomon Collection.

26 For biographical information, on Hart (1768–1852) see Vaugeois, "Moses Hart," *DCB* 8: 367–70.

27 Petition of Moses Hart, 30 October 1797, NA, RG 1, L3, bundle H4/107; Archives of Ontario, *Report*, 1931, 109.

28 Stanley, *Canada Invaded, 1775–1776*, appendix II, 156–7, for Farrand's military service. He was appointed clerk of the Court of Common Pleas for the District of Mecklenburg, 24 July 1788, and deputy secretary of the Luneburg District in 1792: NA, RG 68, Commissions Index, 95, line 32, and 258, line 19. He became registrar for the counties of Glengarry and Stormont in January 1796: J[acob] F[arrand] Pringle, *Lunenburgh or the Old Eastern District* (Cornwall: Standard Printing House 1890), 57; and of the county of Dundas on 1 January 1801: NA, RG 68, Commissions

Index, 305, line 3. In 1800 he had received an additional commission as clerk of the peace for the Eastern District: ibid., 260, line 46. Farrand died on 11 May 1803: Frederick H. Armstrong, *Handbook of Upper Canadian Chronology* (rev. ed.; Toronto and London: Dundurn Press 1985), 154 and 168.

29 Gray's will divided the residue of his estate among his relatives and friends, including Elmsley "in token of my regard and esteem": Robert J. Burns, "Robert Isaac Dey Gray (Grey)," *DCB* 5: 388–9.

30 "Upper Canada Land Book D, 1797–1798," Archives of Ontario, *Report*, 1931, 115–16, 187, for Hart's petitions. Moses Hart to E. Jessy Jr, 16 March 1798; J. Farrand to Moses Hart, 16 April, 2 August, and 17 October 1798; statement of Farrand to Hart, 25 July 1798 – all in ASTR, Fonds Hart, file K–1.

31 D.W. Smith Records, Metropolitan Toronto Reference Library, item B464.

32 Farrand's statement to Hart (25 July 1798, ASTR, Fonds Hart, file K–1) was endorsed: "received payment from Levy Solomons." D.W. Smith's record (ibid.) is endorsed: "8 Mch 1800. To Paid Messrs. Chewett & Ridout Mr Levi's grants." The family of Levy Solomons was commonly known as the Levy family: see pp. 277–8n32.

33 Petition by Colonel Henry Caldwell and Others, NA, RG 1, L3L, vol. 52, 26644. "Isaac Judah of Montreal" owed an account to Aaron Hart of Trois-Rivières in October 1776: ASTR, Fonds Hart, item N–G–3. There are three letters addressed to Isaac Judah in Montreal in 1786 and 1787 in AJA, "The S and M Myers Letter Book, 1785 to 1787," 161, 176, and 225–6.

34 Cornwall town plan, by W. Chewett, 17 February 1792, Ontario, Ministry of Natural Resources, Survey Records Office. Judah is shown on the plan as "J. Judah."

35 Petition by Colonel Henry Caldwell and Others, NA, RG 1, L3L, vol. 52, 26629, 26631, 26659, and 26660A.

36 Index to the Heir and Devisee Commission, Eastern District, NA, mfm H–1151, and vols. 90–92 (mfm H–1133–H–1135); Patent to lot 20, 4th concession, township of Lancaster, County of Glengarry, to "Isaac Judah of the City of Montreal in the Province of Lower Canada, Merchant, dated 17 February, 1804," Ontario, Official Documents Office, QE 21. After obtaining his patent, Judah apparently moved to New York, with his son William. He corresponded with his sister Dorothea every spring until 1811 when the letters stopped: Dorothea Hart to her nephew, John Myers, Norfolk, 11 November 1811, Old Dominion University Archives, Barton Myers Collection, item 1143. His descendants may have been in Toronto. A Sarah Judah married William Vickers at St James Church in Toronto on 27 February 1838: John Ross Robertson,

Landmarks of Toronto (Toronto: the author 1898; reprinted Belleville: Mika Publishing 1974), 3: 458. One of the two witnesses present, John Manuel, was likely a cousin: Isaac Judah's sister, Miriam, had married Emanuel Manuel.

37 This Moses Jacobs was probably the one listed as living at Kent in 1790 in Census A, Rhode Island: see Rosenbloom, *Biographical Dictionary*, 74. Rosenbloom says that Jacobs was probably not Jewish. However, the script of the letters in Jacobs's signatures on his petitions for land is very similar to the Hebraic equivalent – leaving little doubt of his Jewish origins.

38 Petitions of Moses Jacobs, 30 May 1797, and July 1798, NA, RG 1, L3, bundle J10/35–35f.

39 Petition of Moses Jacobs, 30 May 1797, ibid., 35b, endorsement by James Green, the lieutenant governor's civil secretary.

40 For a biography of Moses David (1767–1814), see Katz, "Moses David of Windsor."

41 Petition of Moses David (no 362), NA, RG 1, L3L, vol. 70, 3513–15; referral to land board, 18 July 1799, vol. 1, 58–63, 423; confirmation of land board decision by Executive Council, 3 January 1800, vol. 13, 4528–37.

42 Petitions of Moses David, April 1801 and 8 January 1803, NA, RG 1, L3, bundle D6/23–23f and H4/107b & c. The 1803 petition seems to have been separated by the authorities from David's other petitions and filed with that of Moses Hart: see p. 314n4.

43 Petition of Moses David to Hunter, 9 March 1803, NA, RG 1, L3, bundle D6/23, 23e, & 23f. Russell's letter to the magistrates of the Western District was probably addressed to the Court of Quarter Sessions of the Peace for that district, but the letter has not been found.

44 Endorsement on the back of Petition of Moses David, 9 March 1803, ibid., 23d. See also the records of the meeting of the land board, 10 May 1803: NA, M–59, Upper Canada, Executive Council, Reports, vol. C, 238. The grant to Moses David for lot 7 north side of Centre Road, township of Sandwich, County of Essex, 20 February 1804, is on file as #O/228, Ontario, Official Documents Office.

45 Moses David had lived on the Upper Canada frontier for eighteen years when he married Charlotte, the daughter of Aaron and Dorothea Hart, in 1811. He and his family were the only Jews in the town, and upon his death in September 1814 he was buried behind his house in a corner of his lot which was later officially known for Registry Office purposes as "the Jew Cemetery": deed registered as no 7117 in the Registry Office for Essex County on 9 May 1917. His widow and son, Moses Eleazar David (born 10 March 1813), moved to Montreal after his death. In October 1978, as result of development in the area, David's remains were exhumed and removed to Windsor's Shaar Hashomayim Cemetery.

At that time a collection of goose bones was identified with his grave: Anita Hurwich, "Windsor," in Rome, ed., *Pathways to the Present*, 57. According to Cecil Roth, the "burial of birds in a new cemetery before the first human interments was an old superstitous practice which is occasionally encountered even today": *The Rise of Provincial Jewry*, 73.

46 *The Upper Canada Almanac, 1803* (York: John Bennett 1803), 55–6, lists "Moses Davids" as one of nine ensigns in the regiment commanded by Lieutenant Colonel John Askin. *The Upper Canada Almanac of the Year of Our Lord, 1804* (York: John Bennett 1804), which published the militia list of the preceding year, includes Moses David as one of nine lieutenants in the North East Battalion of the Essex militia. A note in the Askin Papers regarding David indicates that "prior to 1803 he had been an ensign in Askin's battalion of the Essex County militia and in this year he and Charles Askin were slated for lieutenancies when the next vacancies should occur": Quaife, ed., *John Askin Papers*, 2: 645, n. 17.

47 See discussion re Aaron Hart at p. 286n38 and with respect to Jews in the British forces at p. 32.

48 Brock to Sir George Prevost, February 1812, NA, RG 8, series C, vol. 676, 92–6; "Journals of Upper Canada Legislative Assembly 1812," Archives of Ontario, *Report*, 1912, 3–6.

49 The instructions to Gordon Drummond as lieutenant governor of Upper Canada on 29 December 1814 were just as clear as those Dorchester had received on 16 September 1791. Compare Public Archives of Canada, *Report*, 1905, at 56 and 72.

50 Quaife, ed., *John Askin Papers*, 2: 645; also "Return of Essex County Militia at Sandwich," 12 December 1807, signed by Moses David, Captain, Detroit Public Library, Burton Historical Collection, John Askin Papers. David is not shown as an officer in any of the Canadian militias during the War of 1812, however: Irving, *Officers of the British Forces in Canada*. See also Katz, "Moses David of Windsor," 159.

51 Commission to Moses David as coroner, 24 February 1808, NA, RG 68, liber D, 13. David had served as a juror in Upper Canada as early as 31 March 1794: "Records of Court of Common Pleas," Archives of Ontario, *Report*, 1917, 175–6.

52 Petition of Moses Jacobs, 4 June 1816, NA, RG 1, L3, bundle J10/35d–35f.

53 Garrison Orders, Lt. Col. Robert McDougall, Drummond Island, to Military Secretary Foster, 27 June 1816, NA, RG 8, series C, vol. 515, 106–10; printed in *Michigan Pioneer Collections* 16 (1890): 478–9. Jacob Franks (c. 1768–1841) was a son of John Franks and his second wife, Appolonia. After his marriage to Mary Solomons, Levy Solomons's daughter, in 1816, he remained in Lower Canada. See Godfrey, "Jacob Franks," *DCB* 7: 328–9.

54 James Solomons was granted, and by June 1816 occupied, lot 1 on The
Boulevard (or front street) at the new post. "James H. Solomons" was
first recorded in February 1809 as an adult of undetermined age, work-
ing as a clerk for Moses Hart in Trois-Rivières. At the time of his dis-
missal in April 1814 he had worked for Hart for about five years: Bill of
Exchange witnessed by "J.H. Solomons," February 1809, ASTR, Fonds
Hart, N–G–4 and O–C–4–L. Solomons went west to the post at Mackinac
Island, probably in the summer of 1814. On 31 July 1816, he married
Catherine ("Kitty") Hays (1780–1861), second daughter of Andrew
Hays: *Montreal Herald*, 3 August 1816; William D. Reid, *Marriage Notices
of Montreal* (Lambertville NJ: Huntington Press 1980), 10. Their only
child, Myer Solomons, was born later that year. The Solomons returned
to Drummond Island where James Solomons died during the summer
of 1826: B. Frank Emery, *Post Cemetery Drummond* (Detroit: The Old
Forts and Historic Memorial Association 1931), 7. Emery states that
"James Solomon, a merchant," is known to have died in 1826 and that
he was buried in the post cemetery but cites no source for the information. Drummond Island was ceded to the United States by Great Britain
in November 1828. The post cemetery has not been maintained and is
privately owned.

55 There are a number of applicants for crown land in Upper Canada who
may have been Jewish, but further investigation is required. They
include:

• Gilbert Cohen (or Cowen), a military emigrant from Britain, received
a grant of the west half of lot 16, concession B, Murray township in
Northumberland County, on 27 May 1824: NA, RG 1, series C, 13,
vol. 96, 49. He was shown in the annual census for Murray township
beginning in 1819.

• Simeon and Harry Hart, aged 25 and 22 respectively, lately arrived
from New Brunswick with their families, applied on 23 July 1817 for
crown lands as Loyalists. The consideration of their petition was
deferred "to ascertain the terms of leaving New Brunswick & what residence they made in the United States": NA, RG 1, L3, bundles H11/
138 and H11/139.

• Isaac Hart of Ancaster, miller and millwright, was a native of Devon,
England, and the son of a soldier. He came to Canada in 1817 with
his family of five children, applied for land on 28 July 1819, and was
given a crown grant of 100 acres: NA, RG 1, L3, bundle H12/104.

56 Rebecca Franks Kemble (c. 1770–1839), a sister of Jacob Franks, was in
York and Niagara with her husband, William Kemble, from about 1812
to about 1819: Jean-Marie Lebel, "William Kemble," *DCB* 7: 462–3.

57 Lieutenant Barnet Lyon, possibly a son of Benjamin Lyon, was commissioned as a lieutenant in the Indian Department of the Upper Canada

forces at Detroit on 19 June 1813 after participating in the engagement against the Americans at Frenchtown the previous 22 January. He
was transferred to Lower Canada as a lieutenant and interpreter among
the Nipissings and Algonquins at the Lake of Two Mountains on 27
November 1813 and was still there the following year among the
"Indian Warriors": Irving, *Officers of the British Forces in Canada*, 210,
212, 215, 218. He was at Kingston from about 1817, still as a lieutenant in the Indian Department. He returned to Lower Canada about
1820: NA, RG 4, A1.

58 Jacob Jacobs, a young watchmaker recently arrived from England, had
opened a shop at 14 St Lawrence Street in Montreal by 1819: John E.
Langdon, *Canadian Silversmiths, 1700–1900* (Toronto 1960), 87. By
October of that year he was recorded at 134 St Paul Street where he
had leased a shop from Joseph Robillard: Thomas Doige, *An Alphabetical
List of the Merchants Traders and Housekeepers residing in Montreal* (Montreal: James Lane 1819), 114; lease from Robillard to Jacobs, 2 October
1819, ANQ-M, N.B. Doucet, notaire, no. 6672. By 18 June 1821, he had
moved to Kingston. His notice in the *Kingston Chronicle*, 22 June 1821,
advised the public that "J. Jacobs, Watchmaker from England, has commenced his business in the house formerly occupied by Mr. St. GER-
MAIN, a few doors above the Mansion House Hotel," noting "his long
experience in the above line of business." The following spring he advertised "that he is just arrived from Montreal, with a supply of the best
Sheffield plated ware and Jewellery": *Kingston Chronicle*, 12 April 1822.
By 1832 he had returned to Montreal: Jacob Jacobs, merchant, age 33,
was shown as number 11 on the list of Montreal Jews: "Register of British Subjects Professing the Jewish Religion, above the age of 21 years,
11 September 1832 [probably 1830]," 7.

59 Those who stayed included:
• An Isaac Davids lived in York in 1819 with two males over 16, four
  males under 16, two females over 16, and two females under 16: Christine Mosser, ed., *York, Upper Canada Minutes of Town Meetings and Lists
  of Inhabitants, 1797–1823* (Toronto: Metropolitan Toronto Library
  Board 1984), 139. Another Isaac David was elected "pathmaster of the
  East Ward of the Fifth Concession near Kingston" in 1819 (*Kingston
  Chronicle*, 22 January 1819, 3, col. 3) and was appointed highways overseer for Kingston township in 1843 (*Kingston Chronicle & Gazette*,
  7 January 1843, 2, col. 7). This is probably not the same person as
  the Isaac David who signed his name (c. 1839) at Montreal in Hebrew
  as "Itzic David," a trader, aged 31, on the "Register of British Subjects
  Professing the Jewish Religion."
• There was a Henry Nathan living in York in 1819. His family consisted
  of two males over 16, one male under 16, one female over 16, and

one female under 16. Mosser, ed., *York, Upper Canada Minutes of Town Meetings and Lists of Inhabitants, 1797–1823*, 137.

• Alexander Asher, merchand tailor, had a shop in Kingston by 1819: *Kingston Chronicle*, 24 October 1821.

• Jacob William Brinley (Brindley, Binley) died in Kingston of cholera on 30 June 1832: Congregation Shearith Israel, New York, Register, 1759–1834, f. 161; he was previously recorded at the synagogue in New York between 1804 and 1818: "Items Relating to Congregation Shearith Israel, New York," 79. He may have moved to Kingston in the 1820s.

60 Judith or Juda Myers (1759–1831), a daughter of Rachel Myers (see p. 124), had married Alexander Montgomery in New York in 1778 and arrived in Saint John, New Brunswick, in May 1783 aboard the *Hope*. She was baptized as a Anglican at Gagetown on 2 September 1792 along with her children Sarah, Abigail, John, and Alexander: PANB, Gagetown Anglican Church Baptisms, F1140. The Montgomerys were still in Gagetown on 2 August 1801 when their daughter, Juda, was baptized: ibid. In 1803, with eight children in tow, they moved to York, Upper Canada, where Alexander operated a tavern east and south of the corner of Queen and Yonge Streets. Judith lived in York until her death on 3 March 1831: Petition of Alexander Montgomery, 27 June 1806, NA, RG 1, L3, vol. 332, bundle M6; Yetwin, "Myers Family of New Brunswick," 13–18. Her eldest son, John, the owner of Montgomery's Tavern on Yonge Street north of Eglinton, was later convicted for his part in the 1837 rebellion: Edwin C. Guillet, "John Montgomery," *DCB* 10: 529–30. Like a number of other families who settled on both sides of the border with the United States, family members served on both sides of the conflict during the War of 1812, although they appear to have avoided direct combat with each other. Judith's son, John, was with the York militia in its battle at Queenston Heights in October 1812. Her brother, Mordecai, arrived at the conflict after the capture of York by the Americans on 29 April 1813, serving at the Battle of Fort George on 8 July, and was wounded at the Battle of Crysler's Farm in November 1813: Adler and Connolly, *From Ararat to Suburbia*, 4–5.

61 There are many examples of Dissenters who were appointed as officers in the militia and to other non-military offices of the lower rank, in J.K. Johnston, *Becoming Prominent: Regional Leadership in Upper Canada, 1791–1841* (Kingston & Montreal: McGill-Queen's University Press 1989).

62 The appointment of Dissenters as justices of the peace was likely caused by the chronic shortage of magistrates in Upper Canada, identified by J.K. Johnston, ibid., 88.

63 Another example of a device avoiding the law in the appointment of a non-Anglican to office was the deputation of James Howard as collector

of customs for the port of York, on 1 July 1824. William Allan, the collector of customs, was himself appointed by commission and was obliged to be an Anglican by virtue of the royal instructions to the governor, Lord Dalhousie. Howard, a man of unquestioned ability, was the likely replacement for Allan during the latter's absence from the province. As a Methodist, Howard could not be appointed to office without taking the sacrament according to the rites of the Church of England. At the same time, the rules of British common law prevented Allan from ignoring the governor's instructions by delegating his authority to Howard. Instead, Allan "deputized" Howard to exercise the authority of collector of customs, thereby finding another loophole to allow the appointment of an able non-Anglican to office. This appointment is found in a document from a private collection: "Deputation of James Scott Howard as Collector of Customs for the Port of York."

64 Simon Solomon (1767–1839) is "traditionally considered to have been Jewish" according to Joseph R. Smallwood et al, eds., *The Encyclopedia of Newfoundland and Labrador* (St John's: Newfoundland Book Publishers 1984), 2: 901. He came to Newfoundland in 1791. In the St John's census of 1794/5, his religion was indicated as "Protestant," although that circumstance cannot be considered indicative of his actual religion, as the only other choice was "Roman Catholic": Public Archives of Newfoundland, GM 2/3a/A, 3d division, #197. (Hyam Myers, the lay leader of the Congregation Shearith Israel in Montreal, was similarly denoted "Protestant" in a Quebec census in 1773.) Solomon had married Sarah Thomas in an Anglican ceremony on 12 February 1798: Public Archives of Newfoundland, Anglican Church Records. After his death in St John's on 8 December 1839, a newspaper notice advised that "his funeral will take place on Thursday next at 2 o'clock from his late residence on Water Street": *Royal Gazette*, 10 December 1839, 3, col. 4. The fact that his funeral took place from his house rather than from a church is likely significant as an indicator of his religion because there are no records of his burial with the rest of his family in the Congregational Church Records, the Anglican Church Records, or the Records of the General Protestant Cemetery.

65 Public Archives of Newfoundland, A–8–1, Governor's Letter Books, GN 2/1/a, vol. 18, 154–5; Robert H. Pratt, *The Nineteenth Century Postal History of Newfoundland* (New York: Steinway Fund and Collectors Club of New York 1986), 16–21. Solomon's military appointment was made by October 1806: NA, CO 194/45.

66 On 17 June 1824, Abrahams, now known as "William Abrams," was appointed a justice of the Inferior Court of Common Pleas: PANB, RS538, B5, 48, 68, and 80. It is not known whether Abrams was required to swear the state oaths or subscribe the declaration. While the

evidence has not been located, he may have been baptized by the time
of the second appointment. If he was a Jew at the time of these appointments, he can claim the distinction of being both the first Jewish justice
of the peace (1822) and the first Jewish judge (1824) in Canada.
According to the genealogical notes in the William Abrams family file,
in the Manse Library, Douglastown, NB, Abrahams' "descendants claim
that he was an English Jew." He had been born in Plymouth, England,
and had settled in New Brunswick in 1819, followed shortly thereafter
by his family. Within a short time he headed the largest shipbuilding
establishment on the Miramichi River, which was, after Saint John, the
province's most important shipbuilding centre: Spray, "William Abrams,"
DCB 7: 4–5. Abrams was likely related to Chapman Abraham, or
Abrams, also of Plymouth: see Godfrey and Godfrey, "Who Was Who in
Canadian Jewry," Abraham, or Abrams, II.

67 *Montreal Gazette*, 24 January 1831, as cited in Rome, comp., "Challenges
to Equality," 149. However, Upper Canadian Reformers such as the
American-born lawyer, Marshall Spring Bidwell, and even William Lyon
Mackenzie, the leader of the radicals, did not share this liberal view
about the need to be generous to Jews.

CHAPTER THIRTEEN

1 Quoted in Vaugeois, "Moses Hart," *DCB* 8: 368; Marcus, *Early American
Jewry*, 1: 275. Aaron Hart may also have been influenced by the traditional Judaic view that an observant Jew should not seek secular positions of leadership but should accept leadership only in response to
requests by the community or in cases of necessity.

2 "Proceedings Relating to the Expulsion of Ezekiel Hart from the House
of Assembly of Lower Canada," in Doughty and McArthur, eds., *Documents, 1791–1818*, 351–3. The issue is dealt with at some length and all
the relevant sources printed in Rome, comp., "On the Early Harts,"
parts 2–4. See also Sack, *History of the Jews in Canada*, 80–95.

3 Moses Hart never gave up his desire for a political career. He ran unsuccessfully in Saint-Maurice in 1819 and in Upper Town, Quebec, the following year. Finally, at the age of 75, he made a new attempt in Trois-
Rivières against Edward Grieve and then another in Nicolet against
Antoine-Prospère Méthot. Both times he was beaten and contested the
election of his opponents. Vaugeois, "Moses Hart," *DCB* 8: 367–70.

4 The other candidates were Colonel Thomas Coffin, previously member
for Saint-Maurice from 1792 to 1804 (41 votes), Matthew Bell, previously member for the surrounding Saint-Maurice County from 1800 to
1804 (16 votes), and Pierre Vezina, a 35-year-old lawyer and militia
officer: Rome, comp., "On the Early Harts," 218–23.

5 Although the journals of the assembly do not list the names of the members who voted, according to the Quebec *Courier* of 24 February 1808, the five who opposed the resolution were John Richardson, John Mure, John Blackwood, James Cuthbert, and Louis de Salaberry: ibid., 277. The first four were English-speaking Protestants; de Salaberry, who represented Quebec's Lower Town, was a member of an illustrious family of French-Canadian office holders and soldiers.

6 "Observations on the Government of Canada by John Black," 1 October 1806, in Doughty and McArthur, eds., *Documents, 1791–1818*, 323–5. Section 17 of the Constitutional Act had specified that the number of members of the assembly "to be chosen in Lower Canada shall not be less than fifty."

7 Wade, *The French Canadians*, 105–6.

8 Louis-Charles Foucher represented Trois-Rivières in the assembly from 1804 to 1808 while serving as provincial judge for the District of Trois-Rivières, and Pierre-Amable De Bonne represented the County of Quebec in the assembly from 1804 until he was unseated in 1810 while serving as a justice of the Court of King's Bench: Doughty and McArthur, eds., *Documents, 1791–1818*, 170, 342, 370–1.

9 See Lower Canada, Assembly, *Journal*, 1808, 158; also in ibid., 350–1, 370–1. See also Sir James Craig to the earl of Liverpool, 30 March 1810, ibid., 372–8; and Rome, comp., "On the early Harts," 236–7, 337–8.

10 Reid to Ezekiel Hart, 20 April 1807, AJHS, P–18, Hart Papers.

11 Rome, comp., "On the Early Harts," 223.

12 Hart to Jonas Phillips & Sons, 26 May 1808, McCord Museum, Early Hart Papers, files 61 (M18648), 62 (M18647), and 63.

13 In Rex *v.* Bosworth (1739), it had been determined that the manner of swearing was within the discretion of the official before whom the oath was taken.

14 Doughty and McArthur, eds., *Documents, 1791–1818*, 352. The original oath signed by Hart is in NA, RG 1, E 11, vol. 2.

15 Ibid.

16 Rome, comp., "On the Early Harts," 266.

17 Joseph Maingot, *Parliamentary Privilege in Canada* (Toronto: Butterworths 1983), 1–4, 158–9. It is Maingot's opinion as law clerk and parliamentary counsel of the Canadian House of Commons that the privileges and procedures of assemblies in British colonies were based on their inherent power, stemming from the declaration in the English Bill of Rights (1688) that proceedings in parliament shall not be questioned elsewhere than in parliament. On this basis, an assembly has sole jurisdiction to determine rights exercised within it including the right to discipline, expel, and suspend a member. The courts have no power to interfere with that discretion.

18 The debate of 20 February 1808 was reported fully in *Le Canadien*, 2 March. A translation is printed in Rome, comp., "On the Early Harts," 274, 283–6.

19 Richardson (c. 1754–1831) was a successful Montreal merchant who had been appointed to the Executive Council in 1804 and was, during this session, the official representative of the council in the assembly: F. Murray Greenwood, "John Richardson," *DCB* 6: 639–47.

20 Ryland to Ezekiel Hart, NA, RG 7, G 15C, vol. 13, 99. A draft of Hart's petition is in AJHS, P–18, Hart Papers.

21 Rome, comp., "On the Early Harts," 326–7.

22 The law in England on the manner of swearing oaths was well settled before the middle of the eighteenth century: see Henriques, *The Jews and the English Law*, 178–83, 229. Jews were entitled to be sworn as witnesses in court on the Pentateuch or the Old Testament, and they were entitled to be sworn with their heads covered according to their custom. In 1744 the lord chancellor had decided that all persons who believe in a supreme being who will punish them if they swear falsely are competent witnesses and should take the oath in the form binding upon them according to the tenets of their religion. By 1800 the English courts had also decided that a Jew who professed a belief in the doctrines of Christianity might, although never formally admitted to Christianity, be sworn on the New Testament: see Rex *v.* Gilham (1795). There was only one note of caution introduced into the English law on administering oaths. None of the statutes laid down the mode in which the oath was to be administered, the official tendering the oath having the discretion to insist upon its being taken on the New Testament. If this were to be insisted upon, the person sworn would have no right to compel the official to swear him upon the Old Testament.

23 Doughty and McArthur, eds., *Documents, 1791–1818*, 355–6. Ezekiel Hart would not in fact have been bound in conscience by taking an oath in this manner.

24 Rome, comp., "On the Early Harts," 328–54.

25 On 9 February 1808, just before the first debate on Ezekiel Hart's eligibility, a petition had been received by the assembly from Thomas Coffin setting forth that Hart, because he was of the Jewish religion, was incapable of sitting and voting in the House of Assembly and that the votes given him at the by-election ought therefore to be considered null and void and requesting that the petitioner, having the majority of legal votes, be declared elected for the town of Trois-Rivières: Doughty and McArthur, eds., *Documents, 1791–1818*, 352. The petition appears not to have been formally considered by the assembly.

26 Minutes of the Executive Council, 18 April and 10 May 1809, ibid., 356–9.

27 Apart from Sewell, the other judges were De Bonne and Jenkin Williams of the King's Bench: Greenwood, *Legacies of Fear,* 226.

28 Garner, *Franchise in British North America,* 149; NA, series Q, vol. 109, 221; ibid., 229–30.

29 Rome, comp., "On the Early Harts," 388–9.

30 Wade, *The French Canadians,* 107–15.

31 Theodore Hart was apparently well acquainted with a number of observant Jews including Ezekiel and Benjamin Hart and their families, Isaac Valentine, and Benjamin Nunes or Nones of Philadelphia, a commercial broker born in Bordeaux whose clientele were largely French-speaking: Theodore Hart to Ezekiel Hart (in French), 22 September 1810, McCord Museum, Early Hart Papers, folder 28.

32 Theodore Hart to Louis Foy, 16 October 1810, NA, RG 4, B 28, vol. 47, 276–8.

33 On 10 June 1789 Levi Jacobs entered into an apprenticeship agreement for a five-year term with "Dr. James Davidson of Quebec, Surgeon & Apothecary … to learn his Science, Profession, Art, Trade and Mystery." Within a year, Jacobs had run away, breaking the indenture. He was then sent to Detroit to complete his apprenticeship with his brother-in-law, Dr William Holmes, surgeon to the 5th Regiment, who had married Jacobs's eldest sister, Mary Marianne. Jacobs lived in Niagara from 1794 to 1796, possibly as a surgeon. NA, MG 19, A 2, series 3, Samuel Jacobs Papers, vol. 5, 556–66, and vol. 25, 3333–33b, 3340–40b, 3342–43a. In 1800 Jacobs was being considered as successor to "Dr. J. Davidson" as surgeon to the 2nd Battalion of the Royal Canadian Volunteers: NA, series C, 158 (December 1799), 173, 193, 204, 204a (February 1800), mfm C–2843.

34 Theodore Hart told Ezekiel Hart that the examiner, a "Mr McGill," "said to me that a street runner [*coureur des rues*] had more papers to show than I": T. Hart to E. Hart, 22 September 1810, McCord Museum, Early Hart Papers, folder 28; T. Hart to Louis Foy, 16 October 1810, NA, RG 4, B 28, vol. 47, 276- 8.

35 Aaron Hart David, second son of Samuel David of Montreal, was enrolled as Canada's first Jewish physician in 1835. He was on the first board of governors of the College of Doctors and Surgeons when it was incorporated in 1847: Ballon, "Aaron Hart David"; "Obituary," *Canadian Medical Record,* November 1882; Rome, comp., "On the Early Harts – Their Contemporaries, part 1," 98–105.

36 "Unpublished Canadian State Papers Relating to Benjamin Hart," 139; *Montreal Almanac and Lower Canada Register for 1830* (Montreal: Robert Armour 1829).

37 Cochran to Moses Hart, 2 December 1826, ASTR, Fonds Hart, H–B–7. There are ten letters in file H–B that pertain to this issue, which was still unresolved by 1830.

38 According to the *Quebec Almanac* for 1827, "A.P. de Courvalle" was lieutenant-colonel in the Trois-Rivières militia, in which Ezekiel Hart was by
now a captain and "Messire Poulin de Courval" was shown as "aumo-
nier" in the general staff of the sedentary militia of Lower Canada.

39 Vassal de Monviel to de Courvalle, 11 June 1827, ASTR, Fonds Hart,
H–B–9. The adjutant general's actual words were: "Je vous prie de me
répondre à cela aussi tot que possible."

40 According to his biographer, Dalhousie was a Presbyterian: Peter Burroughs, "George Ramsay, 9th Earl of Dalhousie," *DCB* 7: 722–33. He
was nevertheless required to make and subscribe the declaration against
transubstantiation under the Test Act of 1763 in order to assume office:
Commission to Lord Dalhousie as governor-in-chief (12 April 1820),
NA, RG 7, G 18, vol. 4, 26. Article 2 of Dalhousie's instructions of 13
April 1820 required him to "take the several oaths and subscribe the
declaration" referred to in his commission: Public Archives of Canada,
Report, 1905, 49.

41 David David was quartermaster of the 1st Division, Montreal militia, by
1807, lieutenant and quartermaster by 1808, and captain on 28 April
1812: *Quebec Almanac*, 1807, 1808, and 1813; Irving, *Officers of the British
Forces in Canada*, 165. Samuel David was appointed captain and aide-
major of the Longue Pointe militia (2nd Battalion, 3rd Division, Montreal militia) on 7 May 1812 and major second in command of the regiment on 18 November 1813. After the war he was appointed lieutenant-
colonel in command of the Longue Pointe militia: *Quebec Almanac*,
1813; Irving, *Officers of the British Forces in Canada*, 172–3.

42 Ezekiel Hart was an ensign in the North Division of the Trois-Rivières
militia, 1807: *Quebec Almanac*, 1807. He may have been commissioned
ensign as early as 1803: Malchelosse, "Les Juifs dans l'histoire canadienne," 181. He was made a lieutenant in the 8th Trois-Rivières Battalion during the War of 1812, transferred to the 1st Trois-Rivières
Battalion in November 1813, and promoted to captain on 29 June
1816: Irving, *Officers of the British Forces in Canada*, 157–8. He was raised
to colonel with the 1st Saint-Maurice Battalion during the 1830s:
Malchelosse, "Les Juifs dans l'histoire canadienne," 108.

43 Myer Michaels was ensign in the 1st Division, Montreal militia, 1812,
and lieutenant in the same division by 1813: *Quebec Almanac*, 1812, 1813.

44 Isaac Phineas, the son of Heineman Pines or Phineas, was appointed
ensign in Colonel Coffin's division (South Division) on 28 July 1812
and quartermaster of the 3rd Battalion, incorporated militia of Lower
Canada, by 1813: *Quebec Almanac*, 1812, 1813; Irving, *Officers of the British Forces in Canada*, 159.

45 Irving, *Officers of the British Forces in Canada*, 174. Hays had been appren-
ticed to his uncle, Samuel David, at age 14 on 28 September 1798: Marcus, ed., *American Jewry: Documents*, 474–5.

46 Irving, *Officers of the British Forces in Canada*, 240.

47 Ibid., 157–9. According to the *Quebec Almanac*, 1830, the following Jews
were officers in the Montreal militia at that date: 1st Battalion, Captain
B. Hart (appointed 11 January 1825); 5th Battalion, Ensign J. [Isaac]
Valentine (4 February 1828); 6th Battalion, Captain F. David (11 February 1822); and Captain S. David (5 December 1826). The Jewish officers in the Saint-Maurice (Trois-Rivières) militia were: 1st Battalion,
Captain E. Hart (29 June 1816); 2nd Battalion, Lieutenant I. Phineas,
paymaster (19 November 1827). Henry Joseph was captain and paymaster of the militia at Berthier by 1826: Wolff, "Henry Joseph," *DCB* 6:
365–6.

48 See Rome, comp., "Disintegration," 88: "Montreal remained without a
semblance of religious organization" after about 1810. "Most of the
early settlers died or moved away. Only the Judahs, the Davids, the
Hays, the Josephs remained. For forty years Shearith Israel remained
but a memory which proved hard to refresh." According to Sack (*History of the Jews in Canada*, 64), for many years after about 1785, the congregation did not engage a permanent rabbi: "During that period they
were in close contact with the Portuguese congregation in New York,
whose spiritual leader paid frequent visits to Montreal and officiated at
circumcisions, weddings, and other religious ceremonies."

49 AJHS, P–15, Lyons Collection, box 4, Sedaka Offerings. See also "Items
Relating to Congregation Shearith Israel, New York," 78–81.

50 See p. 125.

51 AJHS, P–15, Lyons Collection, box 4, Sedaka Offerings, nos. 245 and
247. There has been no record located to confirm Ezekiel Solomons's
death or burial, although the plaque at Fort Michilimackinac, commem-
orating him as Michigan's first Jewish settler, suggests that he died
about 1808 and was buried at Montreal. The synagogue records that
place him in New York in October 1804 are supported by circumstantial evidence suggesting that he may have died there shortly thereafter:
    First, Solomons is shown on Mackinac Island on 28 June 1803 as
entering into an agreement with Joseph Dupré at page 10 in the
records of Adhémar St-Martin (1800–3) contained in the "Register of
the Post of Michilmackinac *begun & opened* by James Gruet, Notary, June
1st 1785," Mackinac County Court House, Michigan. This is the last
known reference to him at Mackinac.
    Second, accounts for household supplies were opened at the store of
the American Fur Company on Mackinac Island for "Mrs. Solomon" on
31 October 1804 and for "William Solomon" on 5 December 1804.
Both accounts were continued for two or three years in that manner.
There were no entries for Ezekiel Solomons. "Petty Debts" book, American Fur Company Papers, L 4, 1803–6, Burton Historical Collection,
Detroit Public Library.

Finally, there is a document in Michigan Territory Land Claims, Detroit, dated 13 April 1808, and entitled "Claim to the widow and heirs of the late Ezekiel Solomon which had been entered with the former Commissioner of the Land Office at Detroit in Volume 1, page 464 under date December 24, 1805." It was on the basis of this entry that Irving I. Katz infers that the claim was first made by Solomons himself on the date indicated and goes on to suggest that Solomons died between 1805 and 1808: Katz, "Ezekiel Solomon," 252. However, it is equally possible, based upon the wording quoted, that the claim was made on the date indicated, by the widow and heirs of Solomons after his death.

52 Congregation Shearith Israel, New York, Register, 1759–1834, 63.

53 NA, G 24, B 11, mfm M–741.

54 Godfrey and Godfrey, "Who Was Who in Canadian Jewry," David I. The Beaver Club, the élite Montreal organization of fur traders, selected by ballot from those who had wintered in the Upper Country included among its members Myer Michaels by 1793, David David by 1808, and Samuel David by 1811: NA, MG 19, B 3, 5, 68. David David was elected a director of the Bank of Montreal in 1818. About 1814 he appears to have joined the North West Company, and a considerable debt owed by the company to the beneficiaries of his estate appears on the company's books in 1825, immediately after his death: Records of the North West Company, NA, MG 19, B 1, vol. 3. David's will and codicils are in ANQ-M, 06–M, CM1–1/4. According to an observer, his estate was valued at £87,000 at his death: Mary Franks to John Lawe, 11 April 1825, State Historical Society of Wisconsin, John Lawe Papers, box 1, no 2166, 3. See also Senior and Lambert, "David David," DCB 6: 179–81.

55 Journal of Samuel David, NA, MG 24, 1.13.6.

56 ANQ-M, 06–M, CM1–1/4. David David's will was dated 4 October 1815.

57 Will of Elizabeth Nathan, 7 May 1819, ANQ-M, CN601–187, no. 2660; see also Will of 16 October 1817, CN601–134, no. 4617. Elizabeth Nathan was the widow of Moses Nathan. She was licensed in 1807 as an auctioneer, probably becoming Canada's first woman auctioneer. Listed in the *Quebec Almanac* of 1808 (p. 39), as "Elizabeth Nathon," she was the only woman auctioneer in Lower Canada at that time. Her husband Moses Nathan had died in Montreal on 7 March 1804 and was buried in the Jewish cemetery in the St-Antoine suburbs: Rome, comp., "On the Early Harts – Their Contemporaries, part 5," 61. The right to be an auctioneer or vendue master was, for a merchant, a valuable one, given in some jurisdictions by commission from the sovereign. The province of Lower Canada began licensing auctioneers after the passage of the Auctioneer's Act in 1805 (45 Geo. III, c. 13). In 1808, Benjamin Hart and Ezekiel Hart were licensed as auctioneers at Trois-Rivières as well.

58 Woodley, *The House of Joseph*; "Certificate of Marriage of Henry Joseph
to Miss Rachael Solomons 28 Sep 1803," private collection. The wit-
nesses were Judah and Catherine Joseph, Abraham and Hannah Joseph,
Rebekah, Benjamin, and Elizabeth Solomon, Levy Lyons, and Solomon
Benjamin. *Quebec Mercury,* 28 June 1832, 2; Stern, *First American Jewish
Families,* 138 (Joseph II), 95 (Hart I(1)). After the War of 1812 in
which he served in the militia Joseph became directly involved in the
Great Lakes fur trade, spending the winter of 1815–16 in the Upper
Country and continuing to have his own canoes bring furs to Berthier
from the west in conjunction with his brother-in-law, Jacob Franks:
"Harry left this [place] last summer and understand he is in the upper
Country, I believe to the Southward." H. Joseph, Berthier, to Moses
Hart, Three Rivers, 6 March 1816, ASTR, Fonds Hart, O–D–38.

59 The decline of the Trois-Rivières community is documented by the listing of its burial ground: see Gustavus N. Hart, "Memorandum respecting the reburial on Wednesday, the 27th October, 1909, in the
Cemetery of the Congregation of Spanish and Portuguese Jews, at Montreal, of remains brought by Mr. and Mrs. Alfred Belasco, from the
Jewish Cemeteries at Three Rivers," Haddonfield, New Jersey, 1941, CJA,
year files, 1796, Hart Genealogy. According to Sack (*History of the Jews in
Canada,* 147), there may have been a synagogue in Trois-Rivières from
about 1800 until it burned in 1860, but there is no other evidence on
this point.

60 "Samuel David, Excerpts from a Diary, 1801–1841," AJA, Biography
files. This summary notes information from volumes of the "Journal of
the Late Samuel David of Montreal," which could not be located in the
NA.

61 Benjamin Hart, *To the Israelites of the Province of Lower-Canada,* 24 July
1826: copy of pamphlet in ASTR, Fonds Hart, A–H–3.

62 The conditions attached to the bill by the Legislative Council showed a
lack of trust in dissenting sects; they included the filing of a bond or
recognizance by each dissenting minister in the amount of £200, a minimum of 30 families in each congregation, the head of each family was
to have taken the oath of allegiance if not a British subject, and proof
that the minister had been regularly appointed by his congregation:
Lower Canada, Assembly, *Journal,* 1826, 310–14.

63 The bills were entitled An Act for the relief of certain Religious Congregations therein mentioned, An Act to afford relief to a certain Religious
Congregation at Quebec, denominated Presbyterians, and An Act to
afford relief to a certain Religious Congregation at Montreal, denominated Presbyterians.

64 Lower Canada, Assembly, *Journal,* 1828–9, 84. The petition is set out ver-
batim in *CJA* 1 (May 1962): 5–6. Until this time, Jewish communities

had no formal method of recording the births, deaths, and marriages of their congregants, although the Sephardic (or Spanish ritual) congregations sometimes were better organized than the Ashkenazic (or German) ones with the Shearith Israel congregation in New York probably having the most complete records. In a few cases (Abraham I. Abrahams and Jacob Raphael Cohen), circumsion books have survived to supplement other information. Records of vital statistics for Christians were much better preserved, partly because their churches considered it their duty, but mostly because church and state were so closely intertwined that governments relied on the churches to keep such records through an official "parish system" in Quebec as well as in some of the other colonies.

65 The Jewish communal cemetery of Montreal was adjacent to the synagogue built in 1777 on land owned by the David family: Sack, *History of the Jews in Canada*, 60. An additional lot, adjoining "the old Burying Ground," had been purchased by members of the community in February 1798: "Subscription for new Burial Ground," NA, MG 8, G 67, Minutes, Shearith Israel Congregation, vol. 2. The subscribers to the purchase, presumably all the members of the congregation at the time, consisted of: David, Samuel, and Moses David, Levi and Myer Michaels, and Andrew Hays, all of Montreal; Heineman and Isaac Phineas or Pines of Petit Rivière-du-Loup; Judah and Henry Joseph of Berthier; Aaron, Moses, Ezekiel, Benjamin, and Alexander Hart, Uriah Judah, and Simon Lazarus, all of Trois-Rivières; either Barnet Lyons or Benjamin Lyon, simply identified as "Lyon"; and one "Jonas," presumably Lyon Jonas.

66 An Act to extend certain Privileges therein mentioned to Persons professing the Jewish Religion and for the obviating certain inconveniences to which other of His Majesty's subjects might otherwise be exposed, 9 Geo. IV, c. 75 (1829) (Lower Canada). Lower Canada, Assembly, *Journal*, 1830, 26, 36, 151, 165, 310–11, 345, 352, 354, 403.

67 Hart's petition is in Rome, comp., "Samuel B. Hart," 22–3, and in ibid., 1831, 102–3.

68 1 Will. IV, c. 57 (1831) (Lower Canada). Royal assent 1832.

69 Peter Gollick, quoted in Rome, comp., "Samuel B. Hart," 1. He concludes that the act of 1832 "proved to be of even great [*sic*] significance as the catalyst which opened the dams of religious restrictions: legislation followed across the Canadas bringing relief and dignity to all religions." Irving Abella suggests (*Coat of Many Colours*, 7) that the act was not "the Magna Carta of Canadian Jewry," but that with the act of 1832 "Canada became the first colony in the British Empire to emancipate its Jews" and that the act "was almost revolutionary in its implications, a milestone in the battle for civil rights."

CHAPTER FOURTEEN

1 R.J. Morgan, "Laurence (Lawrence) Kavanaugh (Cavanaugh)," *DCB* 6: 370–1.
2 NA, MG 40, D 13, pt 5.
3 Robert Morgan, "Separatism in Cape Breton, 1820–1845," in Kenneth Donovan, ed., *Cape Breton at 200: Historical Essays in Honour of the Island's Bicentennial, 1785–1985* (Sydney NS: University College of Cape Breton Press 1985), 41–3.
4 Peter Burroughs, "Sir James Kempt," *DCB* 8: 458–65. Kempt was required to make and subscribe the declaration under the Test Act by virtue of his commission as lieutenant governor (1 November 1819) and under article 2 of the instructions to Dalhousie as his governor-in-chief of Nova Scotia and Prince Edward Island on 27 April 1820: NA, MG 40, D 13, pts 5 and 6.
5 Garner, *Franchise in British North America,* 141.
6 Nova Scotia, Assembly, *Journal,* 28 February 1822, 139; Nova Scotia, "Journals of the Legislative Council," 28 February 1822 (mss), PANS, RG 1, vol. 218/00, 15323; also Nova Scotia, Assembly, *Journal,* 1 March 1822, 142–3.
7 Nova Scotia, Assembly, *Journal,* 2 March 1822, 144–5.
8 Nova Scotia, "Journals of the Legislative Council," 5 March 1822; Nova Scotia, Assembly, *Journal,* 5 March 1822, 146–7.
9 Nova Scotia, "Journals of the Legislative Council," 9 March 1822.
10 Ibid., 2 April 1823; Nova Scotia, Assembly, *Journal,* 2 April 1823, 288–9.
11 Nova Scotia, Assembly, *Journal,* 3 April 1823, 292–3. Also Garner, *Franchise in British North America,* 142.
12 Three years later, in 1826, the Nova Scotia Assembly unanimously passed an address to the crown requesting the abolition of the declaration against transubstantiation: Garner, *Franchise in British North America,* 142.
13 Kempt to Lord Bathurst, colonial secretary, 20 March 1822, PANS, RG 1, vol. 230, doc. 154, 164.
14 Article 3 of the instructions to Kempt, when he became governor-in-chief of Nova Scotia and Prince Edward Island in 1829, required the declaration of members of the assembly: NA, MG 40, D 13, pt 6.
15 See p. 28. See also Henriques, *The Jews and the English Law,* 251–2.
16 Nova Scotia, *Statutes,* 11 Geo. IV, c. 1 (1830); New Brunswick, *Statutes,* 11 Geo. IV, c. 7 (1830); Prince Edward Island, *Statutes,* 11 Geo. IV, c. 8 (1830). See Garner, *Franchise in British North America,* 147.
17 Goderich to President Tucker, 2 May 1832, NA, CO 195, vol. 18, 50–2 (mfm B–873). The actual commission and instructions to Cochrane

could not be located. They were transmitted under cover of letter from Goderich to Cochrane, 27 July 1832, ibid., 57–80.

18 Ernest Henriques de Souza, *Pictorial* (Kingston, Jamaica: E.H. de Souza 1986), 44–5. The statutes were 7 Geo. IV, c. 23 (1826), 9 Geo. IV, c. 23 (1828), and 11 Geo. IV, c. 16 (1830).

19 An Act to relieve His Majesty's Subjects of the Jewish religion in respect to the Oath of Abjuration, 2 Will. IV, c. 2 (1831). The act provided "that whenever any person professing the Jewish religion shall present himself to take the said Oath of abjuration the said words 'upon the true faith of a Christian' shall be omitted out of the said Oath."

20 Appointments extracted from the *Official Gazette of Jamaica*: Hühner, "Prominent Jews in Jamaica," 164–5. Within a month after the act was passed, Philip Lucas, another Jew, was appointed magistrate and assistant judge of the Court of Common Pleas for the parish of Kingston.

21 Prince Edward Island, *Statutes*, 11 Geo. IV, c. 8 (1830). See, for example, the instructions to Lord Aylmer, as governor-in-chief of Nova Scotia and Prince Edward Island in 1831: NA, MG 40, D 13, pt 6.

22 3 Will. IV, c. 13 (1833) (Upper Canada).

23 Section 4 of the act provided that "notwithstanding any thing contained in any Law or Statute to the contrary, it shall not be necessary from and after the passing of this Act, for any person within this Province, for any such purpose as aforesaid, to take or receive the Sacrament of the Lord's Supper according to the Rites or Usage of the Church of England."

24 In this instance, the colonies once again moved ahead of the metropole. Jews in England were unable to be elected officers of municipal corporations until the passage of the Jewish Disabilities Removal Act in 1845.

25 See, for example, article 3 of the additional instructions to Lord Aylmer as governor of Upper Canada, 8 February 1835; the instructions to William Pitt Amherst, 2 April 1835; and the instructions to the earl of Gosford, 7 July 1835: Public Archives of Canada, *Report*, 1905, 86–8. The instructions to Lord Dalhousie as governor-in-chief of Upper and Lower Canada on 13 April 1820 were incorporated by reference as "standing instructions" in the instructions to subsequent governors of those colonies until 1840: Public Archives of Canada, *Report*, 1905, 86–114. See page 99 for the standing instructions with respect to state oaths.

26 On George Benjamin (1799–1864), see Godfrey and Godfrey, *Burn this Gossip: George Benjamin of Belleville*, esp. 61–2, 73.

27 Ronald J. Stagg and Colin Read, eds., *The Rebellion of 1837 in Upper Canada: A Collection of Documents* (Toronto: Champlain Society 1985), 15n17. Joseph may have been the John Joseph who was a son of Simeon Joseph and Eliza Oppenheim: Will of Samuel Joseph, probated

26 August 1828, PRO, PCC 114. See Godfrey and Godfrey, "Who Was
Who in Canadian Jewry," Joseph IV.

28 Although it does not appear to have affected his actions, Head himself
was of Jewish descent. He was the grandson of Moses Mendes, the celebrated English poet. Mendes' sons had adopted their mother's maiden
name as their surname. Roth, *Jewish Contribution to Civilization,* 101.

29 The quotation appears in Mackenzie's description of a visit to the Colonial Office in 1833, published in the Toronto *Constitution* of 26 July
1837: see Johnson, "John Joseph," *DCB* 8: 444–5.

30 Along with sixty-seven other Jews, John Joseph signed a petition to the
Rt.Hon. Robert Grant, 11 April 1833, requesting relief from the disabilities caused for Jews by the continuing requirement of the state oaths:
see Abrahams, "Sir I.L. Goldsmid and the Admission of the Jews of
England to Parliament," 164–5.

31 Aaron Ezekiel Hart (1803–1857) was a son of Ezekiel Hart and Frances
Lazarus. His application of 22 November 1824 to become a barrister,
advocate, attorney, proctor, and solicitor is in NA, RG 4, B 8, vol. 21, file
1823–24 (mfm H–1416); he completed his examinations on 29 November and was enrolled on 30 November. See also Vaugeois, "Aaron Ezekiel Hart," *DCB* 8: 363–5. Hart thereby became a barrister before any
British Jew. Although Joseph Abrahams had become the first Jewish solicitor in England on 23 January 1770, there were no Jews accepted as barristers by the Inns of Court in England until Francis Henry Goldsmid
was granted his call to the bar by the benchers of Lincoln's Inn on 30
January 1833: Henriques, *The Jews and the English Law,* 203–6.

32 Two weeks later, on 13 December 1824, Thomas Storrs Judah was
enrolled as a barrister and advocate; his brother, Henry Hague Judah,
was enrolled as an advocate on 29 May 1829: NA, RG 68, Registrar General's Index, ff. 12–13. Although their father, Henry Judah, the youngest son of Abraham and Zelda Judah of Montreal, was born Jewish, he
had married a Christian and his children were baptized: see Godfrey
and Godfrey, "Who Was Who in Canadian Jewry, Judah I, I(d)."

33 His oath, sworn on 30 November 1824, is in the NA, RG 1, E 11, vol. 4,
file 1820–30.

34 Rome, comp., "Intergroup," 122. Aaron Philip Hart (1811–1843), the
son of Benjamin Hart, would achieve some prominence after the 1837
rebellion in Lower Canada through his defence of some of the leaders
of the Patriotes.

35 Eleazar David David, Montreal, to Moses Hart, Trois-Rivières, 25 July
1832, ASTR, Fonds Hart, J–P–7. Eleazar David David (1811–1887) was
the son of Samuel David. He was unquestionably of the Jewish faith and
was one of the seven who signed a petition on 11 September 1832
asking for the establishment of a synagogue in Montreal: Rome, comp.,

"On the Jews of Lower Canada and 1837–38, part 2," 93–4. See also Senior, "Eleazar David David," *DCB* 9: 234–5.

36 Rome and Cadloff, comps., "Samuel B. Hart," 13. This correspondence was also published in the *Montreal Gazette* of 11 November 1830, 3.

37 1 Will. IV, c. 57 (1831) (Lower Canada). Royal assent 1832.

38 The commission was actually granted to "David David of Chambly, Esquire": NA, RG 68, vol. 13, 137–45. Evelyn Miller, the former archivist of the Canadian Jewish Congress, has suggested that caution should be exercised in determining whether the person appointed was in fact Eleazar David David. Another possible candidate for this appointment would be a member of the French-Canadian David family from the south shore of the St Lawrence, although no individuals with the given name "David" have been located in that family. Moreover, at the time of his appointment, Eleazar David David would have been six months shy of his twenty-first birthday (born June 1811). Nevertheless, he had sometimes been known as David David after 1824 when he succeeded his uncle, David David, as seigneur of Chambly, and he has been identified as the "Col. David David of St Joseph de Chambly" who was discharged as a commissioner of the peace in 1840 after he eloped with the wife of a fellow officer in 1839: NA, RG 68, vol. 16, 147–8. David was a captain in the cavalry at the time of the 1837 rebellion and was promoted to lieutenant-colonel shortly thereafter: NA, RG 68, Commissions Index, 8 March 1837. See also Rome, comp., "On the Jews of Lower Canada and 1837–8, part 2," 93, 137–8, and Senior, "Eleazar David David."

39 Rome, comp., "Samuel B. Hart," 34 and 64.

40 Ibid., 36–7, 52. Also NA, MG 11, series Q, vol. 209–1, 73.

41 Rome and Cadloff, comps., "Samuel B. Hart," 55.

42 This was the comment of his cousin, Aaron Ezekiel Hart: ibid., 38.

43 Ibid., 70.

44 Ibid., 66–7.

45 Ibid., 67, 69–70.

46 Lower Canada, Assembly, *Journal,* 1834, 229 (8 February, communication from the governor).

47 Jean-François-Joseph Duval (1801–1881), who represented Quebec Upper Town in the assembly from 1829 to 1834, was appointed judge in 1839 and served as chief justice of Quebec from 1864 to 1874: DCB files.

48 Lower Canada, Assembly, *Journal,* 1834, 263 (17 February, information re legal opinions); see also Rome, comp., "Samuel B. Hart," 77.

49 Rome, comp., "Samuel B. Hart," 52–4.

50 "Report of the Special Committee to whom was referred the Message of His Excellency the Governor in Chief, of the 8th February, 1834, relating to the Act 1st William IV. Cap. 57, intituled, 'An Act to declare persons professing the Jewish Religion, entitled to all the Rights and

Privileges of the other Subjects of His Majesty in this Province'," Lower
Canada, Assembly, *Journal,* appendix G.g., 1834. Reprinted in ibid., 84–9.

51 Lower Canada, Assembly, *Journal,* 28 February 1834, 384–5.

52 NA, RG 68, book 14, 510.

53 Robie to Sir Colin Campbell, governor of Nova Scotia, 17 April 1838:
NA, MG 11, vol. 187, pt 2, CO 217, vol. 165, pt 2 (1838), 712.

54 The address of 16 April 1838 was published in Nova Scotia, Assembly,
Journal, 1838, 445. Both the address and the draft bill to which it refers
are in ibid., at 733 and 737.

55 Henriques, *The Jews and the English Law,* 265–6, 254; Hansard, *The Parliamentary Debates,* 3rd series, 39: 508–20.

56 *Bell's Weekly Messenger* (London), 29 June 1834, p. 2, col. 1.

57 Notation by Sir George Grey, approved by Lord Glenelg, 24 May 1838,
on a letter from Sir Colin Campbell to Glenelg, 22 April 1838: NA,
MG 11, vol. 187, pt 2, CO 217, vol. 165, pt 2 (1838), 710.

58 J. Campbell and R.M. Rolfe, law officers, to Glenelg, 12 June 1838: NA,
MG 11, vol. A189, CO 217, vol. 167, pt 1 (1838), 259–61; Garner, *Franchise in British North America,* 147–8.

59 Instructions to Durham as governor-in-chief of Nova Scotia, 10 February 1838, NA, MG 40, B 13, pt 6. While Durham's instructions as governor of Prince Edward Island have not been located, the commission to
Sir John Colborne who replaced him on 13 December 1838 confirms
that by that date the declaration under the Test Act of 1673 was no
longer required. However, notwithstanding the colonial statute of 1830
that had abolished the state oaths, the governor was still required to see
that the state oaths were taken by members of the legislative and executive councils, by the members of the assembly ("and until the same shall
be taken no person shall be capable of sitting though elected"), and by
"every such Person or Persons as you shall think fit who shall hold any
Office or Place of Trust or Profit or who shall at any time or times pass
into the said Island or be resident or abiding therein.": Public Archives
of Prince Edward Island, RG 1, vol. 73, 72–4. In Newfoundland, Governor Thomas Cochrane's instructions (26 July 1832) ordered him to call
the island's first assembly in 1833: *Consolidated Statutes of Newfoundland,*
1916, appendix 1, iii–xxxi. As promised (see p. 195), Catholics were no
longer disabled, and the instructions required only the state oaths (as
modified by Britain's Roman Catholic Relief Act of 1829) as a condition of sitting in the assembly or holding other offices and did not mention compliance with the Test Act (contrary to the case in other
Atlantic colonies). Jews (because of the oath of abjuration) and Quakers (who would not swear) remained disabled, however. The state oaths
were finally replaced by an oath of allegiance in the instructions to Sir
John Gaspard Le Marchant (20 July 1848): Public Archives of Newfoundland, GB 6/1–D.

60 Instructions to Durham as governor-in-chief of Upper and Lower Canada, 2 April 1838: Public Archives of Canada, *Report*, 1905, 92–3 and 53.

61 Anthony Adamson, *Wasps in the Attic: Biographies prepared from Material found in the Attic of the Grove Farm House, Port Credit, Ontario, being the Story of the Direct Canadian Ancestors of Augusta and Anthony Adamson* (Toronto 1987), 231, 258.

62 Ibid., 27.

63 Garner, *Franchise in British North America*, 148.

64 "Upper Canada, Instructions to Governors, 1791–1839," Public Archives of Canada, *Report*, 1905, 93, 99. Head's instructions as lieutenant governor were derived from those of his governor general, Sir John Colborne, who was in turn required to follow the standing instructions, which had not changed since Dalhousie's appointment in 1820. The subsequent paragraph of Head's instructions required him to administer or cause to be administered the oaths and the declaration to all persons "that shall be appointed to hold or exercise any Office, Place of Trust, or Profit in Our said Province, previous to the entering on the duties of such office." Head appears to have ignored this paragraph because it was clearly contrary to the Upper Canada Oaths Act.

65 Knaplund, ed., *Letters from Sydenham to Russell*, 142–3.

66 NA, RG 1, E 11, vol. 17, 87.

67 Paul Knaplund, ed., *Letters from Lord Sydenham to Lord John Russell* (London: Allen & Unwin 1931), 143–4, "private" letter, 12 June 1841. Baldwin's objection had also been based on the precedent of Sir Francis Bond Head who had allowed him and two others to swear only the oath specified in the Upper Canada Oaths Act: Sydenham to Russell, 25 May 1841, NA, G 12, vol. 57, 243–4. In 1850 the provisions of the Upper Canada Oaths Act of 1833 were extended to the area of Lower Canada to make the law uniform in the united province by 13 & 14 Vict., c. 18: An Act for making one uniform provision respecting certain Official and other Oaths to be taken in this Province, and for other purposes therein mentioned.

68 J. Campbell and R. M. Rolfe to Glenelg, 20 September 1839, NA, MG 11, vol. 194, CO 217, Nova Scotia A, 89–92.

69 Baldwin to Rupert Murdoch, chief secretary to Sydenham, 15 May 1841, and Day to Murdoch, 14 May 1841, NA, RG 7, G 20, vol. 1, file 82 (mfm H–1348).

70 Garner, *Franchise in British North America*, 148. The oath referred to was the oath of supremacy although the argument applied equally to the oath of abjuration.

71 Instructions to Durham as governor-in-chief of Upper and Lower Canada, 2 April 1838: Public Archives of Canada, *Report*, 1905, 94.

72 Bagot's commission and instructions were printed in New Brunswick, Legislative Council, *Journal*, 1843, 692–701. The commission to Lord Durham as governor-in-chief of Nova Scotia, 6 February 1838, three years before the law officers' opinion focusing on the royal instructions, used identical wording to Bagot's instructions in New Brunswick: Nova Scotia, Assembly, *Journal*, 1838, Appendix, 194 et seq.

73 Samuel Samuels, a thirty-year-old bachelor, had been in New Brunswick for four years at the time he applied for a grant of land on the Bay du Vin River in 1817: Petition of Samuel Samuels, Miramichi, 8 May 1817, PANB, mfm F9019, 807.

74 Michael Samuel (c. 1786–1862) had married a daughter of Sacker Parker in Halifax. See Godfrey and Godfrey, "Who Was Who in Canadian Jewry," Samuel I, Samuel I(1), Samuel I(2), and Joseph II; also Fraser, *By Favourable Winds*, 290–1.

75 John Joseph (c. 1776–1835) married Sophia, also a daughter of Sacker Parker, in Halifax in 1811, moved to Chatham about 1817, and died 12 March 1835. Although described as a native of Yorkshire, and buried in the Anglican cemetery, he was unquestionably of Jewish origin: Will dated 24 July 1833, Northumberland County Registry Office, vol. 35, 15–20; Godfrey and Godfrey, "Who Was Who in Canadian Jewry," Joseph I.

76 Jacob S. Samuel (c. 1796–1840) returned to England and died in London on 19 March 1840: *Chatham Gleaner*, 6 May 1840; Fraser, *By Favourable Winds*, 290; Godfrey and Godfrey, "Who Was Who in Canadian Jewry," Samuel I.

77 Jonah Samuel ran his uncle's branch store at Dalhousie from 1841 to 1850. On 20 July 1850 he married Julia Esther, a daughter of Joseph and Phoebe Samuel, at the Jewish synagogue on Washington Street in Boston: *Chatham Gleaner*, 19 August 1850. See Godfrey and Godfrey, "Who Was Who in Canadian Jewry," Samuel I.

78 Joseph Samuel (c. 1786–1862) returned to England in 1857, leaving his sons Samuel J. (1812–1890) and Solomon (1814–1869), both bachelors, in Richibuctou. Godfrey and Godfrey, "Who Was Who in Canadian Jewry," Samuel I.

79 Morden S. Levy (c. 1824–1863) was born in England and may have been in New Brunswick as early as 1842: "I was in hope that my Uncle Joe [Samuel] would have been up here with Mordont." Jonah Samuel, Dalhousie, N.B., to Michael Samuel, Chatham, N.B., 18 February 1842: PANB, MC 240, Samuel Family Papers, box 1. As early as 1857, Levy carried on business in Richibuctou in partnership as "Levy & Samuel" with Solomon Samuel, in association with the latter's father, Joseph Samuel: Deed from Joseph Samuel to Solomon Samuel & Morden S. Levy, 1 June 1857, Northumberland County Registry Office, vol. 46, 521–3.

He died at Richibuctou on 28 July 1863 "in the 39th year of his age"; his remains were interred by the Kent Lodge of Masons: *Chatham Gleaner*, 1 August 1863, *New-Brunswick Courier*, 1 August 1863. See Godfrey and Godfrey, "Who Was Who in Canadian Jewry," Levy VII.

80 Simon Aaron came to the Miramichi area along with Michael Samuel and John Joseph in 1814 but returned to Norwich, England, by 1835, leaving his son, H. Maurice Aaron, in Richibuctou carrying on business as Samuel Aaron & Co.: Godfrey and Godfrey, "Who Was Who in Canadian Jewry," Aaron.

81 Michael Samuel Jr (d. 1857), a cousin of Michael Samuel, worked as a merchant in Richibuctou from 1816 to 1838 when he returned to England to marry Emma Jacobs, daughter of Henry Jacobs, at the synagogue in London: *Chatham Gleaner*, 12 June 1838. See also Godfrey and Godfrey, "Who Was Who in Canadian Jewry," Samuel I.

82 Morris Joseph was in Chatham by 1824 but apparently returned to England; Maurice and Hyam Joseph, probably his sons, were in Richibuctou in the 1840s: Godfrey and Godfrey, "Who Was Who in Canadian Jewry," Joseph III.

83 Joseph Levy, tailor, was doing business with Michael Samuel in Newcastle between 1839 and 1842: "M. Samuel's Ledger," PANB, 294. He was likely the same person as "Joseph Levi, tailor," an unmarried man of between 45 and 60 years of age, who gave his religion as "Jewish" and was resident at lot 18, Princetown Royalty, in the northwest area of Prince Edward Island, according to the island's 1861 census (p. 4): see Godfrey and Godfrey, "Who Was Who in Canadian Jewry," Levy VIII.

84 By 1870 Samuel J. Samuel was the only Jew left in the area. His will, dated 5 October 1876, probated 22 May 1890, PANB, mfm 6154, provided that "if I die in Richibucto or Chatham or Elsewhere where there is not a Jewish Congregation that I be buried with Masonic Ceremonies only and that Fifty dollars be paid to the Lodge under whose banner the ceremony may be performed and I further request that although I am of opinion it is a matter of no moment how the dead body is decorated or whether it be at all[,] an old fashioned shroud be used and not your new fangled dress suit." He died on 5 March 1890 and was buried in the Masonic cemetery.

85 *Chatham Gleaner*, December 1842 and 27 March 1843, as cited in notes from "Scenes from an Earlier Day," Samuel Family file, Manse Library, Douglastown, NB.

86 New Brunswick, *Statutes*, 6 Vict., c. 44, An Act to improve the Law relating to the Election of Representatives to serve in the General Assembly, passed 11 April 1843.

87 Nova Scotia, Assembly, *Journal*, 20 March 1846.

88 New Brunswick, Assembly, *Journal*, 6 April 1846.

89 Gladstone to Lieutenant Governor Sir William Colebrooke, 2 June
1846. Letters patent for dispensing with the administration of the state
oaths were transmitted to New Brunswick by the Colonial Office ten
weeks later in Grey to Colebrooke, 18 August 1846: both documents
were printed in ibid., 3 February 1847, 29. The New Brunswick form of
oath, approved 15 February 1847, was: "I, ———, do sincerely promise
and swear that I will be faithful and bear true allegiance to Her Majesty
Queen Victoria, so help me God." The amendment of the state oaths
for Nova Scotia had been confirmed in May: Gladstone to Lord Falk-
land, 5 May 1846: NA, CO 218/33, 188 et seq. (mfm B–1823).

90 Levy was appointed on 27 March 1857: PANB, RG 3, RS538, B1. On
12 April 1859, Levy was stabbed in the abdomen on the main street of
Richibuctou by James Wetmore, who had been dismissed as sheriff of
Kent County three days earlier and who believed Levy to have been
responsible for his dismissal: *Head Quarters* (Fredericton), 20 April
1859; PANB, RG 3, RS538, E17, 6396–401 (petitions for and against Wetmore's removal); *Royal Gazette* (Fredericton), 13 April 1859, 8592
(replacement of Wetmore). Levy may not have been the first Jewish justice of the peace in New Brunswick. William Abrams (or Abrahams) was
appointed justice of the peace in Northumberland County in 1822 and
justice of the Inferior Court of Common Pleas in 1824: PANB, RS538,
B5, 48, 68, and 80. On Abrams's Jewish background, see p. 323n66.

91 For example, see the instructions to Sir Edmund Walker Head, 20 September 1854: "Instructions to Governors," Public Archives of Canada,
Report, 1905, 126.

92 The instructions to Charles Stanley, Viscount Monck, as governor general of Canada, 2 November 1861, required him to take the oath
appointed under the act of 21 & 22 Vict., c. 49 (the Jewish Relief Act
of 1858).

93 Cadloff, "Freedom of Religion," 143–56.

94 Province of Canada, *Statutes*, 1851, c. 75 (royal assent, 9 June 1852).
After Confederation in 1867, section 1 of the Rectories Act was re-
enacted in Ontario and remains on the books as the Religious Freedom
Act, *Revised Statutes of Ontario*, 1980, c. 447. It was also re-enacted in
Quebec: Freedom of Worship Act, *Revised Statutes of Quebec*, 1977, c. L-2.
2: Cadloff, "Freedom of Religion," 155–6. An argument could be made
that the Rectories Act itself is still in force as a law that can be changed
only by the parliament of Canada under the authority of section 129 of
the British North America Act, 30 & 31 Vict., c. 3 (now the Constitution Act, 1867). This argument, originally suggested by Bora Laskin, is
expanded in Godfrey, "Freedom of Religion and the Canadian Bill of
Rights," 60–75.

95 Cadloff, "Freedom of Religion," 149–51.

96 In Prince Edward Island by 42 Vict., c. 19 (1879), s. 10, and in Nova Scotia as part of a general revision of statutes: *Revised Statutes of Nova Scotia*, 1851, c. 170. In New Brunswick it has never been repealed, but its effects appear to have been ended in an evolutionary way by statutes or policies directed at specific manifestations of such establishment: this is the view of Mr. Swarick of the New Brunswick Legislative Library and Professor Acheson of the History Department of the University of New Brunswick, citing as examples the removal of King's College from the control of the Church of England in 1859 and the ending of the right of the bishop of Fredericton to sit on the Legislative Council in 1867.

97 Abraham de Sola (1825–1882) had come from England in January 1847 to serve as spiritual leader of Montreal's Jewish congregation, whose name had been changed the previous year from Shearith Israel to "The Corporation of the Portuguese Jews of Montreal" (Province of Canada, *Statutes*, 9 Vict., c. 96). In accordance with prevailing practice in North America, de Sola was not an ordained rabbi but had been trained as a hazzan or cantor. The scion of a scholarly London Sephardic family that traced its descent back to tenth-century Spain, de Sola became the acknowledged leader of Montreal's Jewish community from the time of his arrival as well as taking part in the wider community. In 1847 he started a congregational Sunday school, organized a Hebrew Philanthropic Society for the assistance of Jewish indigents, and took on duties as lecturer in Hebrew and oriental languages at McGill College. Over the years, he published many works and delivered scholarly papers to a wide range of Montreal's English-language cultural organizations. He was awarded an honorary doctorate of laws by McGill in 1858. On his death in 1882, he was succeeded as spiritual leader of the congregation by his son, Mendola de Sola. See Miller, "Abraham de Sola," *DCB* 11: 253–6; Stern, *First American Jewish Families*, 59–60 (de Sola I); and Tulchinsky, *Taking Root*, 40–9.

98 The badge was a mark placed on the dress of Jews to distinguish them from others. It was made a general order of Christendom at the instigation of Pope Innocent III and adopted at the fourth Lateran Council in 1215. The concept of a badge for Jews was derived from Islam in an earlier period in which the dress of Jews was was distinguished from that of the true believer by a different colour, such as a yellow seam on upper garments. Badges were imposed on Jews by most Christian countries at different periods during the Middle Ages. Badges were frequently yellow, but sometimes red or white. See "Badge," *Jewish Encyclopedia*, vol. 2.

99 Quoted in Sack, *History of the Jews in Canada*, 157–8. Sack gives the *Montreal Herald*, 3 November 1855, as his source, but a complete account of the meeting is unavailable because the *Montreal Herald* for that date has not been located in any Canadian repository.

CHAPTER FIFTEEN

1 "Opening of the Legislature," *British Colonist* (Victoria), 3 March 1860, 1, col. 1.

2 *Victoria Gazette,* 23 August 1859. The article referred to Rolant as "the defaulting Prussian."

3 Ibid., 20 September 1859.

4 It was not in fact finished until 1864.

5 *British Colonist,* 3 March 1860, 2.

6 Ibid. The remark is attributed to Amor De Cosmos in the *British Colonist,* 26 August 1859.

7 The *Victoria Gazette,* 23 June 1859, nicknamed the buildings "fancy bird cages." The buildings were designed by Herman Otto Tiedemann, a German-trained architect: R. Windsor Liscombe, "Herman Otto Tiedemann," *DCB* 12: 1048–9. The last of the "birdcages," as they became popularly known, was destroyed by fire in 1957. A detailed description of the buildings and their subsequent history survives in a 16-page typed account, c. 1957, in BCARS, newspaper clippings on mfm, "Parliament Buildings Old," D–19, reel 108, frame 960 et seq.

8 Lillard, *Seven Shillings a Year,* 109, 178.

9 A watercolour by Owen Staples, "View of Yates Street, 1862," in the collection of the Metropolitan Toronto Reference Library bears the caption: "Most of the figures shown are intended to represent Chinese and natives." Staples's view is a copy of a picture in Mayne's *Four Years in British Columbia and Vancouver Island.*

10 Leonoff, in his *Pioneer Jewish Merchants,* 4, cites Benjamin's account, *Drei Jahre in Amerika,* indicating that the population consisted of "2500 white inhabitants, and more than 5000 Indians."

11 Smith, ed., *Reminiscences of Helmcken,* 173.

12 There are several surviving photographs of the interior of the building in the Picture Collection of the BCARS, although only HP12235 appears to be of the early period.

13 John Sebastian Helmcken (1824–1920) had come to the area as the Hudson's Bay Company doctor, had married Douglas's eldest daughter, Cecilia, in 1852, and had been elected to the first Vancouver Island Assembly in 1856: see Margaret A. Ormsby, "Sir James Douglas," *DCB* 10: 247.

14 "Messrs. Southgate and Green were in San Francisco," *British Colonist,* 3 March 1860, 1, col. 1.

15 James E. Hendrickson, "George Hunter Cary," *DCB* 9: 114–15.

16 Selim Franklin (1814–1883) was born to Lewis and Miriam (née Abraham) Franklin, one of nine sons and two daughters. His brother, Lumley, was probably born in 1812 and died in 1873. Both were bachelors.

See Rome, *Jewish Pioneers on Canada's Pacific Coast*, 52–6; also Leonoff,
Pioneer Jewish Merchants, 13–14; and Leonoff, *Pioneers, Pedlars, and Prayer
Shawls*, 166–7.

17 *British Colonist*, 19 May and 9 June 1860.

18 A partial listing, based on Rome, *Jewish Pioneers on Canada's Pacific Coast*,
6–44, includes: Frank Sylvester, Joseph Boscowitz, Kady Gambitz, Jose-
phus and Lionel Joseph, Lewis Lewis, Samuel Price, Samuel and
Gustave Reinhardt, Emil and Gustave Sutro, Humphrey Abraham
Belasco, Samuel Hyman Cohen, Abraham Blackman, A.J. Brunn, Lewis
Davis, Samuel S. Hyams, Moses Abrahams, Mike Cohen (aka Henry
Moses), S. Elsasser, J.W. Kayser, Morris S. Myers, Alexander Phillips,
Moses Sporberg, Lewis Davy, S. Wolf, I. Tashe, Emanuel Levy, David
Hart, and Lewis Levy. There are a number of other individuals listed in
the *First Victoria Directory of Citizens* who can be counted as Jews since
they, or members of their immediate families, are recorded as buried in
the Hebrew cemetery: "Roll of Persons buried in the Hebrew Ceme-
tery," Congregation Emanuel (1862–1945) [EMC], BCARS, additional
MSS 59. Among these are J. Braverman, Cigar Depot [EMC no. 28];
Joseph Fried, tent & signmaker, Yates Street [EMC no. 34]; D. Kaufman,
tailor [EMC no. 48, Rachel Kaufman, b. Victoria, d. 26 August 1863];
C. Isaacs, fruit and dry goods [EMC no. 57, K. Isaacs]; Philip Lewis,
fruit and tobacco, Yates Street [EMC no. 2, son of Philip Lewis,
d. 1861]; Elias Mark, watchmaker [EMC no. R4 22, Marissa Marks].
Others who are likely Jewish because of their associations include, for
example, Isadore Sherman, who was listed in the *First Victoria Directory of
Citizens* as employed by Selim Franklin & Co. Another fifteen or so individuals can be listed as Jewish based on their names, although satisfactory confirming documentation is lacking: Leonoff, "Victoria: The New
Gold Colony," 15 and 17.

19 Rome, *Jewish Pioneers on Canada's Pacific Coast*, 30–5; *Victoria Gazette*,
9 June 1859, 2, col. 2.

20 Cited in Leonoff, *Pioneer Jewish Merchants*, 4.

21 The inaugural ball was held on Thursday, 23 June 1859: *Victoria Gazette*,
18 June 1859, 3.

22 Levy, "History of the Victoria Community Temple Emanu-El," BCARS
mfm A 71, Congregation Emanuel, rolls 201A and 202A.

23 Smith, ed., *Reminiscences of Helmcken*, 165.

24 Christopher Hanna, "Rot-Gut Liquor Fuelled Fur Trade," and "Jews
Were Fur Trade Pioneers," *Victoria Times-Colonist*, 12 June 1994, M4, M2.

25 The actual election results were Cary, 137; Franklin, 106; and De Cosmos, 91: Rome, *Jewish Pioneers on Canada's Pacific Coast*, 62. See Robert
A.J. McDonald and Keith Ralston, "Amor De Cosmos," *DCB* 12: 237–43.

Born William Alexander Smith in Windsor, NS, in 1825, De Cosmos arrived at the California gold fields in 1853 and commenced work as a photographer. He had his name legally changed by the California legislature in 1854, telling the jeering legislators that he would rather be known as a lover of the universe than as Bill Smith. He followed his elder brother, Charles McKeivers Smith, to Victoria in 1858, founding the *British Colonist* by the end of the year. He remained editor until 1863, regarding himself as a "friend of reform." He died in Victoria, unmarried, in 1897.

26 Douglas, who was also governor of British Columbia, had issued the Oaths Act (1858) as a proclamation relating to the colony of British Columbia, that colony being governed by the governor and council in the absence of an assembly: *Proclamation. By his Excellency James Douglas* ..., 19 May 1859. The proclamation had been motivated not so much by foresight as by the governor's need to remedy a deficiency in the Aliens Act, issued on 4 May 1859, which had inadvertently excluded Jews from its naturalization provisions by specifying a Christian form of oath: Rome, *Jewish Pioneers on Canada's Pacific Coast*, 45–51. The Oaths Act was issued by Douglas two weeks later. The proclamation provided in part: "If ... any person professing the Jewish religion shall at any time be required by any lawful authority, or shall be desirous for any purpose to take ... any form of oath containing the words 'And I make this declaration upon the true faith of a Christian' the said words ... shall be omitted in the form of oath to be taken ... And the taking of every such oath ... shall have the same force and effect as the taking and subscribing by other persons of the oath containing the said words."

27 "Order calling the Elections to the Assembly by Governor James Douglas, 16 June 1856," BCARS, *Third Report*, 1918, 9–10.

28 William R. Sampson, "David Cameron," *DCB* 10: 115–18. Cameron came in for some criticism in Helmcken's *Reminiscences*, 171: "Cameron did all the duties of Judge – and altho perhaps it was not all technical law, still people said he gave justice. He had a pretty good notion of his own capabilities; rather obstinate but not given to loss of temper: perfectly upright and honest." In contrast, Helmcken (p 176) remembered George Hunter Cary, the attorney general, as "a very clever lawyer, as sharp as a needle. He had a very good idea of his talent and importance but occasionally was not a little rash. He was an inveterate opponent of Cameron, passionate and he said he felt degraded at having to appear before Cameron, whom he called an inveterate pigheaded old fool who knew nothing about laws and rules and orders, of which bye and bye I do not think there were any special, but those used in England were supposed to rule when applicable."

29 Franklin advised the house that "I took the oaths this morning, and those now proffered to me.": "Opening of the Legislature," *British Colonist*, 3 March 1860, 1, col. 3.

30 W. Kaye Lamb, "Alfred Penderell Waddington," *DCB* 10: 696–8.

31 In this connection, see "Opening of the Legislature," *British Colonist*, 3 March 1860, 1, cols. 1–4. Additional references to the issue of Franklin's oath are in *British Colonist*, 6 March 1860, 3, col. 1; 8 March 1860, 3, col. 2; 13 March 1860, 3, col. 2; 17 March 1860, 3, col. 2; 20 March 1860, 3, col. 2. See also Hendrickson, ed., *Journals of the Legislatures of Vancouver Island and British Columbia*, 2: 143, 155, 158–68.

32 On 5 March Waddington moved want of confidence in the government following the governor's address to the assembly. He was supported only by James Cooper, member for Esquimalt County: Hendrickson, ed., *Journals of the Legislatures of Vancouver Island and British Columbia*, 2: 160–2; "House of Assembly," *British Colonist*, 6 March 1860, 3, col. 1. In an editorial in the *Colonist* of 10 March entitled "Editorial Misrepresentation," De Cosmos referred to two parties, the "Government party" and the "liberal party." There does not appear to have been any formal party system.

33 Although Crease had supported Franklin's election, he opposed his right to sit without taking the usual oath: *British Colonist*, 3 March 1860, 1, cols. 3–4.

34 "Opening of the Legislature," *British Colonist*, 3 March 1860, 1, cols. 3–4.

35 Ibid., 1, col. 4. Crease labelled himself a "liberal and independent Reformer," but drifted into supporting the government party even before his appointment as attorney general of the colony of British Columbia in October 1861: see Tina Loo, "Sir Henry Pering Pellew Crease," *DCB* 13: 228–31.

36 Hendrickson, ed., *Journals of the Legislatures of Vancouver Island and British Columbia*, 2: 160.

37 Ibid., 2: 159–60.

38 *Victoria Gazette*, 5 March 1860, 2, cols. 1–2.

39 Hendrickson, ed., *Journals of the Legislatures of Vancouver Island and British Columbia*, 2: 163.

40 Ibid., 2: 162–3.

41 Quoted in W. Kaye Lamb, "Waddington," *DCB* 10: 698.

42 Hendrickson, ed., *Journals of the Legislatures of Vancouver Island and British Columbia*, 2: 163.

43 "House of Assembly," *British Colonist*, 8 March 1860, 3, col. 2.

44 Dred Scott *v.* John F.A. Sandford, 60 U.S. 393 (United States Supreme Court 1857).

45 Rome, *Jewish Pioneers on Canada's Pacific Coast*, 61–3; Higgins, *The Passing of a Race*, 167–8.

46 Rome, *Jewish Pioneers on Canada's Pacific Coast,* 95–8; *British Colonist,* 19 May 1860.

47 Henry Hague Judah (1808–1883), the son of Henry Judah and Jane More, was born in London. Although his father was Jewish, his mother was a Christian, and he was certainly a Christian ("one of the pillars of the Anglican communion" – T. Taggart Smyth, *The First Hundred Years* [Montreal: Montreal City and District Savings Bank 1946], 77) and was likely baptized at birth as were his older siblings. Raised in Trois-Rivières, he was admitted to the bar in 1829 and in the same year married the daughter of Dr René-Joseph Kimber. See Godfrey and Godfrey, "Who Was Who in Canadian Jewry," Judah I, Id.

48 Samuel C. Benjamin (c. 1813–1893): "The Spanish and Portuguese Jews of Montreal," *Montreal Daily Star,* 30 December 1893 and Sack, *History of the Jews in Canada,* 141.

49 William Hyman (1807–1882) was re-elected in each of the next twenty-four years: Hart, *The Jew in Canada,* 333.

50 See p. 31.

51 "House of Assembly," *British Colonist,* 17 March 1860, 3, col. 2.

52 David Cameron, chief justice, to the Honourable Mr Speaker Helmcken, 15 March 1860, and attached memorandum, "Oaths to the Government," BCARS, GR 1528, box 2, file 3.

53 The Oaths Act (1858), 21 & 22 Vict., c. 48.

54 "An Act To Provide for the Administration of Oaths in the House of Assembly, and the Production of Evidence before Committees of the same," Colony of Vancouver Island (1860), c. 10 (assented 9 July 1860).

55 Rome, *Jewish Pioneers on Canada's Pacific Coast,* 97.

56 Selim Franklin was defeated at the general election of July 1863 but returned to the assembly in a by-election early in 1864. He opposed the union of Vancouver Island with the colony of British Columbia. When that union was consummated in 1866, he resigned his seat and returned to San Francisco. His older brother Lumley was elected the second mayor of Victoria in 1866: see Leonoff, *Pioneers, Pedlars and Prayer Shawls,* 166–7.

CHAPTER SIXTEEN

1 Letter to the editor, *Philadelphia Gazette,* 12 December 1839; quoted in Leeser, *The Claims of the Jews to an Equality of Rights: Illustrated in a Series of Letters to the Editor of the Philadelphia Gazette,* 51. Isaac Leeser was the spiritual leader of Congregation Mikveh Israel.

2 The phrase is prompted by the title of Henri Bourassa's pamphlet, *Religion, Langue, Nationalité* (Montreal: Imprimerie du Devoir 1910). A fuller discussion of the differences in definition between the ethnic

concept of nationalism based on the adherence of individuals sharing a common religion, language, and culture and the political concept of nationalism based on territory and its boundaries is found in Sheldon J. Godfrey, "John S. Ewart and the Canadian Nation, 1904–1914," master's thesis, University of Rochester, 1961.

3 By 1867 there were organized Jewish communities all across British North America:

- Congregation of Portuguese Jews of Montreal, incorporated by Lower Canada, *Statutes*, 9 Vict., c. 96 (1846) as successor to Congregation Shearith Israel, which had not been incorporated
- Congregation of German and Polish Jews of Montreal, incorporated by Lower Canada, *Statutes*, 9 Vict., c. 96 (1846)
- Toronto Hebrew Congregation (1856)
- Anshe Sholom of Hamilton, incorporated by Province of Canada, *Statutes*, 26 Vict., c. 34 (1863)
- Victoria Hebrew Benevolent Society, formation of the society announced in the *Victoria Gazette*, 9 June 1859, col. 2.
- Baron de Hirsch Institute of Montreal, 1863, the organization of young Montreal Jewish men formed with the object of doing good works for the Jewish poor. Isidore G. Ascher was one of its founders.
- Congregation Emanuel, Victoria (1863). Its building fund was enthusiastically supported by both Christians and Jews throughout the city. The synagogue is the oldest surviving religious institution in Canada west of Winnipeg.

4 Daniel G. Hill, *The Freedom-Seekers: Blacks in Early Canada* (Agincourt ON: Book Society of Canada 1981), 13 and 220. The United States formally ended slavery in 1865.

5 An act to prevent the further introduction of slaves, and to limit the term of contracts for servitude within this province, Upper Canada, *Statutes*, 33 Geo. III, c. 7 (1793). In 1792, Denmark had become the first nation to stop the trade in slaves.

6 An Act for the better establishment and maintenance of Common Schools in Upper Canada, Upper Canada, *Statutes*, 13 & 14 Vict., c. 48, s. 19 (1850) and An Act Respecting Separate Schools, Upper Canada, *Statutes*, 22 Vict., c. 65, s. 1 (1859). Even though the legislation gave black separate schools legal equality on the same footing as Roman Catholic separate schools, in practice black separate schools appear to have been treated as segregated schools with inadequate funding and resources. At the same time, although attendance at black separate schools was optional under the legislation, blacks were frequently denied access to common schools by local school boards: Hill, *Freedom-Seekers*, 147–59.

7 Mifflin Wistair Gibbs (1823–1915), born free in Philadelphia, was the most distinguished of the black pioneers who came from California to Victoria in 1858. A successful businessman, he served on the Victoria City Council from 1866 to 1869. He returned to the United States in 1870, graduated in law, and had a subsequent career that took him from being city judge in Little Rock, Arkansas, to consul in Madagascar: Smith, ed., *Reminiscences of Helmcken*, 246. Abraham D. Shadd was likely the first black to be elected to public office in British North America when he was elected to the council of Raleigh Township in Kent County (Ontario) in 1859. William Parker, a former slave, was elected to the Raleigh Township council in the 1860s: information kindly provided by Alice Newby, curator of the Raleigh Township Museum, North Buxton, Ontario.

8 For example, the widow Phoebe David who ran a shop in Montreal in the 1770s while grooming her children for communal and financial leadership; the widow Rachel Myers who brought her Loyalist family to New Brunswick for five difficult years in the 1780s; and the widow Elizabeth Nathan who became Canada's first licensed woman auctioneer in 1807.

9 Consider, for example, Elizabeth Bertrand Mitchell (c. 1759–1827), a woman of French, Indian, and Scottish blood who achieved remarkable success in leading the Michilimackinac Company in competition with the American Fur Company and the North West Company: see David A. Armour, "David Mitchell," *DCB* 6: 508–11; David A. Armour, "David and Elizabeth: The Mitchell Family of the Straits of Mackinac," *Michigan History* 64(1980): 17–29. See also Elizabeth Mitchell, "The Michilimackinac Company and Its Role in the War of 1812," a paper presented to the Fourth North American Fur Trade Conference, October 1981.

10 According to the *Proposals* of the Canadian government preceding the Charlottetown Accord of 28 August 1992, a new section 25.1 was to be added to the Canadian Charter of Rights and Freedoms allowing the government of Quebec to "promote" the unique culture of the French-speaking majority of Quebec as a "distinct society." The existence of others in Quebec, however, was to be merely "preserved." See *Shaping Canada's Future To-gether: Proposals* (Ottawa: Supply and Services Canada 1991), 14. The Charlottetown Accord was not approved in the subsequent constitutional referendum.

EPILOGUE

1 Isidore Gordon Ascher, *One Hundred and Five Sonnets* (Oxford: Blackwell 1912), 63. Ascher (1837–1933), a member of an observant Jewish

family in Montreal, was widely accepted as a Canadian literary figure. In 1912 it was expected that his sonnet "will be preserved in the Dom. as a masterpiece": Henry James Morgan, "Isidore Gordon Ascher," *The Canadian Men and Women of the Time* (Toronto: William Briggs 1912), 41. For additional poems by Ascher see *Voices from the Hearth: A Collection of Verses* (Montreal: John Lovell 1863). For biographical material, see Speisman, *The Jews of Toronto: A History to 1937*, 31, and A. Levy, "The Origins of Scottish Jewry," *JHSET* 19 (1955–59), 148.

2 *An Autobiography of the Rev. Josiah Henson*, edited by John Loeb (revised and enlarged edition; London ON: Schuyler, Smith 1881), 95.

Bibliography

The sources on which this book are based are widely scattered and often to be found in unlikely places. Many of them are single or at most a few documents buried in the midst of more extensive archives. Many of these documents have not been cited in previously published material. In consequence, and to assist future researchers, our listings of manuscript material offer more detail than is usual in a bibliography. In particular, we have stressed sources relating to the history of the Jews in this period and those documents relating to key moments in the development of civil and political rights for religious minorities.

ARCHIVAL SOURCES

AMERICAN JEWISH ARCHIVES, Hebrew Union College, Cincinnati, Ohio
Chapman Abraham(s) correspondence file
Lucius Solomon Collection, box 2332, including "Levy Solomons His Book
  Albany Septr 2^d 1806" which was published (see below) in "Family Records
  in a Lunar Calendar"
"The S and M Myers Letter Book, 1785 to 1787"

AMERICAN JEWISH HISTORICAL SOCIETY (AJHS), Archives, Waltham MA
Hart Papers (P–18)
Judah Family file (P–78)
Lyons Collection (P–15), box 4, Sedaka Offerings, Shearith Israel, New York
Samuel Oppenheim Collection (P–255)
Contains the research materials and notes of Samuel Oppenheim (1859–
  1928) on colonial American Jewish history. Composed of listings and files
  for some 1100 individual Jews active prior to 1800 as well as notes on the
  Sedaka offerings and other materials held by the Congregation Shearith
  Israel of New York. A 60-page index and finding guide is available.

ANGLICAN DIOCESAN CENTRE, Halifax, NS
St Paul's Church Baptismal Record (re Samuel Hart, 17 March 1793, and
  Moses Montagu Hart, 1 September 1793)

ARCHIVES DU SÉMINAIRE DE QUÉBEC, Quebec City
Ezekiel Solomons, petition, 12 December 1764, no. 16, 261–4

ARCHIVES DU SÉMINAIRE DE TROIS-RIVIÈRES (ASTR), Quebec
Fonds Hart. The Hart family papers, containing about 100,000 items have
been indexed: Hervé Biron, "Index du Fonds Hart" (1950).

ARCHIVES NATIONALES DU QUÉBEC – MONTRÉAL (ANQ-M)
Wills
Chapman Abraham, will of 10 March 1763, probate 11 April 1783, CM1–1,
no. 8
David David, probate 31 December 1824, 06–M, CM1–1/4
Jacob Franks, 14 April 1830, 21 August 1830, 11 June 1834, 5 June 1837, 22
November 1839, 10 December 1839, CM1, no. 3335
Dorothea Hart (née Judah), will of 4 November 1803, CN 601–29, no. 1703;
will of 18 November 1819, CN 601–134, no. 6805; will of 5 July 1824, CN
601–134, no. 11811
Sarah Hart (née David), probate 17 June 1831, 06–M, CM1–1/7
Samuel Jacobs, 1786, 06–M, CM1–1/9
Hannah Joseph (née Lipman), will of 6 February 1821, N.B. Doucet, notaire,
06–M, CN 1–134, no. 8423
Rachel Joseph (née Solomon), probate 30 October 1855, CM1–1, no. 73
Frances Michaels (née David), will of 17 July 1825, CN 601–134; wills and
probate 9 February 1839, CM1–1, no. 178
Catherine Moss (née Joseph), will of 19 December 1818, N.B. Doucet, notaire,
06–M, CN1–134
Elizabeth Nathan (née Lyons), will of 7 May 1819, H. Griffin, notaire, CN601–
187, no. 2660; will of 16 October 1817, N.B. Doucet, notaire, CN601–134,
no. 4617
Rebekah Solomons (née Franks), probate 1812, CN601–126
Phoebe Valentine (née Hays), probate 1841, 06–M, CM1–1/8

Miscellaneous
Jacob Jacobs, lease from Robillard, 2 October 1819, N.B. Doucet, notaire, no.
6672
Gershon Levy, engagement with Pierre Bertrand, 9 December 1761, Étude
Simonet
Hannah Lipman, contract for the apprenticeship of her son, Henry Joseph,
to Samuel Davis, 25 October 1819, N.B. Doucet, notaire, 06–M, CN1–134,
no. 6737
Hannah Lipman, account to her son, Henry Joseph, 28 April 1824, N.B.
Doucet, notaire, 06–M, CN1–134, no. 11653

Benjamin Samuel Solomon (Montreal) and Henry Joseph (Berthier), co-partnership agreement, 29 August 1822, N.B. Doucet, notaire, 06–M, CN1–134, no. 9995

ARCHIVES NATIONALES DU QUÉBEC – QUÉBEC (ANQ-Q), Ste-Foy, Quebec
Anglican Cathedral at Quebec, Parish Register
Fonds Franks (AP–P–764)
Protestant Church records

ARCHIVES NATIONALES DU QUÉBEC – TROIS-RIVIÈRES
Aaron Hart, will, 11 December 1800, Badeaux & Renvoyze, notaires
Judah Joseph, deed from Joseph Bury, 24 April 1787, B. Faribault, notaire

ARCHIVES OF ONTARIO (AO), Toronto
Charlotte David, petition for administration, estate of Moses David (d. 27 September 1814), York, 4 March 1815, RG 22, appendix F, MS 638, series 155 (mfm 45)
Myers Solomons, land grant, RG 1, series A–IV, vol. 8, 54

BAYLISS PUBLIC LIBRARY, Sault Ste Marie MI
Judge Steere Special Collections
Records of Estate of Bte Langlade, 1801–1802, by Adhémar Martin, Notaire de Michilimackinac (re Myer Michaels, Benjamin Lyon, Ezekiel Solomons)
Record Book of Samuel Abbott, Michigan Territory, U.S.A., 1806–1818 (re John Franks)
Partnership agreement of John Franks, Robert Dickson, et al., 16 August 1804 (Miscellaneous file)

BRITISH COLUMBIA ARCHIVES AND RECORDS SERVICES (BCARS), Victoria
Rabbi Jack A. Levy, "A Message From Your Old Home Town, Sixty-Six Years of History of the Victoria Community Temple Emanu-El Oldest Synagogue on the Pacific Coast, 1862 to 1928," mfm reel A 71, Congregation Emanuel, rolls 201A and 202A
Oaths to the Government, report of chief justice, 15 March 1860, GR 1528, box 2, file 3
Roll of Persons Buried in the Hebrew Cemetery, Congregation Emanuel (1862–1945) [EMC], Add. MSS no. 59

CANADIAN JEWISH ARCHIVES (CJA), Montreal
Year files
Biographical files

CHARLESTON COUNTY LIBRARY, Charleston SC
Emanuel Abrahams, will, probate 3 December 1802, in Court File, book 28, 354-5

CONGREGATION SHEARITH ISRAEL, New York City, NY
(Advance permission is required to examine collection)
Register, 1759–1834
Offering Book, 1752–1797

DETROIT PUBLIC LIBRARY, MI
Burton Historical Collection
American Fur Company Papers, L 4, Petty Debts Book (re Solomons family)
John Askin Papers (re Moses David, 1787)

HALIFAX COUNTY COURT OF PROBATE, Halifax, NS
Rebecca Hart estate (1817), file H 44
Samuel Hart estate (1810), file H 42
David Jones estate (1782), file J 25
Joseph Jones estate (1771), file J 29
Isaac Levy estate (1751), "Wills Book Begun 1749"

HALIFAX COUNTY REGISTRY OF DEEDS, Halifax, NS
Israel Abrahams, Joseph Jones, and Emanuel Abrahams, deed to Joshua
    Mauger et al., book 2, 408–10 (1752)
Abraham Andrews, mortgage to Israel Abrahams, book 2, 72 (1752)
Francis Elliott, deed to Nathan Levy, 30 December 1751, book 2, 409 (1755)
Richard Gibbons et al, deed to Joshua Mauger re property of Israel Abrahams,
    Emanuel Abrahams, and Joseph Jones, book 2, 411 (1755)
Samuel Hart, deed from John Turner, book 24, p–10 (1786)
David Jones, sheriff's sale re, book 8, 20 (1766)
Joseph Jones, deed to David Jones, book 5, 277 (1762)
Joseph Jones, deed to John Fraser, book 7, 147 (1765)
Joseph Jones, deed to Abraham I. Abrahams, book 11, 2325–31 (1772)
Joseph Jones, executors of estate of, deed to Thomas Cochran, book 14, 232
    (1774)
Isaac Judah, deed to Israel Abrahams (1752), book 2, 74
Nathan Levy to Ireal [*sic*] Abrahams, 29 January 1752, book 2, 408–9 (1755)
Nathans & Hart *v.* Joseph and Mordecai Jones, sheriff's sale re, book 2, 411
    (1755)

HISTORICAL SOCIETY OF PENNSYLVANIA, Philadelphia
Gratz Papers, case 16, box 11, John Franks file
Mikvah Israel Jewish Congregation, Register, 1776–1834

Stauffer Collection, vol. 8, 590 (re John Franks)
Tench Coxe Papers, 1776 (re John Franks)

KENT COUNTY REGISTRY OF DEEDS, Newcastle, NB
Morden S. Levy, will of 28 July 1863, registered 8 August 1863, book P

LUNENBURG COUNTY REGISTRY OF DEEDS, Bridgewater, NS
Nathan Levy, deed from James Webber, book 1, 315 (1768)
Susannah Levy, deed to Caspar Wollenhaupt, book 3, 531 (1793)

MCCORD MUSEUM, MCGILL UNIVERSITY, Montreal
Early Hart Papers
Thomas McCord Papers
    0207 – Correspondence with Jacques Terroux
    0209 – Solomon[s] family

MACKINAC COUNTY COURT HOUSE, St Ignace MI
"Register of the Post of Michilimackinac *begun* & *opened* by James Gruet,
    Notary, June 1st 1785"

MANSE LIBRARY, Douglastown, NB
William Abrams Family file
Samuel Family file

MASSACHUSETTS ARCHIVES, Boston
Hyam Myers, petition, 13 July 1778, book 168, 444–4a

MEMORIAL UNIVERSITY, MARITIME HISTORY ARCHIVE, St John's, NFLD
Files for Samuel Jacobs, Simon Levi, Peter Ezekiel, Simon Solomon

NATIONAL ARCHIVES (NA), Ottawa
Appointments, Commissions, Letters Patent (RG 68)
David David, commission as justice of peace, 1831, vol. 13, 137–45; discharge,
    1840, vol. 16, 147–8 (mfm C–3926)
David David, commission as lieutenant-colonel, 8 March 1837, Commissions
    Index
Moses David, commission as coroner, 24 February 1808, liber D, 13 (mfm C–
    3916)
John Franks, commissions, November 1768, vol. 89, Commissions and Letters
    Patent, vol. 1 (1764–1775), 208–11 (mfm C–3921)
Benjamin Hart, commission as justice of peace, 13 April 1837, book 14, 510
Moses Judah Hays, commission as justice of peace, 13 April 1837, book 14,
    510

Henry Hague Judah, commission as advocate, 29 May 1829, Registrar General's Index, f. 13

Thomas Storrs Judah, commission as barrister, 13 December 1824, Registrar General's Index, f. 12

Eleazar Levy, appointment as notary public, liber c, part b, Imperial Commissions, 24 December 1766, 31–2 (mfm c–3921)

Benjamin Price, Samuel Jacobs et al., letters patent, liber a, 258–62 (mfm c– 3945)

Instructions/Commissions to Governors, Maritime Provinces (MG 40)

Lord Aylmer, instructions as governor-in-chief of Nova Scotia and Prince Edward Island, 1831, D 13, pt 6 (mfm H–990)

Guy Carleton, commission as governor-in-chief, Nova Scotia, 27 April 1786, D 12, pt 2, 270–99 (mfm H–989)

Guy Carleton, Lord Dorchester, instructions as governor-in-chief, Nova Scotia, Island of St John [Prince Edward Island], and Cape Breton, 23 August 1786, D 13, pt 4 (mfm H–989)

Edward Cornwallis, instructions as governor-in-chief, Nova Scotia, 2 May 1749, B 13, pt 2

Lord Dalhousie, instructions as governor-in-chief, Nova Scotia, 27 April 1820, D 13, pt 5 (mfm H–990)

Lord Durham, instructions as governor-in-chief, Nova Scotia, 10 February 1838, B 13, pt 6 (mfm H–990)

James Kempt, instructions as governor-in-chief, Nova Scotia and Prince Edward Island, 1829, D 13, pt 6 (mfm H–990)

John Parr, instructions as lieutenant governor of Nova Scotia, 25 August 1787, D 13, pt 4

John Wentworth, commission as lieutenant governor, Nova Scotia, 13 January 1792, D 12, pt 2, 302–3 (mfm H–989)

Lower Canada Land Papers (RG 1, L3L)

Colonel Henry Caldwell and Others, 11 petitions and supplementary material, 1792–1801, vol. 52, 26591–728

Moses David, petition, 18 March 1799, vol. 70, 3513–5; referral, 18 July 1799, vol. 1, 58–63; confirmation, 3 January 1800, vol. 13 (mfm c–2520)

John Franks, petitions, 31 May 1765, 10 August 1768, 1 February 1787, 10 October 1792, vol. 87, 42872–81 (mfm c–2526)

Documents re Lyon Jonas and Sarah Jacobs Jonas, 1800–2, vol. 112, 55209–22; vol. 2, 527; vol. 74, 5159, 5166

List of Lots Granted under Tenure, 25 November 1765, vol. 8, 2366 (re Samuel Jacobs)

"Memorial of Isaac Levi ... Levi Solomons, Benjamin Lyon, Gershon Levi, Ezekiel Solomons, and Chapman Abraham ...," 8 February 1768, series s 13, 83–83b (mfm c–2998, 6209–10)

Memorial of Sundry Inhabitants of Montreal for a Grant ... to build a Court House Public offices and a Gaol, 1794, vol. 135, 66351–3 (re David David, Lyon Jonas)

Benjamin Price, Samuel Jacobs, et al., petition, 15 July 1765, vol. 160, 78536–8 (mfm c–2520)

Elias Solomon, petition, 2 April 1792, vol. 185, 88740–1 (mfm c–2563)

Levy Solomons, memorial, 15 November 1784, MG 23, B 3, file 1 (typescript of original in National Archives of the United States)

Miscellaneous Collections

Journal of the late Samuel David of Montreal, vol. 1, 1800–2, MG 24, I 13

Samuel Jacobs Papers, MG 19, A 2, series 3

Shearith Israel Congregation, Montreal, MG 8, G 67, vols. 1 & 2

Miscellaneous Documents

Chapman Abraham, memorial, 11 August 1778, MG 21, series B, vol. 217, 7–9

Gilbert Cohen (Cowen), land grant, 27 May 1824, RG 1, C 13, vol. 96, 49

Lazarus David, purchase of lot, 26 March 1767, MG 24, L 3, vol. 36, 23003–7

Jacob, Esther, and Moses Hart, petitions, 11 November 1783, 5 December 1784, 11 July 1785, Minutes of the Audit Office, London, AO 12/100, 18, 22–3 and AO 12/101, 161, 163, 223–4 (mfm B–1178)

Samuel Becancour Hart, petition, 5 November 1830, RG 4, A–1, vol. 351 (1831), 96–8

Barrak Hays, petition, 4 August 1783, MG 21, series B, Haldimand Papers, vol. 13, 335–6

Eleazar Levy, deposition, 24 November 1766, MG 23, I 13, Joshua Sharpe Papers, vol. 1, 185–6

Eleazar Levy, petition, 1774, MG 11, CO 42, vol. 33, 67 (mfm B–32)

Isaac Levy, deposition, 25 November 1766, MG 23, I 13, Joshua Sharpe Papers, vol. 1, 211–12

Hyam Myers, declaration, 12 September 1778, British Museum Add. MSS 21844, 22 (mfm A–765, 26–8)

Rachel Myers, petition, 3 April 1781, MG 24, B 1, doc. 3427 (mfm M–352)

Elias Solomon, memorial, 3 March 1792, series Q, S 58–1, 231–9

Simon Solomon, appointment as postmaster, October 1806, CO 194, 45

Levy Solomons, memorial, 15 November 1784, MG 23, B 3, file 1 (typescript of original in National Archives of the United States)

MG 11, series A, vol. 11, 170–3 (re David S. Franks, Ezekiel Solomons, May 1775)

MG 11, series Q, vol. 209–1, 73 (re Aaron Philip Hart, Benjamin Hart, Moses Judah Hays, 1833)

MG 19, B 1, vol. 3, Records of the North West Company (re David David 1823)

MG 21, British Museum Add. MSS 35915, 139–54 and 15491, 25–58 (re judgment on Ralph Burton appeal re Eleazar Levy, 26 June 1767)
MG 24, B 11 (re David David 1808) (mfm M–741)
RG 4, B 8, vol. 21, file 1823–4 (re Aaron Ezekiel Hart) (mfm H–1416)
RG 4, B 16, vol. 34 (re Jews serving as jurors, Quebec, 1765)
RG 4, B 28, vol. 47, 276–8 (re Theodore Hart 1810)
RG 7, G 15C, vol. 13, 99 (re Ezekiel Hart 1808)

Oaths of Office (RG 1, E 11)
John Franks, November 1758, vol. 1
Ezekiel Hart, 1808, 1809, vols. 2 and 10
Aaron Ezekiel Hart, 30 November 1824, vol. 4, file 1820–30

Upper Canada Land Papers (RG 1, L 3)
Moses David, petitions, 31 July 1797, 9 March 1803, bundle D6/23–23f (mfm C–1744)
Moses David, petition, 8 January 1803, bundle H4/107b&c (mfm C–2044)
Isaac Hart, petition, 28 July 1819, bundle H12/104 (mfm C–2048)
Moses Hart, petition, 30 October 1797, bundle H4/107 (mfm C–2044)
Simeon and Harry Hart, petition, 23 July 1817, bundles H11/138 and H11/139 (mfm C–2047)
John Levy Jacobs, petition, bundles I-J Misc., 1788–95, vol. 266, 15–15a (mfm C–2116)
Moses Jacobs, petitions (30 May 1797, 4 June 1816), bundle J10/35–35f (mfm C–2109)
Samuel Jacobs Jr, petition, bundle L Misc., 1788–95, vol. 306, 66a–b
Samuel Jacobs Jr, petition, bundles I-J Misc., 1788–95, vol. 266, 15–15a (mfm C–2116)
John Lawe, petition, bundle L Misc., 1788–95, vol. 306, 66a–b
Alexander Montgomery, petition, 27 June 1806, bundle M6, vol. 332
Levy Solomons, petition, 23 October 1797, bundle S4/25 (mfm C–2807)

NEWPORT HISTORICAL SOCIETY, RI
Lopez Papers

NORTHUMBERLAND COUNTY REGISTRY OF DEEDS, Newcastle, NB
William Abrams, will of 5 April 1841, registered as no. 489, vol. 40, 14 March 1845
John Joseph, will of 24 July 1833, registered as no. 7, vol. 35, 15–20, 19 April 1835
Sophia Joseph, will of 6 December 1854, registered as no. 612, vol. 46, 687–9, 6 October 1857
Joseph Samuel, deed to Solomon Samuel and Morden S. Levy, 1 June 1857, vol. 46, 521–3

Michael Samuel, will of 28 May 1862, registered as no. 125, vol. 49, 27 January 1863

OLD DOMINION UNIVERSITY ARCHIVES, Norfolk, VA
Myers Family Papers
 Barton Myers Collection, 5000 mss indexed
 Moses Myers Papers, on loan from Chrysler Museum, Norfolk, indexed

ONTARIO, MINISTRY OF NATURAL RESOURCES, SURVEY RECORDS OFFICE, Toronto
Plan of the town of Cornwall, by W. Chewett, 17 February 1792 (re Isaac Judah)

ONTARIO, OFFICIAL DOCUMENTS OFFICE, Toronto
Moses David, crown grant, 20 February 1804 (#0/228)
Isaac Judah, crown grant, 17 February 1804 (QE21)
Samuel Moss, crown grant, 27 May 1797 (A/44)

PRIVATELY HELD
"Account of 14 Packs Peltries belonging to The Estate of Ezek^l Solomon Seized upon by Edwd. Wm. Gray Esqr. Sheriff–at the request of Alex^r. Ellice & Co. as acting Trustees for said Estate ... dated St. Maries 3d. Augt. 1780." Attached to "Account of 28 Packs of Furs & Peltries Seized upon by Edwd. Wm. Gray Esqr," no date.
"Certificate of Marriage of Henry Joseph to Miss Rachel Solomons, 28 Sep 1803"
Deputation of James Scott Howard as Collector of Customs for the Port of York, 1 July 1824
Letter of Heineman Pines, "River Deloup," to "Mr Wm Dummer Powell, Attorney at Law at Montreal," 21 April 1780
Letter of Heineman Pines, "River Des Loups," to "Messrs Charles Grant & Blackwood, Marchants at Quebec," 26 May 1783
"Petition of the Traders of 1763 to the King's Council of Virginia, Fort Pitt, September, 1775," dealing with the Lancaster Group of traders which included Joseph Simon of Lancaster, Bernard and Michael Gratz of Philadelphia, Levy Andrew Levy of Fort Pitt and others. Copy.
"True Account of Admiral Vernon's Conduct at Cartagena," possibly by a survivor, c. 1745

PROVINCIAL ARCHIVES OF NEW BRUNSWICK (PANB), Fredericton
Commissions
Morden S. Levy, justice of the peace, 27 March 1857, RG 3, RS538, B1
William Abrams, justice of the peace, 11 January 1822, and justice of the Inferior Court of Common Pleas, 17 June 1824, RS538, B5, 48, 68, 80 (mfm F6726)

Land Grants (RS 686)
Samuel Jacobs, 28 May 1760, vol. A, no. 130
Benjamin and Abraham Myers, 14 July 1784, vol. A, no. 98
Rachel Myers, May 1786, vol. 1, no. 41

Land Grants (RS 108)
Joseph Jacobs, 1784, 1786 (mfm F1031)

Miscellaneous
Gagetown Anglican Church Baptisms, F1140 (re Montgomery)
Benjamin Myers, petition, 24 July 1786, mfm F1031
Rachel Myers, petitions, 25 August 1785 and 24 June 1786, mfm F1027 and
   mfm F1031
Samuel Family Merchandizing Papers, MC 240, box 1: correspondence
"M. Samuel's Ledger," mfm F316, 294
Samuel J. Samuel, will of 5 October 1876, probate 22 May 1890, mfm 6154
Samuel Samuels, petition, 8 May 1817, mfm F9019, 807

PROVINCIAL ARCHIVES OF NEWFOUNDLAND & LABRADOR, St John's
Anglican Church records, 12 February 1798 (re Simon Solomon)
Governor's Letter Books, A–8–1, GN 2/1/a, vol. 18, 154–5
Instructions to Sir John Harvey as governor, 20 July 1841, GB 6/1-C-3
Instructions to Sir John Gaspard Le Marchant as governor, 19 July 1848, GB
   6/1—D
St John's census of 1794/5, 3d division, #197 (GM 2/3a/A)

PROVINCIAL CROWN RECORDS CENTRE, Halifax, NS
Halifax Allotment, book 1
Israel Abrahams, p. 25 (1750)
John Franks, pp. 1 and 27 (1749), 65 (1757)
Elizabeth Franks, p. 68 (1757)
Samuel Jacobs, p. 2 (1749)
Joseph Jones, p. 124 (1758)
Isaac Levy, p. 32 (1750)
Isaac Solomon, p. 31 (1749)

Nova Scotia Grant Book 2
Isaac Levy, David Franks, Benjamin Levy, David Salisbury [*sic*] Franks, John
   Franks et al., pp. 178–88 (1786)

Nova Scotia Grant Book 6
Joseph Jacobs, Israel and Benjamin Jacobs et al., pp. 466–7 (1765)

PUBLIC ARCHIVES OF NOVA SCOTIA (PANS), Halifax
Inferior Court of Common Pleas Records (RG 37, Halifax County)
Emanuel Abrahams *u* Mordecai Jones (1753), vol. 2A
Israel Abrahams *u* Samuel Jacobs (1752), vol. 1A (1749–53), no. 39
Israel Abrahams *u* Abraham Andrews (1753), vol. 2
Ball *u* John Franks (1760), vol. 8
Catherwood *u* Judah & Campbell (1751), vol. 1
John Franks *u* Ball (1760), vol. 9 (re Joseph Jones)
Naphtali Hart and Isaac Hart *u* Naphtali Hart Jr and Nathan Nathans (1761), vol. 10
Naphtali Hart Jr *u* Nathan Nathans (1761), vol. 11
Jeffery *u* Jones and Robertson (1762), vol. 15 (re Nathan Levy)
Joseph Jones *u* Trider (1750), vol. 1
Mordecai Jones *u* Nathan Levy (1761), vol. 11
Mordecai Jones, as grand juror (1763), vol. 15; as grand juror (1768), vol. 21B; return to jury notice (1770), vol. 22A
Wood *u* Joseph Jones (1760), vol. 8

Supreme Court Records (RG 39, series C, Halifax County)
Abrahams *u* Scott (1788), vol. 48
Ball *u* Franks (1760), vol. 8
Buckle *u* Isaac Abrahams (1786), vol. 42
Buttar and Bird *u* Isaac Decosta (1771), vol. 9
Fairweather *u* Jones (1755), vol. 2 (re Nathan Nathans, Naphtali Hart Jr)
David Franks *u* Samuel Hart (1788), vol. 51
Kirkham *u* Samuel Hart (1785), vol. 37
Naphtali Hart Jr *u* Nathan Nathans (1768), vol. 7
Jeffery *u* Jones and Robertson (1762), vol. 4 (re Nathan Levy)
David Jones *u* Elizabeth Jones (1772), vol. 10
David Jones *u* Pigott (1768), vol. 7
Jones *u* Gerrish (1756), vol. 2 (re Israel Abrahams and partners)
Nathan Levy *u* Mordecai Jones (1767), vol. 6
R. *u* Joseph Jones (1752), vol. 1
R. *u* Myer Myers (1786), vol. 45
Webb and Ewer *u* John Franks (1752), vol. 1
Wenham *u* Joseph Jones (1759), vol. 3

Miscellaneous
Calnek Family, RG 1, vol. 369, doc. 42, 346
Letters of Cornwallis to Board of Trade, 1749, RG 1, vol. 35
Levy Family, MG 4, vol. 13, 390 (2) and section 2, 17
Levy Family, chart 202 in T.B. Smith Collection, MG 1, vol. 843

H.D. Levy, *History of Sherwood* (1953)
Stayner Collection from Church Records
White Family (mfm w589)

PUBLIC ARCHIVES OF PRINCE EDWARD ISLAND, Charlottetown
Commission to Colborne as governor of Prince Edward Island, 13 December
1838, RG 1, vol. 73, 70–80

ROSENBACH LIBRARY AND MUSEUM, Philadelphia PA
Copy of *The Constitutions of the Several Independent States of America; The Declaration of Independence; The Articles of Confederation Between the Said States; The Treaties Between His Most Christian Majesty and the United States of* America
(Philadelphia: Francis Bailey, 1781) with annotations made by Gershom
Seixas Mendes on 13 January 1783 with respect to the political and civil
rights of Jews in America.

STATE HISTORICAL SOCIETY OF WISCONSIN, Madison
John Lawe Papers, box 1
Morgan Martin Papers, box 1
Grignon, Lawe, and Poirlier Papers

WASHINGTON COUNTY REGISTER OF DEEDS, Fort Edward NY
Administration Papers 1787–1823 (re estate of Henry Hart, 26 December
1788)

WILLIAM L. CLEMENTS LIBRARY, University of Michigan, Ann Arbor
Thomas Gage Papers
James Sterling Letterbook, 1761–1765

PUBLISHED GOVERNMENT DOCUMENTS

Canada, Province of, *Statutes*
– An Act for making one uniform provision respecting certain Official and
other Oaths to be taken in this Province, and for other purposes therein
mentioned, 1850, 13 & 14 Vict., c. 18
– An Act incorporating the Congregation of German and Polish Jews of
Montreal and the Congregation of Portuguese Jews of Montreal, under the
names the Corporation of the German and Polish Jews of Montreal and the
Corporation of Portuguese Jews of Montreal, 1846, 9 Vict., c. 96
– An Act respecting Rectories, 1851, 14 Vict., c. 75
– Incorporation of Congregation Anshe Sholom of Hamilton, 1863, 26 Vict.,
c. 34
– The Marriage Celebration Act, 1856, 20 Vict., c. 66

Delisle, M.D.C. "Register of Protestant Marriages Deaths and Births, 5 October, 1766 to 5 September 1787 [Montreal]." Public Archives of Canada, *Report*, 1885, lxxx–xciv.

Gibbs, Elizabeth, ed. *Debates of the Legislative Assembly of United Canada, 1841–1867*. Montreal: Centre de Recherche en Histoire économique du Canada français, 1981.

"Grants of Crown Lands in Upper Canada, 1787–1791." Archives of Ontario, *Report*, 1928, 7–228.

Great Britain, *Statutes*

– An Act for altering the Oath of Abjuration and the Assurance, 1766, 6 Geo., c. 53

– An Act for explaining and Amending an Act of the last Session of Parliament, Intituled, An Act to oblige all Persons, being Papists, in that part of Great Britain called Scotland, and all persons in Great Britain, refusing or neglecting to take the Oaths appointed for the Security of His Majesty's Person and Government, by several Acts herein mentioned, to Register their Names and Real Estates, and for enlarging the Time for taking the said Oaths, and making such Registers, and for allowing farther Time for the Enrolment of Deeds or Wills made by Papists, which have been omitted to be enrolled, pursuant to an Act of the Third Year of His Majesty's Reign; and also for giving Relief to Protestant Lessees, 1723, 10 Geo. I, c. 4

– An Act for the further Security of his Majesty's Person, and the Succession of the Crown in the Protestant Line, and for extinguishing the Hopes of the pretended Prince of Wales, and all other Pretenders, and their open and secret Abettors, 1701, 13 & 14 Will., c. 6

– An Act to explain Two Acts of Parliament, One of the Thirteenth Year of the Reign of His late Majesty, for naturalizing such Foreign Protestants, and others, as are settled, or shall settle, in any of His Majesty's Colonies in America; and the other of the Second Year of the Reign of His present Majesty, for naturalizing such Foreign Protestants as have served or shall serve, as Officers or Soldiers in His Majesty's Royal American Regiment, or as Engineers, in America, 1773, 13 Geo. III, c. 25

– The Act of Supremacy, 1558, 1 Eliz., c. 1

– The Act of Uniformity, 1558, 1 Eliz., c. 2

– The Constitutional Act, 1791, 31 Geo. III, c. 31

– The Corporation Act, 1661, 13 Car. II, c. 1

– The Jewish Disabilities Removal Act, 1845, 8 & 9 Vict., c. 52

– The Jewish Relief Act, 1858, 21 & 22 Vict., c. 49

– The Jews Naturalization Act, 1753, 26 Geo. II, c. 26

– The Naturalization Amendment Act (An Act to alter and amend 7 Jac. I, c. 2 (1608)), 1825, 6 Geo. IV, c. 67

– The Plantation Act (An Act for Naturalizing such Foreign Protestants and others therein mentioned, as are settled or shall settle in any of His Majesty's Colonies in *America*), 1740, 13 Geo. II, c. 7

- The Quebec Act, 1774, 14 Geo. III, c. 83
- The Religious Disabilities Act, 1846, 9 & 10 Vict., c. 59
- The Roman Catholic Relief Act, 1791, 31 Geo. III, c. 32
- The Roman Catholic Relief Act, 1829, 10 Geo. IV, c. 7
- The Sacramental Tests Repeal Act, 1828, 9 Geo. IV, c. 17
- The Test Act (An Act for preventing Dangers which may happen from Popish Recusants), 1673, 25 Car. II, c. 2
- The Toleration Act (An Act for exempting their Majesties' *protestant* subjects dissenting from the Church of England from the penalties of certain laws), 1689, 1 Will. & Mary, c. 18

Hansard, T.C. *The Parliamentary History of England from the Earliest Period to the Year 1803.* 36 vols. London: T.C. Hansard, 1813. Vol. XIV: *1747–1753* and vol. XV: *1753–1765.*

Hendrickson, James E., ed. *Journals of the Colonial Legislatures of the Colonies of Vancouver Island and British Columbia, 1851–1871.* II: *Journals of the House of Assembly, Vancouver Island, 1856–1863.*

"Instructions to Governors [Quebec 1763–90]." Public Archives of Canada, *Report,* 1904, 191–286.

"Journal and Proceedings of the House of Assembly of the Province of Upper Canada, 1792." Archives of Ontario, *Report,* 1909, 1–20.

Journal of the Commissioners for Trade and Plantations. 14 vols. London: His Majesty's Stationery Office, 1920–38. VIII: *1741–1749.*

"Journals of Upper Canada Legislative Assembly 1812." Archives of Ontario, *Report,* 1912, 1–100.

Lower Canada, House of Assembly, *Journals*
- "A bill to extend certain privileges to Persons professing the Jewish religion," 13th Parliament, 3rd session, 1830
- Kimber Committee report, 14th Parliament, 4th session, 1834, Appendix G.g.
- Petition by the Jews of Montreal for public registers for vital statistics, 13th Parliament, 1st session, 1828
- Petition of Samuel Becancour Hart and others, 14th Parliament, 1st session, 1831, 102–3

Lower Canada, *Statutes*
- An Act to extend certain Privileges therein mentioned to Persons professing the Jewish Religion and for obviating certain inconveniences to which other of His Majesty's subjects might otherwise be exposed, 1829, 9 Geo. IV, c. 75, 1829
- An Act to declare the equality of persons professing the Jewish religion, 1832, 1 Will. IV, c. 57

"Lower Canada, Instructions to Governors, 1791–1839." Public Archives of Canada, *Report,* 1905, vol. 1, 3–54.

"Military Government of Canada: Trois-Rivières 1760–1764." Public Archives of Canada, *Report*, 1918, 143–4.

Munro, James, ed. *Acts of the Privy Council of England, Colonial Series*. IV: *1745–1766*. London: His Majesty's Stationery Office, 1911.

New Brunswick, Legislative Council, *Journal*, 1834, 692–701 (commission and instructions to Bagot as governor general)

Nova Scotia, Assembly, *Journal*, 1838, 194ff (commission to Durham as governor–in–chief, 6 February 1838).

"Order calling the Elections to the Assembly by Governor James Douglas, 16 June 1856." British Columbia Archives and Records Service, *Third Report*, 1918, 9–10.

"Ordinance Regarding Trade to the Upper Country, 1 April 1761." Public Archives of Canada, *Report*, 1918, 43.

A Proclamation to such as are desirous to settle on the lands of the Crown in the Province of Upper Canada; by His Excellency John Graves Simcoe, Esquire; Lieutenant Governor and Commander in Chief of the said Province, 7 February 1792. Reprinted in Archives of Ontario, *Report*, 1906.

Proclamation. By His Excellency James Douglas.... Victoria, 19 May 1859

"Records of Court of Common Pleas, U.C., District of Hesse." Archives of Ontario, *Report*, 1917, 25–177.

"United Provinces, Instructions to Governors, 1840–1867." Public Archives of Canada, *Report*, 1905, vol. 1, 115–35.

Upper Canada, *Statutes*, The Oaths Act, 1833, 3 Will. IV, c. 13

"Upper Canada, Instructions to Governors, 1791–1839." Public Archives of Canada, *Report*, 1905, vol. 1, 55–114.

"Upper Canada Land Book D, 22nd December 1797 to 13th July 1798." Archives of Ontario, *Report*, 1931, 99–194.

Vancouver Island, Colony of. An Act to Provide for the Administration of Oaths in the House of Assembly, and the Production of Evidence before Committees of the same, Colony of Vancouver Island (1860), c. 10

NEWSPAPERS

British Colonist (Victoria), 26 August 1859, 3, 6, 8, 10, 13, 17, and 20 March 1860, 19 May 1860, 9 June 1860

Le Canadien (Quebec City), 20 February 1808 (re Ezekiel Hart)

Chatham Gleaner (Chatham NB), 12 June 1838, 6 May 1840, 19 August 1850, 1 August 1863

Head Quarters (Fredericton), 20 April 1859

Halifax Gazette, 13 April 1752, 9 March 1754, 4 and 11 May 1754

Kingston Chronicle, 22 January 1819, 22 June 1821, 24 October 1821, 12 April 1822

Montreal Daily Star, 30 December 1893
Montreal Herald, 3 August 1816, 3 November 1855
Montreal Gazette, 22 November 1840, 17 April 1935
Montreal Star, 6 November 1926
New-Brunswick Courier, 1 August 1863
Nova-Scotia Royal Gazette, 19 June 1787, 10 October 1810
Quebec Gazette, 23 and 30 August 1781, 6 November 1783, 13 January 1791, 23 May 1805
Quebec Mercury, 28 June 1832
Royal Gazette (Fredericton), 13 April 1859
Victoria Gazette, 9, 18, and 23 June 1859, 23 August 1859, 20 September 1859, 5 March 1860
Weekly Chronicle (Halifax), 3 November 1809

SECONDARY SOURCES

Abella, Irving S. *A Coat of Many Colours.* Toronto: Lester & Orpen Dennys, 1990.
Abrahams, Edmund H., "Some Notes on the Early History of the Sheftalls of Georgia." *American Jewish Historical Society Publications* 17(1909): 167–86.
Abrahams, Lionel. "Sir I.L. Goldsmid and the Admission of the Jews of England to Parliament." *Jewish Historical Society of England: Transactions* 4(1901): 116–76.
Adler, Selig, and Thomas E. Connolly. *From Ararat to Suburbia.* Philadelphia PA: Jewish Publication Society, 1960.
Akins, T.B. *History of Halifax City.* Belleville ON: Mika, 1973.
Annett, Ken. "Quest: Captain George Lawe Sr. and Family, A Summary of the Quest for Information on the Life and Career of Captain Lawe and His Descendants." Unpublished manuscript, 1980.
Armour, David, ed. *Attack at Michilimackinac, 1763.* Mackinac Island MI: Mackinac State Park Commission 1971. Drawn from Alexander Henry, *Travels & Adventures in Canada and the Indian Territories.*
Ballon, Harry C. "Aaron Hart David, MD, 1812–1882." *Canadian Medical Association Journal* 86(20 January 1962): 115–22.
Barka, Norman F. *Archeology of the Jewish Settlement Honen Dalim, St. Eustatius, N.A., An Interim Report.* Williamsburg VA: College of William and Mary, 1988.
Barnett, Richard D. "The Correspondence of the Mahamad of the Spanish and Portuguese Congregation of London during the Seventeenth and Eighteenth Centuries." *Jewish Historical Society of England: Transactions* 20(1964): 1–50.
– "Diplomatic Aspects of the Sephardic Influx." *Jewish Historical Society of England: Transactions* 25(1977): 216–17.

– "Dr Jacob de Castro Sarmento and Sephardim in Medical Practice in 18th-Century London." *Jewish Historical Society of England: Transactions* 27(1982): 84–114.

Benjamin, I.J. *Drei Jahre in Amerika, 1859–1862.* Hannover, Germany, 1862.

Bethencourt, Cardozo de. "Notes on the Spanish and Portuguese Jews in the United States, Guiana, and the Dutch and British West Indies during the Seventeenth and Eighteenth Centuries." *American Jewish Historical Society Publications* 29(1925): 7–38.

Blaustein, Esther I., Rachel A. Esar, and Evelyn Miller. "Spanish and Portuguese Synagogue (Shearith Israel) Montreal, 1768–1968." *Jewish Historical Society of England: Transactions* 22(1970): 111–42.

Blunt, John Elijah. *A History of the Establishment and Residence of the Jews in England; with an Enquiry into Their Civil Disabilities.* London, 1830.

Brodey, Arthur. "Political and Civil Status of Jews in Canada." Master's thesis, Jewish Institute of Religion, Cincinnati, Ohio, 1933.

Burak, Moses Jacob. "Moses Myers of Norfolk." Master's thesis, University of Virginia, Richmond, 1954.

"The Burghers of New Amsterdam and the Freemen of New York." *New York Historical Society Collections* 18(1885): 1–678.

Burt, Alfred L. *The Old Province of Quebec.* Toronto: Ryerson, 1933.

Byars, William Vincent. "The Gratz Papers." *American Jewish Historical Society Publications* 23(1915): 1–23.

Cadloff, Kevin Andrew. "The Freedom of Religion in Ontario and Quebec." *Canadian Jewish Archives,* no 25(1982): 143–56.

Calnek, William Arthur. *The History of the County of Annapolis.* Toronto: William Briggs, 1897.

Canadian Jewish Archives. To date some thirty numbers of the new series (1974–   ) of this periodical have been published. All except number 4 (1975), a memorial issue on B.G. Sack, have been compiled by David Rome. Separate entries for individual items cited in the notes are listed under Rome, David, comp.

"The Case of the Protestant Dissenters, with Reference to the Corporation and Test Acts." *Gentleman's Magazine* (London) (March 1787): 237–40.

Chiel, Arthur A. *The Jews in Manitoba: A Social History.* Toronto: University of Toronto Press, 1961.

– "Manitoba Jewish History, Early Times." *Jewish Historical Society of Canada Journal* 2(1977): 55–74.

– "The Ransom of Ezekiel." *World Over,* 8 April 1960.

Chyet, Stanley F. *Lopez of Newport, Colonial American Merchant Prince.* Detroit MI: Wayne State University Press, 1970.

Corey, Albert B., ed. *The Papers of Sir William Johnson,* vols. 10 and 13. Albany: State University of New York, 1951, 1962.

Corre, Alan D., comp., and Malcolm H. Stern, annotator. "The Record Book of the Reverend Jacob Raphael Cohen." *American Jewish Historical Quarterly* 49(September 1969): 23–82.

Davis, N. Darnell. "Notes on the History of the Jews in Barbados." *American Jewish Historical Society Publications* 18(1909): 129–48.

De Sola Pool, David. *Portraits Etched in Stone: Early Jewish Settlers, 1682–1831.* New York: Columbia University Press, 1952; reprinted 1953.

De Sola Pool, David and Tamar. *An Old Faith in a New World: Portrait of Shearith Israel, 1654–1954.* New York: Columbia University Press, 1955.

Dictionary of Canadian Biography. 13 volumes to date. Toronto: University of Toronto Press, 1965– . Biographies of Jews featured in this book are cited separately under author.

Dinnerstein, Leonard, and Mary Dale Palsson, eds. *Jews in the South.* Baton Rouge: Louisiana State Press, 1973.

Donovan, Kenneth. "The Gradis Collection and the Interpretation of Jewish History at Louisbourg." Paper presented at the Conference of Learned Societies, Laval University, Quebec City, May 1989.

Dorland, Arthur Garratt. *The Quakers in Canada: A History.* Toronto: Ryerson, 1968.

Doughty, Arthur G., and Duncan McArthur, eds. *Documents Relating to the Constitutional History of Canada, 1791–1818.* Ottawa: King's Printer 1914.

Douville, Raymond. *Aaron Hart: récit historique.* Trois-Rivières, 1938.

Dunn, Walter S., Jr. "Lucius Levy Solomons." *Dictionary of Canadian Biography* 4: 718–19.

Dyer, Albion Morris. "Points in the First Chapter of New York Jewish History." *American Jewish Historical Society Publications* 3(1895): 41–60.

"The Earliest Extant Minute Book of the Spanish and Portuguese Congregation Shearith Israel in New York, 1728–1760." *American Jewish Historical Society Publications* 21(1913): 1–82.

Elzas, Barnett A. *A Century of Judaism in South Carolina, 1800–1900.* Charleston, 1904.

– *The Jews of South Carolina from Earliest Times to the Present Day.* Philadelphia PA: Lippincott, 1905.

– *Leaves from My Historical Scrapbook.* Charleston SC, 1907.

– *Monograph on Joseph Salvador.* Charleston SC, 1903.

– ed. *Documents Relative to a Proposed Settlement of Jews in South Carolina.* Charleston: reprinted from Charleston News and Courier, February 1903.

Emanuel, Isaac S. and Suzanne A. *History of the Jews of the Netherlands Antilles.* Cincinnati OH: American Jewish Archives, Hebron Union College, 1970.

Encyclopedia Judaica. Jerusalem: Macmillan, 1971.

"Extracts from the Minute Book of the Spanish and Portuguese Congregation Shearith Israel in New York, 1760–1786." *American Jewish Historical Society Publications* 21(1913): 83–171.

"Extracts from the Note Books of Rev. J.J. Lyons." *American Jewish Historical Society Publications* 27(1920): 251ff.

"Family Records in a Lunar Calendar." In Joseph L. Blau and Salo Baron, eds. *The Jews of the United States 1790–1840.* New York: Columbia University Press, 1963.

Fergusson, C. Bruce. "Jewish Communities in Nova Scotia." *Journal of Education* 11(1961): 45–8.

– ed. *The Diary of Simeon Perkins, 1790–1796.* Toronto: The Champlain Society, 1961.

First Victoria Directory: Comprising a General Directory of Citizens. Also an Official List, List of Voters, Postal Arrangements and Notices of Trades and Professions. Victoria: Edward Mallandaine, 1860.

Firth, Edith G., ed. *The Town of York 1793–1815: A Collection of Documents of Early Toronto.* Toronto: The Champlain Society for the Government of Ontario/University of Toronto Press, 1962.

Frank, Solomon. *Two Centuries in the Life of a Synagogue.* Montreal: [Spanish and Portuguese Jews Congregation], 1968.

Fraser, James A. *By Favourable Winds: A History of Chatham, New Brunswick.* Chatham: The Town, 1975.

F[riedenwald], A.M. "Early Jews in Boston." *American Jewish Historical Society Publications* 29(1925): 153.

Friedenwald, Herbert. "Material for the History of the Jews in the British West Indies." *American Jewish Historical Society Publications* 5(1897): 45–101.

– "Some Newspaper Advertisements of the Eighteenth Century." *American Jewish Historical Society Publications* 6(1897): 49–59.

Friedman, Lee M. *Jewish Pioneers and Patriots.* Philadelphia PA: Jewish Publication Society, 1945.

Garner, John. *The Franchise and Politics in British North America.* Toronto: University of Toronto Press, 1969.

Garrett, Hester, and Robert Grode. "Gravestone Inscriptions, St Eustatius, N.A., 1686–1930." Typescript, 1976. Copy in Library in Oranjestadt, St Eustatius.

Godfrey, Sheldon J. "Freedom of Religion and the Canadian Bill of Rights." *University of Toronto Faculty of Law Review* 22(1964): 60–75.

– "Jacob (John) Franks." *Dictionary of Canadian Biography* 7: 328–9.

Godfrey, Sheldon and Judith. *Burn this Gossip: The True Story of George Benjamin of Belleville, Canada's First Jewish Member of Parliament, 1857–1863.* Toronto: Duke & George Press, 1991.

– "The Jews of Upper Canada." *Jewish Standard* (Toronto), August, September, October, and November 1989.

– "The King vs. Moses Gomez and Others: Opening the Prosecutor's File over 200 Years Later." *American Jewish Historical Quarterly* 80(1991): 397–407.

Godfrey, Sheldon J., and Judith C. Godfrey, comps. "Who Was Who in Canadian Jewry, 1749–1840." A series of genealogical charts documenting family relationships of over one hundred Jewish settlers. To be published.

Goeb, Jan. "The Maritime Jewish Community." Manuscript held by Jewish Historical Society of Nova Scotia, Halifax, c. 1970.

Goldberg, Isaac. *Major Noah, American Jewish Pioneer: The Life of Mordecai M. Noah, 1785–1851.* Philadelphia PA: Jewish Publication Society, 1944.

Goodman, Abram Vossen. *American Overture: Jewish Rights in Colonial Times.* Philadelphia PA: Jewish Publication Society, 1947.

Greenwood, F. Murray. *Legacies of Fear: Law and Politics in Quebec in the Era of the French Revolution.* Toronto: University of Toronto Press, 1993.

Grimwade, Arthur G. "Anglo-Jewish Silver." *Jewish Historical Society of England: Transactions* 18(1958): 121–3.

Grinstein, Hyman B. *The Rise of the Jewish Community of New York, 1654–1860.* Philadelphia PA: Jewish Publication Society, 1947.

Gundry, Eldon P. *The Zacheus Patterson Descendants.* Flint MI: Artcraft Press, 1959.

Gutstein, Morris A. *The Story of the Jews of Newport: Two and a Half Centuries of Judaism, 1658–1908.* New York: Bloch, 1936.

Halchin, Jill Y. *Excavations at Fort Michilimackinac, 1983–1985: House C of the Southeast Row House, The Solomon-Levy-Parant House.* Mackinac Island MI: Mackinac Island State Park Commission, c. 1985.

Hart, Arthur Daniel. *The Jew in Canada.* Toronto: Jewish Publications Limited, 1926.

Hart, Benjamin. *To the Israelites of the Province of Lower-Canada.* Montreal, 24 July 1826.

"The Hart Family of Newport." *American Jewish Historical Society Publications* 38(1948): 86–90.

Hartog, Jan. *The History of St. Eustatius.* Aruba: de Wit, 1976.

– *The Jews and St. Eustatius: The Eighteenth Century Jewish Congregation Honen Dalim and Description of the Old Cemetery.* St Maarten: Windward Islands Bank Limited, 1976.

Hartogensis, B.H. "Notes on Early Jewish Settlers of Baltimore." *American Jewish Historical Society Publications* 22(1914): 191–5.

Heckewelder, John. "History, Manners and Customs of the Indian Nations." *Historical Society of Pennsylvania Memoirs* 12(1876): 257–8; first published as *An Account of the Indian Nations who once inhabited Pennsylvania*, Philadelphia, 1818.

Heineman, David E. "The Startling Experience of a Jewish Trader during Pontiac's Siege of Detroit in 1763." *American Jewish Historical Society Publications* 23(1915): 31–5.

Heldman, Donald P. "Michigan's First Jewish Settlers: A View from the Solomon–Levy Trading House at Fort Michilimackinac, 1765–1781." *Journal of New World Archeology* 6(1986): 21–33.

Henriques, Henry Straus Quixano. *The Jews and the English Law.* Oxford, 1908; reprinted Clifton NJ: Augustus M. Kelley, 1974.

– "The Political Rights of English Jews." *Jewish Quarterly Review* 18(1906): 324–8.

Henry, Alexander. *Travels & Adventures in Canada and the Indian Territories.* New York: I. Riley, 1809; second edition, Boston: Little Brown, 1901. Republished with additional footnotes and index as David A. Armour, ed. *Attack at Michilimackinac, 1763* (Mackinac Island MI: Mackinac State Park Commission, 1971).

"The Henry Gladwin Papers." *Michigan Pioneer Collections* 27(1896): 642–3 and 667.

Hershkowitz, Leo. *Wills of Early New York Jews, (1704–1799).* New York: American Jewish Historical Society, 1967.

Higgins, D.W. *The Passing of a Race and More Tales of Western Life.* Toronto: William Briggs, 1905.

Hill, George W. "History of St. Paul's Church, Halifax Nova Scotia." *Report and Collections of the Nova Scotia Historical Society* 1(1878): 35–58; 2(1879–80): 63–99.

History of the Corporation of Spanish and Portuguese Jews, "Shearith Israel" of Montreal, Canada, Published on the Celebration of Its 150th Anniversary, 5679. Montreal and Toronto: Herald Press and Advertising Agency, 1918.

Holder, Jean M., comp. *Baptisms, Marriages and Burials, 1749–1768, St. Paul's Church, Halifax, Nova Scotia.* Halifax: Genealogical Association of Nova Scotia, 1983.

Hollander, J.H. "The Civil Status of the Jews in Maryland, 1634–1776." *American Jewish Historical Society Publications* 2(1894): 33–44.

– "Documents Relating to the Attempted Departure of the Jews from Surinam in 1675." *American Jewish Historical Society Publications* 6(1897): 8–29.

– "The Naturalization of Jews in the American Colonies under the Act of 1740." *American Jewish Historical Society Publications* 5(1897): 104–17.

Hühner, Leon. "Asser Levy, A Noted Jewish Burgher of New Amsterdam." *American Jewish Historical Society Publications* 8(1900): 9–23.

– "The First Jew to Hold the Office of Governor of One of the United States." *American Jewish Historical Society Publications* 17(1909): 187–95.

– "Jews Interested in Privateering in American during the Eighteenth Century." *American Jewish Historical Society Publications* 23(1915): 163–76.

– "Jews in the Legal and Medical Professions in America prior to 1800." *American Jewish Historical Society Publications* 22(1914): 147–65.

– "The Jews of Georgia in Colonial Times." *American Jewish Historical Society Publications* 10(1902): 65–95.

– "The Jews of New England (other than Rhode Island) prior to 1800." *American Jewish Historical Society Publications* 11(1903): 75–99.

– "The Jews of South Carolina from the Earliest Settlement to the End of the American Revolution." *American Jewish Historical Society Publications* 12(1904): 39–61.

– "The Jews of Virginia from the Earliest Times to the Close of the Eighteenth Century." *American Jewish Historical Society Publications* 20(1911): 85–108.
– *The Life of Judah Touro, 1775–1854.* Philadelphia PA: Jewish Publication Society, 1946.
– "Prominent Jews in Jamaica." *American Jewish Historical Society Publications* 12(1904): 164–5.
– "Some Notes on the Career of Colonel David S. Franks." *American Jewish Historical Society Publications* 10(1902): 165–8.
Hyamson, Albert M. *The Sephardim of England: A History of the Spanish and Portuguese Jewish Community, 1492–1951.* London: Methuen, 1951.
Irving, Lukin Homfray. *Officers of the British Forces in Canada during the War of 1812–1815.* Welland ON: Welland Tribune Print, 1908.
"Items relating to Congregation Shearith Israel, New York." *American Jewish Historical Society Publications* 27(1920): 1–149.
"Items relating to the Jews of Newport." *American Jewish Historical Society Publications* 27(1920): 175–216.
"Items relating to the Newport Synagogue." *American Jewish Historical Society Publications* 27(1920): 404–12.
"Items relating to the Seixas Family, New York." *American Jewish Historical Society Publications* 27(1920): 346–70.
"Items relating to the Solomons Family, New York." *American Jewish Historical Quarterly* 27(1920): 376–8.
The Jewish Encyclopedia. New York and London: Funk & Wagnalls, 1925.
"Jewish Obituaries from the Gentleman's Magazine." Jewish Historical Society of England, *Miscellanies* 4(1942): 39.
Johnson, J.K. "John Joseph." *Dictionary of Canadian Biography* 8: 444–5.
Jones, Charles C., Jr. "The Settlement of the Jews in Georgia." *American Jewish Historical Society Publications* 1(1893): 5–12.
Judah, George Fortunatus. "The Jews' Tribute in Jamaica,' *American Jewish Historical Society Publications* 18(1909): 149–77.
Katz, Irving I. *The Beth El Story.* Detroit MI: Wayne State University Press, 1955.
– "Chapman Abraham: An Early Jewish Settler in Detroit." *American Jewish Historical Society Publications* 40(1950): 81–6.
– "Ezekiel Solomon: The First Jew in Michigan." *Michigan History* 32(1948): 247–56.
– "Moses David of Windsor and His Family." *Michigan History* 47(1963): 156–60.
Kay, Jeanne. "John Lawe, Green Bay Trader." *Wisconsin Magazine of History* 64(1980): 3–28.
Kennedy, W.P.M., ed. *Statutes, Treaties and Documents of the Canadian Constitution, 1713–1929.* London: Oxford University Press, 1930.
Kohler, Max J. "The Civil Status of the Jews in Colonial New York." *American Jewish Historical Society Publications* 6(1897): 81–106.

– "The Jews in Newport." *American Jewish Historical Society Publications* 6(1897): 61–80.
– "Phases in the History of Religious Liberty in America, with Special Reference to the Jews." *American Jewish Historical Society Publications* 11(1903): 53–73.
Kohut, George Alexander. "Martyrs of the Inquisition in South America." *American Jewish Historical Society Publications* 4(1896).
Koven, Marcia. *Weaving the Past into the Present: A Glimpse into the 130 Year History of the St. John Jewish Community.* Saint John: Jewish Historical Museum, 1989.
Labaree, Leonard Woods, ed. *Royal Instructions to British Governors, 1670–1776.* 2 vols. American Historical Association, 1935; reprinted New York: Octagon Books, 1967.
Lebowich, Joseph. "Jews in Surinam." *American Jewish Historical Society Publications* 12(1904): 169.
Leeser, Isaac. *The Claims of the Jews to an Equality of Rights: Illustrated in a Series of Letters to the Editor of the Philadelphia Gazette.* Philadelphia PA: C. Sherman, 5601 [1841].
Leonoff, Cyril E. *Pioneer Jewish Merchants of Vancouver Island and British Columbia.* [Vancouver]: Jewish Historical Society of British Columbia/Jewish Western Bulletin, 1983.
– *Pioneers, Pedlars and Prayer Shawls: The Jewish Communities in British Columbia and the Yukon.* Victoria: Sono Nis Press, 1978.
– "Victoria: The New Gold Colony." *The Scribe* 12(winter 1991): 14–15, 17.
Lillard, Charles. *Seven Shillings a Year: The History of Vancouver Island.* Ganges BC: Horsdal & Shubart, 1986.
McAleer, J. Philip. *A Pictorial History of St. Paul's Anglican Church, Halifax, Nova Scotia.* Halifax: Resource Centre Publications, Technical University of Nova Scotia, 1993.
McKinley, Albert Edward. *The Suffrage Franchise in the Thirteen English Colonies in America.* Philadelphia, 1905.
Malchelosse, Gérard. "Les Juifs dans l'histoire canadienne." *Les Cahiers des Dix,* no. 4(1939): 168–95.
Mann, Harvey. "The Jew of St Denis: An Introduction [Samuel Jacobs]." *Canadian Jewish Historical Society Journal* 8(1984): 85–9.
Marcus, Jacob R. *The Colonial American Jew.* 3 vols. Detroit MI: Wayne State University Press, 1970.
– *Early American Jewry, 1649–1794.* 2 vols. Philadelphia PA: Jewish Publication Society, 1961.
– "The Jew and the American Revolution." *American Jewish Archives* 27(1975): 103.
– ed. *American Jewry: Documents, Eighteenth Century.* Cincinnati: Hebrew Union College Press, 1919.

Marsh, William R. "Montgomery and Myers Families." In *The Ancestors and Descendants of F.A. Marsh and Ivy Crites.* Baltimore MD: Gateway Press, 1990, 36–49.

Maseres, Francis. *Additional Papers Concerning The Province Of Quebeck: Being An Appendix To the Book entitled "An Account of the Proceedings of the British and other Protestant Inhabitants of the Province of Quebeck in North America, in order to obtain a House of Assembly in that Province".* London: sold by W. White, 1776.

Mayne, R.C. *Four Years in British Columbia and Vancouver Island.* London, 1863.

Mendelssohn, Sidney. "Jewish Pioneers of South Africa." *Jewish Historical Society of England: Transactions* 7(1914): 180–205.

Mentzer, Raymond A. "The Marranos of Southern France in the Early Sixteenth Century." *Jewish Quarterly Review* 72(April 1982): 303–11.

Michener, James. *The Caribbean.* New York: Fawcett, 1989.

Miller, Carman. "Abraham de Sola." *Dictionary of Canadian Biography* 11: 253–6.

"Minute Book of the Spanish and Portuguese Congregation Shearith Israel in New York, 1760–1786." *American Jewish Historical Society Publications* 21(1913): 83–171.

Moir, John S., ed. *Church and State in Canada, 1627–1867: Basic Documents.* Toronto: McClelland & Stewart, 1967.

Montefiore, Joshua. *A Commercial Dictionary: Containing the Present State of Mercantile Law, Practice and Custom.* London, 1803.

Morris, Richard B. "Civil Liberties and the Jewish Tradition in Early America." *American Jewish Historical Society Publications* 46(1957): 20–39.

Namier, Sir Lewis, and John Brooke. *The House of Commons, 1754–1790.* 3 vols. London: Her Majesty's Stationery Office, 1964–70.

Newman, Aubrey. "The Expulsion of the Jews from Prague in 1745 and British Foreign Policy." *Jewish Historical Society of England: Transactions* 21(1968): 30–41.

"Obituary [Aaron David Hart]." *Canadian Medical Record* (November 1882).

Osborne, E.H. "The Migration of Voyageurs from Drummond Island to Penetanguishene in 1828." *Ontario Historical Society, Papers and Records* 3(1901): 123–66.

"Personal Narrative of Capt. Thomas G. Anderson." State Historical Society of Wisconsin, *Collections* 9(1882): 136–206.

Phillips, N. Taylor. "The Congregation Shearith Israel: An Historical Review." *American Jewish Historical Society Publications* 6(1897): 123–40.

– "Family History of the Reverend David Mendez Machado." *American Jewish Historical Society Publications* 2(1894).

– "The Levy and Seixas Families." *American Jewish Historical Society Publications* 4(1896): 208.

Picciotto, James. *Sketches of Anglo-Jewish History.* London, 1875. Revised edition by Israel Finestein. London: Soncino Press, 1956.

Plaut, W. Guenther. "Two Notes on the History of the Jews in America." *Hebrew Union College Annual* 14(1939): 580–1.

Pratt, Robert H. *The Nineteenth Century Postal History of Newfoundland.* New York: The Steinway Fund and the Collectors Club of New York, 1986.

Quaife, Milo M., ed. *John Askin Papers.* 2 vols. Detroit, 1928–31.

"Registry of Circumcisions by Abm. I. Abrahams from June 1756 to January 1781 in New York, in Hebrew and English." *American Jewish Historical Society Publications* 27(1920): 150–6.

Reznikoff, Charles, and Uriah Z. Engelman. *The Jews of Charleston.* Philadelphia PA: Jewish Publication Society, 1950.

Rome, David. "Adolphus Mordecai Hart." *Dictionary of Canadian Biography* 10: 337–8.

– *The First Two Years: A Record of the Jewish Pioneers on Canada's Pacific Coast, 1858–1860.* Montreal: H.M. Caiserman, 1942.

– "Jacob Raphael Cohen." *Dictionary of Canadian Biography* 5: 193–4.

– ed. *Pathways to the Present: Canadian Jewry and the Canadian Jewish Congress.* Toronto: Canadian Jewish Congress, 1986.

Rome, David, comp. "Barrak Hays." *Canadian Jewish Archives,* no. 20(1981).

– "Benjamin Hart and 1829." *Canadian Jewish Archives,* no. 24(1982).

– "Challenges to Equality." *Canadian Jewish Archives,* no. 16(1980): 146–9.

– "David Salesby Franks in Montreal." *Canadian Jewish Archives,* no. 22(1982): 94–100.

– "David Salesby Franks: American." *Canadian Jewish Archives,* no. 22(1982): 101–5.

– "Disintegration." *Canadian Jewish Archives,* no. 23(1982): 88.

– "The First to Sit?" *Canadian Jewish Archives,* no. 16(1980): 150–61.

– "The Hays Family." *Canadian Jewish Archives,* no. 20(1981): 237.

– "Heineman Pines." *Canadian Jewish Archives,* no. 23(1982): 47–8.

– "Hyam Myers." *Canadian Jewish Archives,* no. 23(1982): 41–5.

– "Intergroup." *Canadian Jewish Archives,* no. 16(1980): 122–33.

– "Lyon Jonas." *Canadian Jewish Archives,* no. 23(1982): 49.

– "Mauger." *Canadian Jewish Archives,* no. 23(1982): 22.

– "On the Early Harts." published in four parts as *Canadian Jewish Archives,* nos. 15–18 (1980) with consecutive pagination.

– "On the Early Harts – Their Contemporaries." *Canadian Jewish Archives,* nos. 19–21 (1981) and nos. 22 and 23 (1982).

– "On the Jews of Lower Canada and 1837–38, part 2." *Canadian Jewish Archives* no. 29(1983).

– "The Partners: Ezekiel Solomon." *Canadian Jewish Archives,* no. 21(1981): 1–47.

– "Samuel Becancour Hart and 1832." *Canadian Jewish Archives,* no. 25(1982).

– "Samuel Judah." *Canadian Jewish Archives,* no. 20(1981): 121–36.

Rosenbach, Abraham A.S. "Notes on the First Settlement of Jews in Pennsylvania." *American Jewish Historical Society Publications* 5(1897): 191–8.

Rosenbach, Abraham S. Wolf. "Documents Relative to Major David S. Franks while Aid-de-Camp [*sic*] to General Arnold." *American Jewish Historical Society Publications* 5(1897): 157–89.

Rosenberg, Louis, comp. "The Prothonotary's Register of British Subjects in Montreal Professing the Jewish Religion, above the age of 21 years, as prescribed by the Act of 9 & 10 Geo IV c. 75." *Canadian Jewish Archives*, old series, 1(May 1962): 7–42.

Rosenbloom, Joseph R. *A Biographical Dictionary of American Jews from Colonial Times to 1800.* Lexington: University of Kentucky Press, 1960.

Rosendale, Simon W. "An Early Ownership of Real Estate in Albany, New York by a Jewish Trader." *American Jewish Historical Society Publications* 3(1895): 61–71.

Roth, Cecil. "The Challenge to Jewish History." *Jewish Historical Society of England: Transactions* 14(1940): 1–38.

– *The Jewish Contribution to Civilisation.* London: Macmillan, 1938.

– "Jews in the Defence of Britain, Thirteenth to Nineteenth Centuries." *Jewish Historical Society of England: Transactions* 15(1946): 3–28.

– *The Rise of Provincial Jewry: The Early History of the Jewish Communities in the English Countryside, 1740–1840.* London: Jewish Monthly, 1950.

– "Some Jewish Loyalists in the War of American Independence." *American Jewish Historical Society Publications* 38(1948): 81–107.

Sack, Benjamin G. *The History of the Jews in Canada: From the Earliest Beginnings to the Present Day.* Volume I: *From the French Regime to the End of the Nineteenth Century.* Montreal: Canadian Jewish Congress, 1945.

– "A Suit at Law Involving the First Jewish Minister in Canada." *American Jewish Historical Society Publications* 31(1928): 181–6.

Samuel, Edgar Roy. "Anglo-Jewish Notaries and Scriveners." *Jewish Historical Society of England: Transactions* 17(1953): 113–59.

Samuel, Wilfred S. "A List of Persons Endenized and Naturalized, 1609–1799." *Jewish Historical Society of England: Transactions* 22(1970): 111–44.

– "Review of the Jewish Colonists of Barbados, 1680." *Jewish Historical Society of England: Transactions* 13(1936): 1–111.

Scott, Kenneth, comp. *Rivington's New York Newspaper: Excerpts from a Loyalist Press.* New York: New York Historical Society, 1973.

Senior, Elinor Kyte. "Eleazar David David." *Dictionary of Canadian Biography* 9: 234–5.

– and James H. Lambert. "David David." *Dictionary of Canadian Biography* 6: 179–81.

Senior, Hereward. "George Benjamin." *Dictionary of Canadian Biography* 9: 44–6.

Shaftesley, John M. "Jews in English Regular Freemasonry, 1717–1860." *Jewish Historical Society of England: Transactions* 25(1977): 150–209.

Shortt, Adam, and Arthur G. Doughty, eds. *Documents Relating to the Constitutional History of Canada, 1759–1791.* 2 vols. Second revised edition; Ottawa: King's Printer, 1918.

Smith, Dorothy Blakey, ed. *The Reminiscences of Doctor John Sebastian Helmcken* Vancouver: University of British Columbia Press, 1975.

Smith, Shirlee Anne. "Ferdinand Jacobs." *Dictionary of Canadian Biography* 4: 383–4.

Solis-Cohen, J., Jr. "Barrak Hays: Controversial Loyalist." *American Jewish Historical Society Publications* 45(1955/6): 54–7.

"The Spanish and Portuguese Jews of Montreal, Shearith Israel – An Interesting and Venerable Record: Their 125th Anniversary Today." *Montreal Daily Star,* 30 December 1893.

Speisman, Stephen A. *The Jews of Toronto: A History to 1937.* Toronto: McClelland and Stewart, 1979.

– "Judah George (Gershom) Joseph." *Dictionary of Canadian Biography* 8: 445–6.

Spray, W.A. "William Abrams." *Dictionary of Canadian Biography* 7: 4–5.

Stanley, George F.G. *Canada Invaded, 1775–1776.* Toronto and Sarasota: Samuel Stevens Hakkert, 1977.

Stern, Malcolm H., comp. *First American Jewish Families, 600 Genealogies, 1654–1988.* Baltimore MD: Ottenheimer, 1991. This is the most recent of Stern's books on this subject. It is essentially the second reprint of his 1960 volume, *Americans of Jewish Descent,* but new information is included as an update at pages 320–41.

Straus, Oscar S. "New Light on the Career of Colonel David S. Franks." *American Jewish Historical Society Publications* 10(1902): 101–8.

Sutherland, D.A. "Samuel Hart." *Dictionary of Canadian Biography* 5: 409–10.

Thorpe, Francis Newton, comp. and ed. *The Federal and State Constitutions, Colonial Charters, and Other Organic Laws of the States, Territories, and Colonies Now or Heretofore Forming the United States of America.* 7 vols. Washington: Government Printing Office 1909.

Tovey, D'Blossiers. *Anglia Iudaica or the History and Antiquities of the Jews in England.* Oxford, 1738; reprinted New York: Burt Franklin, 1967.

Tulchinsky, Gerald. *Taking Root: The Origins of the Canadian Jewish Community.* Toronto: Lester, 1992.

"Unpublished Canadian State Papers Relating to Benjamin Hart." *American Jewish Historical Society Publications* 23(1915): 137–40.

Universal Jewish Encyclopedia, edited by Isaac Landman. New York, 1941.

Vaugeois, Denis. "Aaron Hart." *Dictionary of Canadian Biography* 4: 331–2.

– "Aaron Ezekiel Hart." *Dictionary of Canadian Biography* 8: 363–5.

– "Benjamin Hart." *Dictionary of Canadian Biography* 8: 365–7.

– "Ezekiel Hart." *Dictionary of Canadian Biography* 7: 386–9.

– *Les Juifs et la Nouvelle-France.* Trois-Rivières: Éditions Boréal Express 1968.

– "Moses Hart." *Dictionary of Canadian Biography* 8: 367–70.

– "Samuel Jacobs." *Dictionary of Canadian Biography* 4: 384–6.

Wade, Mason. *The French Canadians, 1760–1945* (New York: Macmillan 1955).

Wallace, W. Stewart, ed. *The Maseres Letters, 1766–1768.* Toronto: Oxford University Press, 1919.

Wolf, Edwin, II, and Maxwell Whiteman. *The History of the Jews of Philadelphia from Colonial Times to the Age of Jackson.* Philadelphia PA: Jewish Publication Society, 1957.

Wolf, Lucien. "American Elements in the Resettlement." *Jewish Historical Society of England: Transactions* 3(1899): 76–100.

– "Henry Straus Quixano Henriques, K.C., 1866–1925." *Jewish Historical Society of England: Transactions* 11(1928): 247–51.

Wolff, Annette R. "Henry Joseph." *Dictionary of Canadian Biography* 6: 365–6.

Woodley, E.C. *The House of Joseph in the Life of Quebec: The Record of a Century and a Half.* Quebec: The Joseph Company, 1946.

Woolf, Maurice. "Joseph Salvador 1716–1786." *Jewish Historical Society of England: Transactions* 21(1968): 104 et seq.

Yetwin, Neil B. "American Jewish Loyalists: The Myers Family of New Brunswick." *Loyalist Gazette* 27(1990): 13–18.

Zitt, Hersch L. "David Salisbury Franks, Revolutionary Patriot (c. 1740–1793)." *Pennsylvania History* 16(1948): 77–95.

Index

The letter "t" after a page number indicates that the information is in a table.

Women are indexed by both their married and their maiden names, if known. Their birth (b.) name or married (m.) name is in parentheses.

References to notes indicate substantive additional information.

McGill-Queen's Studies in Ethnic History
Donald Harman Akenson, Editor